NOTHING PURE

Nothing Pure

Jewish Law, Christian Supersession, and Bible Translation in Old English

MO PARELES

UNIVERSITY OF TORONTO PRESS
Toronto Buffalo London

© University of Toronto Press 2024
Toronto Buffalo London
utorontopress.com

ISBN 978-1-4875-5067-7 (cloth)   ISBN 978-1-4875-5069-1 (EPUB)
                                    ISBN 978-1-4875-5070-7 (PDF)

Library and Archives Canada Cataloguing in Publication

Title: Nothing pure : Jewish law, Christian supersession, and Bible
   translation in Old English / Mo Pareles.
Names: Pareles, Mo, author.
Description: Includes bibliographical references and index.
Identifiers: Canadiana (print) 20230470793 | Canadiana (ebook)
   20230470920 | ISBN 9781487550677 (hardcover) | ISBN 9781487550691
   (EPUB) | ISBN 9781487550707 (PDF)
Subjects: LCSH: Aelfric, Abbot of Eynsham – Criticism and interpretation. |
   LCSH: Wulfstan, Archbishop of York, – 1023 – Criticism and interpretation. |
   LCSH: Jewish law – History – To 1500. | LCSH: Bible. Old Testament –
   Translations into Old English – History and criticism. | LCSH: Christian
   literature, English (Old) – History and criticism. | LCSH: Christianity
   and other religions – Judaism – History – To 1500.
Classification: LCC BS1199.L3 P37 2024 | DDC 296.1/809021 – dc23

Cover design: Val Cooke
Cover image: *Judith* by Gustav Klimt. Fine Art / Alamy Stock Photo

We wish to acknowledge the land on which the University of Toronto Press operates. This land is the traditional territory of the Wendat, the Anishnaabeg, the Haudenosaunee, the Métis, and the Mississaugas of the Credit First Nation.

This book has been published with the help of a grant from the Federation for the Humanities and Social Sciences, through the Awards to Scholarly Publications Program, using funds provided by the Social Sciences and Humanities Research Council of Canada.

University of Toronto Press acknowledges the financial support of the Government of Canada, the Canada Council for the Arts, and the Ontario Arts Council, an agency of the Government of Ontario, for its publishing activities.

 Canada Council for the Arts / Conseil des Arts du Canada

 ONTARIO ARTS COUNCIL
CONSEIL DES ARTS DE L'ONTARIO
an Ontario government agency
un organisme du gouvernement de l'Ontario

Funded by the Government of Canada / Financé par le gouvernement du Canada

For Rose, critical reader

Contents

Acknowledgments ix

List of Abbreviations xiii

Introduction: A Brief History of Supersessionary Disgust   3

1 Exsanguinating Leviticus: Supersessionary Translation in the *Old English Heptateuch*   19

2 Men as Meat: Jewish Law and Orders of Being in Ælfric's Translations of Maccabees and Job   42

3 The Benedictine Invention of Heterosexuality: Jewish (Law's) Sexual Difference in Time   66

4 *Ænlic Wimman*: Judith and the Exception   93

5 Like Dogs and Wolves: Wulfstan as Biblical Translator   118

Afterword: Cleansings   139

Notes   149

Bibliography   201

Index   249

Acknowledgments

I must begin this book by thanking three dear friends who have supported and encouraged me throughout the writing of this book and read many, many drafts. The first of these is Haruko Momma: the best of teachers; the wisest, kindest, and strictest mentor; proof that the era of sages and prophets has not ended. I cannot begin to repay you, Hal. The second is my beloved UBC colleague Vin Nardizzi, who has been guide, editor, and master of practical advice. Ben Saltzman was there at the book's inceptive moment and has provided years of unstinting encouragement and wise feedback, even when we were, supposedly, in competition. *Runwitan* and *rædboran*, all three of you are models of what scholars and colleagues should be. I do not know what I have ever done to deserve you in my corner.

My research and writing have been supported by several grants and a pre-tenure sabbatical from the UBC Faculty of Arts, and just as importantly, by three years of UBC Childcare. Without year-round, subsidized early childcare, which should be universally available but remains a rare privilege, this book could never have been written. I also thank my superb colleagues, the faculty and staff of the UBC Department of English Literatures and Language, for a thousand acts of collegiality, generosity, and labour beyond the call. I am particularly grateful to those colleagues whose wise mentorship has guided my path, and to those whose hospitality and friendship has made UBC (and Vancouver) such a congenial home. The brilliant, radical Y-Dang Troeung *z"l* lives in my heart.

For your help with this project – reading of drafts and proposals, advice and practical help, incessant cheerleading and check-ins, discussion of ideas, and provision of references – I especially thank Patsy Badir, Kim Bain, Dennis Britton, Siân Echard, Rob Rouse, and Danielle Wong. I am grateful to my extraordinary graduate research assistants,

Sarah-Nelle Jackson and Allen Fulghum, who found the unfindable and made sure everything was in order.

For postdoctoral funding to research and write this book, I am also grateful to the Mellon Foundation and to Barbara Newman, whose generosity allowed me to spend a postdoctoral year at Northwestern University in 2014–15, to the NYU Department of English for a wonderful postdoctoral year in 2015–16 and for travel funding, and to the Northeast Modern Language Association for a small but crucial grant that allowed me to travel to the Bibliothèque Royale in Brussels in 2014. Thank you also to the medievalists and other faculty and staff at Northwestern, and to the colleagues in French and Italian who supplied me with office space, hot drinks, and warm conversation. I would also like to thank the members of the NYU Department of English, especially Jini Watson, for support and many productive conversations during my postdoc in 2015–16. Nick Matlin, my office mate, was a brother-in-arms and always ready with jokes and hard-to-find books. Thank you to Lissette Flores for absolutely everything at NYU.

I have benefited greatly from the generous questions, feedback, and conversation of my scholarly communities as I worked on this book. Thank you to the organizers and members of the University of Chicago Medieval Studies Workshop, the New Chaucer Society, the Oecologies Collective, IONA (Islands of the North Atlantic), the Making Early Middle English Conference, the Modern Language Association, BABEL, the International Society for the Study of Early Medieval England (formerly ISAS), the Friends of the Saints Seminar at CUNY Graduate Center, the International Conference on Medieval Studies, the Colloquium for Early Medieval Studies (formerly ASSC), Endnotes at UBC, the UBC Medieval Workshop, the UBC Department of English Faculty Research Series, the Northwestern University Medieval Colloquium, the NYU Medieval Studies Society, and Jay Gates's "Law and Literature" seminar at John Jay College for allowing me to present early versions of these chapters. The suggestions and criticisms I received at these talks were invaluable. For funding to attend these conferences and workshops, I thank the UBC Faculty of Arts and Department of English, the Lynne Grundy Memorial Trust, the New Chaucer Society, ISSEME, the Oecologies Collective, and the Oxford Centre for Research in the Humanities.

This project started when I was still in coursework for my PhD, and my earliest work on it was generously funded through grants and fellowships by the NYU Faculty of Arts, the NYU Provost's Global Research Initiative, the NYU Department of English, and the Mellon Foundation. It was also fostered by the inspiring faculty, staff, and students of the NYU Department of English and of the NYU Medieval and

Renaissance Center. I am grateful to Emily Apter, Kathleen Davis, Carolyn Dinshaw, Jaques Lezra, Elizabeth McHenry, Ann Pellegrini, and Robert J.C. Young, who helped me frame the questions and read early drafts. Thank you to the wild and wonderfully supportive community of medievalists and scholars in and around New York, especially at the Graduate Center (and elsewhere), including those mentioned above. I owe an enormous debt to my entire graduate cohort and to my Mellon Summer Seminar classmates, and particularly to my faithful comrades Dan Remein and Gerald Song, as well as to Carla Thomas, Jen Little, and Liza Blake. Many thanks to Martin Foys and to the members and organizers of BABEL and the Colloquium for Early Medieval Studies for nurturing my graduate work. I am grateful to Adrienne Clay, who taught me to research; Tom La Farge *z"l*, who taught me (*cnihtwesende*) to write and to be a medievalist; and Jill Muller, who introduced me to English literature. James Simpson, Leah Middlebrook, Pelagia Goulimari, and Michael Denning encouraged my work at a formative time.

Thank you to my wonderful students at UBC, NYU, and Northwestern for discussing these ideas with me throughout the years.

Particular thanks are due to my editor at University of Toronto Press, Suzanne Rancourt; to the two anonymous readers; and to Janice Evans and Elizabeth Ferguson at UTP. I also owe many thanks to the librarians of Cambridge University's Parker Library, NYU's Bobst Library, UBC Libraries, the Bibliothèque Royale de Belgique Manuscripts Collection, British Library, Bodleian Library Special Collections, Cambridge University Library, and Durham Cathedral Library for special assistance and for generous access to crucial texts.

An early version of chapter 2 appeared as "Men as Meat: Exploiting Jewish Law in Ælfric's Translation of Maccabees," *Exemplaria* 27.3 (2015): 187–204, https://www.tandfonline.com/journals/yexm20. It is reproduced here by permission of Taylor & Francis through Copyright Clearance Center, Inc. An early version of chapter 3 appeared as "Jewish Heterosexuality, Queer Celibacy? Ælfric Translates the Old Testament Priesthood," *postmedieval* 8 (2017): 292–306, https://www.palgrave.com/gp/journal/41280, and is reproduced here by permission of Springer Nature. A small portion of the introduction is adapted from "Giving Yiddish the Devil: How Missionary Translation Reckons with Demons in the Yiddish New Testament," *Literature and Theology* 26.2 (2012): 144–59, https://academic.oup.com/litthe, and is reproduced with permission of Oxford University Press. I am grateful to the editors of these publications.

Friends and family in New York, Vancouver, and elsewhere have made the impossible seem possible – and, more than that, worthwhile. My study buddy Anna Robinson has kept me caffeinated and optimistic.

Ilana Danzig, Caitlin Delohery, Alli Kraus, Miriam Miller, Tamar and Ajit Pyati, and other precious friends have provided constant encouragement and commiseration in the later stages of this project. Thank you to the Livingstones for generous hosting in London. Thank you to the Hip Mamas of Chicago and to the queer and academic parenting groups that were crucial to my happiness and connectedness from 2014 to 2020, and to the many friends-with-kids who have so enriched my life. Jon Kief and Jini Bae, you have been the kindest and most erudite of friends (and sometimes roommates) as well as family. Donna Russo, I could never have done my work without your loving care for Rose (and for Nicole and me). Sue Freedman, you are the best mom (and Bubbe) anyone could ask for, and you know everything you have done. I owe much thanks to the rest of my family, especially Mike Pareles and Jen He, Mary Gilroy *z"l*, Stephen Pareles *z"l*, and the Russo and Freedman clans, and to all of my Jewish and queer/trans ancestors. My deepest gratitude goes to those who have looked after my child, especially Natalie Vo, J.S., and Aimee Kubes.

Nicole, thank you for calling the SuperShuttle and for every act of heroism and wisdom since – and for saying you thought this would be fun. Rose, my favourite author, thank you for your indomitable creativity and peerless advice. Thank you both for your sustaining love and your ferocious belief.

I gratefully acknowledge that this book was written primarily on Lenapehoking, the unceded ancestral lands of the Lenape peoples, and on the unceded, ancestral, and traditional territories of the xʷməθkʷəy̓əm (Musqueam), Sḵwx̱wú7mesh (Squamish), and səlilwətaɬ (Tsleil-Waututh) Nations.

Abbreviations

CHI	*Ælfric's Catholic Homilies: The First Series Text*
CHII	*Ælfric's Catholic Homilies: The Second Series Text*
CHIntro	*Ælfric's Catholic Homilies: Introduction, Commentary and Glossary*
DOE	*Dictionary of Old English*
DOEWC	*Dictionary of Old English Web Corpus*
DR	Douay-Rheims Bible
EETS	Early English Text Society
JPS	Jewish Publication Society
LS	*Ælfric's Lives of Saints*
NOAB	*New Oxford Annotated Bible*
OEH	*The Old English Heptateuch and Ælfric's Libellus de veteri testamento et novo*
OEM	*Old English Martyrology*
PL	*Patrologia Latina*

NOTHING PURE

Jewish Law, Christian Supersession, and
Bible Translation in Old English

Introduction: A Brief History of Supersessionary Disgust

Like any ancestor, Judaism provides Christianity with an inheritance, which is always, Derrida suggests, spectral … "If the readability of a legacy were given, natural, transparent, univocal, if it did not call for and at the same time defy interpretation, we would never have anything to inherit from it … One always inherits from a secret – which says 'read me, will you ever be able to do so?'" If Christianity works radically to reduce the "heterogeneity" of Judaism, to claim for itself the one proper "reading" of the Jewish "legacy," and a reading that denies validity to Jewish readings, the felt necessity of keeping Judaism and Jews in play … allows for a Jewish presence that is spectral.

(Kruger, *The Spectral Jew*, 11)

Jewish centrality to early English culture goes beyond the representation of Jews *qua* Jews. Old English writers grappled with the part of Jewish tradition that is allegedly most definitely thrown off by Christianity, most irrelevant and tedious – that is to say, Jewish Biblical law.[1] This system of law has, to borrow Kruger's term, a "spectral" presence in pre-Conquest English literature and theology, and the mechanism of this spectrality is the doctrine of supersession, which impossibly rejected Judaism, attempting to suppress it, control its legacy as ancestral, and keep it alive as a foe.[2] Supersession is the idea that Christians have inherited the Jewish covenant with God, displacing Jews, and possess the only correct "reading" of the Hebrew Bible and even of Jewish laws. Since supersession and the Hebrew Bible have been so important to Christian self-definition, many Christianities have been unable to live with Judaism and, so often, unable to live without it.[3] Or, in Joseph Litvak's memorable description of another renounced Jewishness, "if one must keep on kicking the habit, then of course one must keep on indulging in it – with all the abuse that both the kicking and the indulgence suggest. In other words, the abuse may be a kind of cultivation."[4] Medieval exegesis and translation are not immune to this contemptuous passion for superseded Jewish laws.

Pre-Conquest England had no known Jewish population and was geographically removed from the rich tumult of Ashkenaz and from larger Jewish centres. Yet in the final period before the Norman Conquest, English Christian cultural translation of Jewish law proved surprisingly central to religious and political thought. This book presents a new reading of works by the prolific Old English monastic writer and translator Ælfric, Abbot of Eynsham (ca. 955–1010), and to a lesser degree the legist Wulfstan, Archbishop of York (d. 1023), with ample reference to the *Old English Heptateuch*, a vast translation project to which Ælfric made primary contribution. The period spanned by this study is best described as "late Old English," a literary rather than a historical locator, as the book focuses primarily on texts that date from between 987, the probable year of Ælfric's first compositions at Cerne Abbas, and Wulfstan's death in 1023.[5] Of course, I also spend considerable time on sources and influences, as well as on manuscripts that postdate the period in question and later reverberations.

These works are exemplars of what I call *supersessionary translation*, an ethics and aesthetics of translation that grapples with the Christian relationship to Judaism. I define supersessionary translation as a philosophy of interlinguistic and cultural translation that not only refers to but also models Christianity's triumph over and resignification of Judaism. Supersessionary translations are methodically diverse, but always take a path of enacting and communicating supersession: of appropriating rather than erasing Jewish material, of affirming the temporal and spiritual ascendancy of Christianity over Judaism.[6] I argue that supersessionary translation, rather than a natural consequence of the irrelevance of Jewish law to Christian life and spirituality, was instead a sophisticated literary-theological mode in which Old English translators influenced by the Benedictine Reform appropriated Jewish law. Abjection of Judaism was central to this project, as scholars of Christian supersession and of English anti-Judaism have demonstrated, but my goal is not to trace attitudes towards Jews as Jews (as others such as Janet Thormann, Andrew P. Scheil, and Samantha Zacher have so skilfully done), even in their capacious fictional roles, but rather to reframe the vernacular intellectual projects of tenth- and eleventh-century England as productively dependent upon the appropriation of Jewish concepts, indeed as impossible without such appropriations.[7] Late Old English writers put Jewish laws about purity, food, and sexuality to counterintuitive and wide-ranging uses: Jewish law becomes both a basis for early English Christian sexual norms and a foil for monastic chastity, the Old Testament heroine Judith anchors a political theology that undergirds ecclesiastical sovereignty, and Jewish distinctions between unclean and clean animals structure early English ideas of purity and difference. At the same time, Ælfric and other translators weaponize these laws against the pollution of Christianity by its own Jewish ancestry, characterizing Jewishness as superseded, past, and even dead.[8]

Why another book about England and the English? This book treats late Old English literature primarily because it presents an extraordinary and, in the Latin West, unrivalled corpus of vernacular Biblical translation that has fascinated me for many years; when properly considered, this literature forces a reckoning with some of the earliest institutional ties between Christian ethnocentrism and the English language. This study works against several myths about Bible translation and about Old English. First, scholars sometimes read the style of early English prose Bible translations as clumsy and crude, the primitive first drafts of a (teleologically developing) English literary language, despite the many witnesses to an exquisitely complicated Old English poetic tradition several centuries older than these prose texts. As Kathleen Davis and Rebecca Stephenson have amply demonstrated, however, the "simplicity" and "brevity" of Benedictine English prose relative to the Latin of its intertexts must instead be seen as a politicized aesthetic that, far from decentralizing interpretive authority, concentrates it in skilled hands while also designating its texts as plain, contemporary, urgent, and essential.[9]

Moreover, As Gil Anidjar observes, scholars (particularly Jewish and other religious minority scholars) must still "attend to the peculiarly Western, singularly Christian, history of knowledge and power that lingers on (would that it only lingered!) to this day."[10] Although this literary history is not solely about anti-Judaism, the Benedictine cultural translation of Jewish law represents an important chapter in the prehistory of English anti-Semitism and therefore of European racism in general, shedding needed light on the genocidal developments of the twelfth and thirteenth centuries.[11] It also demonstrates the relationship between early experiments in theological dehumanization (associating Jews with animals) and the formation of English Christian corporate identity. As such, while in no way implying an inevitable continuity between pre-Conquest anti-Jewishness and the ethnic cleansing and Jewish Expulsion of the thirteenth century, the book suggests that appropriation of Jewish law and culture, and in particular the temporal operations of supersessionary translation and reading theorized by Ælfric and Wulfstan, provide an essential basis for later legal and cultural work that write Jewish people out of the English present and future.[12]

Supersessionary Translation as Cultural Translation

Where supersession is the theory, Bible adaptation and translation are, in medieval terms, the practice. A teleological narrative of Bible translation history has obscured this glaring principle of vernacular Biblical material. It is not at all the case that an all-powerful medieval Church prohibited vernacular Bible translation, as has long been taught in English-speaking countries that, as James Simpson notes, portray the Reformation as the beginning of vernacular literacy; as Andrew Colin Gow has demonstrated, this was not even true of Germany, where Luther popularized this claim.[13] This myth is itself an example of the extraordinary power of supersessionary thought in national cultural identity: this imaginary event of first translation conveys that the English language became public property as the result of liberal Protestant supersession of medieval Catholic regimes of prohibition.[14] By understanding the range of Biblical translation, and by regarding as a spectrum various forms of written dissemination, from the most faithful translations to the most free or concise adaptations, as well as by viewing Old Testament translation as a translation of specifically Jewish literature within various (usually formally and aggressively anti-Jewish) Christian cultures, it is possible to place medieval Biblical translation within the history of cultural translation as a whole.[15] Instead of appearing as the romantically liberated fragments of a suppressed mode of literacy, these authorized and semi-authorized vernacular works can then be seen as privileged texts appropriating a Jewish source culture into an English Christian host culture.

Cultural translation – adapting texts, concepts, and structures to a target culture from a source culture – tends to reify the power differential between two cultures.[16] When the source culture controls the translation and this power differential is extreme, cultural translation may colonize or assault the receptor culture. Translation of the Bible throughout the British Empire provides countless examples. Musa W. Dube has written on the missionary Setswana Bible's translation of demons and devils by the word *badimo*, meaning revered ancestor spirits, and the first Setswana-English dictionary's substitution of *badimo* for the correct Setswana words describing evil spirits. The violence of these missionary, colonial mistranslations, argues Dube, lies not only in denigrating the readers's honoured ancestors but also in perverting her relationship to her own Setswana language and culture – here "*Badimo* are equated with demons and devils, when any Motswana reader expects them to be friends with Jesus, or with divine powers."[17] In her discussion of German evangelism to the Ewe in (what is now) Ghana, Birgit Meyer finds this problem to be precisely the point: "The mission's preaching was thus characterized by the following paradox: on the one hand, terms from the non-Christian religious framework had to be integrated into the Christian Ewe discourse through translation, while on the other hand, a strict boundary was drawn between the two religions by diabolisation."[18]

When the receptor culture controls translation, cultural translation may conceal or vitiate aspects of the source culture. In the latter case, sometimes translation comments on the *existence* of the source culture. Tejaswini Niranjana locates translation as one way that colonizers create their fantasized colonial subjects (fantasies that, as Edward Said notes, take on dangerous material existence), defining colonial translation as the "transparent presentation of something that already exists, although the 'original' is actually brought into being through translation."[19] For the purposes of this book, the metaphor of the captive woman is particularly relevant to conceptualizing cultural translation. The influential Alexandrian exegete Origen identified translated texts with the war captive of Deuteronomy 21:10–13, a law describing how foreign women captured and enslaved in battle might be legally made into wives.[20] Origen, in one of his Levitical homilies, transforms the Biblical passage as follows to explain how Christians should read Jewish law:

> But nevertheless, I also frequently "have gone out to war against my enemies and I saw there" in the plunder "a woman with a beautiful figure." For whatever we find said well and reasonably among our enemies, or we read anything said among them wisely and knowingly, we must cleanse it also from the knowledge which is among them, remove and cut off all that is dead and worthless – namely all the hairs of the head and the nails of the woman taken from the spoils of the enemy – and so at last make her your wife when she has nothing of the things which are called dead through infidelity. She has nothing in her head, nothing in her hands, lest she bring something unclean or dead either in her thoughts or in her deeds. For the women of our enemies have nothing pure because there is no wisdom among them with which something unclean was not mixed.[21]

> Verumtamen et ego frequenter exivi ad bellum contra inimicos meos, et vidi ibi in praedam mulierem decora specie. Quaecunque enim bene et

rationabiliter dicta invenimus apud inimicos nostros, si quid apud illos sapienter et scienter dictum legimus, oportet nos mundare id, et ab scientia quae apud illos est auferre et resecare omne quod emortuum et inane est, hoc enim sunt omnes capilli capitis et ungulae mulieris ex inimicorum spoliis assumptae, et ita demum facere eam nobis facere eam nobis uxorem, cum jam nihil ex illis quae per infidelitatem mortua dicuntur, habuerit, nihil in capite habeat mortuum, nihil in manibus, ut neque sensibus, neque actibus, immundum aliquid, aut mortuum gerat. Nihil enim mundum habent mu[l]ieres hostium nostrorum, quia nulla est apud illos sapientia, cui immunditia aliqua sit admista.[22]

This metaphor approvingly describes the process of cultural translation as akin to cultural genocide and forced marriage,[23] so that supersession appears as an act of salutary and redemptive sexual violence by Christian interpreter upon humiliated Jewish text and supersessionary texts as the sacred progeny of forced reproduction.[24] The image, which in the writing of Jerome and Augustine came to describe the relationship between Christian and Gentile classical texts, became what Audrey Walton describes as a *"locus classicus"* of translation discourse in the medieval Christian West and appears in the work of Hrabanus Maurus, Peter Damian, Pope Gregory IX, Petrarch, and Chaucer.[25]

When speaking of medieval Bible translation, it is helpful to imagine a third case, in which the dominant culture acts as intermediary between source and ultimate host cultures. Such is the case when writers of a prestige language – medieval Latin or imperial British English – translate the Bible into a minority vernacular for pastoral use. In reality, my examples from the first case belong to this third category, because Latin and English are not the Bible's first languages.[26] Supersession has been particularly salient in these cases of double cultural translation, for such translators face an enhanced imperative to de-Judaize the Christian Bible in order to make it more accessible.[27] As Eugene Nida notes, not without chagrin, "in Bible translating it is quite impossible to remove such foreign 'objects' as *Pharisees*, *Sadducees*, *Solomon's temple* ... for these expressions are deeply imbedded in the very thought structure of the message."[28] Scrubbing the New Testament of its "foreign" Jewish valences becomes a matter of (im)practicality – one would wish to do so to aid universal comprehension of the Christian message, but one cannot do so because to lose Judaism is to rob Christian meaning. Moreover, some terms (*"Pharisees, Sadducees"*) are important for the very work they do in repudiating Judaism – a repudiation that may be necessary for Christian readers to understand even if, as in so many cases, they have no prior knowledge of Jewish beliefs. As theologian

William James Jennings observes, colonial missionary translation relies upon the myth that Christianity is universal and non-racial while Jewishness is particular and ethnic, a myth that ironically reinforces white supremacy.[29]

The instructive limit case of a particularistic theological attempt to remove Judaism from Christianity is the Institute for the Study and Eradication of Jewish Influence on German Church Life, founded in 1939 in Nazi Germany. The name of this group indicates an irresolvable tension, in which the imperatives of "study" and "eradication," while optimistically joined, are in fact diametrically opposed, and in which "Jewish influence" is central to the definition of the group charged with eradicating it. (This has been the fate of Nazism in general – its legacy is to be remembered primarily as part of the history of the major group it tried to eradicate.) As Susannah Heschel chronicles, the Institute prepared a new translation of the New Testament that did just what Nida pronounces desirable but impossible: it eradicated Jewish references. Indeed, it went even further: the popular German Christian movement, as it was known, rejected the Old Testament entirely, and so *Die Botschaft Gottes* (God's Message) was designed to be read entirely independently of that corpus. However, this solution would not be acceptable to most translators facing the problem of supersession – and not only because it is too anti-Semitic, as the German Christians' opponents, the Confessing Church movement, demonstrated when they argued for retaining the Old Testament on the grounds that the Hebrew Bible is actually anti-Semitic (thus proving the relevance for theology of Sartre's axiom about anti-Semitism). Rather, this solution resulted in such a transformation of the New Testament that, absent the kind of political pressure the Protestant churches felt in Nazi Germany, the product is difficult to recognize as a Christian Bible. For instance, as Heschel notes, the gospels had to be integrated into a single narrative and much of Paul's work had to be eliminated because it revealed his Jewish origins; as Gerdmar observes, most of the Gospel of John was retained because of its apparently anti-Semitic character, but the translators found concepts such as the Word and the Lamb of God too Jewish for inclusion.[30] Even the most anti-Jewish translators have been reluctant – have indeed been unable – to go this far. Erasing Judaism not only erases the contexts, references, and messages of early Christianity; it also makes impossible the message of supersessionary rebirth.

The falsely neutral principles of universality, relevance, and transparency have travelled unmarked into Western translation discourse and, indeed, often pervade the tools we use to analyse Christian translation in the secular academy. Derrida's "What Is a 'Relevant' Translation?"

demonstrates the centrality of Christian repudiation of Judaism to the Western concept of "relevant" translation, which converts both text and human other. Venuti excoriates the falsely universal principles of relevance and transparency in translation, locating the importance of Derrida's essay in exposing their "ethnocentric violence."[31]

The Gag Reflex: Revulsion in Time

I am aware of the difficulties in presenting Hebrew Biblical law as an attractive subject for sustained contemplation. Its unattractiveness has a history, however, that is not at all irrelevant to the argument of this book. Perhaps Origen instantiated the tradition that some Jewish law is too alienating and tedious for Christian reading.[32] Leviticus, the topic of chapter 1 of this monograph and the place where my research began, is the most legalistic book of the Hebrew Bible; it contains most of the food law and sexual law, as well as very considerable instructions regarding agriculture, sacrifice, and worship. It is in the unique position of directly inspiring a considerable amount of medieval Christian law and *also* figuring as synecdochic for the aspects of Judaism that Christianity most needs to reject. Origen notes that in contrast to the easily digestible historical and wisdom books of the Hebrew Bible, "Si vero legatur ei liber Levitici, offenditur continuo animus, et quasi non suum refugit cibum. Qui enim venit ut disceret Deum colere, justitiae ac pietatis ejus praecepta suscipere, audit mandata de sacrificiis dari, et immolationum ritus doceri"[33] (But if the book of Leviticus is read to him, his mind immediately stumbles and he flees from it as from something that is not his own food. For the one who had come to learn how to worship God and how to receive his commandments concerning justice and piety, hears precepts given about sacrifices and the rites taught that concern immolation).[34] Although Origen also writes of the boredom inspired by these laws, what he is actually describing is revulsion – a visceral repulsion at the foreign that manifests like an involuntary seizure at the mere thought of accepting it – that proves inconvenient for the evangelizer who has a relatively easy time spreading the Christian message without the burden of Jewish law.[35] This is not just a figure of speech. To early Christians as bearers of Jewish and Roman tradition, the idea of theology as food, and vice versa, was in John Penniman's words "no mere metaphor"; the two concepts were, as Gillian Feeley-Harnik notes, inseparable.[36] This relationship is complicated, as I have suggested above, both by the inextricable association of Jewish law with rejected food practices, and by the impossibility of stripping Jewish law from the theological food that nourishes Christianity. As Heschel notes, "Dejudaizing Christianity was a kind of theological bulimia ... an example of the daughter religion, Christianity, engaging in a constant, repeated process of taking in the symbolic mother, Judaism, and then regurgitating her."[37] Judaism is here the mother whose milk is essential for the daughter she has produced, but the daughter deliberately vomits it. How, then, to ensure enough nourishment is taken?

As Sara Ahmed has skilfully demonstrated, such forms of revulsion should be understood as public feelings, shared cultural affects that regulate the bounds of a social body by attaching to persons and things to be excluded.[38] The work of nineteenth-century English historian and cleric Henry Soames demonstrates how exclusion of Jewish law in the form of Anglo-Saxonist distaste for its translation serves an account of English national progress. In his 1834 history of early English Christianity,[39] Soames notes: "Of religious peculiarities incidentally discovered in Egbert's *Penitential*, no one is more striking than Anglo-Saxon reception of that compromise with Jewish prejudices which apostolic authority established early in the Christian era. Our forefathers were enjoined a rigorous abstinence *from blood, and from things strangled*: nor did they disregard Levitical distinctions between the clean and unclean among animals."[40] Our "forefathers" are the English lay subjects who abide by the "remarkable prohibitions" of the penitential. A further passage bears quoting at length:

> Anglo-Saxon prejudices appear never to have been relaxed upon the subject of such aliments as the most venerable of councils, that of Jerusalem, had forbidden. Although Jewish prejudices no longer needed conciliation, yet this was apparently quite overlooked. Ecclesiastical authorities implicitly followed Egbert's example in prohibiting the tasting of blood or of strangled animals. A legal defilement was attributed even to the water into which such substances had fallen. In the *Penitentials*, accordingly, are provided penances apportioned to all these breaches of the ceremonial law, whether accidental or otherwise. It is this peculiarity which has made many regard certain canonical sanctions, occurring in Anglo-Saxon monuments, as irresistibly ludicrous. Readers have been unable to contain their laughter, on encountering grave denunciations against water that had come into contact with a dead mouse or weasel. Those who think, however, of Mosaic prohibitions and the council of Jerusalem, will recognize in such peculiarities interesting links connecting modern times with ancient ...[41]

As I describe in chapter 1, the blood prohibitions have a continuing (if conflicted) moral logic in the English church, which Ælfric scrupulously upholds, while distaste for drinking water contaminated by dead rodents was not a peculiarity limited to the early English. But the term "legal defilement," while not entirely accurate, does important work here by collapsing the penitential into a very specific theological error associated with Pharisaic Judaism and firmly repudiated by early Christianity, which it now makes synecdochic for Jewish law itself: the belief that contaminated substances ritually contaminate those who ingest them.[42] What is erroneous about avoiding water containing dead rodents is not, presumably, the unreasonable fastidiousness of the hygienic standard. Instead, it is that – in Soames's mind – it is almost as though the early English forgot that they "no longer" had to accommodate "Jewish prejudices" as earlier Christians once did.

That Soames describes Judaism dismissively, characterizing Jewish law as "Jewish prejudices" and as "ceremonial," that is, ethically irrelevant, is no more (or less) than one expects, for we are all aware by now of the compact between medievalism and the nineteenth century's deadly racial categories, and moreover of the casual anti-Semitism of polite Anglo-American culture in this and other eras (even "polite" and its synonyms, such as "genteel," carry a whiff of exclusion).[43] Nor is it particularly unexpected that anthropological relish seems to enter into the equation – the banishment of English food laws, on account of their Jewishness, to the exotic "air" of the "Orient" where they can be enjoyed as foreign, is a standard Orientalist move that aligns the scholar with modernity. More notable is the reassertion of Jewish law's unassimilability in order to retain a fictive Christian English continuity from early pre-Conquest ecclesiasts, here described more generally as Anglo-Saxon forebears, to Victorian scholars. Here, overzealous "compromise with" rejected "Jewish prejudices" appears as an atavistic flaw in the English church, comparable to the superstitious practices of contemporary non-Western peoples. In categorizing it among the "religious peculiarities" of medieval Christians and treating it as a source of exotic amusement, the Anglo-Saxonist locates the difference between medieval and modern English churches in Judaism improperly brought forward and made foreign, accidental to an essential Christianity. ("[L]aughter" is the genteel answer to gagging, another somatic event of instantaneous rejection.) Like Origen, he worries about the place of (potentially revolting) Jewish law in his Christian spiritual nourishment. Meanwhile, the Jewish rejection of idolatry remains an essential antecedent, passed into Christianity, which can be used to validate the authenticity of the early English church, repudiate Catholicism, and draw a specious distinction between them.

Johannes Fabian and Edward Said have demonstrated the process by which contemporary Eurocentrism rests on an idea of time that Fabian

Introduction: A Brief History of Supersessionary Disgust 13

calls the "denial of coevalness," the belief that cultural others exist in a time prior to the subject's time.[44] Other societies are primitive, occupying an earlier stage of social evolution, frequently frozen there and timeless. Denial of coevalness to Judaism is foundational to Christian supersessionism, which sees the world in terms of a sacred, universal time divided into eras based on revelations of divine law: a time before Jewish (Mosaic) law, the age of Jewish law before the coming of Christ, and the time after Christ's advent, crucifixion, and resurrection, in which the New Dispensation swept away the Old Law, bringing the possibility of salvation and the expectation of final judgment to everyone. Although on the face of it, Christian salvation history is universalizing and encompasses all of world history, Christian time is in practical terms a totalizing system imposed on – and meant to stamp out – non-Christian conceptions of time. For Protestant and post-Protestant secular historians, additional eras may supersede those listed above, but the event of the Incarnation still anchors a universal temporal regime (*anno domini* or Common Era), which globalizes the Christian calendar.[45] Denial of coevalness to non-European, non-Christian peoples is foundational to many modern university disciplines, and is, to slightly misquote Malory Nye's provocative critique of religious studies, the "poisoned tree" from which Euro-American scholarship and pedagogy continue, even in resistance, to draw fruit.[46] Soames is chronologically and geographically distant from Origen, although like Origen he practised theological bulimia in a society that included real, law-observing Jews as his coevals. In his overt chauvinism, he may seem distant as well from twenty-first-century medieval studies, but I include him here as a cautionary tale: it is not so easy, really, for many readers to shake off the notion that religious laws are "ludicrous," or disgusting, or superstitious – that they belong in the past. As Davis, Kathleen Biddick, and others in and out of medieval studies observe, supersessionary thinking is intertwined with notions of progress and rationality, as well as with national thinking and periodization.[47] Secular scholarship has not banished the supersessionary assumptions and the denial of coevalness to Jews evident in Soames's discussion of English history; assumptions about Jewish particularity and Christian universality, for instance, or the desirability and rightness of typological reading, or self-evident periodizations and disciplinary categories, still have the potential to cloud our thinking about English reception of Jewish law.[48] So does simple disgust. Moreover, supersession is highly seductive because it allows us to master and overcome an embarrassing past. Indeed, one lesson of this book is that eagerness to suppress one's cultural or scholarly inheritance – in this case, the inheritance of supersessionary thinking – can lead to a profoundly mistaken sense that one has broken with or triumphed over that inheritance.

The question, then, has never been whether Jewish Biblical laws are revolting or boring, but whether they are assimilable to Christian theology, sociality, and temporality, or to their secularized sequels.[49] These questions are not posed only by anti-Semites, or even by committed Christians. Even Jewish and secular scholars have adopted attitudes of temporal embarrassment towards the ancient Jewish laws. As the feminist Jewish commentator S. Tamar Kamionkowski notes, "the first parts of Leviticus … [feel] alienating, if not downright offensive, to many modern Westerners … Jewish and Christian clergy tend to flounder for good sermonic material in this part of the Bible. We tend to read the text as reflecting primitive thought, an aspect of our past for which we must produce apologetics." The referent of "We" is ambiguous, perhaps deliberately: is it "[m]any modern Westerners" who find the material "primitive," or only those sermonists who feel compelled to defend the Jewish "past"? Almost certainly both – even "kids in Hebrew school" see Leviticus as "gross and barbaric."[50] Kamionkowski, a scholar of Leviticus who (like Radner) defends the book's relevance after this feint, presumably makes this elision among "modern Westerners," modern rabbis, and naïve Jewish children, in opposition to the primitive past, not in order to question whether "modern Westerners," here emphatically including Jews, are in fact hygienic and progressive but in order to defend the Jewish theological place in Western modernity.

The Bad Bits: Leviticus in Old English

When it comes to translation, then, abbreviation must come as a relief. As Richard M. Marsden observes in his brilliant 1995 study *The Text of the Old Testament in Anglo-Saxon England*, "Leviticus is entirely concerned with law, including the elaborate procedures laid down for the making of sacrificial offerings, and repetition is frequent. The Old English translator edited heavily, usually with considerable intelligence, and excised more than three quarters of the book."[51] This statement, which appears in a magisterial monograph on Old Testament manuscript sources in pre-Conquest England, implies that Jewish law is of little thematic or symbolic importance to the Bible as a whole – the book is "entirely concerned with law," that is, it is not concerned with anything else other than law; it presumably yields no other insights. As an example of the allegedly negligible relevance of Levitical law, Marsden mentions "sacrificial offerings" – a topic symbolically central to medieval Christian theology. The tedium reduced by the prudent translator is exemplified by "elaborate procedures" and "frequent" "repetition" – two literary devices the Hebrew Bible uses precisely to call attention to its most central passages and principles.[52] Even the narrowest reading of this praise, that is, that "considerable intelligence" refers only to the translation *style* that renders the translation apparently seamless, takes nothing away from the overall approval towards gutting the Book of Leviticus. However, within a work dedicated entirely to the Old Testament in pre-Conquest England, in which careful manuscript and philological evidence is laid out in minute detail, this praise is unconvincing. The Old English translator who has cut out the poetic repetitions and mysterious elaborations of Jewish law, and thereby also perhaps removed desirable evidence for the Latin sources, cannot be dear to the scholar. On the contrary, this praise expresses a reflexive affirmation of what everyone knows about the ordinary reader's inability, then and now, to stomach this book.

Yet there is an aesthetic argument for reading Leviticus holistically. Mary Douglas, reading Leviticus as literature, demonstrates that the work bears a ring structure that integrates every chapter and law. As Douglas observes regarding the elaborations of Leviticus, "Leviticus' literary style is correlative, it works through analogies. Instead of explaining why an instruction has been given, or even what it means, it adds another similar instruction, and another and another, thus producing its highly schematized effect."[53] The accumulation of parallel laws and statements creates an orderly world view within which individual verses make sense. The overall structure works the same way: "the ring form dominates the whole composition, every couple of chapters, or four or five chapters, form a clearly defined ring, and [the] book is a maxi-ring containing all the constituent rings."[54] Rather than comprising a list of laws with a linear logical relationship, the argument of Leviticus proceeds in a literary way – through the analogical structure of the prohibitions, which echo one another and indicate the parallels among body, sanctuary, and creation. There is no distinction between ethical and ritual prohibitions – purity safeguards and demonstrates holiness. Even given that Leviticus is a composite work, it has a single message – to imagine, as centuries of Christian and secular interpretation do, that the gruesome minutiae of the sacrifice regulations intrude upon its ethical program is to miss the signals of its literary integrity.

A closer look reveals that the translators of the *Old English Heptateuch*, a selective Old Testament translation unprecedented in its scope within Western European vernaculars, like Douglas, *also* see Leviticus as literature. They recognize that it is composed of a story, hence the heavy emphasis on the narrative portions. This is not to say that they recognize every piece as being integral to the whole – far from it – only that the new and improved Old English Leviticus is also a piece of narrative and *conceived* as narrative. As Withers notes of the Heptateuch manuscript, "even where a succession of large omissions has been made, continuity of narrative is maintained."[55] Looking carefully at the Old English Leviticus, where omitted and included portions form a pattern that demands analysis, it is impossible to sustain the belief that the principle of translation is simply the dissemination of laws relevant to Christians and omission of other laws, bound up with the need for brevity.[56] Irrelevancies are not omitted. Numerous laws relevant to a Christian audience are obfuscated, elided, or omitted. Moreover, Moses, Aaron, and God are continually marked as actors and speakers, even when they do little that is new. The translated text now resembles historical narrative rather than sacred code, and thus portrays the lawgiving primarily as historical event, situating Jewish law in a past time. The supersessionary tradition of Leviticus as disgusting and boring intersects with what Davis has identified as the brevity trope in Old English homiletic literature, a style that constitutes an apocalyptic "politics of time" in which (particularly Old Testament) exegesis must for reasons of urgency be abbreviated to commentary.[57] However, this does not mean the translators – or any supersessionary translators – simply avoid the unsavory parts. The limits of millennial time, of the unlearned mind, and of the allegedly easily provoked Christian gag reflex require a new style of translation, an exegetical style that masticates and digests (and masticates and digests), and thus transforms, the raw material that offends.

Structure of the Book

This monograph explores the distinct, yet mutually conversant, strategies of several contemporary Old English translators in this process of Christian digestion. The first part of the book, chapter 1, "Exsanguinating Leviticus: Supersessionary Translation in the *Old English Heptateuch*," examines direct and faithful transmissions of some parts of the Hebrew Bible, where "faithful" indicates a degree not of completeness but of Christian discernment. The *Old English Heptateuch*, a compilation of the Pentateuch, Joshua, and Judges in Old English prose by Ælfric and an anonymous translator or group of translators, provides an opportunity to contrast two divergent approaches to translating Jewish law. In the aggressively brief Old English translation of Leviticus (the first translation of this text in a Western European vernacular), the anonymous translator's method appears mysteriously arbitrary. Seemingly irrelevant laws are retained and relevant laws excluded or distorted. The anonymous source has, unlike Ælfric, left no statement of principles. By focusing the lens of supersession on the repeated Biblical prohibition against consuming blood, I unlock this puzzle and uncover the guiding impulse of this pattern. In a mode of supersessionary translation I playfully call *exsanguination*, the anonymous translator deliberately flaunts the otherness of Jewish law, while showing the Christian supersession of Old Testament sacrifice at work.

The second part of the book, chapters 2 through 4, takes as its primary subject Ælfric's translations of Jewish law in his Old Testament homilies and in the First Old English Letter to Wulfstan, and begins to explore the uses of supersessionary translation for agendas beyond Christian supersession. Chapter 2, "Men as Meat: Jewish Law and Orders of Being in Ælfric's Translations of Maccabees and Job," engages with critical animal studies to explore early English ambivalence about kosher law. Although officially rejected by the Church, the Hebrew Bible's taxonomies of gustatory purity subvert the food taboos observed in Christian English and European penitentials. This chapter demonstrates that, drawing on this ambivalence, Ælfric makes canny use of kosher law to entangle Christian–Jewish and human–animal difference. Ultimately, the abbot responds reassuringly to English anxieties about hunger and predation by defining meaningful life as what is proper to humans and Christians. Chapter 3, "The Benedictine Invention of Heterosexuality: Jewish (Law's) Sexual Difference in Time," argues that in the writings of Ælfric, Wulfstan, and other English Benedictines on the priesthood and on circumcision, as well as in the anonymous Old English Life of St. Smaragdus, Old Testament Jews represent a reproductive heterosexuality valid in its time but now superseded by the chastity and non-reproductive familial life of the monastery. This argument revises histories of medieval sexuality and gender by demonstrating that long before what scholars such as Daniel Boyarin call the "invention of heterosexuality," which figured Jews and other groups as "queer," the Benedictines had already produced and weaponized a coherent vision of Jewish heterosexuality.

Chapter 4, "*Ænlic Wimman*: Judith and the Exception," demonstrates that Ælfric retranslates the Book of Judith as a meditation on sacred sovereignty. Ælfric opposes Holofernes's *anweald* (rule, i.e., imperial sovereignty) to Judith's **ænlicnyss* (singularity, i.e., independence), reconfiguring these terms as concepts in a Reformist political theology. Using the multivalent Old English *clæne* (pure) to translate Judith's observance of Jewish law as Christian chastity, Ælfric makes chastity the precondition for self-rule. Reading Ælfric's *Judith* as an unconventional hagiography further reveals that it is only through a translated

Jewish heroine, not a Christian saint, that Ælfric can model embodied sacred sovereignty.

In the final section of the book, I advance a new reading of Wulfstan's best-known sermon, *Sermo Lupi ad Anglos*, as a piece of Bible translation *sub rosa*. Chapter 5, "Like Dogs and Wolves: Wulfstan as Biblical Translator" traces Wulfstan's canny redeployment of several modes and figures of translation, all of them centring on scenes of humiliation, conquest, and abasement. In his politicized translation praxis, Wulfstan forges a passage of the Hebrew Bible, subverts the well-known translation trope of the captive woman until it is nearly unrecognizable, and uses dogs as figures of both supersession and of bad pastorship. What unifies these modes is an apparent multivocality straining towards univocality, where the voice of the people, the voice of the author, and the voice of God become indistinguishable. For the episcopal author, supersessionary translation serves and expresses a political theology in the sense Miguel Vatter uses the term, as "an answer to the question of who or what represents and bears the person of the state or of God."[58]

It is a book for strong stomachs.

1 Exsanguinating Leviticus: Supersessionary Translation in the *Old English Heptateuch*

Reading the Old Testament on its own, one could almost think that God wanted people to follow Jewish law. By the eleventh century, centuries of Christian interpretation had roundly refuted this so-called literal reading – more or less, since (as I discuss below) in fact Christian societies and the Church adopted many Biblical sexual regulations and some Biblical food regulations.[1] As a result, the central creative problem for Ælfric and the other translators of the massive prose translation project known as the *Old English Heptateuch* is probably not the difficulty of faithfully translating God's word in the vernacular, but that of accurately representing God's word while also conveying that God means something other than what He said. This problem, which, following Stanton's influential discussion of Ælfric's apparently agonized and apologetic *Preface to Genesis*, we conventionally refer to as "anxiety," is, as Menzer suggests, specific to Christian supersessionary reading of the Old Testament.[2] This chapter reframes the apparent anxiety of translating Scripture as an anxiety of *cultural* translation that arises from the irreducible problem of Jewish–Christian inheritance/rejection, and most of all from the inheritance and rejection of Jewish law, the continuing observance of which is itself associated with an inappropriate form of fidelity.

Several reparative translation strategies suggest themselves to address this knotty problem. In Ælfric's late translations of Old Testament historical books, he will, as Stanton notes, choose open transformation, altering the material and littering it with commentary. As Rebecca Stephenson observes, Ælfric often finds great narrative power in limiting nuance and multivocality.[3] In his contributions to the *Old English Heptateuch*, he uses a version of his concise, precise "plain style" and abbreviates and redacts the text while adding very little original language.[4] The result is, as Stanton notes, "far from slavishly literal."[5]

The anonymous translators of Leviticus, who face the most harrowing challenge to a Christian translator anxious about Judaism, also use a simple style and enthusiastic redaction. They add nothing, or almost nothing, to the text.

Yet the anonymous translators avoid the easiest possible solution to their own particular problem. Leviticus is the book riddled with Jewish laws, laws that have the potential to mislead Christians and (as I have discussed at length in the Introduction to this book) that notoriously alienate and disgust Christian naifs. It would be possible, more or less, to simply delete those laws that Christians no longer follow and include those that are still relevant. The eighth- or ninth-century Hiberno-Latin *Liber ex lege Moysi* adapts much of the Pentateuch according to this logic, which Sven Meeder describes as "presenting the biblical rules, stripped from their biblical context, as a collection of practical laws that were to be taken literally and seriously in their own right."[6] A similar principle, with greater emphasis on the glamour of Biblical authority, animates Alfred's Old English Prologue to the *Domboc*, which translates much of Exodus 20–3, and Wulfstan's sermon *Be Godcundre Warnunge*, an adaptation of Leviticus 26 that claims to be a close translation.[7] But this is not the route these translators have chosen. On the contrary: the pattern of what the translators choose to include and exclude is at first indecipherable, apparently haphazard. The answer lies in their own particular ethics of supersessionary translation, which I call *exsanguination*: a skilled demonstration of Jewish otherness, which enacts through translation the Christian supersession of Old Testament sacrificial ritual.

The Texts

The *Old English Heptateuch* is an eleventh-century translation from Latin of the Pentateuch, Joshua, and Judges, translated partially by Ælfric and partially by the later anonymous compilers, with an additional preface (the *Preface to Genesis*) and treatise (*Libellus de veteri testamento et novo*) by Ælfric. Of the Biblical material, Ælfric likely translated Genesis 1–3, 5:32–9:29, and 12:1–24:10; Numbers 13–26; Joshua; and Judges; the other source provided the remaining material as well as intervening in Genesis 23–4, Numbers 13, and Joshua 1 and 12.[8] Two of the manuscripts include the entire Pentateuch: Oxford, Bodleian Library, MS Laud Misc. 509 (the complete *Old English Heptateuch*, ca. 1075) and London, British Library, MS Cotton Claudius B.iv (the *Illustrated Hexateuch*, eleventh century).[9] Neither of these is the original exemplar; they are sibling texts, or copies of sibling texts, of which MS Laud Misc. 509 (sometimes called the Heptateuch, a term that I generally reserve for the project as a whole) is more faithful to its parent; that parent text was probably a direct copy of the original.[10] These two manuscripts are the only vernacular witnesses to the books of Leviticus, Numbers, and Deuteronomy from pre-Conquest England. Leviticus, translated by the anonymous compilers, appears in both manuscripts; however, chapters 12–17, 21, 22, and 27 of Leviticus are entirely absent;[11] what remains is substantially redacted. For example, chapter 19 is abbreviated from thirty-seven to twenty-one verses, some of which are also shortened.[12] As Richard Marsden, the text's most recent editor, notes, only three of the book's chapters (1, 8, and 26) can be considered to have "received a fairly full treatment."[13]

Latin sources for the Book of Leviticus were scarcely more plentiful in pre-Conquest England. Biblical manuscripts circulated in parts, and few such books seem to have included Leviticus. We know of five exceptions: four complete Bibles, three of which are extant,[14] and two nonconsecutive leaves of another Leviticus fragment that survive in Durham Cathedral Library, C. IV. 7, where they have been folded to make a cover for a Boethius manuscript.[15] That the surviving Latin Leviticus witnesses tend to appear in full Bibles, when the manuscript norm was partial Bibles such as psalters and gospel-books, may simply be the results of a distorted record, since many such books did not survive.[16] Most likely, it indicates that even within the circulation of Latin Bibles a form of literary selection was already at work, and that Leviticus was considered less useful or valuable than others that circulate in part-Bibles.

Supersession

Problems of omission and interpolation do not arise only in relation to the Old English translations. The extant Anglo-Latin Bibles from this period also make minor emendations. For instance, the tenth-century Northumbrian Royal Bible (MS London, BL, Royal 1. E. VII + VIII) already omits certain portions of Leviticus,[17] although by the standards of the Old English Bibles these are conservative changes: for instance, Leviticus 19:2 and 3 of the Royal Bible omit *"et dices ad eos"*[18] and abbreviate *"patrem suum, et matrem suam timeat"* to *"matrem et patrem suum timeat,"* changes that, except for an inversion of parental gender, omit only what is already implied and so do not change the literal meaning.[19]

In contrast to the conservative changes the Anglo-Latin Bibles make to their probable source material, the emendations of the Old English translation are radical and broad. A survey of the Latin material included and excluded from the Old English Leviticus reveals a great deal of apparent randomness, but there are some general rules. For one thing, there is almost no sexuality; chapter 15 is omitted and chapters 18 and 20 almost entirely excised. There are also few explicit references to uncleanness; although the concept pervades the Book of Leviticus and the word *inmundus* (as *immundus* and its declensions) appears approximately sixty times in the Vulgate Leviticus, this word is translated only *once* into the Old English Leviticus, in regards to prohibited fish: "Ne ete ge nanne fisc, buton þa þe habbað finnas and scilla; þa oðre synd unclæne" (11:9–12; Do not eat any fish except those that have fins and scales; the others are unclean).[20] Likewise, not a single *immundus* is translated from the Latin Numbers or Deuteronomy (where the word is abundant), or Joshua or Judges (where it is scarce) into Old English. The very question of uncleanness is eliminated – it becomes a question only of what is prohibited and not prohibited – as if the very notion of uncleanness were religious esoterica not appropriate, in the minds of the anonymous translators, for a vernacular text. Although it is impossible to entirely eliminate the structures of pollution and purity from the Pentateuch, since this system is in fact, as Douglas notes, a major organizing metaphor through which the Pentateuch explains the Jewish covenant with God,[21] eliminating the *word* unclean is a neat supersessionary solution, enacting in translation the theological ideal in which the New Dispensation removes the label of uncleanness from the physical world, physical practice, and reserves it for the world of evil spirits and intentions.[22] Leviticus is thus defanged – its law exists as a semi-anthropological window onto Old Testament practice, but loses the power to label obedience pure and violation impure.[23]

The (Missing) Sexual Prohibitions

The most obvious rule of the Old English translation of Leviticus is the excision of sexuality. This principle presents the anonymous translator's somewhat extreme solution to a problem that plagued Ælfric in his translation of Old Testament materials in general and of the prose in Genesis in particular. The sexual behaviour of the patriarchs (and perhaps of ancient Israel in general) was to Ælfric a key problem of sharing the Old Testament, particularly the Pentateuch, with unlearned clerics and lay people. As Hugh Magennis notes, it is ironically Biblical material that proves most "intractable" in the overall trend in Old English monastic translation of purifying sources, particularly Latin sources, of their most "prurient" content.[24] Ælfric writes of this difficulty in the *Preface to Genesis*:

> Nu þincð me, leof, þæt þæt weorc is swiðe pleolic me oððe ænigum men to underbeginnenne, for þan þe ic ondræd gif sum dysig man ðas boc ræt,

oððe rædan g[e]hyrþ, þæt he wille wenan þæt he mote libban nu on þære ni[wan] æ swa swa þa ealdan fæderas leofodon, þa on þære tide ær þan þe seo ealde æ gesett wære, oþþe swa swa men leofodon under Moyses æ. Hwilon ic wiste þæt sum mæssepreost, se þe min magister wæs on þam timan, hæfde þa boc Genesis and he cuðe be dæle Lyden understandan. Þa cwæþ he be þam heahfædere Iacobe þæt he hæfde feower wif: twa geswustra and heora twa þinena. Ful soð he sæde, ac he nyste, ne ic þa git, hu micel todal ys betweohx þære ealdan æ and þære niwan. On anginne þisere worulde nam se broþer hys swuster to wife, and hwilon eac se fæder tymde be his agenre dehter, and manega hæfdon ma wifa to folces eacan. And man ne mihte þa æt fruman wifian, buton on his siblingum. Gyf hwa wyle nu swa lybban æfter Cristes tocyme swa swa men leofodon ær Moises æ, oþþe under Moises æ, ne byð se man na cristen, ne he furþo[n] wyrðe ne byð þæt him ænig cristen man mid ete. (*OEH* 3–4)

Now it seems to me, dear friend, that this [translation] work is very dangerous for me or for anyone to undertake, because I fear that if someone ignorant reads this book, or hears it read, that he will think that he should live now in the New Law just as the ancient fathers lived in that time before the Old Law was established, or just as people lived under Moses's law. Once I knew a mass-priest, who was my teacher at that time, who had the book of Genesis and could partly understand Latin. He said then of the patriarch Jacob that he had four wives: two sisters and their two maids. He told the truth, but he did not know, nor yet did I, how much difference there is between the Old Law and the New. At the beginning of this world a brother took his sister as a wife, and sometimes also a father begot by his own daughter, and many also had more wives [than one] for the people's increase. And a person might not then take a wife at the beginning, except among his sisters. If anyone will now live after Christ's coming just as people lived before Moses's law, or under Moses's law, then that person is no Christian, nor is he even worthy that any Christian should eat with him.

Sexual behaviour among the patriarchs included incest and polygamy (as well as the combination, marriage of a man with two sisters, that troubles Ælfric in Jacob's life), and in fact at the very beginning of time (presumably among the children of Adam and Eve), implies Ælfric, incest was the only possible means of procreation. It is probably not literally the case that Ælfric's teacher so misunderstood Biblical example as to sanction unrestrained polygamy and incest, although in monastic eyes such a slur against married priests might be close enough to the truth.[25] Rather, as Melinda J. Menzer notes of the preface as a whole, this passage must be taken as an "admonition" about reading the Old

Testament without the New Testament – that is, without understanding that the New Testament supersedes the Old.[26] Although this preface could read as distinguishing between the laws before and after Christ's advent, Ælfric is actually talking about three distinct time periods, each with its own regime of laws: the wild and woolly period before Moses's law (which includes all of Genesis), the time of the Old Law (Judaism before Christ, when priests could marry and procreate), and the time since Christ's advent. Each regime has, but is not reducible to, its own forms of sexual propriety.

Managing the misbehaviour of pre-Mosaic figures is indeed a key translation principle in the Ælfrician Genesis. This operation usually occurs through omission, since, as Rebecca Barnhouse notes, "Old Testament patriarchs often engage in deeds that are difficult for a translator to interpret figuratively by adding a word or phrase. Whole paragraphs or pages of exegesis would be needed to explain some of these acts – murder, rape, deceit, sexual licentiousness."[27] Thus Rachel's untruth about menstruation disappears from the translation,[28] and Sarah emerges explicitly "ungewemmed" (uncorrupted, Genesis 20:14), Ælfric's interpolation, from the harem of Abimelech, in which her husband (and perhaps half-brother) Abraham willingly if temporarily places her.[29]

In general, however, Ælfric does not censor polygamy among the pre-Mosaic patriarchs, even when it would be possible to do so – for instance, in the case of Lamech's wives, who are not integral characters.[30] However, the story of Lot, who offers his daughters to a mob intent on sexual assault, demonstrates that some patriarchal behaviours are too grievous for a complete translation. This is evident when Ælfric censors the climactic crimes in the story of Sodom. In the Biblical original, the men of Sodom try to force Lot to surrender his angelic guests so that they may sexually assault them (in the Vulgate, "ut cognoscamus eos," that we may know them, Genesis 19:5), and Lot offers his two daughters as substitute victims: "Educam eas ad vos, et abutimini eis sicut placuerit vobis dummodo viris istis nihil faciatis mali, quia ingressi sunt sub umbraculum tegminis mei" (Genesis 19:8; I will bring them out to you, and abuse you them as it shall please you so that you do no evil to these men, because they are come in under the shadow of my roof). Ælfric's substitution replaces the description of the crime with a more circumlocutionary explanation: "Se leodscipe wæs swa bysmorfull þæt hig woldon fullice ongean gecynd heora galnysse gefyllan, na mid wimmannum ac swa fullice þæt us sceamað hyt openlice to secgenne, and þæt wæs heora hream þæt hig openlice heora fylþe gefremedon."[31] (That people was so depraved that they wished to filthily satisfy their lusts against nature, not with women but so filthily that it shames us to say it openly, and that was their disturbance of the peace, that they openly performed their filth.) At first glance, this explanation seems to censor the sexual material, but if Ælfric means to keep his audience's minds from sex, he chooses his words poorly. The wrong described in the Biblical text is a (potential) rape; Lot's response indicates that he must protect his male guests (because they have come under his protection), even at the cost of his daughters. This response is certainly open to interpretation – is sexual contact between men, or specifically anal intercourse, an important aspect of the crime's abhorrence? – and it would later become standard to reduce this crime against hospitality to its gender configurations.[32] Ælfric's euphemistic but hardly discreet explanation makes just this move, reducing the potential multivalence of the Sodomites' sin to sexual irregularity rather than the abuse of guests. The point of all this ambiguity and obfuscation is not, perhaps, to keep the reader from sexual speculation; it is hard to see how it would successfully do so. Rather, in keeping with Ælfric's agenda elsewhere, it is probably to occlude Lot's suboptimal response, a move consistent with his overall interest in sanitizing the patriarchs.

A comparison to the Old English poetic *Genesis A* accentuates this ambiguity: the Sodomites of this poem

>   Heton lædan ut
> of þam hean hofe   halige aras,
> weras to gewealde,   wordum cwædon
> þæt mid þam hæleðum   hæman wolden
> unscomlice   – arna ne gymden   (lines 2457b–61b)

[c]alled [for him] to bring out the holy messengers from that lofty house, [to deliver] the men into their power, and declared that with those warriors they shamelessly desired to have intercourse – taking no care for honour.

Lot responds with equal frankness:

> Her syndon inne   unwemme twa
> dohtor mine.   Doð, swa ic eow bidde
> – ne can þara idesa   owðer gieta
> þurh gebedscipe   beorna neawest –
> and geswicað þære synne   (lines 2466a–70b)

Here inside are my two uncorrupted daughters. Do as I ask you – neither of these ladies yet knows intimacy with men in bed – and turn away from this sin.[33]

26   Nothing Pure

Magennis notes that the poet is less squeamish than the Old English norm in his approach to sexually scandalous source material; however, the poem generally attempts "to absolve good characters from criticism with regard to questions of sexual behaviour and attitudes," displacing blame onto villains.[34] The sin of the Sodomites shines through here, but the narrative does not gloss over Lot's attempt to sacrifice his daughters, although the language of his offer is prettier than that in the Vulgate.[35] The Book of Genesis, then, appears in Ælfric's translation to abbreviate and euphemize sexuality when possible, but not to eclipse it entirely. It is most concerned with altering the material that Ælfric objects to in his *Preface to Genesis* – that is, with the sins of the patriarchs, who are supposed to be righteous. The translation principles of Leviticus as regards sexuality are so extreme as to be in fact quite different – the solution of the anonymous Leviticus translators is to excise nearly all reference to sexuality without regard to relevance or attribution of blame.

The Book of Leviticus contains the portions of Mosaic law that strictly regulate marriage and sexuality. Douglas argues that sexuality, symbolized by circumcision, is the third pillar of Levitical theology (in addition to God's justice or righteousness and the covenant): "Leviticus is an elaborate teaching of the difference between sexual and ritual reproduction. It opposes natural fertility to the ritual for making heirs to God's promise. Descent by the seed of the loins on the one hand, and the cut and blood of the circumcised penis on the other, its laws keep the two bodily fluids, semen and blood, meticulously apart."[36] Although it might seem natural for the Old English translation of Leviticus to emphasize laws about sexual purity, particularly because many of them overlap with and indeed give rise to Christian sexual mores, and because, as Calum M. Carmichael notes, they correct some of the behaviours of the patriarchs described in Genesis,[37] the Old English translator in fact does quite the opposite with these sexual laws, as in Leviticus 18. This thirty-verse chapter, which deals primarily with prohibited sexual partners, loses more than twenty-seven verses in translation:

[18:6] Ne hæme nan man wið his magan, [16] ne wið his mæges wif. [30] Healdað mine bebodu. Ne do ge þa þing þe þa didon þe beforan eow wæron, þe læs ge beon besmitene. Ic eom Drihten eower God.[38]

Let no one lie with his relative, nor with his relative's wife. Keep my commands. Do not do the things that they who were before you did, lest you be defiled. I am the Lord your God.

Both verses 6 and 16 are abbreviated. Verse 6 retains the essence of the original, while 16 functions more as a summation of the prohibitions against sex with in-laws that appear in verses 8, 14, 15, and 16 than as a strict translation of Leviticus 18:16 (in the Vulgate: "Thou shalt not uncover the nakedness of thy brother's wife, because it is the nakedness of thy brother").[39] Conspicuously absent are the details of the incest regulations and the prohibition referring to sex between male partners, although these would not be lifted by the New Dispensation. Also gone is the prohibition against sex with one's wife's sister, "Sororem uxoris tuae in pelicatum illius non accipies, nec revelabis turpitudinem eius adhuc illa vivente" (Leviticus 18:18; Do not take your wife's sister into concubinage [in supplement to] her, nor should you expose her nakedness while [your wife] is living).[40] As Milgrom notes, the original prohibition, which he translates as "And you shall not marry a woman producing rivalry to her sister, uncovering her nakedness during her (sister's) lifetime" apparently refers to a second marriage,[41] thus implicitly accepting the general rule of polygamy – a potential problem for Christian translation that is already obviated in the Vulgate, which misleadingly turns it into a prohibition against adultery with a sister-in-law. Even the more general prohibitions against adultery (with one's neighbour's wife) and bestiality are omitted from the Old English version of Leviticus 18; indeed, they are omitted from the entire Old English Leviticus (for instance, the additional prohibition against adultery in 20:10). To understand how unusual this brevity is, we might compare this chapter to the same chapter in the *Stjórn*, a compilation of Old Testament materials in Old Norse similar in scope to the amount of Old Testament material available in Old English. The translation of Leviticus, which occurs in a portion of the *Stjórn* dating from the thirteenth century or earlier, is extraordinarily brief but contains a much fuller version of chapter 18 than does the *Old English Heptateuch*. In the *Stjórn*, chapter 18 comprises a long list of prohibited degrees of incestuous relation, adding grandsons, stepmothers' sisters, and daughters (only implicitly included in the original prohibition on wives' daughters).[42] This list accords more or less with the prohibitions on incest that were current in Iceland after the New Christian Laws of 1275, although they are not identical.[43] The difference is unlikely to reflect a greater tolerance of incest in pre-Conquest England than in medieval Iceland, and indeed the Church's rules on incestuous marriage were liberalized between the dates of the Old English and Old Norse translations, at the Fourth Lateran Council of 1215.[44] Like the Old English version, this translation also excludes prohibitions on intercourse between men, adultery, mingling of seed, and sex with beasts.

28   Nothing Pure

The Old English Leviticus minimizes the original's references to sexual behaviour and intimate body functions: omitted are chapter 12, on the circumcision of infants and the impurity and purification of women after childbirth; chapter 15, on impurity and purification after nocturnal emissions and menstruation, which includes references to the sexual communicability of uncleanness; most of chapter 18, on sexual prohibitions, as above; the parts of chapter 19 that refer to sexual relations with enslaved women, along with much of the rest of 19, although not the injunction against prostituting one's daughter; most of chapter 20, which prohibits ritual fornication and adultery and adds penalties to chapter 18's prohibitions on incest with relatives and in-laws, homosexuality, and bestiality; and all of chapters 21 and 22, which detail the purity/impurity of priests and include references to sexual matters. In fact, Leviticus's originally ample commentary on sexual matters is reduced to the two umbrella verses of chapter 18 and to this abbreviated version of 19:29: "Ne læt þu þine dohtor beon myltestre, þe læs þin land sig mid mane gefylled" (Do not let your daughter be a prostitute, lest your land be filled with wickedness).[45]

In some cases, the omitted verses are no more graphic than events in the narrative of Genesis (to some of which Ælfric refers fairly clearly in his preface), and, as I have mentioned, indeed act as a corrective to some of those events. It seems unlikely that a motive in censoring sexuality out of Leviticus was to avoid condemning the sins of the patriarchs, since it is precisely the danger of endorsing the behaviour of the patriarchs that has caused such anxiety in the translators. Leviticus 18 in its original form prohibits adultery between men and married women (a danger to which Abraham repeatedly exposes Sarah),[46] incest (practised by Noah's sons, Lot and his daughters, Reuben and his stepmother Bilhah, and others),[47] and fornication between men (ostensibly practised by the Sodomites). The prohibition on prostituting daughters is a corrective to Lot's actions, and in a reversal of the other patriarchal sin/Levitical prohibition pairs, the corrective prohibition rather than the initial sin appears in the translation. This latter example is, in other words, the only time that inclusion of sexual matters works in the way we might expect it to: by rendering what is most morally relevant to Christian readers.

Why include these three verses about sexual matters and no others? Perhaps in the translator's pristine world view they sum up all that needs to be said about preventing sexual iniquity: no incest, no promiscuity – or else. What is clear is that relevance to contemporary Christianity is not the principle of inclusion or omission. Sexuality is, in fact, a crux at which Christianity imperfectly expresses its repudiation of Jewish law. The laws excluded were in many cases still in effect. Those regarding incestuous marriages were particularly important; the Church justifies many such prohibitions by means of Leviticus. In fact, as Carmichael notes, "the incest rules of the Bible ... have had greater effect on Western law than any comparable body of Biblical rules."[48] In Gregory's responses to Augustine of Canterbury, for instance, Gregory answers a question about marriage with stepmothers and sisters-in-law negatively, noting, "indeed, union with a stepmother is a heavy sin, since it is written in the Law: 'You shall not expose your father's nakedness'" (Cum noverca autem miscere grave est facinus, quia et in lege scriptum est: "Turpitudinem patris tui non revelabis"); the same passage even justifies the Church's prohibition against cousin marriage, not in fact specified in the Old Testament, by noting, "sacred law forbids that one expose the nakedness of his kin" (sacra lex prohibet cognationis turpitudinem revelare) even while treating the Old Testament regulations about post-childbirth isolation and purification as superseded.[49]

Given that so many relevant and influential laws disappear in Old English translation, and that therefore relevance is not a viable explanation for this pattern of translation, one motivation for excision may have been fear of the provocation of inappropriate desires through sexual knowledge. That is, it may be that many Levitical prohibitions were too racy for general circulation. As Allen J. Frantzen observes regarding Old English penitentials, religious authorities were circumspect about mentioning specific forms of sexual perversion, particularly homosexuality, because they understood as we do that texts can provoke physical desires and that prohibitions can bring about the actions they prohibit. As Frantzen notes, "Early Irish and Anglo-Saxon penitentials warned confessors to use discretion, to avoid scandalizing penitents by asking inappropriate questions that might suggest sins, and to protect their own purity. These warnings are reminders that questions about sexual sins, if too explicit, might lead penitents to commit sins they had not previously known about."[50] Likewise, the details of Biblical sexual prohibitions might have been reserved for those at the highest level of understanding, that is, those literate in Latin.

How do these examples, and how well does the data on Leviticus, fit in with existing theories about the translation strategy of the Heptateuch? The first scholar to theorize about principles of selection in the *Old English Heptateuch* may have been the late nineteenth-century scholar Caroline Louisa White. White's explanation provides an early

30 Nothing Pure

example of how the survival of supersessionary attitudes can complicate contemporary scholarship on translation of the Hebrew Bible:

> The principle of omission with Ælfric is here unmistakable.[51] He wishes to furnish a practical, easily-understood rendering of the parts which are most important for the laity to know. All else he passes over … almost all catalogues of names … the abstruse passages in the practical portions … The other omissions are either short passages which repeat what is given elsewhere, or parts less essential for carrying forward the history … [M]ost of the single Levitical laws, are omitted, and the book of Judges, except the life of Samson, is given only in brief abstracts.[52]

In fact, White's explanation puts forward two distinct, although not necessarily contradictory, principles. One of these casts Leviticus as a narrative beholden to the imperatives of storytelling: "carrying forward" the plot, disregarding what distracts. This explanation has some merit, since the redacted Leviticus subordinates the content of the commandments to the structure – the interaction of Moses and Aaron with the commanding God – that frames them. Stripped of much of the legal content, the narrative nonetheless retains ample variations on "Drihten spræc to Moise and þus cwæð" (The Lord spoke to Moses and said as follows) and follows the movements of Moses, Aaron, and their kin while receiving the commandments. Nonetheless, this is a relatively weak explanation, even if it is partly true. It is unlikely that the anonymous translator of Leviticus saw their text as a good story that simply needed a bit of streamlining to keep a reader's attention, and a narrative motive would only partially explain, at best, the selection of included laws.

White points to a second principle of translation, the "rendering of the parts which are most important for the laity to know." The principle of eliminating irrelevant, outmoded material fits in with the overall project of vernacular translation of the Hebrew Bible in the sense that it follows the motive behind most Old English treatment of the Old Testament: to present that body of Scripture in its typological and historical relevance to the New Testament, rather than focusing on old laws that have been lifted by the New Dispensation. The problem with this explanation, as noted above, is that many of the commandments eliminated in Leviticus – for instance, many of the sexual prohibitions in Leviticus 18 – are not outmoded. Moreover, this explanation does not explain the *inclusion* of numerous rules, laws, and instructions that no longer apply to Christians; these prescriptions, which include the sacrifice procedures concentrated in Leviticus 1, 8, and 9, as well as the taboo against shaving one's beard in Leviticus 19, in fact make up most of the included material. (The interest of Old English prose translators in Old Testament sacrifice is evident in the existence, as Marsden notes, of three distinct Old English prose translations of Exodus 12:2–11.)[53]

Several other explanations have been posed. Marsden persuasively posits the capitular division of the Old Latin original as a main principle for the omissions and redactions. Capitular divisions were not standardized until late in the Middle Ages, but several systems existed, including the Turonian, to which many of the Heptateuch's emendations appear to correspond. Marsden notes, however, that this pattern breaks down notably in Leviticus largely because of the extent of the omissions.[54]

Alternatively, the brevity of these translations may be a goad to further reading by clerical audiences. Discussing the redaction of the story of Rebecca in the Laud Misc. 509 and Cotton Claudius B.iv manuscript versions of Genesis, a redaction marked by an unusual reference to the full version in the Latin Bible ("And he þær Isaace wif gefette, swa hyne hys hlaford het and him God wisode, swa hit on þære Ledenbec awriten ys: ræde þær se þe wylle"; And from there he fetched a wife for Isaac, just as his lord had ordered him and God directed him, as it is written in the Latin book; read it there, whoever wishes to),[55] Withers suggests that the "interpolation refers the reader back to the plenitude of the Latin, to the fullness of the stories found there."[56] This argument has considerable merit. The gaps in Genesis (Rebecca, Sodom) are marked as referring to information not suitable for the abbreviated Heptateuch, thus marking the Heptateuch as partial. We can think of the Old English Leviticus as dramatizing, in its own way, a similar distinction between the unexpurgated book and what is accessible in English. Certainly, even if the expurgated Leviticus cannot be said to have provoked the reader's desire for a full version – a reader interested in the sexual prohibitions, for instance, may indeed have been motivated to turn to the Vulgate – it does mark the omitted laws as a special kind of knowledge, a kind that goes beyond a priest's necessary Bible knowledge (for example), one for which it might after all be fitting to read Latin. As Liuzza notes of the Latin glossing of the Old English Gospels, "one can see the Latin text exerting a kind of gravitational pull on the English versions, keeping them in the role of gloss rather than text, supplement rather than substitute ... The translation, originally free-standing, was drawn back into the orbit of the Latin text of the Gospels."[57]

Several principles may be simultaneously at play. Rebecca Barnhouse points to some of the translators' potential motives: "to streamline the text," "to simplify passages whose complex figural meanings made them susceptible to misinterpretation" in order "to control the reading and interpretation of the biblical text,"[58] "to make the text more accessible to an Anglo-Saxon audience,"[59] including by simplifying the language; overall, Barnhouse notes, the translators "turn God's words into something more palatable and understandable for the audience of Anglo-Saxon Christians" "with the intent of saving readers from error and helping them towards salvation."[60] These are important aims for Ælfric in particular throughout his large-scale translation project. Although not all of the included material would necessarily be actually attractive to pious English Christians, making the Old Testament "palatable" simply means breaking down the alien and difficult food of Judaism into a more familiar and therefore more easily salvific form. Also worth noting is the distinction between sections geared towards priests and towards Israel as a whole. The distinction between priestly and lay concerns does not correspond precisely with the distinction between included and excluded material in the *Old English Heptateuch*, but it is helpful. Jacob Milgrom points to the inclusion in Leviticus (in the P parts) of *tôrôt*, "documents ... that constitute the special lore of the priesthood." Milgrom notes those portions of Leviticus "addressed to the priests (chaps. 6–7, 13–14, 16)" and those that "involve sacrificial rites, the domain of the priests (chaps. 12, 15)." He also argues for the inclusion of chapter 11 in this priestly material, since "though addressed to the laity, [it] is a concern for the priests, for it is their responsibility to distinguish between 'the pure and the impure' (10:10)." The Old English translator includes small portions of chapters 6 and 7 (to do with the sacrifice), excludes 12–16, and includes a considerable portion, relatively speaking, of 11. Milgrom identifies the material that lies outside this realm, that is, does not contain *tôrôt*, as "narrative portions (chaps. 8–10)" and the first five chapters, which "deal[]with the lay person's role in the preliminary rites of the sacrifices."[61] Large portions of 1–5 and of 8–10 are included in the *Old English Heptateuch*. It is fair to say, then, that both narrative material and material relating to lay involvement take precedence, in the translator's eyes, over priestly matters. However, once again, some of the material most precisely relevant to the laity is not included (chaps. 18–20); the ancient Israelite laity were not, of course, similar in their pastoral needs to a turn-of-the-millennium English lay audience.

As for audience, Marsden speculates that, in light of the dedication to Ælfric's patron Æthelweard, the *Old English Heptateuch* "may perhaps be seen, therefore, along with Ælfric's other spiritual works in the vernacular, as part of a programme of adaptation of monastic materials for the devotional life of pious (and noble) laymen" (not that, as

Marsden points out, Æthelweard himself needed such a translation), and that additionally "[t]he use of translation in a preparatory and educative role for novice monks or for secular clergy and others should not be overlooked."[62] In this case, we must ask whether the omission of priestly directives is an important part of the latter mission. Judging from Ælfric's concerns about the mistakes of priests, perhaps it is. It would be a mistake to assume that the translator identifies information for the ancient Hebrew priestly audience as appropriate for priests in England and, likewise, information directed at lay Israelites as appropriate for contemporary Christian laypeople. It is just as likely to be quite the opposite – we are particularly familiar with Ælfric's concerns about clerics getting the wrong idea about priestly marriage, and the translators are more likely to have considered the lay behaviour prescribed in Leviticus enlightening for Christian priests than worthy of imitation by lay Christians. So perhaps the correct (from a translator's point of view) alignment of text and audience is lay Jewish law for a clerical Christian audience.

The Prohibition on Blood Consumption

The first mention of the prohibition against blood consumption is in Genesis 9, the establishment of the Noahic covenant. In this covenant, God binds himself to both humans and animals never again to send them a great flood. In return, he institutes what we might call a new biological regime:

> And God blessed Noah and his sons. And he said to them, "Increase, and multiply, and fill the earth. And let the fear and dread of you be upon all the beasts of the earth and upon all the fowls of the air and all that move upon the earth. All the fishes of the sea are delivered into your hand. And every thing that moveth and liveth shall be meat for you. Even as the green herbs have I delivered them all to you, saving that flesh with blood you shall not eat, for I will require the blood of your lives [*animarum*] at the hand of every beast, and at the hand of man, at the hand of every man and of his brother will I require the life [*animam*] of man. Whosoever shall shed man's blood, his blood shall be shed, for man was made to the image of God" (Genesis 9:1–6).[63]

Urging humans to reproduce and to dominate animals, and giving humans permission to eat animals for the first time (Adam and Eve were restricted to food that grew in the garden), he indicates the special nature of blood, announcing that he will avenge the spilling of human blood by both humans and animals and forbidding humans from consuming animal blood. Blood functions both symbolically and physically in the covenant – in the former prohibition it is metonymic for gross violence, and in the latter it is the material object of a taboo. The border between symbolic and material fails, however, almost as soon as the exegete attempts to institute it: Is the material taboo itself the result or expression of a symbolic importance? God makes this covenant with all people and indeed all flesh, emphasizing the universal and exceptionless nature of this rule. Ælfric, translator of Genesis 9, translates this chapter relatively closely, as follows:

> God bletsode þa Noe and his suna and cwæð him to: "Weahxað and beoþ gemenigfilde and afyllaþ þa eorðan. And beo eower ege and oga ofer ealle nitenu and fugelas and ofer ealle þa þing þe on eorðan stiriað. Ealle sæfixas sindon eowrum handum betæhte, and eall þæt þe styrað and leofað beo eow to mete; swa swa growende wyrta, ic betæhte ealle eow, buton þam anum, þæt ge flæsc mid blode ne eton. Eower blod ic ofgange æt eallum wilddeorum and eac æt þam men. Of þæs weres handa and his broþor handa ic ofgange þæs mannes lif. Swa hwa swa agit mannes blod, his blod byð agoten. Witodlice to Godes anlicnisse ys se man geworht. Weaxe ge nu and beoð gemenigfilde and gaþ ofer eorðan and gefyllaþ hig." God cwæð eft to Noe and to his sunum: "Efne nu ic sette min wedd to eow and to eowrum ofspringe, and to eallum þam libbendum nytenum þe of ðam arce eodon, þæt ic nateshwon nelle heononforð eall flæsc adydan mid flodes wæterum, ne heononforð ne biþ flod tosencende þa eorðan … Ðis biþ þæt tacn mines weddes þæt ic gesette betwux me and eallum flæsce ofer eorþan." (*OEH* Genesis 9:1–11, 9:17)[64]

God then blessed Noah and his sons and said to them: "Increase and be many and fill the earth. And awe and terror of you shall be over beasts and birds and over all the creatures that move on land. All fish of the sea are committed into your hands, and all those that move and live shall be food for you, and so too the growing herbs. I have committed all of them to you, except for one thing, that you not eat flesh with blood. I will require satisfaction for your blood from all wild animals and also from people. From a man's hands and his brother's hands I will require satisfaction for a person's life.[65] Likewise, if anyone sheds human blood, his blood shall be spilled. People are truly made in God's likeness. Now grow and be many and spread over the earth and fill it." God said again to Noah and to his sons: "Equally now I establish my covenant with you and with your offspring, and with all the living beasts that went from the arc, that I will never from now on destroy all flesh with the waters of a flood, nor from now on will flood dissipate the earth ... This [rainbow] is the sign of my covenant that I establish between myself and all flesh on earth.

The prohibition on blood consumption that is first made explicit in the Noahic covenant is, as David Biale notes, reiterated in Leviticus 3:17, 17:10–16, and 19:26, and in Deuteronomy 12:23.[66] As Milgrom observes, "In the priestly view, [the blood prohibition] stands even higher than the ten commandments: the Decalogue was given solely to Israel, but the blood prohibition was enjoined on all humankind. It alone, according to the priestly legists, forms the basis of a viable human society."[67] As Laurie Shannon notes, the Noahic covenant explicitly includes animals in this society, prohibiting them from shedding human blood just as it protects their own blood from human consumption.[68]

The taboo creates a limit not only on bloodshed but also on the enjoyment of bloodshed. The symbolic importance of this passage, that is, the marking of bloodshed and its enjoyment as a particular taboo at the boundaries of animals, humans, and God, and the nascent political theology in which God – in his position as Israel's leader – requites blood for blood and killing for killing, may be what motivates the inclusion of this passage in the very freely translated *Genesis A*:

> Eow is eðel-stol
> and holmes hlæst   and heofon-fuglas
> and wildu deor   on geweald geseald,
> eorðe ælgrene   and eacen feoh.
> Næfre ge mid blode   beod-gereordu
> unarlice   eowre þicgeað,
> besmiten mid synne   sawl-dreore.
> Ælc hine selfa   ærest begrindeð
> gastes dugeðum   þæra þe mid gares orde
> oðrum aldor oðþringeð   ... ic monnes feorh
> to slagan sece   swiðor micle,
> and to broðor banan,   þæs þe blod-gyte,
> wæll-fyll weres   wæpnum gespedeð,
> morð mid mundum.   Monn wæs to Godes
> anlicnesse   ærest gesceapen.
> Ælc hafað mag-wlite   metodes and engla
> þara þe healdan wile   halige þeawas   (lines 1514b–31a)

Homeland and the ocean's goods and the birds of the air and wild animals are given into your power, as well as the green earth and tame beasts.

36 Nothing Pure

> Never shall you unrighteously eat your feasts with blood, polluted with sin by life-blood. Everyone first deprives himself of his soul's gain who with the point of a spear forces away another's life ... Even more will I seek man's life from a homicide and from a brother's killer, for bloodshed, who speeds with weapons the slaughter of men, murders with his hands. Man was first created in God's likeness. Everyone who will keep holy customs has the form of the creator and the angels.

The language cites the concept of pollution by blood, seeming to convey an understanding of Jewish law. In fact, however, the passage conveys pollution "mid synne" by means of blood – with the concept of sin spiritualizing the harm of the taboo. Moreover, there is little elaboration on what it means to eat with blood: animal blood is not specified (the animals who shed human blood are missing), much less does the Apostolic wording about strangled meat appear. In the context of the elaborated main point – God requites the human slaughterer of men; do not eat your feasts stained with sin by blood – this translation makes the blood taboo a statement on the avoidance of violence between people.

The Old English Leviticus minimizes, but does not entirely eliminate, the prohibition on blood consumption. Instead, the translators' moves apparently restrict these laws to their sacrificial contexts. For instance, Leviticus 3:16–17 in the Vulgate ("And the priest shall burn them upon the altar for the food of the fire and of a most sweet savour. All the fat shall be the Lord's by a perpetual law for your generations and in all your habitations; neither blood nor fat shall you eat at all"[69]) becomes "Ælc rysel sceal Drihtne to leohte. Ne ete ge naðer ne rysel ne blod"[70] (All of the fat shall be light for the Lord. Eat neither fat nor blood). The context straddles the sacrificial context and perpetuity, although it is clearly set within the sacrificial context, where fat is forbidden (as opposed to outside of it, where fat can be consumed in meat).[71] By eliminating the portion of 3:17 that names this rule as eternal for the generations of Israel, the translation eliminates any potential for a continued claim on the descendants of this covenant.

The Old English Leviticus also omits all of chapter 17, in which the crime of eating blood is laid out independent of the sacrifice:

> If any man whosoever of the house of Israel and of the strangers that sojourn among them eat blood, I will set my face against his soul and will *cut him off* from among his people because the life of the flesh is in the blood and I have given it to you that you may make atonement with it upon the altar for your souls and the blood may be for an expiation of the

soul. Therefore I have said to the children of Israel, "No soul of you nor of the strangers that sojourn among you shall eat blood."

Any man whosoever of the children of Israel and of the strangers that sojourn among you, if by hunting or fowling he take a wild beast or a bird which is lawful to eat, let him pour out its blood and cover it with earth, for the life of all flesh is in the blood. Therefore I said to the children of Israel, "You shall not eat the blood of any flesh at all because the life of the flesh is in the blood, and whosoever eateth it shall *be cut off.*" (Leviticus 17:10–14)[72]

This passage makes clear that the prohibition is independent of the sacrifice and emphasizes three times that it applies to "the strangers that sojourn among you" – that is, that it pertains to Jews and Gentiles alike.

The blood consumption prohibition appears again in chapter 19 of Leviticus, a collection of apparently miscellaneous holiness directives that includes honouring parents, avoiding agricultural crossbreeding and witchcraft, and loving the stranger.[73] The final verses include the following heterogenous section:

> You shall not eat with blood. You shall not divine nor observe dreams. Nor shall you cut your hair roundwise, nor shave your beard. You shall not make any cuttings in your flesh for the dead, neither shall you make in yourselves any figures or marks. I am the Lord. Make not thy daughter a common strumpet lest the land be defiled and filled with wickedness. Keep ye my sabbaths, and reverence my sanctuary. I am the Lord. Go not aside after wizards, neither ask any thing of soothsayers to be defiled by them. I am the Lord your God. Rise up before the hoary head, and honour the person of the aged man, and fear the Lord, thy God. I am the Lord. (19:26–32)[74]

The Old English renders the blood prohibition and most of the rest of these verses, omitting the prohibition on markings and the injunction to keep the sabbath. In addition to keeping the blood prohibition, this passage of the Old English is notable in that it is the only direct reference to sexuality the translator renders from all of Leviticus. Note that the prohibition is reiterated alongside the prohibition against the shaving of beards, which is superseded.

The *Old English Heptateuch* entirely omits Deuteronomy 12, which enjoins the rejection of idolatry and describes appropriate sacrifices, except for this final and (under the circumstances) inapt verse: "Wirceað ealle þa þing þe Drihten eow bebead and ne ice ge nan þing þærto, ne ne waniað" (12:32; Perform all the things that the Lord commanded you and do not add anything to them, nor diminish [them]).[75] The original Vulgate chapter repeats the injunction against blood consumption as follows: "Only beware of this: that thou eat not the blood, for the blood is for the soul, and therefore thou must not eat the soul with the flesh" (12:23; Hoc solum cave: ne sanguinem comedas, sanguis enim eorum pro anima est, et idcirco non debes animam comedere cum carnibus). This appears in the context of a discussion of clean and unclean animals and is followed by an explanation of the proper uses for blood – the Israelites should pour blood on the ground rather than eating it; the blood should be poured on the altar.

In each case in which it appears in the Old English Leviticus, the blood prohibition trails alongside a superseded regulation rather than being marked as a prohibition that remains in effect. The most prominent example of this is the translation of Leviticus 7:25–7, which bans eating the fat of animals sacrificed to God, then elaborates on the blood prohibition: "If any man eat the fat that should be offered for the burnt sacrifice of the Lord, he shall perish out of his people. Moreover, you shall not eat the blood of any creature whatsoever, whether of birds or beasts. Every one that eateth blood, shall perish from among the people" (Leviticus 7:25–7).[76] The Old English translation compresses the three verses in this way: "Gif hwa þæt smeru oððe þæt blod [ytt], þe bið Gode geoffrud, he sceal forwurðan" (Leviticus 7:25[–26]; If anyone eats the fat or the blood that is offered to God, he must perish).[77] By rendering this particular prohibition against eating blood as part of the instructions on animal sacrifice, the translation interprets the ban within an economy of supersession. Although the Old English Leviticus elsewhere translates the taboo more or less accurately, in this instance it expressly folds the prohibition against eating blood into the prohibition dealing with sacrificial flesh, thus inaccurately portraying it as part of a superseded practice.[78] I call this rendering inaccurate not because it misrepresents the source (although it does), but because it incorrectly gives the impression that the blood consumption taboo itself is a Jewish practice from the past, now superseded. In fact, the taboo remained a troubled and controversial aspect of Christian practice well into the time of the Old English translation.

The Jewish taboo against blood consumption would be interpreted in Judaism to mandate kosher slaughter (via incision in the neck) and the thorough draining of blood from meat before cooking – practices that provoked horror in European Christian neighbours, leading them ironically to associate Jews with bloodthirstiness.[79] The prohibitions were interpreted differently in insular sources, which see them as banning the consumption of undercooked meat – the Scriftboc and the Old English Penitential both call for modest penance for eating "blodig ðicge in healfsodenum mete" (bloody pieces in half-cooked meat)[80] – and the actual drinking of blood – prohibited in so many varying iterations in the penitentials that some, including the Scriftboc and Old English Penitential, include the following qualification: "[S]e ðe his sylfes blod in spatle mid ungewisse forswelge nis þæt nænig fyren" (If anyone unwittingly swallows his own blood in his spit, this is no crime).[81]

It is clear that Ælfric endorses the ban. In his *Letter to Brother Edward*, for instance, Ælfric vigorously reinforces a prohibition on blood consumption, liberally quoting God's pertinent injunctions to Noah and Moses as justification:

> Her geswutelað on ðysum gewrite hu God ælmihtig forbead mancynne ælces cynnes blod to etenne. God cwæþ to Noe æfter þam mycclum flode: "Þære sæ fixas and þære eorðan nytenu ic sylle eow to bigleofan, buton þæt ge heora blod ne þicgon. Witodlice þæra nytena blod ic ofgange æt eowrum handum, and þæs mannes lif þe ofslagen byð ic ofgange æt his slagan. Swa hwa swa mennisc blod agyt, his blod byð agoten." Eft cwæð God to Moysen: "Ic eom eower God ðe eow lædde of Egypta lande. Ne þicge ge nanes nytenes blod on eowrum mettum ne fugela ne oðra nytena. Ælc ðæra manna ðe blod ytt sceal losian of his folce, beo he inlenda, beo he ælðeodig, forþan ðe on þam blode is þæs nytenes lif. Swa hwa swa fehð fugel oððe deor, þæra þe mannum to metum synd alyfede, ageote heora blod on ða eorðan and swa hwa swa þæs blodes hent and him to mete macað he losað of his folce." Eft we rædað on canonibus þæt nan nyten þe to mete sceal ne byð clænlice acweald, buton þæt incunde blod ðe anbutan þære heortan is ut yrne.

> Now this letter explains how God almighty forbade mankind to eat any kind of blood. God said to Noah after the great flood: "Of the fish of the sea and the beasts of the earth I give you for food, except that you not consume their blood. Certainly I will require [satisfaction for] the blood of beasts at your hands, and of a man's life I will require that the one who slays him be slain. So too if anyone spills human blood, let his blood be spilled." God also said to Moses: "I am your God who led you out of the land of Egypt. Do not consume the blood of any beast in your meat nor of birds nor of any other beasts. Any man who eats blood shall be lost from his people, whether he be native or foreign, because a beast's life is in the blood. Just so, if anyone captures a fowl or wild animal of which men are permitted to eat, spill its blood on the ground, and similarly anyone who seizes this blood and makes it food for himself shall be lost from his

people." We also read in the canons that no beast that is for food is killed cleanly unless the internal blood that is around the heart has run out.[82]

Despite support from Ælfric and perhaps other monastics, ecclesiastical officials rarely commented on and did little or nothing to enforce such bans. According to Ann Hagen, who views the blood and corollary strangulation bans as protective of public health ("[I]f an animal was strangled, the supposition is that blood would remain in the tissues and, as this is a perfect medium for microbes, decay would set in quickly"), ordinary people were probably aware but not particularly observant of the taboo (for "blood is an extremely valuable source of nutrients, and the danger of infection would be destroyed by cooking"). They slaughtered according to the regulations (that is, by blood-letting: "pole-axing and/or cutting the throat") but often disregarded them when it came to consumption. One leechbook prescribes sheep's blood as a remedy, and blood commonly went into puddings and sausages, "where it was not recognisable as a forbidden substance."[83] It is possible, then, to see the blood taboo as a locally rather than centrally authorized ecclesiastical observance, honoured for the most part in the breach, and in the confessional practices that shaped the idea of sin on the part of those who confessed and took confession. But the Church probably had no motivation to revoke it. In addition to the health considerations for which Hagen argues, the prohibition, which also appears in the *Old English Heptateuch* as "Ne eton ge blod" (Leviticus 19:26; Do not eat blood), is likely useful as a figurative injunction against bloodthirstiness. Indeed, this seems to have been the meaning for the ancient Jews, for whom the prohibition was explained in terms of life and death, even invoking the penalty of excommunication: "for the life of all flesh is in the blood. Therefore I said to the children of Israel, 'You shall not eat the blood of any flesh at all because the life of the flesh is in the blood, and whosoever eateth it shall be cut off'" (Leviticus 17:14).[84]

The overall pattern of translation of the blood ban is based in this ambivalence. The difference between the lengthy translation of the ban in the Noah passage (Genesis) and the translations in Leviticus points to a disjunction in the translators' attitudes. As I have demonstrated, when Leviticus translates the ban, it usually places it alongside or even folds it into more obviously superseded regulations; sometimes it omits the ban entirely. In chapter 7, the translation affirms the taboo, in a limited way, by repeating it; it also rejects it by folding it into superseded practice. In the Old English translation of Leviticus, then, the ambivalent positioning of the taboo between Old Law and New may communicate ambivalence about the place of the taboo in real practice. In some places (in the text and in the culture) it is affirmed, in others eliminated. As a textual strategy, it may mirror the aim that I have suggested regarding the redacted translation of sexual prohibitions. Gesturing or standing in for a whole constellation of unknown Jewish dietary laws and carnal attitudes absent from this translation, it delicately removes the reader from the carnality of Judaism while stimulating interest in that carnal world – for the purpose, as with Kruger's spectral Jewish body, of summoning and then once again repudiating it.

The ambivalent status of the blood prohibition provides not only an example of but also a potent metaphor for the supersessionary translation strategy of the Old English Leviticus. As the Hebrew Bible suggests and the New Testament affirms (in its way), there is a connection between the life and the blood; by exsanguinating flesh, one preserves that distinction. Blood that remains in dead flesh renders that flesh, in some way, undead; as a result, it pollutes both the meat and those who eat it. Kruger suggests that Judaism is, for medieval Christians, undead: corporeal, bloody, and in constant need of reburial. The violence of this summoning and reburial is, for now, a violence of translation. It is at the heart of supersessionary translation, a strategy that animates every word in the Old English Leviticus. This strategy explains the inclusion of seemingly unimportant details of dialogue and character in the otherwise succinct translation – we see now that these portray Leviticus as a story, a narrative of interaction between man and God in the distant past. It explains the tantalizing inclusion of some of the carnal prohibitions and the excision of most of the others. Without understanding it, we will not understand the coherence of this apparently potshot Old English translation of Leviticus; indeed, we will not understand why it needed to be translated at all.

2 Men as Meat: Jewish Law and Orders of Being in Ælfric's Translations of Maccabees and Job

Ælfric's passion of the Maccabees begins with a band of imperial thugs tormenting an old scholar – a harrowing scene that might come from the Danish attacks on monasteries or, indeed, from persecutions of nearly any era. It is a moving scene of defiance by a person who is defenceless only in his body, and – inconveniently for a Christian translator – it is a particularly, specifically Jewish story:

> Þa wolde Eleazarus werlice sweltan
> ær ðan þe he Godes æ forgegan wolde,
> and nolde forswelgan ðæs spices snæd
> þe hi him on muð bestungon, forðan þe Moyses forbead
> swyn to etenne ...   (lines 86–90)

> Then Eleazar wanted to die manfully instead of violating God's law, and he would not swallow the bit of pork that they pushed into his mouth, because Moses forbade [them] to eat pigs.[1]

How is it that Ælfric, so concerned to distinguish the Old Law from the New, so explicitly includes Jewish dietary law in what is clearly an exemplum of pious martyrdom?

Ælfric's approach to supersessionary translation, as I will argue in this chapter and in the two following, makes maximum use of Jewish law for Christian ends. This is not easy. As Malcolm Godden notes, "too many of the practices which had been acceptable in the Old Testament world were perilously close to practices which Church officials considered pagan or at least objectionable," including food taboos, polygamy, and priestly marriage.[2] Sometimes, although noticeably less frequently than other Old English translators, Ælfric erases such material. In his homily on Esther, he ignores Esther's after-the-fact denunciation of nonkosher food and of the bed of an uncircumcised man, and in the homily on Judith he omits the circumcision of Achior. In his homily on 1 and 2 Maccabees, too, he omits the Biblical books' numerous references to circumcision.[3] However, although Ælfric sometimes prefers not to call attention to Jewish laws and practices mentioned in the Old Testament, this is not an absolute position. In the case of 1 and 2 Maccabees, where Jewish dietary law is integral to the martial plot, Ælfric's extensive translation-homily engages with the problem almost preemptively. This chapter argues that Jewish food laws present a unique problem and opportunity for Ælfric. The struggle with Jewish attitudes towards flesh and food at large proves a central theme of Ælfric's translation of Maccabees. Ælfric ably confronts these difficulties, ultimately appropriating the Jewish food laws and practices at issue in Maccabees and reorienting the message of the book of Job to create hierarchical distinctions not only between Christians and Jews but also between humans and animals.

Ælfric's Old English translation of Maccabees, a homiletic and hagiographic exemplum of resistance against heathen oppressors, appears in his *Lives of Saints*, a collection of primarily hagiographical homilies (ca. 993–8) that survives as British Library, MS Cotton Julius E.vii, ff. 3r–230r.[4] The work paraphrases the Old Testament books 1 and 2 Maccabees, deuterocanonical histories that describe in contrasting terms the successful second-century (BCE) rebellion of a small band of Judean Jews against the Seleucid emperor Antiochus IV Epiphanes, who outlawed Jewish practices, including circumcision, sacrifices, and food restrictions, and maliciously invaded the sanctity of the temple.[5] Although somewhat incongruous in its subject matter, this passion shares, like the homiletic translations of Esther and Judith, the prevailing investment of the Lives of Saints collection in struggle against polytheistic persecutors who seek to defile the faith, customs, and holy places of God's people.[6] With his typically canny narrative use of Biblical originals, Ælfric opens the paraphrase of 1 Maccabees with a dramatic vignette borrowed from 2 Maccabees: the cruel execution of Eleazar, a Jewish elder who chooses this fate rather than violate his religious principles. In Ælfric's telling, this heroic martyrdom and the additional wave of martyrdoms it inspires spur the Judaic revolt, which culminates in military victory against the empire, the routing of the polytheists, and the cleansing of Judaea's holy sites. Eleazar, a figure from later in the rebellions, thus replaces the less sympathetic instigator Matthias, a zealous elder who in 1 Maccabees plays a parallel role but, rather than martyring himself, kills both a heretic and a polytheist before running for safety. Ælfric uses the figure of Eleazar, then, as the key to an inspirational and culturally relevant hagiographic exemplum. As Stuart D. Lee observes, the Maccabean passion "was the section of the story that held most interest for a Christian audience. That a people should accept death rather than relinquish the laws of their religion was a stirring model of behavior."[7] In order to fully serve its inceptive narrative role in this politically important exemplum, however, Eleazar's heroic deed requires some cultural translation for an English audience. Unlike other saints in the collection, Eleazar goes to the death not for the sake of his chastity or for faith in Christ, but rather for refusing to eat pork, a food perfectly acceptable to Christians.[8]

In narrating Eleazar's self-sacrifice, Ælfric must thus explain "þone fulan mete þe Moyses forbead / Godes folce to þicgenne for þære gastlican gatacnunge" (lines 35–6; the filthy meat that Moses forbade God's people to eat because of its spiritual signification). Ælfric begins by introducing the crucial concept of cleanness under Jewish law:

> We moton nu secgan swutellicor be ðysum:
> hwylce mettas wæron mannum forbodene
> on ðære ealdan æ þe mann ett nu swaðeah.
> Moyses forbead for mycelre getacnunge
> on ðære ealdan æ, æfter Godes dihte,
> þa nytenu to etanne þam ealdan folce
> þe heora cude ne ceowað and het ða unclæne   (lines 37–43)[9]

> We must now speak more clearly about these things: which meats were forbidden to people in the old law that one now nonetheless eats. In the old law Moses forbade, on account of great significance, according to God's commands, the ancient people to eat the beasts that do not chew their cud and called them unclean.

Scholarship on this translation has emphasized the foreignness of Jewish dietary law to the early English as the motive for this addition. Noting that this explanation is a paraphrase of Leviticus 11, Lee contends that Ælfric inserted this passage into his translation of Maccabees out of "respect and understanding" for his listeners, because he knew that "the importance of [Eleazar's] torture would be lost on a Christian audience."[10] John Halbrooks, similarly, observes that Ælfric "is using an additional source … to explain potentially confusing episodes to an uninformed readership."[11]

After this fairly neutral, informative addition, the Passion takes a pointedly interpretive turn, as Ælfric explains the typological meaning of the Levitical rules. In the following passage, a paraphrase of the Jewish dietary laws of Leviticus 11 and Deuteronomy 14 influenced by Pseudo-Bede,[12] the Jewish distinction between clean and unclean animals is transmuted into the Christian distinction between Christians and Jews – with Christians occupying the position of cleanness and Jews of uncleanness:

> Þa clænan nytenu þe heora cudu ceowað
> getacniað þa men þe on heora mode smeagað
> embe Godes willan, syððan hi his word gehyrað
> of lareowa muðum, swylce hi heora mete ceowan …
> Swa swa ða Iudeiscan þe urne Drihten forseoð
> and his god-spel-bodunge to bysmre habbað
> syndon unclæne and Criste andsæte
> þeah ðe hi Moyses æ on heora muðe wealcon,
> and nellað understanden butan þæt steaflice andgit   (lines 46–9, 69–73)

> The clean beasts that chew their cud signify the people who ruminate on God's will in their minds after they hear his words from the mouths of teachers, as if they chewed their food … Likewise, the Jews who scorn our Lord and make a mockery of his gospel message are unclean and hateful to Christ, although they roll Moses's law around in their mouths and wish to understand nothing but the literal sense.[13]

This passage makes practices from a now-alien Jewish culture legible in the service of Christian piety. Rather than passively illuminating this dead past, it deploys Jewish tropes and history to delegitimize Judaism. Ælfric's swift appropriation of Jewish food laws for a supersessionist analogy challenges any initial impression that his introduction of kosher law in the translation of Maccabees primarily serves an informative purpose. In inserting background material on kosher law, Ælfric is not innocuously introducing his audience to unfamiliar customs, but rather deliberately establishing Jews as others – indeed, as enemies. In discussing both halves of this passage, Andrew P. Scheil has established the tradition of anti-Jewish interpretation that lies behind Ælfric's explanation of dietary laws and demonstrated that explaining the foreign practices of Jews is itself part of an othering anthropological discourse: "Jews are beyond the actual experience of the English and invite explanation."[14] In this reading, the two aims – introducing alien customs and constructing the alien – are complementary, and the anthropological aim lends itself to the anti-Jewish conclusion to which Ælfric, with such painful irony, brings the litany of forbidden foods.

Scheil argues that this description of the carnal rules of Israel, because of the distance it creates between Christians and Jews, lends itself to that typological use of the oppositions between clean and unclean that ironically descends into "anti-Judaic invective."[15] Jonathan Wilcox also sees this explanation as deliberately rather than incidentally anti-Jewish; as he notes, condemnation of contemporary Jews who cling to the Old Law offsets the text's potentially confusing endorsement of Jewish heroes righteous under that same Law.[16] While I agree with Scheil and Wilcox that Ælfric's apparently neutral anthropological mode is never innocuous but rather powerfully enables his anti-Judaic turn, I argue nevertheless that since a remnant of Jewish law survives in early English culture, it is likely this survival, rather than ignorance, that calls forth the necessity to explain and repudiate Jewish law.

Ælfric's discussions of Old Testament sacrifice and of the human–animal relations of the Bible appropriate Jewish law to produce a definition of humanity that excludes and animalizes non-Christians. This strategy is not only or even primarily a matter of anti-Judaism but rather of reifying a hierarchical divine and natural order, deeply imbricated with divisions between English Christians and others, which are crucial and threatened distinctions in times of privation and invasion (and therefore in need of defence). Critics of liberal humanism ranging from Sylvia Wynter to Giorgio Agamben have observed that the modern human–animal divide is not natural and external to the human, but is rather a racialized and gender-inflected division within the human (and a manmade division within the animal) that makes possible the very concept of the human.[17] So too, through the process of supersession, is the division between Jew and Christian an internal division that makes Christian texts and identities possible. As Agamben, Kenneth R. Stow, Claudine Fabre-Vassas, and others have demonstrated, this is not an analogy, but indeed an interlocking process with that of the human/animal division; that is, the division between Jew and Christian is also a division between beast and human.[18] Likewise, Stow has documented that the long association between Jews and dogs is a primary channel of Christian supersession over Judaism.[19] Jewish food laws and practices, as culturally and theologically distant as they may seem from Ælfric's program of educating English laypeople and clergy in the orthodoxies of Christian faith, are, as Joyce E. Salisbury notes, also based on the separation of orders of being, particularly the classification and separation of animal orders;[20] this shared interest provides irresistible opportunities for Ælfric to shore up Christian humanity against its human and animal others, including Jews. Because separations lay at the heart of kosher laws and because in practice they separated Gentile followers of Christ from Jewish followers, these laws were in fact ready to hand for anti-Jewish use.

Identifying Judaism and its laws with the body and the physical world and Christianity with the spirit is crucial to the project of supersession. Indeed, Ælfric must consign Jewish law to the dead past – hence the rapid repetition of "ealdan" (old) – in order to explain the relation of Christianity to Jewish law. John Halbrooks notes the importance of Ælfric's supersessionary rhetorical move for the larger aims of the text: by "emphasiz[ing] the difference between the old Jewish law and the new Christian law," Ælfric can use a martial, physical, heroic story to signify "the spiritual war that Christians must now fight" against their heathen invaders.[21] As Steven F. Kruger writes, "A Jewish past ... that has been taken away from Jews is here revivified, reawakened *as* Jewish, to be activated in a situation of present distress."[22]

Kosher Laws and Food Taboos

The kosher laws that Ælfric excerpts in *Maccabees* are part of the holiness code received by Moses and expounded in the Pentateuch, primarily in Leviticus and Deuteronomy. These rules distinguish between clean and unclean animals, the latter of which are never acceptable as food; specify appropriate methods of slaughter and prohibit consumption of blood and carrion (all of which reinforce the prohibition against eating blood earlier revealed to Noah, the first licit carnivore); enjoin various food customs such as eating the bread of affliction at Passover; prohibit other customs that appear to be against the spirit of separating the holy and the profane (such as boiling a kid in its mother's milk or eating the first fruits of the harvest); and give thorough guidelines on the offering and consumption of food sacrifices.[23] Mary Douglas has demonstrated that the separation of clean and unclean animals in Leviticus 11, as well as other practices and stories of "uneven complementarity," in which one person or thing is consecrated or sacrificed while its fellow is excluded, ritualizes and emphasizes a crucial organizing principle of Leviticus: the covenant binds Israel to God, constrains it, and separates it from Gentiles.[24]

Kosher laws, because they separated Jews from non-Jews, were a source of bitter controversy in the early evangelization of the Gentiles. The compromise in Paul's Letter to the Romans, which in fact urges reconciliation between advocates and detractors of the laws and condones continuing observance among those who previously obeyed them, is nevertheless considered to have lifted the taboos: "I know and am confident in the Lord Jesus that nothing is unclean of itself, but to him that esteemeth any thing to be unclean, to him it is unclean" (Romans 14:14; Scio et confido in Domino Iesu quia nihil commune per ipsum, nisi ei qui existimat quid commune esse, illi commune est).[25] Nevertheless, the Acts of the Apostles exhorts the Gentiles who follow Christ to avoid certain categories of food: "that you abstain from things sacrificed to idols and from blood and from things strangled" (Acts 15:29; ut abstineatis vos ab immolatis simulacrorum et sanguine et suffocato). As Salisbury and Bernadette Filotas have observed, the Apostolic Decree endured: bans on strangled food, carrion, and any other meat from which blood has not been properly shed appear in many early medieval penitentials.[26] Sometimes these bans are explicitly attributed to the ban in Acts, as in the Canons of Theodore: "Ða feower heafodcwidas in *Actibus apostolorum* þus be beodað [sic], þæt man hine forhæbbe fram dyrnum geligrum, and fram awyrgedum nytene, and fram blode, and fram deofolgylde" (A-11 [italics in original]; the four main decrees in the Acts of the Apostles command as follows: that man abstain from secret fornication, and from strangled beasts, and from blood, and from devil-worship) and in the Scriftboc: "Fugelas and oðre nytenu þa ðe on nette beoð awyrgede, ne synt hi to etanne … forðan swa is in Actibus Apostolorum beboden: Abstinete uos a fornicatione et a suffocato sanguine et idolatria" (XVII.34c; Birds and other animals that are caught in nets are not to be eaten … because it is thus commanded in the Acts of the Apostles: Abstain yourselves from fornication and from things strangled and from consuming blood and from idolatry).[27]

The food rules, practices, and metaphors of the Hebrew Bible have shaped both Jewish and Christian identities. As Karl Steel neatly summarizes, "As early as the Maccabean revolts, both adherents and enemies of Judaism had identified its food laws as a synecdoche for the whole of Jewish faith and culture. Christianity differentiated itself from Judaism – and later, from Islam and various heresies – by imagining itself unburdened by alimentary laws, or, at least, by alimentary laws that distinguished between licit and illicit foods."[28] Although this fantasized distinction loomed large in Christian identities, comestibles like meat, bread, and wine were never matters of insignificance to Christians in late antiquity and the early Middle Ages. Nor was early Christianity so separable from Judaism, or what we might call other forms of Judaism. Citing the significance of food language in Christ's words to his disciples, Gillian Feeley-Harnik notes, "At the time of Jesus Christ, food was the word, and food law was the law," such that "most of the time his disciples do not understand what he is saying until he finally speaks to them in food."[29] The nature and consumption of food and drink always marked the boundaries between Christ-believers and their human and animal others. Freidenreich, Feeley-Harnik, and many others have demonstrated the centrality of food and eating, manifested particularly in the sacrament and communal meals, to early and medieval Christian identities. Freidenreich demonstrates that this centrality is a direct consequence of the emergence of Christianity among Hellenistic Judean Jews, for whom food regulations virtually constituted cultural identity, so that even eating with non-Jews was for them a boundary violation.[30] He notes that table-fellowship between Jewish and Gentile Christians was by no means a rejection of the importance of eating with coreligionists according to common standards; instead, it performed the symbolic work of bringing Gentiles into the tent of holiness.[31] Outside that tent were Gentile idolators, who performed sacrifices and ate sacrificial meat rejected by both Judaism and nascent Christianity.[32] Non-Christ-believing Jews, who after the destruction of the Second Temple had given up animal sacrifices, and Muslims also became excluded from Christian commensality.

Writers of Old English inherited and elaborated the attitude that Christians and non-Christians should be separated at table. In the *Preface to Genesis*,[33] perhaps his clearest statement on the translation of the Old Testament, Ælfric warns, "Gyf hwa wyle nu swa lybban æfter Cristes tocyme swa swa men leofodon ær Moises æ, oþþe under Moises æ, ne byð se man na cristen, ne he furþo[n] wyrðe ne byð þæt him ænig cristen man mid ete" (3–4; If anyone will now live after Christ's coming just as men lived before Moses's law, or under Moses's law, then that man is no Christian, nor is he even worthy that any Christian man should eat with him). Likewise, the Scriftboc instructs, "ne mot gefullad mid þæne gecristnodon etan, ne hine cyssan, swa mycele ma swa he ne mot mid þæne hæðenan" ([since] a baptized person must not eat with a person to be baptized, nor kiss him, so much more must he not with a heathen). This is a distinction between Christians and all others, not between righteous people and sinners, as evidenced by the penitential's subsequent comment, "Swa hwylc se ðe hafað gemanan oððe wifgyfte unalyfedlice, swa þeah he mot swa hwylcne mete þicgean swa he hafað, forðam se witega cwæð: *Domini est terra and plenitudo ejus*" (XIII.16g; Whoever has unlawful intercourse or nuptials, nevertheless a person may eat whatever food he has, for the Scripture says, *The earth is the Lord's and its abundance is his*).[34] According to this logic, food is not contaminated by association with sinners, but commensality with non-Christians violates a certain necessary separation.

The Apostolic Decree was the most important source for Christian food regulations after the time of Christ, such that Christian refusal to eat meat sacrificed to idols became a key marker of Christian identity in the Roman Empire.[35] However, Freidenreich observes that with the Christianization of the empire, insistence on the Apostolic Decree gave way to a concern to differentiate proper Christianity not from polytheistic beliefs but rather from Judaism.[36] Augustine influentially repudiated observance of the Apostolic Decree's ban on blood in his *Contra Faustum*.[37] Meanwhile, many early medieval Christian writers found more horror in Jewish than in Gentile foods. Patristic sources and medieval penitentials enjoined against eating Jewish matzoh, the unleavened bread of Passover eaten by the disciples at the Last Supper, and even, in some cases, against consuming food slaughtered or prepared by Jews.[38] And despite the absence of a Jewish community in pre-Conquest England, pseudo-Theodore's penitential indicates that if Jewish butchers and cooks materialized there, their meat and matzah would be forbidden to the Christian faithful. This originally Carolingian penitential, which according to Meens enjoyed "considerable influence" in tenth-century England,[39] enjoins forty days of penance upon anyone who "takes from the faithless Jews their unleavened bread – or any other food or drink – and participates in their impieties … because it is written, 'For the pure all things are pure but for the defiled and unbelieving nothing is pure' [*Tit* 1.15], but rather all is profane."[40] About this rationale, Freidenreich comments, "For Christians, all things are pure; for Jews, who reject the Christian belief that all things are pure, nothing is pure; therefore Christians must avoid Jewish food as impure – despite the fact that for Christians all things are pure!"[41] Both pre-Conquest English witnesses to the penitential (Brussels, Bibliothèque Royale 8558–63 and Cambridge, Corpus Christi College 190) include this facially irrelevant injunction against eating Jewish food.[42]

Augustine's influence notwithstanding, the Apostolic Decree exerted significant influence on Frankish, Irish, and English penitential literature in the early Middle Ages. According to Filotas, about three-quarters of extant penitentials from this period boast food prohibitions, and many of these penitentials specifically mention the Decree.[43] Steel argues that the persistence and popularity in these penitentials of taboos against carrion performed a necessary role in defining humanity as the only licit killer of animals.[44] Perhaps in the spirit of the Apostolic Decree, an additional category of taboos seems to repudiate the practices of contemporary polytheists. For instance, bans on and, particularly in Old English penitentials, mere discouragement from eating horsemeat responded to this apparently accepted dietary practice among non-Christian northern Europeans.[45]

Ælfric addresses the survival of food prohibitions uneasily in the homily-translation on Maccabees. After citing Paul's maxim, "*Omnia munda mundis.* / 'Ealle ðincg syndon clæne þam clænum mannum'" (lines 76–7; all things are clean to clean people), he admits:

> Sume wæron þa fule þe nu synd eac fule,
> ac hit biþ to langsum eall her to logigenne
> be ðam clænum nytenum oððe be þam unclænum
> on ðære ealdan æ þe mann ett nu swaðeah   (lines 82–5)

> Some were foul then that are also foul now, but it is too long to list here all the clean beasts or the unclean ones, according to the old law, that one nevertheless eats now.[46]

Although Ælfric does not specify where Old Testament and early English food avoidances overlap, it is clear in this translation and elsewhere that he considers some food taboos legitimately to constrain his own Christian community. In his "Letter to Brother Edward," as noted previously, Ælfric champions a prohibition on blood consumption, liberally quoting God's pertinent injunctions to Noah and Moses as justification:

> Her geswutelað on ðysum gewrite hu God ælmihtig forbead mancynne ælces cynnes blod to etenne. God cwæþ to Noe æfter þam mycclum flode: "Þære sæ fixas and þære eorðan nytenu ic sylle eow to bigleofan, buton þæt ge heora blod ne þicgon. Witodlice þæra nytena blod ic ofgange æt eowrum handum … Ne þicge ge nanes nytenes blod on eowrum mettum ne fugela ne oðra nytena. Ælc ðæra manna ðe blod ytt sceal losian of his folce, beo he inlenda, beo he ælðeodig, forþan ðe on þam blode is þæs nytenes lif…" Eft we raedað on canonibus þæt nan nyten þe to mete sceal ne byð clænlice acweald, buton þæt incunde blod ðe anbutan þære heortan is ut yrne.

> Now this letter explains how God almighty forbade mankind to eat any kind of blood. God said to Noah after the great flood: "Of the fish of the sea and the beasts of the earth I give you for food, except that you not consume their blood. Certainly I will require [satisfaction for] the blood of beasts at your hands … Do not consume the blood of any beast in your meat nor of birds nor of any other beasts. Any man who eats blood shall be lost from his people, whether he be native or foreign, because a beast's life is in the blood…" We also read in the canons that no beast that is for food is killed cleanly unless the internal blood that is around the heart has run out.[47]

Ælfric thus attributes the blood ban not only to the Apostolic Decree but also directly to the Old Testament – both the ostensibly universal Noahic covenant,[48] from which the Apostolic Decree draws much of its rationale, and the Mosaic laws, which pertain to the covenant between God and the Jews and allegedly do not bind Christians. He does not, for the purposes of this letter, distinguish between the relevance of the two covenants. In eliding the two, he demonstrates the potential of kosher law to reach beyond the limits ostensibly set by supersession and serve, when called upon, to reinforce a point of Christian doctrine. To make use of Kruger's metaphor regarding "Jewish corporeality," the Old Law may be interred, but it is not really gone.[49]

Likewise, in an homily on the Lenten Fast that follows Gregory the Great in connecting Old and New Testament fasts (those of Moses and Christ) to each other and to the contemporary fast, Ælfric demonstrates a capacity to affirm the inextricability of spiritual and ethical meanings from a material fast without calling for a supersession of the physical observance: "Unrihtlic bið þæt se cristena mann flæsclice lustas gefremme, on ðam timan þe he flæscmettas forgan sceal" (It is unlawful for a Christian person to indulge in fleshly desires in the time that he must forgo flesh meats).[50] Ælfric is thus not only well aware but also a vigorous proponent of the Christian legitimacy of some food regulations within his own culture. Nevertheless, in the translation of Maccabees it does not serve his aims – the differentiation of Jews and Christians and of humans and animals[51] – to explore this legitimacy any more fully.

Early English Christians were by no means, then, completely unaware of Jewish food laws, nor did they entirely disregard them. In addition to pseudo-Theodore's generalized assertion of the difference of Jewish food, the Old Testament's clean/unclean distinction among animals appears more than once in Old English literature. For instance, in the Old English translation of Bede's *Ecclesiastical History*, Cædmon's composition of hymns evokes a comparison to kosher animals: "swa swa clæne neten eodorcende in þæt sweteste leoð gehwerfde" (just as clean beasts ruminate he turned [them] into the sweetest songs).[52] As Scheil observes, this is the rumination trope that appears in Ælfric's Maccabees.[53] Similarly, Ælfric's *Colloquy* imagines a teacher asking a fisherman, "Hwæt gif hit unclæne beoþ fixas?" (What if the fish are unclean?). The fisherman replies, "Ic utwyrpe þa unclænan ut, and genime me clæne to mete" (lines 94–5; I throw the unclean ones out, and take the clean for food).[54] Most notably, Alfred's translation of Psalms 16:14 explicitly if parenthetically addresses Jewish avoidance of pork: "Weorþen hi swa geðræste mid hungre, þæt hi eton swynen flæsc (þæt Iudeum unalyfedlic ys to etanne)" (They grew so worn out with hunger that they ate swine's flesh, which is unlawful for the Jews to eat).[55] This cursory explanation, which would have been well-known to Ælfric, emphasizes by contrast the deliberateness of Ælfric's interpretive turn, signalled in his initial characterization of food law ("þone fulan mete þe Moyses forbead / Godes folce to þicgenne for þære gastlican gatacnunge") as a matter for exegesis.

Jewish food taboos were thus not radically foreign to English Christians, not even in the vernacular alone. The English works of learned authors make offhand use of them (as in the translation of Bede and in the *Colloquy*) and they manifest as surviving practices and objects of anxiety in influential penitentials. As David Grumett and Rachel Muers observe, Ælfric's apparently passing admission about the continuing foulness of some unspecified food items indicates a profound unease stemming from his inability "to escape the facts that choices are made, and continue to be made, about which foods are acceptable, and that there is some continuity between Christian and Jewish food practices."[56] They also represent the legacy of Christianity's struggle to differentiate itself from Jews, Muslims, and polytheists through food consumption, a struggle that is linked to the establishment of human supremacy over animals. Thus, Ælfric's explanation of Jewish food laws was unlikely to have been motivated solely by the need to inform an ignorant audience; it was more likely a response, in part, to the uneasy and at times oppositional similarity between Christian and Jewish prohibitions, which although not coextensive were deeply entangled.

Men as Meat

The Aristotelian hierarchy of the natural world, of which man is the earthly apex because of his relationship to the divine, anchors Ælfric's vision of humanity. In a passage of his homily "On the Lord's Ascension," Ælfric translates from Gregory's Homily 29 an explanation of the place of humanity in creation:

> Gærs and treowa lybbað buton felnysse; hi ne lybbað na þurh sawle, ac þurh heora grennysse. Nytenu lybbað, and habbað felnysse buton gesceade. Hi nabbað nan gescead, for þan ðe hi sind sawullease ... Nu hæfð se man ealra gesceafta sum þing: him is gemæne mid stanum þæt he beo wunigende, him is gemæne mid treowum þæt he lybbe, mid nytenum þæt he gefrede, mid englum þæt he understande ... ðæt godspel bið gebodad eallum gesceafte, þonne hit bið þam menn anum gebodad, for þan ðe ealle eorðlice þing sind gesceapene for þam men anum.[57]

Grass and trees live without feeling; they live not by a soul, but by their greenness. Beasts live and have feeling, without reason; they have no reason, because they are soulless ... Now the human has something of all creatures. He has in common with stones that he exists; he has in common with trees that he lives, with beasts that he feels, with angels that he understands ... the gospel is proclaimed to all, when it is proclaimed to humans alone, because all earthly things are created for humans alone.[58]

This conception of the hierarchy of being and of human dominion on earth (with angels on the rung above humans) was almost universally accepted in medieval Christianity, and finds support in God's first words to humanity: "Increase, and multiply, and fill the earth, and subdue it, and rule over the fishes of the sea and the fowls of the air and all living creatures that move upon the earth" (Genesis 1:28; Crescite, et multiplicamini, et replete terram, et subicite eam, et dominamini piscibus maris et volatilibus caeli et universis animantibus quae moventur super terram).[59] The above passage is notable not only because of its careful attention to the respective beingness of inanimate, animate, and sensible creatures, but also because it locates humanity's earthly dominion and indeed the basis for the gospel message in the *use* of other creatures – they are "ealle ... gesceapene for þam men anum." Simultaneously, it acknowledges that some form of animal identity is also implicated in human identity ("hæfð se man ealra gesceafta sum þing") because a certain form of beingness is "gemæne," common to and shared by humans and animals.

The assertion that the purpose of animal life is to serve and be used by humanity allows a safe distance from which to acknowledge the similarity of humans and beasts. As Agamben comments about Aristotle's taxonomy of kinds of life, "what has been separated and divided (in this case nutritive life) is precisely what – in a sort of *divide et impera* – allows the construction of the unity of life as the hierarchical articulation of a series of functional faculties and oppositions."[60] Shared characteristics are thus the basis not of mutuality but of hierarchical order. Humanity becomes defined as everything within "man" that he does not share with the other creatures.[61]

Humanity includes not only the soul, but also intellectual and physical mastery over beasts. But this order of things is prone to upset. Magennis's argument that Old English writers found eating distasteful, since "eating itself is ... a bodily function that human beings have in common with animals,"[62] is pushed to the limits in the case of the Jewish brothers of the *Passio*: how much worse it is to share with animals the function of *being* eaten. The uneasiness of the distinction between human and animal flesh pervades this initial story of martyrdom, as the heathen oppressors follow their execution of the heroic Eleazar, who would not eat sacrifice-bacon, by torturing and murdering seven nameless Jewish brothers in ways that recall the slaughter and cooking of animals for consumption. These brothers have also refused to eat pork, declaring that they would rather die than break God's law. Accordingly, the executioners carry out commands, regarding the first brother, to

> forceorfan his tungan,
> and hine behættian and his handa forceorfan,
> and eac befotian and … feccan ænne hwer
> and hine þæron seoðan oðþæt he sawlode (lines 116–19)

> cut out his tongue and scalp him and cut off his hands and also sever his feet and to fetch a pot and boil him therein until he gave up his soul.[63]

The brothers are tortured "þæt hi etan sceoldon, ongean Godes æ, spicc" (line 112; so that they would eat bacon against God's law) – and killed as if they themselves are meat because they refuse.[64] It is a particularly cruel punishment, from a Jewish perspective, because the kosher laws are based on and seek to maintain the distinctness of orders of being (and orders of people, covenanted and heathen), and this type of murder elides even the most important of such distinctions, the separation between humans and animals established in Genesis far prior to the dietary laws.[65]

When the human body is treated as meat, it moves into what Gilles Deleuze has called "a *zone of indiscernibility or undecidability* between man and animal … the common zone of man and beast."[66] Deleuze defines meat in this context not necessarily as dead flesh but rather as the condition in which the body descends conceptually from a kind of formal unity (the person) into a collection of suffering parts.[67] Humanity's difference from animals is elided, as is the difference between life and death. In this formulation, it is the capacity to suffer and die as meat, not *gefred[nes]*, feeling and sensibility in general, as Ælfric's homily on the Lord's Ascension claims, that represents what is truly common to humans and animals.[68] Edibility is, in other words, a deep form of dehumanization.

The brand of degradation that removes supremacy over animals as a source of human identity intensifies when a man not only suffers as if meat but also actually becomes food for animals. The capacity to be eaten belongs properly to animals and nonliving things; as Kyla Wazana Tompkins observes, "to be completely other with relation to the human,

56 Nothing Pure

is one of the conditions of being edible."[69] Such an expulsion from the human community also finally befalls the emperor Antiochus, oppressor of the Maccabees. Antiochus's appropriate punishment for defiling the temple with heathen "fylðum" (line 539; filth, in this case offerings to idols) is a death by rotting alive, eaten by worms:

> Him weollon þa wurmas of ðam gewitnodan lic-haman,
> and he stanc swa fule þæt man hine ferian ne mihte,
> and he ða yfele and earmlice geendode   (lines 545–7)

> Worms then swarmed from his tortured body, and he stank so foully that no one could carry him, and then he badly and wretchedly perished.[70]

Ælfric selects for translation, then further condenses, lines specifying worms and stink[71] from a long, gory passage that is itself only one version of Antiochus's overdetermined fate.[72] Daniel R. Schwartz reads the copious horror of this Biblical passage as serving the interests of "poetic justice," a preoccupation of 2 Maccabees: "the fact that the illness affected [the Biblical Antiochus's] stomach fits the fact that he sinned by requiring Jews to eat forbidden foods, and … the circumstances of his death are like those he imposed upon others."[73] Worms and "fule" smell are, of all these disgusting and painful details, appropriate to Ælfric's more concise narrative because they connect the categorical uncleanness that the tyrant forced on others to the uncleanness of his body in death. Generally speaking, living humans eat and are not eaten; flesh lives until it dies, and then is food for worms, a dynamic spelled out, for instance, in the Soul's Address to the Body in *Soul and Body II*. Michelle Hoek writes of this gruesome transition: "Death has removed the body from any associations with human society. It now belongs to the gluttonous community of the worms."[74] In a double alienation from the human, Antiochus's reduction to food for worms removes him from human society while he still lives; the smell of his putrefaction excludes him from human touch.[75]

Job: The Consumed

Being eaten alive by worms is a fitting punishment for the defiler Antiochus, but when this fate strikes a righteous man in Ælfric's works, it signifies a breakdown of moral order. In Ælfric's homily-translation of Job, "Dominica I. in Mense Septembri," Satan receives God's permission to afflict Job's flesh with wounds and putrefaction, and as Job's skin rots, he sits on a heap of dung and laments: "Min flæsc is ymscryd mid forrotodnysse, and mid dustes horwum. Min hyd forsearode, and is forscruncen. Me habbað geswencednysse dagas, and on niht min ban bið mid sarnysse ðurhðyd, and ða ðe me etað ne slapað." (My flesh is clothed with putrefaction and with the grime of dust. My skin is withered and shrivelled. Days of affliction have me, and at night my bone is pierced through with pain, and those that eat me do not sleep.)[76] The "forrotodnysse" that afflicts Job represents, in its philological context, a particularly fleshly and horrible form of decay.[77] Old English derivatives of *forrotian*, as opposed to those of the milder *rotian*, tend to implicate animal matter, flesh or blood or corpses; this is true, for instance, in the Old English Hexateuch, which applies derivatives of *forrotian* to manna rotted and crawling with worms (Exodus 7:18) and to the Nile turned to blood and choked with the bodies of dead fish (Exodus 7:21). The withering of the body is also, as John Aberth notes, a real-life consequence of starvation.[78] The transformation of Job, like that of Antiochus, is more abject for all that it is less absolute than that of a corpse: the horror of Job is that he experiences the change while he still lives. From one who owned animals to one without possessions, from one who eats meat to one who *is* meat, he becomes the food of worms while he is still alive. As Besserman notes, the trajectory of the story of Job, from ancient to medieval iterations, was towards increasing levels of physical degradation. The original Job, the Job of the Masoretic (Hebrew) text, is not even afflicted with worms; he gains them only in the Septuagint and they do not appear in the Vulgate. Yet Job's worms became essential to his patience, pathos, and dignity: that is, his popular appeal. The medieval (Christian) Job, writes Besserman, was "venerat[ed] as the patron saint of sufferers from worms, various skin diseases including leprosy, venereal disease, and melancholy … In medieval Latin and German charms against worms, Job is invoked."[79] Job's suffering becomes existential; as Gene M. Tucker comments of the message in this passage, "What is the place of human beings in the natural order? They could be food for eagles, carrion."[80]

Of this homily, Ælfric writes in his *Libellus*, "Be þam ic awende on Englisc sumne cwide iu, and hit ys eac witegung witodlice be Criste and be his gelaþunge" (I previously turned a certain homily about this into English, and it is also certainly a prophecy about Christ and about his church).[81] Here Ælfric interprets Job typologically, an interpretation made standard by Gregory the Great's *Moralia in Job*. Ælfric's most complete Old Testament life in either collection of *Catholic Homilies*, the sermon on Job apparently constituted a relatively safe text for the edification of the unlearned. Neither a seductress, nor a warrior, nor a leader of dubious morals – nor, indeed, a circumcised Jew – the suffering and putatively

58 Nothing Pure

blameless Job was apparently such an unproblematic Christian type that, save a few comments on the sacrificial practices of Job's friends, this homily mentions neither Judaism nor repudiated Jewish practices.

Job's potential as a Christian type may not be immediately obvious from all parts of his narrative, but his identity as a non-Jew and the depth and horror of his suffering have made him a far more universal target for interpretation and identification than the more intransigently ethnic Maccabees. Job is a pious non-Israelite whom Satan[82] convinces God to test through awful material afflictions – the deaths of Job's children, the destruction of his animals and property, and finally the corruption of Job's own body. Job's friends come in order to comfort him, although in fact they do the opposite, and a long conversation about theodicy ensues among them, followed by a dialogue between Job and God in which Job challenges God's apparent injustice and God asserts the limitations of Job's understanding of the divine. Finally Job's possessions are returned twofold and he is given a new set of children. The book of Job, a more or less unified text since about the sixth century BCE, exists in two parts, likely from two distinct sources: the brief chapters of Job's story, which involve mostly material loss and gain, and the long wisdom poem that comprises the conversations and dialogues about divine justice. As Steven J. Vicchio notes, this division reveals two Jobs and two Gods: "The Job of the prose (ch. 1 and 2 and 42.7–17) is a patient and holy man, one who fears God and shuns evil; the Job of the poetry (ch. 3–42.6) is angry, at God and at his friends."[83] Likewise, the God of the framing narrative, always called Yahweh in the original Hebrew, "is anthropomorphic, irascible and easily duped"; the poetic God, usually known as "El, Eloah, Elohim, and El Shaddai ... is powerfully foreboding and unknowable."[84] Ælfric's homily-translation, like most medieval Christian treatment of the book of Job, is primarily concerned with the frame narrative, but also incorporates material from the poem.

As well as being preyed upon, Job has a dietary problem of his own – one that Ælfric does not expound upon, although it appears in both the Vulgate Job and Gregory's *Moralia in Job*, his main sources.[85] Sitting upon his dunghill, Job reflects on his suffering: "The things which before my soul would not touch now through anguish are my meats" (Job 6:7).[86] Conspicuous even within the notorious interpretive maelstrom that is the book of Job,[87] this verse has historically been difficult to translate and understand. Part of the difficulty appears to stem from the inherent tense ambiguity of the Biblical Hebrew verb system,[88] so it has been a matter of interpretation whether Job is saying that he formerly found the food loathsome and now eats it, or that he currently finds the food loathsome (and now does not eat it). In the second sense, it is usually taken as a metaphor for the bitter words of his friends, which he cannot accept: the standard English translation of the Masoretic text (JPS), for instance, has "I refuse to touch them; / They are like food when I am sick." Robert Alter's translation highlights the comparison between food and Job's own flesh: "My throat refuses to touch them. / They resemble my sickening flesh."[89] Alter paraphrases the first phrase as "For Job in his suffering, all food has become nauseating," and notes of the second line, "The translation is an educated guess. The syntax of the Hebrew is crabbed, and the last word of the line, *la[kh]mi* [לַחְמִי], could mean either 'flesh' or 'bread.'"[90] As Jack H. Kahn and Hester Solomon note, "In Hebrew, the word for soul is often used for appetite. In this context, it means that Job's whole being revolts against the food that he needs for his physical nourishment."[91] The Vulgate translation, however, very clearly supports the first interpretation ("Quae prius tangere nolebat anima mea nunc prae angustia cibi mei sunt"), which as Heidi O. Lee notes also resonates with Proverbs 27:7: "A soul that is full shall tread upon the honeycomb, and a soul that is hungry shall take even bitter for sweet" (Anima saturata calcabit favum, et anima esuriens et[iam] amarum pro dulci sumet).[92] This is also the meaning followed by Gregory, Ælfric's source.

It is difficult to determine what Job, as a Gentile, would previously have found loathsome to eat, and what exactly this "conversion of the appetites," as Heidi O. Lee describes this verse in another iteration, would have entailed.[93] To Alter, Job means all food on account of its resemblance (physical and perhaps conceptual) to his own rotting flesh. In the most literal terms, Job appears to be talking about the food of starvation, food that in his earlier affluence (or in his earlier observance of taboos, if any) he would not have eaten. This interpretation is supported by 6:5–6: lamenting his affliction, Job asks: "Will the wild ass bray when he hath grass? Or will the ox low when he standeth before a full manger? Or can an unsavoury thing be eaten that is not seasoned with salt? Or can a man taste that which when tasted bringeth death?"[94] For one problem of starvation, as Job and those familiar with famine would know, is that rather than simply depriving one of food, it first brings those it afflicts into newly intimate contact with foods that were previously (and in many cases still are) repugnant.

Early medieval people were familiar with the phenomenon of extreme hunger. Starvation, like invasion, was a matter of perennial anxiety in early England. Ælfric gives a poignant view of the sufferings of his time in his homily on the Second Sunday in Advent, which describes the "tacna" (signs) of the coming Day of Judgment with an urgency that seems borne not only of concern for men's souls but also of longing: "Sume þas tacna we gesawon gefremmede, sume we ondrædað us towearde ... Mid cwealme and mid hungre we sind gelome geswencte, ac we nateshwon gyta swutele tacna on sunnan and on monan and on steorran ne gesawon." (Some of these signs we have seen performed, some we fear are coming ... With plague and with hunger we are continually afflicted, but we have by no means seen plainly yet the signs in the sun, and in the moon, and in the stars.)[95] Hunger weakened previous convictions about what was and was not edible. Indeed, as Filotas notes, many Old English penitentials, such as the Scriftboc and Theodore's penitential, frankly acknowledge the problem of eating forbidden and repugnant foods out of hunger and necessity, and to a certain degree even excuse the practice. As Filotas writes, "Necessity in the form of threats of violence and perhaps hunger was tacitly accepted as a partial excuse" for illicit consumption.[96] The Scriftboc, which lists numerous categories of unclean food, has this: "Se man se ðe unclæne neat þigeð for his þearfum, ne eglað þæt nawiht" (XVIII.34.i; If someone of necessity eats an animal that is unclean, that is no harm to him).[97] In the Canons of Theodore, although a consumer of carrion must ordinarily do penance, "Gif hine hunger to drifð, þonne ne dereð hit him na" (If hunger drives him to it, then it does not hurt him at all).[98] This penitential also states, "And se ðe for nydþearfe þigeð þæt nyten þe unclæne bið gesewen, fugel oððe wilde deor, ne sceðeð him þæt" (And he who because of necessity eats any apparently unclean beast, a bird or wild animal, that does not injure him).[99] As Ann Hagen notes, "taboos play little part when existence is at stake"; according to her interpretation of the penitentials and other early English texts, desperate people likely ate spoiled meat and other previously unattractive foods during famines, despite their ill health effects.[100] Early English culture (like perhaps all others) also distinguishes between food for animals and for humans, and the homilies contain instances in which humans are reduced to eating, or degraded by the offer of, food fit for animals. For instance, in Ælfric's Deposition of St. Basil, which is largely concerned with the nature of food, particularly the sacrament, Emperor Julian requites the ascetic Basil's gift of barley loaves with grass in order to insult him: "Horse mete is bere / þæt he us forgeæf – underfo he gærs!" (lines 215–16; The barley he gave us is horsefeed; let him accept grass!); Basil replies,

> We budon þe, casere, þes þe we sylfa brucað
> and þu sealdest us togeanes þæt þæt ðe ungesceadwyse nytena
> habbað him to bigleofan, gebysmriende us   (lines 218–20)[101]

> We offered you, emperor, what we ourselves eat and in reply you gave us what unreasoning beasts have for their nourishment, mocking us.

It is no surprise that the emperor spurns the loaves; more notable is that even the ascetic, vegetarian Basil is capable of offence when offered what he considers animal feed. Yet in times of hunger, the dictates of religion, taste, and health all, to a certain degree, lose their powers to separate suitable and unsuitable foods.[102]

Job is a sick, hungry person who suffers much in common with many medieval people. Yet Gregory, reminding the reader that the words of this verse "would never have gone on commanding such deep veneration even to the very ends of the world, if they had not been pregnant with mystical meaning" (7.10), turns from a physical reading in his *Moralia in Job*. For Gregory, whose *Moralia* exerted so much influence on Ælfric's interpretation, Job 6:7 signifies the true relation between Jews and Gentiles and the supersession of the Hebrews as God's elect:

> these words agree with the voice of Judaea ... [who] looked down upon all the Gentiles as brute creatures. But because, when instructed by the precepts of the Law, she disdained to admit to herself the communion of the Gentiles, what did she but loath to take "unsavoury food?" For the Divine decree had forbidden, on the menace of death, that the Israelitish people should join in a league with strangers, and pollute the way of life in holy religion.[103]

This passage demonstrates that what Kruger taxonomizes as "allegorical readings that invert the biblical text's literal opposition between Jewish believers and non-Jewish unbelievers to make the believers Christian types and the unbelievers Jewish infidels"[104] – a characterization that accurately describes Ælfric's discussion of food laws in his Maccabees homily – do not originate with Ælfric, but rather run through the veins of medieval Christian Old Testament exegesis. Bound to the letter of the law, says Gregory, Jews did not want to be spiritually defiled by Gentile ways. The taste of the Church (previously Judaea) undergoes a conversion, however, when many of the Jews reject Jesus, and out of necessity she must take that which (those whom), as Judaea, she loathed:

> For Judaea, having disdained the life of the Gentiles, refused as it were for long to touch her, whose society she scorned to admit; but on coming to the grace of the Redeemer, being rejected by the unbelieving Israelites, while by the Holy Apostles she stretches out herself for the gathering together of the Gentiles, she as it were takes that for food with a hungry appetite, which before with loathing she disdained as unworthy ... for her "straitness" she ate the food which she had for long despised, in that being rejected by the obduracy of the Jews, she yearns to take to her the Gentile folk, whom she had contemned.[105]

Necessity, then, in the form of hunger, includes in the broader sense the necessity to repudiate Judaism in order to attain salvation.

Gregory appropriates food and hunger as vehicles of supersession, and his interpretation set a medieval standard. As Vicchio and Besserman note, it is difficult to overestimate the influence of Gregory's interpretation in the Latin West. Vicchio observes that the *Moralia* was second only to Augustine's work in its reach among monks, so influential that "at least in the early medieval western Christian tradition, it was simply taken for granted that what the book of Job meant was identical to what Gregory had to say about the text."[106] The extraordinarily long commentary did not confine itself strictly to reflecting on the book of Job, but explicated so many additional points of Christian theology and Scriptural interpretation that, in Vicchio's words, it "achieved a kind of canonical status usually reserved for the books of the Bible themselves."[107] In addition to its many glories, the book applies considerable creativity to what Vicchio calls "a sustained attack on the Jews," finding in many of Job's adversities references to supersession of Jewish law and to the sinfulness and unbelief of Jews.[108]

The Restoration of Human Mastery

The Maccabee heroes restore the temple by eradicating the remnants of polytheistic offerings and instituting Jewish sacrifice:

> þa fylðe adydon ut
> of ðam godes huse and godes lof arærdon
> æfter moyses æ mid mycelre blysse
> and offrodon gode lac mid geleafan and sange   (lines 381–4)

> they cleared the filth out of the house of God and raised up the praise of God in accordance with Moses's law, with great rejoicing, and offered sacrifices to God with faith and song.

The sacrifice as described in the Old Testament retains a particular importance in late Old English prose writing, since it is important theological background to Christ's self-sacrifice and to the Eucharist. As Richard Marsden notes, Exodus 12:2–11, the instructions for sacrificing the first paschal lamb in Egypt, circulates in three distinct late Old English prose translations: those of the *Old English Heptateuch*, Ælfric's *Sermo de sacrificio in die Paschae*, and Byrhtferth's *Enchiridion*.[109] The replacement of polytheistic with Jewish offerings is a prerequisite to the Christian supersession of Jewish sacrifice, a final step that Ælfric explains succinctly at the conclusion of the homily on Job. When Job's friends offer an atonement sacrifice of bulls and rams, Ælfric explains these sacrifices ("seo offrung") as "gewunelic on ealdum dagum" (customary in the old days) but "nu unalyfedlic æfter cristes / ðrowunge" (now unlawful after Christ's passion).[110]

It is appropriate for the ancients of the story, says Ælfric, to sacrifice. In fact, it is incumbent upon them because of God's command. But this kind of carnal sacrifice has been replaced by the eternal sacrifice, that of Christ's passion – a sufficient sacrifice, in theory, henceforth to expiate all the faithful.[111] We are reminded here of the difference that the meat of food and sacrifice makes in dividing Jewish (Old Law) and Christian (New Law) identities: Christians are allowed to eat the swine that Jews are forbidden. Christians are forbidden the animal sacrifices that (Biblical) Jews are permitted. This is also an object lesson in the way Jewish ideas about the flesh, although they initially present a problem for the homilist, can in skilled hands be an opportunity to reassert the supersession by Christianity of Judaism. More than that, they can provide the opportunity to demonstrate anew the distinctions between orders of being – those things that live in the flesh only (animals) and those with access to eternal life. The sacrifice of the animals restores a balance, man's proper relationship to animal meat: now again, humans kill animals rather than being preyed upon by them. Job's animal and material possessions are restored twofold. He is given a new set of children, but not in double quantity, explains Ælfric, because while animals as physical life can be utterly destroyed, Job's deceased first round of children "him wæron gehealdene"[112] (were kept for him) in the afterlife. The book ends in a feast, which Nathan MacDonald notes is a gustatory symbol of Job's full restoration to prosperity and community.[113] This restoration entails a reestablishment of value, a resegregation of the human and the animal and a reassertion of power over the animal – over animals and over our nature as animals. It is also a reestablishment of God's authority. As in the Schmittian theory of the state of exception elaborated by Agamben, in which sovereign power manifests through a suspension of law that withdraws all protection from the vulnerable figure,[114] God's authority consists in demonstrating that just as he has apparently suspended the laws of divine justice that putatively protected Job's humanity from punishment, so too can he easily reinstate those laws by providing a liberal reward for pious suffering. God was present all along, and his divine laws of hierarchy and of justice always in force, although temporarily suspended. This fantasia might well have offered comfort in a time of privation and uncertainty.

To appreciate the flawlessness with which Ælfric achieves this arc, it is helpful to understand the extent to which the homily (and indeed the medieval Christian understanding of Job as such) counters the apparent thrust of much of the Biblical book of Job. Job as a whole seems to be a reflection on the troubled relationship between God and his physical creation, and a revelation of the insignificant place of man in the physical world. In the wisdom poem at the heart of the book, Job rebels in his faith, challenging God, who after long silence answers unsympathetically. In what Tucker calls the Bible's "most forceful and compelling critique of the idea that humanity is the pinnacle of the natural order," God mockingly compares Job's anthropocentric view of him – as a deity occupied at the most granular level with the fate of individual humans – to the vastness of his natural works.[115] In Job 40, God taunts Job with his power over the leviathan, an awesome beast identified variously with the whale or a sea monster:[116]

> Canst thou draw out the Leviathan with a hook, or canst thou tie his tongue with a cord? Canst thou put a ring in his nose or bore through his jaw with a buckle? Will he make many supplications to thee or speak soft words to thee? Will he make a covenant with thee, and wilt thou take him to be a servant for ever? Shalt thou play with him as with a bird or tie him up for thy handmaids? Shall friends cut him in pieces? Shall merchants divide him? (Job 40:20–5)[117]

The set of rhetorical questions highlights the impossibility of reducing the leviathan to human use or subjecting it to human intimacy or power. It also highlights an intimacy between God and animals from which humans are excluded. If the prose narrative of punishment and reward demonstrates God's sovereignty by setting Job's suffering in a temporary state of exception to the rules of divine justice as humans know them, then the wisdom poem disrupts this plot, in passages such as this, by suggesting that no such rules are in play at all; they are a human invention, representing a frustrated anthropocentric wish for God to be close enough for absolute sovereignty.

Ælfric's translation of Maccabees, although highly selective and particularly creative in its approach to chronology, contains little original material. His other significant addition, after the passage explicating kosher law, is an explanation of the elephant, which he describes as an "ormæte nyten mare þonne sum hus" (line 566; a huge beast larger than a house) that has no need to recline, gestates for two years, and lives three hundred years. In all dimensions, the elephant is greater and more enduring than humans, yet

> hi man mæg wenian wundorlice to ge-feohte.
> Hwæl is ealra fixa mæst
> and ylp is eallra nytena mæst
> ac swa-þeah mannes gescead hi mæg gewyldan (lines 571–3)
>
> man may wonderfully train them for war. The whale is the largest of all fish and the elephant is the largest of all beasts, but nevertheless they may be tamed by man's reason.[118]

Although the Bible asserts human dominion (Genesis 1:28), the level of confidence revealed in Ælfric's explanation is not inherent in the Biblical source material. More explicitly than the conclusion of Ælfric's homily on Job, the elephant passage is a statement of mastery over the animal world consistent with the ability of the spirit (and the New Testament) to tame, exploit, and transcend the flesh (and the Old Law). It could hardly contradict God's speech to Job more.

The care with which Ælfric reifies these distinctions, however, underlines how fragile they are, precisely because of the frailty of the flesh. As Scheil indicates, the elephant is "beyond the actual experience" of the English. Flesh, however, and the problem of the resemblance between meat and human flesh in a time of embattlement and privation, is by no means beyond their experience. Like the rebellious Maccabees, Ælfric's audience can make certain distinctions – between Christians and others, humans and animals, what the community will and won't eat – but such distinctions may seem constantly in danger of collapse, as one may be figuratively eaten alive by the enemy or, more concretely, confronted by the reduction of the human to degraded and destroyed flesh. Taming animals, managing food prohibitions, anthropologizing Jews – all of these are necessary and interlinked in maintaining Christian humanity's identity and place in the world. Reduced to prefiguration of the distinction between the Old Law and the New, unsaved and saved, Jewish food taboos become not simply an anthropologically or historically interesting aspect of the difference between Christians and non-believers (or an effect of that difference); they become the very index of that difference. This is so even in spite – or precisely because – of the lack of distinction, at times, between old taboos and new.

3 The Benedictine Invention of Heterosexuality: Jewish (Law's) Sexual Difference in Time

Sexuality, like food, proves a potent site for Jewish/Christian resignification through translation. Its centrality both to Abrahamic theologies and to eleventh-century ecclesiastical politics (and therefore to English politics as such) makes sexual regulation a natural arena for Ælfric's intervention. This chapter demonstrates that Ælfric's translations of Biblical laws about marriage and supersession, echoing and echoed by other Benedictine thinkers, demonstrate an early medieval English articulation of sexual difference between Jews and Christians. Departing from the more mainstream tradition, dating from the patristic period and continuing intermittently through the present, that forges Christian purity and gender propriety in opposition to Jewish sexual perversion and gender deviance, Ælfric sees ancient Jews as model heterosexuals whose way of life is superseded by a more perfect Christian chastity.

Regulating sexual life is fundamental to Christian and Jewish theologies, as well as to processes of national and racial formation. The preoccupation of normative institutions with gender and sexuality makes it unsurprising that Christians and Jews have frequently articulated their mutual differences and antagonisms, in addition to many internal differences, in sexual terms.[1] Similarly, the study of Christian–Jewish difference and of sexual difference has productively created and used similar tools. As Daniel Boyarin, Daniel Itzkovitz, and Ann Pellegrini note, it is impossible to separate the formulation of queer theory and its antecedents from "the Jewish question" – the question of Jewish racial and sexual difference, and how state and society manage this difference, within Christian Europe and its (post)colonies.[2] This book finds its genealogy in queer/Jewish scholarship that, at this intersection, uses classic and emerging queer methodologies to examine Jewish difference as such within Christian and Christian–secular societies.

Of particular interest to queer/Jewish thinking, for many years now, is the distinction between "minoritizing and universalizing" models of sexual difference best articulated by Eve Sedgwick, whose joyful and explicit discussion of gay coming-out proceeds in part, as Naomi Seidman observes, through a fascinating confession and "disavowal" of the author's Jewishness and of the parallels between Jewish and queer identities.[3] In Sedgwick's schema, the fictive "homosexual-heterosexual" binary operates simultaneously through a "minoritizing" model in which same-gender desire is the province of a "discrete category of persons," and a contradictory "universalizing" model in which nearly everyone harbours latent same-gender desire, bolstered evidentiarily by the majority's "paranoid insistence" on abjecting such desires. In this "indisseverable girdle of incongruities" that maintains hierarchical sexual difference, the majority "may require for their maintenance the scapegoating crystallization of a same-gender male desire that is widespread and in the first place internal."[4] Although Sedgwick forcefully rejects the parallel between Jewish and queer identities, scholars in both queer and Jewish studies have returned to their failed dissociation in this "primal scene of queer studies"[5] and insisted that, on the contrary, Jewishness has always been sexed and gendered in the anti-Semitic imaginary and that these sexual fantasies about Jews are not "minor" issues for majority Christian gender regimes.[6] As a result, the matrix Sedgwick describes is more than apt when describing the "Jewish question" in an anti-Semitic society. For any crude model of Jewish/Christian difference – that is, most of the models that have animated various anti-Jewish church–state imaginaries – relies on Jewishness to signify both an identifiable minority and, as Claudine Fabre-Vassas notes, a quality or essence that dangerously "inhabits ... every Christian."[7] This paradoxical model of Jewish otherness/endemic potentiality, as well as numerous other insights from queer theory, has guided scholars who trace Jewish abjection in the establishment of Euro-Christian sex and gender forms.[8]

In these histories, Jews figure as sexual deviants from the dominant culture's norms: as queer, as nonbinary or gender non-conforming, sometimes as dangerous perverts.[9] The medieval emblem of this queerness is the menstruating Jewish man, who embodies undesirable corporeal fluidity in a spectacular confluence of pollutions.[10] Such histories are rightly discontinuous and often skip over early medieval Britain, where ideas of Jewish sexual difference were available from sources such as Chrysostom but surfaced rarely.[11] Within this chapter, I return to the question of how sexual difference and Jewish difference intersect in the creation of Christian sexual ideals. This analysis would be impossible without the alignment of queerness and Jewishness finely traced by Jewish/queer theory, yet in reading the English Benedictines I find that the usual patterns do not apply. In a nearly inverse dynamic to that traced by Steven F. Kruger, Daniel Boyarin, and Susanna Drake, temporally distant Biblical Jews represent a procreative, kinship-oriented heterosexuality that has been superseded by Christian chastity and asexual, spiritual reproduction.[12]

Before progressing, a brief remark on how the terms "heterosexuality," "kinship," and "queer" appear in this chapter. I use "heterosexuality" with self-conscious anachronism to refer to what many call *heteropatriarchy*, a term I avoid here because the monastic familial system my primary texts champion in opposition is also frequently patriarchal. In the term "heterosexuality" I include the social institutions and intimate practices (marriage; procreation, defined as legitimate or illegitimate; sexual relations between men and women, defined as marital, premarital, or extramarital) that link, and naturalize the links among, sexuality, gender assignment and identity, procreation, family and kinship, lineage and legacy, status and value of women, and property transfer. I do not refer to an erotic orientation or to erotic and affective relationships between men and women. (Eve experiences the difference, most chillingly distilled, when she emerges from the garden with her husband and is cursed with perpetual desire for and submission to him – and, in the Old English *Genesis* poem, fear of all men – as well as pain and labour in child-bearing, conditions that did not apparently attach to their prelapsarian relationship.) It is not hard to notice, as David Clark does, the "almost complete absence"[13] of heteroeroticism in the literature of elite pre-Conquest England.

I recognize kinship as what Damien W. Riggs and Elizabeth Peel call a "technology" of social formation, through which "particular human kinship practices produce particular modes of personhood"[14] and particular institutions and affective modes, all of which seem perfectly "natural" by the logic of kinship. When, therefore, I discuss relations such as "fatherhood" in this chapter, I do not distinguish between "real" vs. synthetic or metaphorical fatherhood – distinctions that obscure the constructed and narrative nature of all kinship – but among spiritual, legal, biological, and ancestral forms.

My definition of "queer" will unfold with my readings to include, without being reducible to, the chastity of the regular life.

Monasticism as a Queer Mode of Life

Twentieth- and twenty-first-century critiques of heterosexuality have posed queer models of affiliation and reproduction as superior and necessary alternatives to heterosexual models of reproductive kinship. Queer and lesbian-feminist critics have observed that heterosexual kinship is maintained by, as Jane Ward notes, "force, both through cultural propaganda targeting girls and women and more directly through sexual assault, incest, compulsory marriage, economic dependence, control of children, and domestic violence."[15] Lee Edelman criticizes the "reproductive futurism" in which the valorization of heterosexual reproduction guarantees a cycle in which "the future is mere repetition and just as lethal as the past," while Andrea Long Chu describes heterosexual life as "a mode of diminishment and slow death for women."[16] Medieval writers also viewed reproduction with horror and heterosexual time with dread. *Hali Maiðhad* propagandizes chastity to the upper classes by describing the degrading conditions under which many married women produce children – sexual coercion and domestic abuse, painful and humiliating childbirth – and the unbearable time of solitary motherhood: "to feskin ant to fostrin hit se moni earm-hwile, ant his waxunge se let, ant se slaw his thriftre!" (so many miserable hours to swaddle and feed [a child], and its growth so slow, and its development so gradual!). A mother "nis ha neaver bute care leste hit misfeare" (is never without anxiety that [her child] will come to harm),[17] and the more she loves her children and husband, the more pain she will inevitably suffer at their ingratitude, misadventures, and deaths. Medieval critics of the reproductive family do not share the ideals of modern feminists and queers: they do not, for one thing, seek full sexual and gender freedom; they do not note, explicitly, that heterosexuality as an institution reproduces capitalism, settler colonialism, and white supremacy.[18] But they do share suspicion of heterosexuality as a worldly practice that reproduces a detrimental fixation on material investments, that inhibits the expansion of care to those who need and deserve it, and that keeps women and men leashed to their gendered bodies and, in many cases, to unwanted and degrading sexual exchanges and to lives without equality or companionship. In the age of Christ, the champions of monastic and clerical chastity stress, this not the best way to create ties of kinship and care.

This Christian critique of the heterosexual family dates to St. Paul, whose movement from "Israel in the flesh" to "Israel in the spirit" Daniel Boyarin persuasively interprets as a statement precisely on the ethnocentric limitations of heterosexual kinship. To Paul, argues Boyarin, universality demands a rejection of this form of kinship, even if rejecting ethnocentricity, sex, and sexuality also effectively devalues both the Jewish and the feminine elements they ostensibly subsume.[19] As Drake observes, Paul at times uses "flesh" (σάρξ, *sarx*) to represent "a former way of life, one characterized by sexual reproduction and endless cycles of life and death: 'bearing fruit for death.'"[20] For Paul, as Boyarin notes, "bear[ing] fruit for death" is an inevitable outcome of fulfilling the commandment to be fruitful: "that is to have children and thus to participate in the whole disaster of human mortality ... Dying to the law through the body of Christ relieves one of the obligation to produce children ... and thus frees one to bear only spiritual fruit, fruit for God."[21] Drake characterizes Paul's use of sexuality to differentiate Gentiles and Christians as part of a larger body of Hellenistic Jewish writings on the sexual immorality and idolatry of Gentile Romans; as she observes, "Subsequent Christian authors reformulated Paul's arguments to contend that it was Jews themselves who were guilty of sexual immorality and Christians who upheld the mantle of sexual purity."[22] Benedictine English writers, without any specific need for anti-Jewish polemics, further develop these Pauline and patristic ideas in order to criticize the theory and practice of heterosexuality and to offer chastity as a preferable alternative orientation.

Monastic celibacy offers a robust alternative to biofamilial kinship by providing fraternal, reproductive, and temporal structures that disrupt and attempt to replace those of the sexually reproductive family. Monasticism adopted, as Pasternack observes, a patristic "devaluation of procreative sexuality and the related families and the absorption of the individual into the structures of the Church as if into an alternative family."[23] These "alternative" familial structures, in theory, severed and replaced both the generative ("procreative sexuality") and affiliative ("related families") connections of heteropatriarchal family life. In practice, secular familial bonds both competed with and complemented monastic kinship ties; Lisa M.C. Weston's study of *amicitia* in Anglo-Latin nuns' letters, for instance, demonstrates that Leoba calls upon both spiritual and secular kinship ties to address Boniface, and that Eangyth, mother of many spiritual daughters, shares a privileged bond with Heaburg, who is also her biological child.[24]

Monastic affiliation also qualifies as a "mode of life" in the sense that Michel Foucault uses this term. In the 1981 *Gai Pied* interview "De l'amitié comme mode de vie (Friendship as a Way of Life)," Foucault argues for a "homosexual mode of life" (*un mode de vie homosexuel*) defined neither by identity politics nor by genital sexuality but by the multiplication and intensification of friendships among men. Monasticism is one potential answer to Foucault's question: "how is it possible for men to be together? To live together, to share their time, their meals, their room, their leisure, their grief, their knowledge, their confidences?"[25] In monastic life, these issues are central and have explicitly taken the place of heterosexual and kin relationships. The question echoes the debate within early medieval monasticism about the propriety of intense friendships between monks, typified on the one hand by Ælred of Rievaulx, whose work glorifies spiritual love between men, and on the other hand the Benedictine Rule, which forbids close relationships on the grounds that they subvert order and equality (see in particular sections 2, 22, 69).[26] As Benjamin Saltzman notes, "Kinship – a tie that for the Anglo-Saxons was of utmost importance … must be severed upon entering the monastery, forming the monks into a homogeneous community of spiritual brothers, united under a spiritual father. Hence, Benedict foresees one monk defending his kinsman or friend (though he avoids this word) as a devastating act against the equilibrium of solitude and community."[27] As Foucault observes of this tension, "The institution is caught in a contradiction; affective intensities traverse it which at one and the same time keep it going and shake it up."[28] The most passionate, contested, and discussed human affective investments of this life are primarily same-gender. In monastic life, the issue of life within the fellowship is central and has explicitly taken the place of heterosexual and biofamilial kin relationships.[29] The resonance of the problems of early medieval European monastic life in twentieth-century queer theory reveals monasticism as a fully non-heterosexual, indeed anti-heterosexual, "mode of life."

The *Regularis Concordia*, which supplemented the Benedictine Rule in rigorously governing the schedule of English monastic life, in fact provides specific and detailed answers to each of these questions, describing how monks are to sleep and eat communally, to avoid the temptations of intimacy with women and youth, to mourn, and to teach one another and avoid gossiping. *Sharing time* emerges as the rule's greatest concern: to be "united in the fellowship of the monastic life" (§67; unitus in ordinis communione)[30] with brethren, the words with which one hopes to be eulogized, is to be occupied night and day in highly ritualized communal activity. The temporal regimen of monastic life contrasts profoundly with the chaos and unrelenting, lonely anxiety that *Hali Maiðhad* describes as a secular woman's lot in life, although in practical terms monastic life also involved much care work and many tedious, urgent, and unpredictable duties.[31]

Thus monastic life replaces kinship by providing alternative fraternal structures, by providing alternative filiative structures, and by occluding the heterosexual. Pasternack and Ruth Mazo Karras have demonstrated that the monastic ideal of chastity is a sexual orientation.[32] I argue that in monastic texts, particularly Ælfric's, there emerges an Old Testament heterosexual orientation; that is, a set of endorsed and tolerated practices, including circumcision, polygamy, priestly marriage, and feminine adornment, specific to the Old Testament and oriented around ensuring the continued survival and distinctive identity of the Jewish people. This orientation is not in itself sinful, but it is superseded by the Christian ideals of monastic chastity and universal membership. As Karma Lochrie has influentially noted, the medieval Christian West was not characterized by a normative heterosexuality. However, the cluster of "cultural appurtenances" ("the sexual act of intercourse, the social and legal rights of marriage, ideas of domesticity, doctrines of procreation, concepts of parenting and child rearing," and so forth) that Lochrie and other queer theorists describe as coalescing into heterosexuality as late as the nineteenth century appears in late Old English writing in the form of Jewish (Old Testament) sexuality.[33] The English monastics, in other words, although neither heterosexual or homosexual themselves, had already invented a heterosexual antagonist.

Aldhelm: Monastic Reproduction

As a committed lifestyle with no equivalent in medieval Judaism or Islam, Christian monastic chastity is an orientation to sexuality with its own pleasures and reproductive practices. As Pasternack has noted, the late seventh-century Anglo-Latin treatise *De virginitate*, by Aldhelm, Abbot of Malmesbury, portrays chastity as both pleasurable and fertile, qualities embodied in the figure of the bee, a scripturally authorized (according to Aldhelm) type of the Church who "produces her sweet family and children, innocent of the lascivious coupling of marriage, by means of a certain generative condensation of a very sweet juice." Just so, "the Church, striking vitally into the hearts of men with the double-keen sword-edge of the (two) Testaments, fertilizes through the chaste seed of the Word the offspring who are lawful heirs of eternity."[34] In this form of generation, *Ecclesia* penetrates the Christian heart with a textual rather than sexual organ of fertilization. Also unlike a traditional phallus, this virginal organ is doubled rather than singular (bringing to mind Luce Irigaray's connection between doubled genitalia and textual femininity);[35] the Word it produces in lieu of semen is, as we well know, part of the masculine godhead. Queer reproduction, like much else in Aldhelm's extended complex of metaphors, resists a single reading:

here the feminine penetrates, here chastity fertilizes, here Christians appear to be their own offspring. All tends not towards a dull futurity but towards an excessive eternity. Celibacy, like the queer temporality proposed by José Esteban Muñoz, offers not just the rejection of heterosexual futurity and relationality, but also a potentially fuller and more loving existence than this one, a hopeful although by no means predetermined alternative futurity.[36]

The fruits of chaste reproduction are sweeter than worldly things: not only is this honey more delicious than "all dishes of delicacies" (*cuncta deliciarum*) and more fragrant than "sweet ambrosia and the odour of fragrant balsam, but [it] also ... may exceed all delights of worldly sweetness and the exquisite pleasures of sumptuous gourmandising and may leave far beneath it the gulping down of sweet wine."[37] These delights lie beyond the reach of secular people engaged in reproductive sex. Nuns are the products of this spiritual conception, which is just as fruitful as sexual reproduction: they are "adoptive daughters of regenerative grace brought forth from the fecund womb of ecclesiastical conception through the seed of the spiritual Word."[38] The Church reproduces as easily as, and with more pleasure than, the world of marriage and secular sin. As Weston notes, in portraying the reproductive monastery as a multi-celled honeycomb where bees gather to joyfully share nectar, Aldhelm creates a "sensuous fertility [that] is by definition communal and collective – and effectively homonormative."[39]

Spiritual procreation and filiation are not merely metaphorical. To draw a binary distinction between social ("synthetic") and genetic forms of kinship is to ignore the importance of marriage, a synthetic relation understood as both binding and real, in creating heteropatriarchal families. Legal fatherhood was, in the Middle Ages, based largely on marriage and not at all on verifiable genetic relationship (since such verification was not available and would, in many cases, not have coincided with legal and social fatherhood), and the non-biological kin status of "step-father" or "father-in-law," a relation that enjoys full legal and social recognition, is as socially constructed as monastic fatherhood. To put it another way, a monastic vow is as just as real and binding as a marriage vow; whether that vow succeeds in creating a legible (to others) kinship relation depends on the strength of monasteries, and of marriages, as public institutions and on their productive capacities. In addition to producing spiritual families, monasteries were also sites of large-scale child-rearing. It is not necessary to romanticize life within the monastery to note that care and authority that would be gendered in secular life cannot be so in the minster. Indeed, V.A. Kolve has demonstrated twelfth-century monasteries' self-conception as potential sites of male maternal love for the boys in their care.[40]

This pleasurable production of spiritual children can be considered queer in the proper sense, since as Clark notes it is not only "predicated on the *absence* of physical union between man and woman," but also upon the (properly) non-sexual affective bonds within the body of the monastery.[41] The idea of the monastery as queer space is hardly new. Kolve, Lochrie, Weston, Valerie Traub, and many others have noted the homoaffectivity of monastic communities, an affectivity that includes, in Carolyn Schroeder's words, both the "presence of homoeroticism and anxieties about the homoerotic," as well as, in some cases, sanctioned love bonds of various sorts within same-gender pairs and clusters.[42] (It must be emphasized that monastic rules attempted, however successfully, to avert any physical expression of these affections. While most expressed "anxieties about the homoerotic" were aimed at what we would call sexual abuse, consensual sex was *also* an abuse within the chaste ideology of the monastery.[43]) Monastic life also allowed for the possibility of different-gender pair-bonding without sexual expectations, reproduction, or any of the structures of marriage; some such couples were blood siblings like Benedict and Scholastica, but some were solely spiritual kin. As Lisa Weston observes, the mixed-gender Boniface Circle addressed one another in the effusively affectionate language of *amicitia*; this language, which Weston argues was the hallmark of their elite "extended *familia*," crossed genders but bore little resemblance to heterosexuality.[44]

Monastery as Genderqueer Space

The monastery was also imagined by early medieval writers as a space of gender transformation, particularly (although not exclusively) as a space of trans masculinity. As Roland Betancourt notes, a corpus of mostly Byzantine transgender saints' lives that circulated throughout the Christian world in translation in the ninth through eleventh centuries describe saints who, "assigned female at birth … chose to live most [of] their lives as monks, usually presenting and passing as eunuchs within male monastic communities."[45] Two such lengthy hagiographies, Ælfric's *Life of St. Eugenia* and the anonymous *Life of Smaragdus* (conventionally called the *Life of Euphrosyne*), appear in Old English; the Old English Martyrology also describes the transmasculine and gender fluid lives of, among others, Saints Eugenia, Perpetua, and Thecla. These hagiographies place various forms of transmasculinity, as Betancourt notes, "within the normative practices of Christian worship, aescetisicm, and empire."[46] While such hagiographies in Old English and other insular sources locate their trans protagonists in distant times and places and do not, therefore, tell us anything about the quality of trans life in English monasteries, they demonstrate that what Betancourt calls a "vocabulary" for gender transformation and trans life was available in monastic spaces.[47] This includes not only the sites where relevant texts were translated from Latin (having been already translated, in most cases, from Greek), but also those where they were copied, circulated, and read out in either Latin or the vernacular.

One indication of the queer imaginative role of trans saints' lives is their eroticism, which has attracted much scholarly enthusiasm.[48] Almost all of these lives depict transmasculine and other gender-variant people as extraordinarily attractive and posit that when they inhabit a cloister, confessional, or other holy space, this becomes a place of irresistible erotic temptation.[49] As a result, most of these lives include fantasies about the overwhelming excitement men and women feel while cloistered with a trans person who is generally just trying to pray.[50] The transmasculine saint Smaragdus is so attractive that "ða broðra ... wurdon þearle gecostnode þurh his fægernysse and ... wurdon astyrode wið þone abbod forþam swa wlitigne man into heore mynstre gelædde" (lines 160–4; the brothers were badly tempted by his beauty and all became agitated against the abbot because he had brought such a lovely person into their monastery).[51] Two kinds of disorder occur here: sexual temptation and (perhaps more seriously) a threat to the abbot's authority. Yet there is no indication that the monks' agonized attraction to Smaragdus is considered taboo; on the contrary, they apparently discuss it freely and indicate that the abbot should have foreseen the problem. At no point does anyone seem to blame the brothers or, as Clark notes, Smaragdus, although naturally it is Smaragdus who suffers the consequences.[52] Even less happily, in Ælfric's life of St. Eugenia, the saint who has entered a monastery "on þam wærlicum hiwe" (line 89; in masculine presentation) and "mid wærlicum mode þeah þe heo mæden wære" (line 93; with a masculine spirit although she was a girl) eventually loses their position as abbot because a wealthy laywoman takes advantage of one-on-one spiritual instruction to sexually harass, assault, and then falsely accuse them.[53] In these texts, the eroticism of trans bodies is not truly separable from the erotics of the cloister or minster, for it is in these spaces that trans people are imagined to be located.[54] The erotic fantasies in these texts are not liberatory or, to my mind, worthy of celebration. They describe unwanted attention that creates unpleasant consequences for the trans saints who are the objects of desire: Smaragdus must be isolated from his fellows, and Eugenia is forced to out and expose themself and thus loses both home and abbatical position. These scenarios are quite similar, in fact, to the real traumas and fears of real trans people, who are so often punished for the desires they inspire in others. In describing them as fantasies, what I am particularly interested in is the self-evident (to hagiographers) idea that if one were to encounter a transmasculine person and become so overwhelmingly attracted to him as to fall into evil lusts, this would naturally occur in a monastery, where he would be engaged in prayer, sacred study, and monastic brotherhood or fatherhood. The implication is that monasteries are a commodious setting for (real or imagined) trans lives. As a result, these two hagiographies and their many intertexts imagine the monastery as a space where trans and genderfluid people flourish, not merely as unwilling erotic objects, but also as subjects of admiration, imitation, and identification.

Despite the threats and extreme inconvenience posed by other people's lusts, neither Eugenia and Smaragdus ultimately suffers lasting blame or stigma for these episodes, or for living a trans or genderfluid life. On the contrary, both ultimately prevail in chaste sanctity through spiritual kinship. Eugenia's loss of status as abbot is profound, but ultimately they find another way into the chaste intimacies of Christian life with their father Philip, now converted and a bishop, and another holy woman, Basilla:

> Þa wurdon gelome þa leofan mædenu
> Eugenia and basilla and eac se biscop
> on sunder-spræce swiðe gebysgode
> and digel-lice on nihtum hi symble geneosodon
> and hæfdon heora gerihtu mid þam halgen biscope (lines 338–42)

Then the beloved virgins Eugenia and Basilla and the bishop [Philip] were often very occupied in private conversation, and secretly by night they often visited and had their rites with the holy bishop.

Rather than avoiding the private meetings and attachments that led to their previous downfall, Eugenia spends frequent nighttime visits in secret conversation and prayer with a holy new family, including a beloved friend and a secular father now converted to spiritual father, and this mixed-gender group is a vehicle for sacred learning and for turning others to *clænre drohtnunge* (344, chaste living). Ultimately, Eugenia causes many conversions and demonstrates spectacular spiritual power at their martyrdom.

The queerness of monastic sexuality and affectivity is thus, in my view, not defined primarily by homoeroticism, however widespread, or by gender fluidity and transformation, however desired and imaginatively explored by monastic thinkers, nor by the homoaffectivity that, as C. Stephen Jaeger has amply demonstrated, suffused secular as well as religious aristocratic life.[55] Nor indeed is it defined by non-normativity, queerness's now ubiquitous gloss, which we would have to measure by making the secular life ascendant and the regular life abject. As I hope is evident by now, it is also very far from equivalent (in my usage) to sexual or personal liberation, ideals that had no place in medieval Christian monasticism. I locate this queerness, instead, in the absolute orientation away from biological reproductivity and its secular institutions, and the formation of other durable kinship and affective structures against which, even when they appear ritually or superficially similar, the heterosexual reproductive family seems a pale and undesirable alternative.[56]

Jewish Heterosexuality: The Dangerous Example of Married Priests

The Benedictine writers demonstrate that heterosexuality is outmoded by aligning sexual difference with Jewish–Christian difference, to be explicitly understood as temporal difference. In its fullest form, this theory proposes, as Cubitt notes, that "Chastity and Christianity were ... coextensive; Christ's incarnation embodied a new sexual code which at times almost seems to be identified in Ælfric's writings with Christianity itself. This established an opposition, both temporal and spiritual, between the old order and the new ... between the old Jewish law and Christianity."[57] This theory, originally proposed by Jerome, did not enjoy much influence in either mainstream theology or local belief, but it provides an ingenious solution to certain on-the-ground problems for the Benedictine Reform in England, as well as to the glaring contradictions long presented by Old and New Testament pronouncements on sexuality.

The Hebrew Bible endorses universal marriage, both monogamous and polygynous, for followers of the commandments, as well as the overlapping practice of concubinage; these relations promote and organize patriarchal descent, which structures kinship and history in the Hebrew Bible.[58] At the theological heart of this system, as Jeremy Cohen has observed, is the "primordial blessing" of the first creation story: in the Vulgate, "Crescite, et multiplicamini, et replete terram, et subjicite eam, et dominamini piscibus maris, et volatilibus caeli, et universis animantibus, quae moventur super terram" (Increase, and multiply, and fill the earth, and subdue it, and rule over the fishes of the sea and the fowls of the air, and all living creatures that move upon the earth; Genesis 1:28). While this principle (Hebrew פְּרוּ וּרְבוּ, Be fertile and increase) retained its centrality to Jewish traditions, early and medieval Christian thinkers struggled to reconcile it with Pauline exaltation of chastity and celibacy.[59] As Cohen chronicles, Eusebius and later Jerome suggested that perhaps Genesis 1:28 could be grouped with other commandments superseded partially or entirely by the New Dispensation.[60] This did not become an orthodox point of view, however, probably because of Augustine's more moderate (late) position sanctifying sexual difference and childbearing, although not sexual pleasure.[61] Ælfric clearly takes Jerome's position, explaining in his homily on the Chair of St. Peter that the apostle abandoned his marriage when

> he wære
> gecyrred to Cristes hirede …
> forþan þe crist astealde clænnysse on worulde
> and ealle his folgeras ferdon on clænnysse (lines 201–5)
>
> he was converted to Christ's household … because Christ established chastity in the world and all his followers took to chastity.

In other words, becoming Christian leads Peter to turn from his secular household, from sexuality, and from biofamilial ties to Christ's household with its chaste ties alone. In contrast to any interpretation that would make chastity a special calling of the disciples and of monastic life while other Christians continued to observe the blessings of marriage, Ælfric emphasizes,

> On anginne middan-eardes cwæð se ælmihtiga God:
> "Beoð gemenigfylde and gefyllað þas eorðan."
> And Crist wolde on his tocyme clænnysse aræran
> and his halgan hired heold on clænnysse (lines 210–14)[62]
>
> At the beginning of the world, the almighty God said, "Be abundant and fill the earth." And Christ at his advent wanted to establish chastity and kept his sacred household in chastity.

Rather than being set apart from the world by the practice of chastity, then, Christ's household is an exemplum of the new order of chastity that he wishes to establish in the world in supersession of the reproductive order.[63]

Ælfric exploits this ideological inheritance in his arguments for a celibate English priesthood, ultimately developing a model of justified Jewish heterosexuality to which Christian celibacy is a natural and superior successor. Chastity held particular importance to the monastic reform, not just as a virtue within the regular life but, as Cubitt notes, as an index of monastic superiority over the lay priesthood and over secular leadership.[64] In Ælfric's First Old English Pastoral Letter to Wulfstan (1006), which focuses largely on chastity and the problem of clerical sexuality, Ælfric demonstrates how central clerical chastity is to Christian difference from the Jewish past, and how central this difference is, in turn, to Christian knowledge.[65] Characteristically, he exhorts, "Ge sceolan witan, gif ge wisdom lufiað, hwæt sy betwux þam twam gecyðnyssum, þære ealdan æ, ær Cristes to-cyme, and þære niwam gecyðnysse"[66] (You should know, if you love wisdom, what is between these two testaments: the old law, before Christ's advent, and the new testament). Knowing the difference, knowing it *as* temporal difference, is crucial if one is to know anything of value.

The problem at hand is priestly marriage, which its practitioners apparently justify with recourse to Biblical example (or which Ælfric fears they will justify in this way): "Nu mæg eaþe getimian, þæt eower sum ahsige, hwi he ne mote wif habban, swa-swa Aaron hæfde" (*Hirtenbriefe*, IV, §147; Now it might easily happen that one of you asks why he may not have a wife just as Aaron had). The solution is a full supersessionary understanding of the difference between Jewish priests and their Christian successors:

> Þonne secge we eow, þæt seo ealde æ wæs ær Cristes to-cyme eall getacniendlic. And hi þa wif hæfdon, forþon-þe hi wæron flæsclice and hi næfre ne mæssedon and mihton þa swa don. Nu is seo ealde æ eall awend on oþer to gastlican þingum, and Godes þenas sceolon healdan hyra clænnysse, swa-swa Crist hit astealde. And se-þe nu hilt þa ealdan æ æfter Cristes tocyme on þa ealdan wisan, he bið amansumod. (*Hertenbriefe*, IV, §148–51)

> Then we say to you that before Christ's advent the old law was completely symbolic. And they had wives then because they were carnal, and they never performed mass and could do it then. Now the old law is subsequently changed entirely to spiritual matters, and God's ministers must keep their chastity [*clænnysse*] just as Christ established it. And anyone who now keeps the old law in the old way after Christ's advent will be excommunicated.

Giorgio Agamben's conception of (Franciscan) monasticism as a unique *forma vitae* that "attempt[s] to realize a human life and practice absolutely outside the determinations of the law"[67] explains in part why these practices under the Old Law are so inadequate to monastic life; they represent a biofamilial management of desire and reproduction from which the religious body must utterly withdraw. This reproductive regime even included incest (as Ælfric notes at length in the *Preface to Genesis*), a practice that Ælfric explicitly links to priestly marriage in the Chair of St. Peter homily:

> Menn hæfdon on frymðe heora magan to wife
> and swa wel mosten for ðære wifleaste,
> and gif nu hwa swa deð næfð he Godes bletsunge.
> Under Moyses æ moste se bisceop habban
> an geæwnod wif, for þære gewissan æfter-gencgnysse,
> þæt is þæt se sunu sceolde symle fon to þam hade
> æfter his fæder geendunge and nan oðer ne moste.
> Hit mihte þa wel swa forþan þe hi ne mæssodon næfre,
> ac hi offrodon nytenu on heora lacum Gode.
> Ne husel næs gehalgod ær þam ðe se hælend com
> and þa niwan gecyðnysse mid Cristendome arærde
> and geceas þa clænan to his clænum þeowdome,
> na to nytena offrunge ac to his agenum lic-haman.
> And bisceopas ne beoð nu be gebyrdum gecorene,
> ac seo halige gelaðung lufað þa clænan (lines 214–28)[68]

At the beginning people had their relatives as wives, and they could rightly do so because of the lack of women, but if anyone does that now, he will not have God's blessing. Under the law of Moses, the bishop needed a wedded wife for the purpose of sure succession – that is, that the son always had to take the office after his father's death, and no other could. It might properly be that way then, because they never performed mass, but they gave beasts in their sacrifices to God. Nor was the Eucharist sanctified before the Saviour came and established the new covenant with Christendom and selected the chaste for his chaste servitude, nor [did he choose] for his sacrifice beasts but his own body. And bishops are now not chosen for their lineage, but the holy church loves the chaste.

According to this passage, priestly marriage is of a piece with animal sacrifice: both are Old Testament practices swept away by Christ's sacrifice, which replaces them with chastity and the Eucharist, Christian institutions that are not merely parallel but in practice inseparable, since the Eucharist requires priestly sexual purity. For Christian priests to marry as Jewish priests did would be as foolish and sinful as for Christians to make incestuous marriages because the first humans were compelled to; when Ælfric notes with wry understatement that God does not bless the incestuous, he indicates that marriage is an obstacle to divine blessing for clerics. (This dig resonates with Stafford's observation that in the Letter, "Ælfric comes close to the brink of disqualifying 'unclean priests' and their sacraments."[69]) In the Letter to Wulfstan and in the homily on St. Peter, the superseded carnality of old law and practices both rhetorically excuses the marriages of Old Testament priests and implicitly institutes a prohibition on using practitioners of the old law as sexual role models.

Ælfric describes contemporary clerical marriage as a theological error, when those who "nu hilt þa ealdan æ æfter Cristes tocyme on þa ealdan wisan" profoundly misunderstand Christian temporality. The present is here doubly free of Jewish carnality – liberated both by its chronological place in revelation history ("æfter Cristes tocyme") and by its participation, as Kathleen Davis's discussion of Ælfric's tedium topos suggests, in the elongated "nu" of what Agamben calls messianic time.[70] The doubleness of this formulation – its doubled doubleness – is not a matter purely of emphasis or rhetorical flourish but of the compounded error of keeping the old law *in the old way*, without the exegetical understanding that would transform it into the liberatory law of chastity. As Davis notes, "Periodization, if it is to have a historical legacy, results from a *double* movement: the first, a contestatory process of identification *with* an epoch, the categories of which it simultaneously constitutes ... and the second a rejection of that epoch identified in this reduced, condensed form."[71] Ælfric's repetitions underscore the process by which he reifies the time of Mosaic law in order to reject it in favour of a superseding Christian present.

While Ælfric extends the same logic of celibacy across all clerical groups, the distinction between monastic chastity and priestly chastity is relevant to secular ecclesiastical writers and manifests with particular starkness in Wulfstan's treatment of Ælfric's writings on priestly celibacy. Compare Ælfric's emphasis on theological and temporal error to Wulfstan's later formulation of clerical marriage as adultery, filth, and evil, and his particular vilification of priests' wives, who wear the jewels that belong to the altar: "Nis preostes cwene ænig oðer þing butan deofles grin"[72] (A priest's woman is nothing except a devil's snare), where the epithet *deofles grin* gains power from the more mundane assertion that such women are *nis ænig oðer þing*: nothing, no one. In revising Ælfric's letter for his own pastoral use, Wulfstan excises the above portion explaining the difference between old and new law.[73] Wulfstan's location of conjugal temptation in women as sexual objects, and Ælfric's attribution of the sin to theological error, are characteristic of the treatment of sexuality in their work: while Wulfstan habitually objectifies women and typically condemns sexual sins as widespread,[74] Ælfric's many discussions of chastity generally treat illicit sexual activity as characteristic of the especially perverse – evil tyrants seeking the virginity of saintly Christians, etc. – and the spiritually ignorant. As Clare Lees's reading of Ælfric demonstrates, the homilist hardly relishes discussing sexual activity, however licit, involving Christian women.[75] Regardless of any other reasons for this difference, as a rhetorical strategy it dovetails nicely with Ælfric's perpetual recuperation of the past as exemplum; while Jewish heroes participate in licit heterosexuality, polytheistic villains exemplify illicit and unruly sexuality.

Yet the carnality of the old law does not fully explain why those priests, holiest of their own age, married. The answer is found in Jewish particularity:

> Þa moste se Aaron and his æfter-gengan niman him to gemacan, æfter Moyses æ an clæne mæden. Forþan-þe nan ne moste of oþrum cynne becuman to þæm hade, þæt he bisceop wære, butan of Aarones cynne. Hi ne mostan na wifian on nanre wudewan ne on forlætenan wife be Godes leafe þa, ac on clænum mædene. And hyra clænnysse healdan, swa oft swa hi offredon þa ælican onsægdnysse. Hy moston þa wel wif habban, þæt ne wurde ateorad þæt mære bisceop-cyn, þe com of Aarone. Forþan-þe nan cyn ne moste becuman to þam hade butan þæt an cyn þe com of Aarone. And hit stod æfre swa on þære ealdan æ.[76]

> Then, according to Moses's law, Aaron and his descendants had to marry clean maidens, because no one from another line could attain the rank of bishop, except from Aaron's line. They could not by God's permission marry any widow or abandoned wife then, only clean maidens, and maintained their cleanness as often as they offered the lawful sacrifice. They might well have wives then, so that the illustrious line of bishops that came from Aaron did not flag, because no group could attain that rank except for the line that came from Aaron. And so matters always stood according to the Old Law.

The purpose of these marriages was the physical continuation of the priestly tribe; "þæt mære bisceop-cyn, þe com of Aarone" represents a patrilineally inherited priesthood, the ecclesiastical structure proper to Biblical Jews in Temple times. In the Letter, Ælfric is careful to incorporate a vision of these priests as sexually restrained in their own way – marrying only virgins and abstaining prior to sacrifice – in order to procreate. As Ælfric observes in his *De initio creaturae* (On the Origin of the Created World), periodic rather than regular sexual relations are the prelapsarian ideal; if not for the Fall, "sceolde adam and his ofspring tyman on asettan tyman, swa swa nu doð clæne nytenu" (153–4; Adam and his offspring had to have intercourse/reproduce at appointed times, as clean animals do).[77] Through these visions, Ælfric extends the descriptor "clæne" to priests' wives, the very group Wulfstan describes in a contemporary context as worthless "butan deofles grin" – except as vehicles for temptation. Cleanness then describes not only marital chastity – a conventional if somewhat less common use – but also priests who are, at the appointed times, sexually active with such women. That both groups are also Jewish extends the unconventionality of this move, for neither group is under Christ's umbrella, but also provides its mitigating logic – these guardians of the old law were clean in their way, in their time. As both Daniel Anlezark and Catherine Karkov note, Ælfric describes Abraham's marriages according to the same logic; his translation of Genesis, for instance, emphasizes that Abraham's polygamous second wife Hagar was a concubine (*cyfese*), entirely omitting the verse (Genesis 16:3) that refers to her as a wife. In so demoting her and restoring the proper hierarchy of Abraham's marital relations, Ælfric rationalizes even concubinage (although not polygamy) in terms of Abraham's sacred fatherhood, which makes a Christian future, and not just Jewish and Muslim futures, possible.[78]

Jewish Paternity, Christian Parenthood: Abraham's Circumcision

Sometimes Ælfric demonstrates an appreciation for the material details of Old Testament law where another exegete might ignore the historical meaning (to use a conventional exegetical term). We see this in the *Letter to Brother Edward*, where Ælfric designates the ban on consuming blood not only as spiritually valuable in itself, but also as binding for his fellow Christians. Ælfric also finds historical meaning in circumcision, which he establishes as a spiritually consequential material practice in its Old Testament context, not as mere forerunner of Christian "circumcisio cordis in spiritu" (circumcision ... of the heart in the spirit; Romans 2:29).[79] Ælfric's early homily on the Lord's Circumcision describes the practice frankly to establish circumcision as an aspect of Jewish heterosexuality that founds the sacred identity of ancient Israel, which is to be inherited, evacuated, and superseded by Christianity. Circumcision, in this homily, spiritually signifies true Christian descent from Abraham, possible only through a heterosexual, marital, sovereign paternity that passes through the Jews and is no longer in effect.

Circumcision is not only a permanent visible mark that designates a full member of the covenant, what Zacher terms "a visible sign of nationhood";[80] it signifies what is in Biblical terms an obvious link between the covenant and cis men's reproductive bodies.[81] The key phrase, as it appears in the Vulgate, is "Eritque pactum meum in carne vestra in foedus aeternum" (And my covenant shall be in your flesh for a perpetual covenant; Genesis 17:13), in which "in carne vestra" (Hebrew בִּבְשַׂרְכֶם, Greek ἐπὶ τῆς σαρκὸς) merges references to individual bodies, their sexuality and mortality, and their generations of cis male children, who have been promised in the recitation of the bond and who will be likewise bound.[82] David Biale calls Biblical circumcision a "symbolic sacrifice in gratitude for God's blessing of fertility," although the sacrifice is more than symbolic. As Leonard B. Glick notes, placing infants at the centre of this dangerous ritual means that Abraham and his descendants make a potential sacrifice of "men's most precious possessions": "male progeny" and "patrilineal continuity," which God then rewards with a greater flow of these deeply desired goods: "grandsons, great-grandsons," perpetuity of descent. As Glick observes, from a historical/anthropological view, "the circumcised penis was an ideal symbol of the Lord's covenant, and of everything that the priests intended to promote with their new rite of initiation: male reproductive success, continuity in the male line, male-defined ethnic identity and exclusiveness, acknowledgment of patrilineally legitimated priestly authority."[83] As Ælfric notes in the (scurrilously anti-Jewish) homily on the Fifth Sunday in Lent, adapting from Augustine a passage about Isaac taking a vow on Abraham's thigh,

> Hwæt belamp abrahames ðeoh to ðam heofenlican gode? … Witodlice þæt ðeoh getacnode his cynn, and abraham ðurh witeg unge stafode þone að, þa ða he geseah drihtnes dæg toweard of his sæde[84]

> What does Abraham's thigh have to do with the heavenly God? … Certainly that thigh signifies his descendants, and through prophecy Abraham dictated that vow, when he saw that the lord's day is coming from his seed.

Without understanding where on the body circumcision takes place, it is difficult to understand the vast theological compact circumcision emblematizes for various readers of Genesis. Several roadblocks to Christian pastoral aims inhere in a detailed description, including the dangers of inciting imitation (Judaizing) and of endorsing a particularistic (Jewish) and therefore incorrect view of the covenant. Ælfric frankly addresses the first problem in his comprehensive prose translation of the relevant lines in (what would become) the Heptateuch Genesis:

> Ðis ys þæt wedd þe ge healdan sceolon, betwux me and eow and þin ofspring æfter þe, þæt ælc hysecild betwux eow beo ymbsniden, and ge embsnidað þæt flæsc eowres fylmenes, þæt beo tacn mines weddes betwux me and eow ... And beo min wedd on eowrum flæsc on ecum wedde. Se werhades man þe ne byþ ymsniden on þam flæsce hys fylmenes, his sawul bið adilegod of his folce, for þan he aidlode min wedd. (*OEH* Genesis 17:10–14)[85]

> This is the covenant that you must keep, between me and you and your descendants after you: that every male child amongst you be circumcised, and you will circumcise the flesh of your foreskin: that will be a sign of my covenant between me and you ... And my covenant will be in your flesh as an eternal covenant. The male person who is not circumcised in the flesh of his foreskin, his soul will be blotted out from his people, because he voided my covenant.[86]

In this passage, Ælfric mentions the foreskin twice, repeating the formula describing circumcision in a demonstration that Ælfric both understands and at times cooperates with the Biblical composition principle of conveying importance through repetition.[87] But Ælfric does not interpolate an explanation of the foreskin, which was not required in the Biblical text. He is more concerned to ward off the theological error of imitation, placing it in the distant Jewish past. After the circumcisions of Abraham and Ishmael, Ælfric inserts the original note: "Nu secge we betwux þisum þæt nan cristen man ne mot nu swa don" (Now we declare between these that no Christian may now do this).[88] Here he doubles the temporal move, placing both his declaration ("*Nu* secge we") and his audience's Christian obedience ("ne mot *nu* swa don") at a supersessionary remove from a practice that does, of course, continue to bind other Abrahamic peoples in the present.

Fortuitously, Ælfric had already found a solution in the connection between circumcision and kinship. Ælfric's homily for 8 January (The Lord's Circumcision), already in circulation by the time he translated the prose Genesis, comprises his first translation of and commentary on Genesis 17:1–23, the story of Abraham and Sarah's blessing of fertility and Abraham's reception of the covenant and circumcision on behalf of his descendants. Ælfric leans heavily on Bede's homily on the same topic, which also contextualizes Christ's circumcision by explaining the importance of that practice to the covenant between Israel and God solemnized in Genesis 17.[89] As usual, he goes beyond his sources. Writing with a frankness unusual for the vernacular of the details of circumcision, Ælfric observes:[90]

> Wen is þæt eower sum nyte hwæt sy ymbsnidenys; God bebead abrahame þæt he sceolde and his ofspring his wed healdan þæt sum tacen wære on heora lichaman to geswutelunge þæt hi on god belyfdon; and het ðæt he name scearpecgedne flint, and forcurfe sumne dæl þæs felles ætforeweardan his gesceape.[91]
>
> It is likely that some of you don't know what circumcision is. God commanded Abraham that he and his descendants keep his covenant such that there was some sign on their bodies as a manifestation that they believed in God and ordered that he take a sharpened rock and cut off a certain piece of the foreskin of his member.

Here, where Ælfric has a mixed audience and the scope to explain circumcision in its temporal context, "sumne dæl þæs felles ætforeweardan his gesceape" takes a pedagogical tone, describing the appearance and location (the bit of skin at the end of one's member) of the foreskin to those who might not understand the decontextualized word *fylmen*, which can be used in other anatomical contexts. As Zacher demonstrates, Ælfric seems in this homily to have "developed or adopted a fuller phallic vocabulary" than other Old English writers, possibly drawing on botanical vocabulary in the Vulgate Leviticus, in order to discuss circumcision.[92] As Marsden notes, the description of the knife also borrows from other descriptions in the Pentateuch.[93] This attention to detail contrasts with the fulsome but vague wording in *Genesis A*:

> Sete sigores tacn   soð on gehwilcne
> Wæpned-cynnes,   gif þu wille on me
> hlaford habban   oððe holdne freond
> þinum from-cynne.   Ic þæs folces beo
> hyrde and healdend,   gif ge hyrað me
> breost-gehygdum   and bebodu willað
> min fullian.   Sceal monna gehwilc
> þære cneorisse   cildisc wesan

```
wæpned-cynnes,      þæs þe on woruld cymð,
ymb seofon-niht     sigores tacne
geagnod me,         oððe of eorðan
þurh feondscipe     feor adæled,
adrifen from duguðum                        (lines 2313a–25a)
```

Set the true sign of victory on everyone of male sex, if you want to have a lord in me, or a generous friend to your descendants.[94] I will be shepherd and guardian of this people, if you follow me in [your] thoughts and wish to fulfil my commands. Every child in your tribe of the male sex who comes into this world, must after a week be claimed for me with the token of victory or separated far from the land with enmity, driven away from the multitude.

In the poetic *Genesis*, the term *wæpned-cynnes* (of the male sex, *lit.* of the armed kind) cues what is ultimately an enthymic association between men and *sigores tacn*. That is, the reader (primed by the association of sex, gender, and martial matters) easily, although incorrectly, understands that only men need bear this sign because it is men who are concerned with matters of politics, war, and "victory." The poem thus expends considerable rhetorical skill on obfuscating the nature of circumcision – so much so that, as Zacher observes, it is barely clear that the poet understands what they are describing.[95] Ælfric, while not graphic in his description of the operation (he does not specify male descendants or even the penis; *gesceap*, which also means creation or thing, can be used for any genitals), is much more straightforward; in using the word "ætforeweard," he communicates that God is commanding removal of the foreskin. The original covenant between God and Israel is tied, for better or worse, to the reproductive body.

The covenant's relationship to Abraham's sacred fatherhood, and to Sarah's sacred motherhood, is crucial to Ælfric's interest in circumcision. He is particularly concerned to establish their authority not only as a reproductive marital couple but also as patriarch and matriarch. According to Bede, from whose homily on the circumcision Ælfric translates this passage, Abraham's and Sarah's names indicate a (limited) sovereign relation to Abrahamic peoples that operates through their authorization by God:

Abrahames nama wæs æt fruman mid fif stafum gecweden abram. þæt is healic fæder. Ac god geihte his naman mid twam stafum and gehet hine abraham þæt is manegra þeoda fæder; Sarai wæs his wif gehaten. þæt is gereht min ealdor; ac god hi het syðþan sarra þæt is ealdor; þæt heo nære synderlice hire hiredes ealdor geciged; ac forðrihte ealdor; þæt is to understandenne.[96]

> Abraham's name was at first written with five letters: Abram – that is, great father. But God augmented his name with two letters and called him Abraham – that is, father of many peoples. His wife was called Sarai – that is interpreted as my leader, but afterwards God called her Sarra, which is leader, so it is to be understood that she was not addressed privately as her household's leader, but as leader outright.

The covenant transforms Abraham from biological to sacred father, while Sarah's status as a (miraculous) mother of ancient Israel is not merely reproductive, nor is it reducible to authority over her kin and over unfree people such as Hagar.[97] This line is a strange crux – what sort of sole authority, not over her marital household, could a mother have? Bede, hagiographer of many abbesses, answers this question explicitly in his own homily, converting domestic to spiritual motherhood: Sarah is "omnium recte credentium feminarum … parentem" (the parent of all rightly believing women).[98]

Ælfric only obliquely answers the question at the homily's first supersessionary turn, which clarifies the importance of circumcision for Christians and (implicitly) of Abraham and Sarah as models of Christian fatherhood and motherhood. Creatively translating Bede, Ælfric makes the traditional move of associating circumcision with baptism, and then ties the circumcision once again to Abraham's fatherhood in a way that converts Jewish paternity to spiritual patriarchy.[99] He borrows a brief passage from Bede that culminates in an interesting sidenote about Abraham's protection of his kin in hell:

> And þæt tacen wæs ða swa micel on geleaffullum mannum. swa micel swa nu is þæt halige fulluht buton þam anum þæt nan man ne mihte godes rice gefaran ær þan ðe se come þe þa ealdan æ. sette and eft on his andwerdnysse hi to gastlicum þingum awende; ac gehwilc halgan andbidodon on abrahames wununge buton tintregum. þeah on hellewite; oð þæt se alysend com þe ðone ealdan deofol gewylde. and his gecorenan to heofenan rice gelædde.[100]

> And that sign was then so great amongst believing people, as great as the holy baptism is now, except for one thing: that no one could arrive in God's kingdom before He came who might establish the old law(s) and then in his time turn them [it] into spiritual matters, but anyone holy

waited in Abraham's dwelling without torments, although in hell, until the redeemer came who [over]powered the old devil and led his chosen ones to heaven.

In Bede's telling, the patriarchs are saved by circumcision as if by baptism,[101] but not until Christ's intervention; until then, "in sinu abrahae post mortem beata requie consolati supernae pacis ingressum spe felici expectabant" (consoled in the bosom of Abraham by a blessed rest after death, they awaited with blissful hope their entry into heavenly peace).[102] Ælfric reframes Abraham's protection in hell as a *wunung*, a home, rather than a *sinu[m]*, bosom or lap, and dramatizes the dangers outside this home. Abraham's authority in this *wunung* is the traditional authority of the head of the household to protect guests – the same authority that his nephew Lot invokes in Sodom to protect the angels from rape: "quia ingressi sunt sub umbraculum tegminis mei" (Genesis 19:8; because they are come in under the shadow of my roof). In this case, what lies outside the barred doors is not a violent citizenry but the devil, hell, and all the torments thereof. Abraham's house protects his kin from what will later be the inevitable consequences of Jewish practice (that is, he holds the space between old law and old devil, the latter cannily introduced here by Ælfric) by holding them in a particular temporal position, anticipating the new law that these old Jews were too early to observe. Jesus and God are initially elided, so that Jesus is named as the one who created and later mastered the old law, but in the next sentence this is revised, so that Jesus, who by the same logic also created and later mastered the devil, only "appears" at the incarnational moment (in fact, at the post-Crucifixion moment of the Harrowing). When in Ælfric's addition Christ takes charge of Abraham and those he protected, "heofenan rice" / "godes rice" supersedes "abrahames wununge," transforming the meaning of "his gecorenan" from the chosen people to those newly chosen (and saved) by Christ.

But it is more than this, because the ideal Christian family life that Ælfric envisions is not biofamilial or secular. Rather, as Ælfric will amply demonstrate in his correspondence with Wulfstan, in his sermon on the Chair of St. Peter, and in much of his other work, the forms of generativity and of kinship that he envisions in the time of Christ are chaste and monastic. This explains why Ælfric moves from the baptismal supersession of circumcision to Abraham's protective fatherhood over the faithful in enclosure while waiting for Christ, and why he specifies that Sarah's motherhood is not to be understood as a domestic authority but as leadership "forðrihte." In the time of Christ, Abraham and Sarah's sacred parenthood undergoes a conversion from kinship-based paternity and maternity to spiritual, hierarchically gender-segregated patriarchy and matriarchy, the form of ideal family life found in the monastery and, ideally, the clergy. Although Ælfric does not pursue this unusual connection – the translation of sanctified Old Testament married life into monastic chastity – any further in this homily, he will do so, as I demonstrate in the following chapter, in his daring translation of the Book of Judith.

In Ælfric's translation, Jewish sexual difference is thus not absolute, nor is it a difference among kinds and combinations of bodies, connections, affections. It is difference in time – old sexual law, new sexual law – and in ideology.[103] By explaining Old Testament procreative practices, including marriage and circumcision, and monastic chastity as two parallel but not equivalent holy paths, one old, Jewish, and abrogated, and the other new, Christian, and flourishing, Ælfric describes two incommensurable sexual orientations, each with its own technologies of kinship.

Purity in Translation

While patristic and medieval Christian writings tend to portray early Christians as rejecting Jewish forms of holiness, in fact the New Testament's debates on food purity and circumcision focus on the inclusion of Gentile Christ-followers under the social umbrella of Jewish purity.[104] Instead of rejecting the Jewish ideas of purity and impurity, the New Testament largely translates this distinction from the physical realm to the spiritual. This shift is particularly clear in the Vulgate. In Latin versions of the Old Testament, *mundus* and *inmundus* ("clean" and "unclean") largely gloss Old Testament טָהוֹר and טָמֵא (*tahor* and *tame*, ritually "pure" and "impure"); they appear most often in the context of the holiness code that regulates eating, sacrifice, the containment and expression of bodily fluids, handling of the dead, and so forth in the life of ancient Israel. In the New Testament, on the other hand, they typically emerge in expressions such as *Beati mundo corde* ("Blessed are the clean of heart," Matthew 5:8) and *immundus spiritus* ("unclean spirit," i.e., demon; Matthew 12:43, Luke 11:24, etc.), glossing forms of Greek καθαρός and ἀκάθαρτος (*katharós* and *akáthartos*, "clean" and "unclean"). The continuity between Old and New Testament forms of *mundus/immundus* arises authentically from the Biblical Greek, for καθαρός and ἀκάθαρτος are also, within the Septuagint, the translated forms of טָהוֹר and טָמֵא.

Ælfric, primary Old English translator of the Old Testament, translates the Vulgate's *mundus* and *inmundus* into Old English *clæne* and *unclæne*.

When translating Genesis in the *Old English Heptateuch*, he does this in 7:2 and 8:20 when referring to clean and unclean beasts.[105] In contrast, other Old English translators shy away from linking *clænnys* to the Old Testament. For example, although the concept pervades (and indeed organizes) the Book of Leviticus and the word *inmundus* (as *immundus* and its declensions) appears approximately sixty times in the Vulgate Leviticus, this word is translated only *once* into the version of Leviticus that appears in the *Old English Heptateuch*, in regards to prohibited fish: "Ne ete ge nanne fisc, buton þa þe habbað finnas and scilla; þa oðre synd unclæne" (11:9–12; Do not eat any fish except those that have fins and scales; the others are unclean).[106] Likewise, not a single *immundus* is translated from the Latin Numbers or Deuteronomy, where the word is abundant, or from Joshua or Judges, where it is scarce, into Old English. Ælfric, apparently responsible for many of these omissions, does translate two of the three instances in which the beasts on Noah's ark are separated into clean and unclean (7:2, 8:20). In contrast, Old Testament poems pointedly avoid not only the word but also the concept: *Genesis A* refers not to clean and unclean beasts on the ark but to "ælcum æfter agenum eorðan tudre" (each according to its terrestrial kind),[107] while the Biblical heroine Judith's devotion to Jewish dietary law, a crucial plot point in the Biblical narrative and in Ælfric's prose translation of the story, is nowhere in the poem.[108]

Vernacular writers instead use *clænnyss* to translates a cluster of Latin synonyms for chastity, including *castitas*, *pudicitia*, *caelibatus*, and *pudor*.[109] In Ælfric's context and in Old English generally, *clænnyss* tends to mean "chastity": in Benedictine homiletics, as Pauline Stafford and Charles D. Wright have observed, it is primarily associated with clerical or sanctified chastity.[110] Within the poetic corpus, *clæne* nearly always means morally or sexually pure; more often than not, it refers to Mary's virginity or the chastity of a saint. In Ælfric's works *clænnyss* can be more broadly defined, in Shannon O. Ambrose's terms, as "spiritual and bodily purity."[111] Ælfric is in fact the main vernacular source for this term in its various forms – as Ambrose notes, he uses the terms *clænnyss* and *unclænnyss* more than fifty-five times in the homilies alone.[112]

In Ælfric's writing and in the Old English corpus as a whole, *clænnyss* is inseparable from the valorization of monastic celibacy and saintly virginity. Yet in his discussion of Old Testament priests and their wives, women he optimistically calls *clæn[e] mæden[u]* rather than *deofles grin*, Ælfric expands the term's remit across both temporal and sexual difference. Jews, by means precisely of their relegation to a superseded model of the law, can now receive the appellation *clæne*, an ordinarily Christian sexual and spiritual term, for their own historically sufficient arrangements. This discussion differs not only from some of the patristic sources, such as Origen and Chrysostom, who represent Jewish law and sexual formation as a manifestation of carnal misreading and a screen for sexual sin,[113] but also from Ælfric's monastic and ecclesiastical contemporaries (and predecessors) who view marriage and sexuality solely as snares, distractions, and objects of distaste.[114]

Unlike those Heptateuch translators who would avoid using *clæne* or *clænnyss* to describe Jewish ritual purity, perhaps in order to avoid any confusion with Christian spiritual and sexual purity, Ælfric finds a reason to grant a kind of vernacular theological dispensation to those benighted Jews whose reproductive heterosexuality, in the darkness before the New Dispensation, made Christ's birth ultimately possible. Ælfric thus transmutes Jewish purity into Christian sexual purity. Terms from the Hebrew Bible that, when translated into Greek and Latin, assume equivalence to New Testament terms for spiritual purity thus undergo a further conversion in the writings of Ælfric, who diverges from other Old English writers in linking the word *clæne* not only with the Old Testament but also, specifically, with Jewish sexuality. Ælfric's linguistic choices forge a largely fictive continuity between ancient Jewish and Christian monastic sexual purity systems, while also authorizing their decisive temporal break.

4 Ænlic Wimman:
Judith and the Exception

In opening his translation of the Vulgate Book of Judith with the comment, "We secgað nu ærest on þisum gewritum þæt twegen cyningas wæron gecweden on Leden Nabochodonosor, swiðe namcuðe begen" (lines 2–4; Now we say first in this treatise that two kings were called Nebuchadnezzar in Latin, both very much so named), Ælfric supplies an ironic context for the insecure and bellicose emperor Nebuchadnezzar/Cambisus, whose goal is complete sovereignty over conquered peoples.[1] The Nebuchadnezzar of the Judith story, whom Deborah Levine Gera calls an "imperialist tyrant who attempts to rival God," "[w]olde þæt hi ealle sceoldon him anum abugan, þæt he ana wære heora cyning" (lines 26–8; wanted them all to have to bow to him alone, so that he alone would be their king).[2] In framing the distinction between the two kings as, initially, a matter of comparison, and by placing them together at the head of the homily, Ælfric is also subverting the spirit, if not the letter, of his own translation principle, laid out in the Latin preface to *Lives of Saints*: that he will never produce a translated piece so that two kings rule simultaneously: "nollem alicubi ponere duos imperatores sive caesares in hac narratione simul sicut in Latinitate legimus, sed unum imperatorem in persecutione martyrum ponibus ubique, sicut gens nostra una regi subditur, et usitata est de uno rege non de duobus loqui" (I have not wished to record anywhere in this narrative two emperors or caesars at the same time, as we read in the Latin, but we have recorded one emperor engaged in the persecution of the martyrs everywhere, just as our people is subject to one king and is accustomed to speak of one king not two.)[3] Although this passes, more or less, as a principle of cultural translation (to use political titles and ideas as they are commonly used in English), it is most centrally a principle tying translation to God's sovereignty and to proper rule, key themes of that collection. As Ælfric notes in the

Old English preface, the saints are God's "halige þenas" (line 6; holy retainers), supporting his rule:

> An woruld-cynincg hæfð fela þegna
> and mislice wicneras; he ne mæg beon wurðful cynincg
> buton he hæbbe þa geþincðe þe him gebyriað
> and swylce þening-men þe þeawfæstnysse him gebeodon.
> Swa is eac þam ælmihtigan Gode (lines 1–5)

> A terrestrial king has many attendants and various ministers; he cannot be an esteemed king unless he has the honours due to him and similarly the attendants offering him obedience. So it is too for almighty God.[4]

But *Judith* is singular among Ælfric's hagiographies, although it fits very much into that genre. (I will, however, refer to it by its conventional title, the *Judith*-homily, which distinguishes it from the anonymous Old English *Judith*-poem.) The breach that reveals Nebuchadnezzar, would-be omnipotent sovereign, as one of two barely distinguishable tyrants is a political aesthetic tied to the translation's primary purpose – to explore and undermine imperial sovereignty and oppose to it the independent, sacred exception.

Ælfric's work demonstrates, as discussed in chapters 2 and 3, that the productivity of supersessionary translation for pre-Conquest Christian intellectual and political projects stretches far beyond Christian identity vis-à-vis Jews. The Hebrew Bible's inexhaustible but ill-fitting resources for political theology, for law, and for philosophies of sex and the body put it into agonized and fruitful relationship with the English Christian socius. Ælfric finds in Biblical translation a matrix for intertwined theologies of sovereignty and sexuality, and in the English language an arena for the conversion of Hebrew Biblical concepts into Benedictine monastic ideals: Jewish purity into Christian chastity, and in *Judith*, martial heroism into abbatical sovereignty.

Ælfric freely translates the *Judith*-homily from the Vulgate version, which derives from the Greek Septuagint rather than the Hebrew Bible. Like the Old English *Judith*-poem of the Nowell Codex, the homily varies considerably from the Biblical text; Marsden and Stuart D. Lee attribute most of the many interpolations to Ælfric rather than to intermediate texts.[5] The earlier (fragmentary) manuscript witness to the *Judith*-homily, British Library, MS Cotton Otho B.x, and the fuller witness, the twelfth-century homiletic collection Cambridge, Corpus Christi College, MS 303, place the homily among other saints' lives and martyrdoms translated from various Latin sources. Ælfric takes the Book of Judith as theologically rich source material for a treatise on sovereignty, both self-rule and unjust imperial rule.[6] McCracken, in discussing women's "fantas[ies]" of "self-sovereignty" in medieval French romance, uses Patchen Markell's definition: "being subject only to those forms of authority to which you have yourself consented, and whose purpose is to protect your domains of independence."[7] I find this definition, taken out of its secular contexts, particularly apt for those who gain their authority through a rigorous submission to divine will – a chosen people, for instance, or abbots and abbesses, or in Judith's case a woman who exceeds others in piety. Although all are subject to God, it is in this form of special voluntary submission that one becomes free from all sorts of secular authorities and commands, justified even in resisting imperial power, which appears within this framework as improper usurpation of God's total power.

Imperial Sovereignty: *Geweald* **and** *Anweald*

The form of power initially at issue in the Judith-homily is *anweald*, rulership or sovereignty, defined by the *Dictionary of Old English* principally as "power, sovereignty, sway," as well as "authority," "dominion," "possession," "command," and many similar uses.[8] The prefix *an-* is, as Joseph Wright and Elizabeth Mary Wright note in their classic grammatical text, the "stressed form of the preposition on, *on*"[9] and is unrelated to the nearly homonymous stressed *an*, "one," another favourite word of Ælfrician tyrants, which can also be combined with *weald* to make the infrequently attested homonym *anweald (an-weald)*, "sole rule." It is sometimes difficult to distinguish the two words in prose texts; the *Dictionary of Old English* identifies the latter only in "element-by-element glosses of *monarchia*" but concedes that this might be overly conservative.[10] As Haruko Momma argues, the distinction might have been equally, and perhaps productively, blurry to some readers of Old English.[11] Scott Smith glosses *anweald* as "political power and dominion over a group of territories and peoples," with particular connotations (in the Anglo-Saxon Chronicle and other secular documents) of imperial, "expansive," "dynastic," "secular," "royal" power.[12] The *Dictionary of Old English* attributes the imperial sense particularly to the expression "*gereccan in anweald/gewyldan to anwealde* 'to subjugate, bring (a nation or country) under domination.'"[13] *Anweald* and its semantic relations emerge in profusion in the *Orosius* when humanity begins to practise kingship and territorial war: first the Assyrian Ninus, "manna ærest ricsian on ðysum middangearde ... mid ungemætlicre gewilnunge anwaldes he wæs heriende and feohtende fiftig wintra, oð he hæfde ealle

Asiam on his geweald genyd" (the first person on the earth to rule ... with excessive desire for *anw[e]ald*, he was plundering and making war for fifty winters, until he had forced all of Asia under his dominion). This territory, which extends from the Red to the Black Seas, then comes "on ... gewealde" (under the rule) of his even more rapacious widow Semiramis; "hyre þagyt to lytel þuhte þæs *anwaldes* ðe se cyningc ær gewunnen hæfde" (the *anw[e]ald* that the king had conquered earlier still seemed to her too small).[14] *Anw[e]ald* in these two instances means *empire* or *imperial rule*.

Ælfric frequently uses *anweald* and its cognates *geweald* (noun) and *gewealdan* (verb) similarly to describe God's sovereignty over the earth and its creatures, an imperial power that He can distribute or share with deputies without diminishing it.[15] Ælfric translates the Vulgate's "dominamini" as the periphrastic "habbaþ on eowrum gewealde" (have under your rule) in God's instructions to the man and woman of the first Genesis story: "Wexaþ and beoð gemenigfilde and gefillaþ þa eorðan, and gewildaþ hig and habbaþ on eowrum gewealde þære sæ fixas and ðære lyfte fugelas and ealle nytenu þe stiriaþ ofer eorðan" (*OEH* Genesis 1:28; Increase and be multiplied and fill the earth and rule [*gewildaþ*] it, and have in your power [*gewealde*] the fish of the sea and the birds of the air and all the beasts that move across the earth).[16] In Ælfric's *De Falsis Diis*, God gives humans "anweald ofer eorðlice gesceafta" (line 30; dominion over earthly creatures),[17] and in his *Old English Hexameron* "anweald ... ofer eallum fixum and ofer fugolcynne / and ofer wildeorum and ofer eallum gesceafte (lines 333–5; dominion over all fish and over birdkind and over wild animals and over all creation).[18]

It is the same right to rule that, in cursing Adam and Eve to mortal married life, He gives Adam over Eve: "Ic gemenigfilde þine yrmða and þine geeacnunga; on sarnysse þu acenst cild and þu bist under weres anwealde, and he gewild ðe" (*OEH* Genesis 3:16;[19] I will multiply your miseries and your childbirths; you will birth children in pain and you will be under man's dominion, and he will rule you), where "under weres anwealde" translates the Vulgate's *sub viri potestate*. The imperial nature of these Hexameral and lapsarian gifts of *geweald* and *anweald* helps flesh out the word's theo-political connotations of sovereignty that can be delegated and shared: in ruling over the creatures, man and woman partake in God's power at His will without replacing or diminishing it. It is only in God's words to Eve that we first get the sense that such power or supremacy – already mentioned numerous times in the first chapter of Genesis as a gift to humanity and creation – can be a curse to those under it.

In Old English poetry, the noun *geweald* and verb *gewealdan* often pertain to God's rule, although they may also refer to other forms of dominion; for instance, of the nineteen individual appearances of these words in the poetic *Genesis*, most refer to divine sovereignty, but two occur in the alliterative formula *wif to gewealde* (woman under [a husband's] authority). In prose, Ælfric often uses *geweald/gewealdan* to describe divine sovereignty ("god ælmihtig ... ðe ah geweald heofenas and eorðan" [God almighty ... who holds authority over heavens and earth]).[20] In the secular sphere, he also frequently applies the words to both Christian and non-Christian imperial rule:

Constantinus se æþela wæs ærest Cristen
of eallum þam kaserum þe to criste gebugon,
and he ana ahte ealles middaneardes geweald (lines 7–9)

The noble Constantine was the first Christian of all the emperors who submitted to Christ, and he alone had dominion over the entire earth.[21]

The same word can have negative or positive connotations in Ælfric's writing, depending on the ruler: "Aurelianus andwyrde orgelice swiðe, Ic ana gewealde, ealles middaneardes" (Aurelianus answered very arrogantly, "I alone rule, over all the earth").[22] In these contexts, Ælfric uses *gewealdan* to distinguish between imperial, deputizable sovereignty (whether righteous or tyrannical) and the lesser powers of client rulers: for instance, the Roman emperor Decius, persecutor of Abdon and Sennes,

Ana geweold ealles middan-eardes,
and ealle oðre cyningas to him cneowodon
and heora rice wunode swa swa he ana wolde (lines 5–7)

alone ruled [*geweold*] the entire earth, and all the other kings knelt to him, and their rule [*rice*] lasted just [as long] as he alone willed.[23]

According to *The Dictionary of Old English*, "Wulfstan prefers *geweald*" to *anweald*; unlike Ælfric, however, the archbishop does not use the terms interchangeably.[24] To Wulfstan, *geweald* has the connotation of tyrannical or illegitimate rule – he uses it frequently in the context of the devil or of foreigners controlling the land as a result of English sin; like the *Genesis A* poet, Wulfstan uses *geweald* to refer to power over or improper possession of another's body, often for abuse or violence. In *Be Godcundre Warnunge*, for instance, Wulfstan warns, "ge beoð gesealde feondum to gewealde, þa eow geyrmað and swyþe geswencað" (lines 66–7; you will be delivered into the power of enemies, who will make you miserable and severely oppress you).[25] In the *Sermo Lupi*, the dog-like English rapists deliver an English woman into the *geweald* of foreigners for the purpose of sexual abuse, just as the men of Sodom, in the *Genesis* poem, seek to put "weras to gewealde" (line 2459; men into their power), for the same purpose.[26] Contrast this with the Old English Martyrology entry on Abdon and Sennes, whom Decius "het … nacode sendan on wildra deora geweald. Þa weop eall Romana dugoð for þære dæde, forþon þa weras wæron wlitige ond fægres lichoman. Ða noldon þa wildan deor him onhrinan for Godes ege" (ordered to be sent naked into the power of wild beasts. Then all of the Roman senate cried about that action, because the men were beautiful, with lovely bodies. Then the wild beasts would not touch them because of fear of God).[27] Here, the sense of *geweald* is that of power over lovely naked bodies, in this case given up to real beasts (as opposed to the figurative dogs of *Sermo Lupi*) for real consumption; the mildly sexualized connotations suggest the same tie between *geweald* and improper authority over other bodies.

What Nebuchadnezzar desires is *anweald*: unrestrained imperial authority over conquered peoples, robust enough to be shared with powerful deputies such as his general and true believer Holofernes. In the *Judith*-homily, *anweald* therefore never describes God's power (although, as mentioned above, Ælfric frequently uses the term elsewhere to refer to divine authority); it can signal only that power of conquest that Nebuchadnezzar wishes to extend over Israel and the nations. In the planning stages, he "gegaderode his witan ða, and wið hi ealle rædde, cwæð, þæt him swa þuhte þæt he sylf wolde ealne middaneard to his anwealde gebigean, and hi him andwerdon, þæt he ænlice spræce" (lines 34–7; then gathered together his counsellors and consulted with them all, saying that it seemed to him that he himself wished all the earth to submit to his rule, and they answered him that he spoke peerlessly).[28] Imperial ambition over one's neighbours is not inherently ignoble in Old English literature, even for polytheistic kings; it seems to be precisely what Scyld is praised for achieving in the opening lines of *Beowulf*, when he fights fiercely abroad until

>   …him æghwylc   þara ymbsittendra
>   ofer hronrade   hyran scolde,
>   gomban gyldan   (lines 9a–11a)

>   every one of the neighbours over the whale-road had to submit to him, to pay tribute.

This behaviour earns Scyld the famous and almost certainly unironic epithet "god cyning" (line 11b; good king). Yet more than a hint of irony emerges from the counsellors' suggestion in the *Judith*-homily that this emperor Cambisus speaks, or does anything else, peerlessly. He is, after all, only the second of the two easily confused Nebuchadnezzars whom Ælfric has just listed, and his glorious ambitions are destined for humiliating defeat by the "ænlic wimman" of the Hebrews.[29] Nonetheless, at first Nebuchadnezzar's plans appear to succeed in the capable hands of his general Holofernes. Summarizing more than a chapter of the Book of Judith (Judith 2:18–3:15), Ælfric writes:

> nan folc ne mihte his fyrde wiðstandan, ac comon him to of fyrlenum landum, mid fyrhte fornumene, friðes biddende. Cwædon þæt him leofre wære, þæt hi libbende þeowdon þam mæran cyninge Nabochodonosor ðonne hi swyltende samod forwurdon. And hi swa abugan þa þam breman heretogan mid eallum heora æhtum to þæs cyninges anwealde (lines 47–53)

> no people could withstand his army, but [they] came to him from distant lands, consumed with fright, suing for peace. They said that it was preferable to them that, living, they serve that illustrious king Nabochodonosor than that they altogether perish. And so they then bowed to that fine warleader, surrendering with all their goods to his king's power.[30]

This cycle of intimidation, submission, and tribute, expanding the king's *anweald* and confirming the sense that this Gentile army is invincible, provides a template for what Holofernes will expect from the Hebrews, expectations that the *ænlic wimman* Judith will use against him and his men.

The main obstacle to imperial *anweald* is the claim of Israel (later represented by Judith, whose name indicates her representative relationship to her people)[31] to be a free and sovereign nation ruled only by their God. Holofernes's retainer Achior explains this, to unwelcome reception:

> ne mihte nan mann naht þisum folce, swa lange swa hi heoldon heora God on riht … Ic bidde þe nu, hlaford, þæt þu læte ofaxian gif ðis folc nu hæbbe ænige unrihtwisnysse oððe gylt geworhtne ongean heora God, and hi beoð underþeodde þonne þinum anwealde (lines 102–4, 117–20)

> no one could hold onto this people, as long as they clung to their God in righteousness … I petition you now, lord, that you let me inquire whether

this people has now committed any unrighteousness or crime against their God, and is [therefore] subject to your *anweald*.

Achior avers that God's jealousy and vengeance against his chosen people are such that, if they have broken His laws, Holofernes can expect to be able to conquer them, but Holofernes repudiates this strategy:

> Wite ðu nu, Achior, þæt ðu weorþan sceal mid urum swurdum ofslagen mid him, þonne we hi ealle ofsleað swa swa ænne mann, þæt þu mage tocnawan þæt ure cynehlaford Nabochodonosor is soðlice God, and he nu Israhel ealle eaðelice fordeð. (lines 129–30)

> Now know, Achior, that our swords must kill you along with them, when we slay them all just like anyone [else], so that you might know that our king Nebuchadnezzar is truly God, and now he will easily destroy all of Israel.

Achior's logic offends Nebuchadnezzar's imperial arrogance, because while Nebuchadnezzar demands sole sovereignty, Biblical theodicy as Achior accurately presents it would make Assyrian conquest, and thus the empire itself, only an instrument of God's punishment, destined to be overcome whenever the chosen people repent once again. This unacceptable vision of limited *anweald*, subject to the all-powerful Hebrew God's whims and permissions, requires Holofernes's insistence that "ure cynehlaford Nabochodonosor is soðlice God" and that he will be able not only to conquer but to destroy Israel. And thus the death penalty for Achior, who in championing this Jewish theodicy commits a form of blasphemy.[32]

According to Judith, it is morally impossible for the Jews to submit to Holofernes's *anweald* just because everyone else has done so. Narratively and theologically speaking, the importance of resistance lies precisely in the capitulation of all the other peoples. Since, as Achior has explained, obedience to God's law is the guarantee of Israel's sovereignty, the wise and pious Judith views with alarm the local authorities' intention to surrender within five days and functionally to transfer their obedience from God to the tyrant. While the Biblical Judith, convening the elders in her home, delivers a learned and lengthy (Judith 9:11–27) exposition of the plan's flaws, earning the men's submission to her point of view, Ælfric's Judith briefly objects only that surrender demonstrates insufficient faith and that the five-day deadline inappropriately places an ultimatum on God:

> Ðeos Iudith ofaxode hu Ozias gespræc, and cwæð þæt hit wære witodlice unræd, þæt mann sceolde settan swylcne andagan Gode, þæt he binnan fif dagum þam folce gehulpe, oððe hi woldon gesecan þone Syriscan here and þone ealdorman to his anwealde (lines 177–81)
>
> This Judith found out how Ozias had spoken and said that it would certainly be ill-advised if they imposed such a deadline on God: that [either] He would help the people within five days or they would approach the Syrian army and the lord to submit to his authority [*anwealde*].

This represents a summary rather than a direct translation of Judith's speech to King Ozias (Uzziah) in the Vulgate, but it captures an essential point. Ælfric meaningfully alters even this short speech, replacing Judith's accusation that the elders will approach Holofernes "trad[ere] civitatem" (Judith 8:9, 8:10; to betray the city) with the more thematically apt reminder that they will do so in order to submit to human *anweald* – that is, that they intend to betray not only the city but their submission to God.

Ænlic: Sovereign Singularity

That Nebuchadnezzar can harbour such an ambitious goal as sole dominion over the Jewish people is possible only because he denies God's sovereignty and the conformation of salvation history to His will. The effect of inserting the story of the first Nebuchadnezzar, who does not appear in the Book of Judith, at the beginning of the homily is not only to obviate the possibility of this would-be sovereign's singularity at the outset, but also to establish the lesson that Holofernes will elect to ignore when his man Achior later explains it.[33] As Achior tells Holofernes, conquest and liberation of Israel proceed only as instruments of God's cycle of vengeance and mercy towards His chosen people:

> An wæs se Chaldeisca þe acwealde Godes folc on Iudea lande for heora geleafleaste, þa þa hi wurðodon wolice hæþengyld and deofolgyld beeodon heora drihtne on teonan. Ða towænde se cyning heora winsuman burh, Hierusalem gehaten, and þæt halige templ – ðe Salomon geworhte mid wundorlicum cræfte – and towearp hi grundlunga, and þæt Godes folc

ofsloh, and þa herelafe to his lande adraf to Babiloniam, heora micclan byrig; and hi þær wunedon on his wælhreowan þeowte, gecnæwe heora synna wið þone soþan God. Hundseofontig geara hi wunedon þær on þeowte, oðþæt Cyrus cyning hi asænde eft ongean to Iudea lande, þanon þe hi alædde wæron, and het hi eft aræran þæt ænlice templ: swa swa se ælmihtiga God on his mod asænde, þæt he his folce mildsode æfter swa micelre yrmþe. (lines 4–18)

There was a certain Chaldean who decimated God's people in the land of Judea, because of their infidelity when they perversely turned to idolatry and observed devil-worship as offence to their Lord. Then that king destroyed their pleasant city, called Jerusalem, and the holy temple that Solomon built with wonderful skill, and destroyed them to the foundations and slaughtered the people of God and drove the remnant to his land, to Babylon, their great city, and they lived there in his cruel bondage, conscious of their sins against the true God. A hundred and seventy years they lived there in slavery, until King Cyrus sent them again to the land of Judea, from which they had been taken, and called them again to raise up the singular temple. Just as the almighty God had sent them away in His anger, so He took mercy on his people after such great misery.

Here, polytheistic kings are the proximate physical agents of Israel's exile and return. However, these exiles take place only when the Jewish people stray and God decides to punish them, so the conquering forces function as little more than militarized moving companies. In referring to the *ænlice templ* (which he also calls the *halige templ*), Ælfric introduces a term that will operate as an alternative to *anweald*, and which will recur in the naming of Judith as *ænlic wimman*. As Rebecca Stephenson observes of this instance, "The word *ænlic* is strange here and deserves further comment."[34] *Ænlic* appears to be a keyword in this homily,[35] twice describing what is proper to royal or sovereign individuals: Nebuchadnezzar's speech, according to the incorrect estimation of his counsellors, and Judith's purple and gold clothes: "hi sylfe geglængede mid golde, and mid purpuran, and mid ænlicum gyrlum" (lines 192–3; she decked herself with gold and with purple and with singular garments). In three additional cases, *ænlic* refers to what is independent or self-sovereign, beyond the control of other people: Judith, the temple, and finally the victory of Israel: "Israhela folc þa mid ænlicum sige wendon him hamweard, and þa herelafa dældon betwux him on deorwurðum sceattum, swa þæt hi wurdon swiðe gewelegode" (lines 316–19; With singular triumph the people Israel then travelled home and shared out the spoils amongst them in the form of valuable treasure, so that they became very rich).

Singularity and exception, described as *ænlic*, may elsewhere signify Christ's and the Church's unique sovereignty. For instance, in Ælfric's *Passion of St. Thomas*, the apostle Thomas presents himself to the Indian royal retainer Abbanes as an enslaved builder in Christ's service. Abbanes, who has not heard of Christ, remarks, "Ænlic is se wer / þe swilce wyrhtan hæfð; he is selra þonne sum kynincg!" (lines 65–6; The man who has such craftsmen is singular; he is better than a king!) and Thomas responds, echoing the language of singularity,

> Ænlice þu spræce.
> Kyninges Sunu he is, an-cenned his Fæder;
> and hylt his Fæder rice on healicum muntum   (lines 67–9)

You speak singularly; he is a king's son, the only one born from his father, and he guards his father's kingdom in the high mountains.

where *an-cenned* nods also to Christ's singular means of birth and to his singular right, on earth, to rule in his father's realm.[36] The *Dictionary of Old English* lists "single, one and only" as the first definition of *ænlic/anlic*, and includes the following example from the anonymous Old English homily on the Seven Sleepers: "we andettað þe leofa hælend, þu þe ænlic eart þæs lyfigendan Godes bearn" (lines 805–6; we praise you, dear Saviour, you who are the only child of the living God).[37] The theological importance of singularity also manifests in the following *Dictionary* entries: "in glosses referring to the one and only church or faith" (1.c.), including "glossing *catholicus* 'universal; catholic, orthodox'" (1.c.i.) as, for instance, in "ic gelyue on gast haligne halige gelaþuge anlice" (I believe in the Holy Spirit, in the singular holy congregation [the holy Catholic Church]). This latter glosses "*Credo in spiritum (sanctum) sanctam ecclesiam catholicam sanctorum communionem*" in the Apostolic Creed in the Salisbury Psalter.[38] These primary linguistic associations between *ænlic* and sacred singularity underwrite the connection to divinely authorized sovereignty that becomes apparent in the *Judith*-homily.

When Ælfric uses *ænlic* to describe women, the word usually confers the connotations of sacred or royal authority. *Ænlic wimman*, his epithet for Judith, is a unique phrase in his extant work.[39] These connotations can be excavated in other Old English texts, although they are sometimes obscured by the gendered assumptions of scholarship.

For instance, when *Beowulf* condemns queen Modthryth for executing subjects, the speaker comments,

> Ne bið swylc cwenlic þeaw
> idese to efnanne, þeah ðe hio ænlicu sy,
> þætte freoðuwebbe feores onsæce
> æfter ligetorne leofne mannan. (lines 1940b–43b)

Such a custom is not queenly for a lady to perform, although she be singular – for a peaceweaver to strike against a valued person's life on account of false fury.[40]

Here the demands of sixth-century queenship as filtered through the poet's imagination – that one be *freoðuwebbe*, an officer of peace, pardons, and diplomacy – conflict starkly with the rights over life and death that Modthryth incorrectly sees as her own. In accordance with a general trend, traced deftly by Josephine Bloomfield, of depoliticizing *Beowulf*'s queens, this *ænlicu* is generally glossed as a comment on Modthryth's appearance.[41] The *Dictionary of Old English*'s *ænlic* entry, too, includes this line under the definition "of humans or angels and their physical appearance: peerless, beautiful."[42] But given the pairing of *ænlic* and *cwenlic*, so that the person described as *ænlic* is condemned for acting in a way that is not *cwenlic*, this cannot refer merely to the beauty that has prompted men's glances – it must describe Modthryth's misrecognition of her political power, her confusion of **ænlicnyss* (a form of sovereignty appropriate to queens and holy women) with *geweald* (rule over bodies, including the unqueenly power to abuse them).[43]

Ælfric uses *ænlic* in the hagiographies to mark out various kinds of singular sanctity. For instance, in his passion of St. Agnes, the saint describes the spiritual adornments granted to her by the bridegroom Christ, which she prefers to those of her polytheistic suitor: "He æteowde me eac his ænlican hordas, / ða he me gehet gif ic him gelæste" (lines 38–9; He also showed me his singular treasures, which he promised me if I followed him).[44] A comparison of the two *ænlic* wardrobes affirms the exceptionality – indeed the singularity – of Judith as a Jewish heroine. In what Cubitt calls a "a stock narrative structure" for virgin passions, Agnes passively resists a polytheistic nobleman's escalating sexual predations, culminating in her execution.[45] Ælfric dwells on the treasures she rejects and those she embraces instead: her suitor's family offers precious clothing and expensive things, but

seo eadige Agnes þæt eall forseah
and þæra maðma ne rohte þe ma þe reocendes meoxes.
Ða brohte se cniht to ðam clænan mædene
deor-wurða gimmas and woruldlice glencga
and behet hire welan gif heo wolde hine. (lines 17–23)

the blessed Agnes despised it all and valued the treasures as no more than stinking dung. Then the young man brought fine jewels and worldly ornaments to the chaste girl and promised her riches if she would [have] him.

She replies "an-rædlice" (line 24; resolutely), telling him about the "bæteran frætegunga" (line 29; better ornaments) – the "deor-wurðum stanum" (line 33; precious stones), "scinendum gimmum" (line 33; shining jewels), and "orle of golde awefen" (line 36; garment of woven gold) – that her suitor Christ has already spiritually given her, and about the bliss of their lovemaking: "Of his muðe ic underfeng meoluc and hunig. / Nu iu ic eom beclypt mid his clænum earmum; / his fægera lic-hama is minum geferlæht / and his blod geglende mine eah-hringas" (lines 45–9; From his mouth I take milk and honey; now I am long held in his clean arms; his lovely body is united with mine and his blood adorns my eyelids).[46] As is conventional for cloistered women and saints, Agnes must reject all physical adornment in order to receive God's glory and glamour. Judith, in contrast, arranges a pretended political and sexual submission to her people's heathen pursuer, and for this occasion, she first prays and then "sylfe geglængede mid golde and mid purpuran and mid ænlicum gyrlum." As Mary Clayton notes, "The familiar pattern of the virgin martyr opposed to the lustful tyrant seems to determine the way in which Ælfric views this scene, but it is one which is at odds with the biblical story. Whereas martyrs resist temptation, Judith tempts and, while martyrs reject ornate clothing and all the trappings of sexual adornments, Judith adopts them."[47] While Ælfric claims that she is "geglenged for nanre galnysse" (line 242; adorned for no lustful purpose), a phrase he borrows from elsewhere in the Vulgate text, this is true only the very narrowest sense.[48] Judith dresses glamorously for no lustful purpose of her *own*, but rather to appeal to Holofernes's sexual tastes and, as a crucial side benefit, to disarm his men by embodying a fatal (for the aggressors, in this instance) fantasy of surrendering peoples as submissive, sexually vulnerable, and welcoming. Zacher's description of this outfit as a killer's "disguise"[49] indicates that Judith's singular garments, the gold and jewels, represent not only peerless beauty but a singular exception to several rules of pious behaviour and, in the

English context, of hagiographic narrative. This exceptionality is the heart of Judith's *ænlicnyss.

Judith as Political Theology: Feminine Sovereignty and the State of Exception

The leadership of a singular woman in wartime is an original concern of the Book of Judith, which scholars such as Tal Ilan associate with the reign of Queen Shelamzion (Salome Alexandra) of the Hasmonean Dynasty, who succeeded her husband Jannaeus Alexander in 76 BCE and was the only reigning queen of an independent Judaea.[50] Judith has no official position within the patriarchal governance of her city, but comes to leadership rather through her beneficial intervention at a point when male community leaders are on the verge of surrendering the city. Armed with unique wisdom and piety, Judith publicly challenges them, substitutes her own judgment for theirs, and carries out her own successful military expedition with their consent.[51] As Gera has observed, Judith demonstrates a model for proper leadership during an invasion: "active resistance should go hand in hand with prayer and trust in God. Jerusalem and its temple must be protected at all costs, there is to be no submission to a foreign power, and all means, including deception and killing, are legitimate in this context."[52] In publicly correcting her people's course and in seeking counsel and consent for her bold actions, and in her continual recourse to God's will to support deeds that would be otherwise impossible, Judith contrasts the operations of legitimate authority from the many examples of bad imperial rule and kingship in her intertexts. There could be no starker contrast with the lecherous and impious queen Jezebel of the Book of Kings, evoked by some medieval theo-political writers as a rebuke of, among other things, female authority and bad counsel.[53] The Book of Judith demonstrates what Gera calls a "double causation" of divine and human agency,[54] in which the fate of God's covenanted people relies essentially on the capacity of its leadership to align their own will and actions with God's. To the question of whether an exceptional woman can lead a whole people with appropriate wisdom and strength, the Book of Judith answers yes: its readers and interpreters must struggle to understand what conditions make this singular circumstance possible, even desirable.

As a matter of political theology, Judith's singularity offers a rich provocation to medieval monastics concerned with abbatical sovereignty and monastic independence. Women's rule, for instance, inappropriate in most secular settings, requires absolute obedience within a women's minster, and indeed there is no getting around the historical role of double monasteries in which early English abbesses ruled over and taught the most learned monks. Women's sovereignty is, in fact, a perfect demonstration of *divine* sovereignty because, as Päivi Salmesvuori observes of Birgitta of Sweden's establishment of women's abbatical authority, it embodies a divinely created "exception" to masculine supremacy over women.[55] In her boldly named *Rule of the Savior*, Birgitta allocates herself the Virgin's exceptional power in the name of Christ, writing as his amanuensis that the abbess "should be the head and leader, for the Virgin, whom the abbess represents, was the head and queen of my apostles and disciples after my ascension into heaven."[56] The Book of Judith asserts, to put the problem in terms of political theology, that female sovereignty is a state of exception to female subjection, through which God demonstrates His own power of decision.[57] Here I use Carl Schmitt's concept of the exception as proof of sovereignty, although I dispense with the ahistoric supersessionary relationship he proposes, much critiqued by medieval and Jewish studies scholars, between the "theological" and the political.[58] (As Susannah Heschel notes, "Theology is always political.")[59] Keeping in mind that, as Zacher observes, political theology is an inherent quality of the Biblical and medieval texts that does not require secularized interpretation, Schmitt's articulation of the sovereign exception (encapsulated in the infamous axiom, "Sovereign is he who decides on the exception"[60]) is uniquely useful to our understanding of Judith.[61] It is this exception that the Book of Judith theorizes as underlying Judith's victory, and which Ælfric's homily on Judith exalts as the sign of legitimate self-sovereignty, impossible without and inseparable from chastity. As Miguel Vatter notes, "Political theology is possible only as an answer to the question of who or what represents and bears the person of the state or of God. Political theology depends on representation and is impossible without it."[62] Any discussion of Judith must reckon with the question of why (and how) she alone is authorized to act for God and Israel in this situation of crisis.[63] Ælfric makes this exceptionality and its conditions the subject of his translation.

The Biblical book of Judith, read as a work of political theology, theorizes the divine exceptionality of a woman's lethal violence. In the Vulgate translation (which already differs in some crucial respects from the Septuagint text), Judith urges God to destroy Israel's enemies through her, "erit enim hoc memoriale nominis tui cum manus feminae deiecerit eum" (Judith 9:15; for this will be a glorious monument for thy name when he shall fall by the hand of a woman [italics removed]). In triumphing through her conspicuously unpromising body, He demonstrates a power far beyond superior military might (9:9–16).[64] Judith announces her victory in the same terms, exclaiming at her return: "nobiscum est Deus, qui fecit virtutem in Israhel ... interfecit in manu mea hostem populi sui hac nocte ... per manum feminae percussit illum Dominus, Deus noster" (God is with us, who hath shewn his power in Israel ... he hath killed the enemy of his people by my hand this night ... the Lord, our God, slew Holofernes by the hand of a woman, 13:13–19). As Gera, noting close parallels to Jael's victory in Judges, observes, "Death at the hands of a mere woman adds to Holophernes' shame, points to Judith's bravery, and indicates God's involvement at one and the same time."[65] The rejoicing crowd declares, "Benedixit te Dominus in virtute sua quia per te ad nihilum redegit inimicos nostros" (13:22; The Lord hath blessed thee by his power because by thee he hath brought our enemies to naught) and Ozias announces, "Benedicta es tu, filia, a Domino, Deo excelso, prae omnibus mulieribus super terram" (13:23; Blessed art thou, O daughter, by the Lord, the most high God, above all women upon the earth). The first reaction is to praise God, to recognize in His use of Judith a miraculous humiliation and reversal of the oppressor's power, and the second is to affirm that Judith is an exception among women, in whom the sovereignty of God is manifest. Authorized by her deed and by this affirmation, Judith leads the people in a successful military campaign against the cowed invaders, which they follow with a song of thanksgiving. Judith rejoices: "Dominus ... omnipotens nocuit eum et tradidit eum in manus feminae et confodit eum ... Adonai, Domine, magnus es tu et praeclarus in virtute tua, et quem superare nemo potest" (16:7, 16:16; the almighty Lord hath struck him and hath delivered him into the hands of a woman and hath slain him ... O Adonai, Lord, great art thou and glorious in thy power, and no one can overcome thee). She praises God's almost unlimited power to defend His faithful people against arrogant enemies and to destroy these enemies through whatever means He chooses. As Achior has explained, Israel is not, however, therefore powerless in this matter; God extends or withdraws protection depending upon its righteousness. Judith's unlikely victory over Holofernes, which is now the triumph of the besieged Jewish people, provides living proof of God's sovereignty and of Israel's status as God's people.

If Judith's extreme piety is the Biblical explanation for her ability to act as God's exceptional instrument and as a defender of her people, one aspect of this piety – chastity – eclipses any other in Ælfric's homily. As the high priest Joachim tells Judith: "Tu gloria Hierusalem; tu laetitia Israhel; tu honorificentia populi nostril, quia fecisti viriliter, et confortatum est cor tuum eo quod castitatem amaveris et post virum tuum alterum non scieris, ideo et manus Domini confortavit te, et ideo eris benedicta in aeternum" (Judith 15:10–11; Thou art the glory of Jerusalem; thou art the joy of Israel; thou art the honour of our people, for thou hast done manfully, and thy heart has been strengthened because thou hast loved chastity and after thy husband hast not known any other, therefore also the hand of the Lord hath strengthened thee, and therefore thou shalt be blessed forever). This is the first time the Book of Judith explicitly describes Judith as chaste. In his homily, Ælfric affirms Judith's chastity as the source of her power, rendering this as follows:

> Þu eart wuldor soðlice ure byrig Hierusalem and Israheles bliss, ures folces arwurðness, forþan þe þu wunodest æfter þinum were wiflice on clænnysse, and God þe gestrangode for þære clænnesse, and forðan þu sylf bist gebletsod on worulde! (lines 325–30)

> You are truly the glory of our city Jerusalem and Israel's joy, our people's honour, because you lived in womanly chastity [*clænnysse*] after your husband['s death], and God strengthened you on account of your chastity [*clænnesse*], and therefore you yourself are blessed throughout the world!

Ælfric removes the reference to Judith's virility, emphasizing chastity as the sole reason the people bless her and God strengthens her. Indeed, according to this logic, the apparent plot actually conceals its reverse: while Judith's military success appears to proceed directly from her seduction campaign, the underlying truth is that she succeeds only because of her exceptional chastity, through which she earned God's support. Ælfric notes, citing the gospels,

> On hire wæs gefylled þæs hælendes cwyde: "Ælc þe hine ahefð sceal beon geeadmet, and se ðe hine geeadmet sceal beon ahafen." Heo eadmod and clæne, and ofercom þone modigan, lytel and unstrang, and alede þone miclan. (lines 341–5)

> In her was fulfilled the saviour's utterance: "Everyone who exalts himself shall be humbled, and he who humbles himself shall be exalted." She [was] humble and chaste, but overcame the arrogant one, small and weak, but she put down the mighty one.

In this way, Ælfric converts the Biblical message about Judith's exceptionality into a fulfilment of Luke 14:11 (Quia omnis qui se exaltat humiliabitur, et qui se humiliat exaltabitur; Because everyone that exalteth himself shall be humbled, and he that humbleth himself shall be exalted). He then concludes the homily by addressing women under vows and, indirectly (as Stephenson argues) male monastics on the subject of chastity and Christian temporality: "Nimað eow bysne be þyssere Iudith, hu clænlice heo leofode ær Cristes acennednysse, and ne leogað ge na Gode on ðæs godspelles timan þa halgan clænnysse þe ge Criste beheton" (lines 365–8; Seize the example of this Judith, how chastely [*clænlice*] she lived before Christ's birth, and do not deceive God in the time of the gospels about the holy chastity [*clænnysse*] you promised to Christ).

Within the Benedictine Reform, self-rule and independence were linked to the power of monasteries and to the purity of monastic life. What Pauline Stafford calls the "charismatic authority" that "[a]t its fullest … expressed itself in the abbess or saint," and what I am referring to as sovereign exceptionality, was so potent that such a person could serve as a corporate sovereign body.[66] Chastity is key to this equation. A female ruler's chastity demonstrates – through the theory of the sovereign's "two bodies," in which the ruler maintains an immortal corporate body – that the nation or land she protects need not submit to any other.[67] Without secular or sacred office, the Biblical Judith embodies the nation in just such a way; as Musa W. Dube observes, the Book identifies the Jewish people with her chaste body, demonstrating that Israel "is desired but … cannot be taken."[68] As Virginia Blanton notes, this is precisely how the male monastics of Ely deployed the immortal body of Æthelthryth, their founder, centuries after her death, to support Ely's "independence, sovereignty and impenetrability": "not only is this female body virginal and sanctified, it is also royal. As such, the royal body allows the monks to imagine Ely as a theocratic space." Under this banner of Æthelthryth as royal, sovereign, chaste, and inviolable, the *Liber Eliensis* "suggests that the monastic polity enjoyed special privileges separate from the secular polity … God sanctioned Æthelthryth's governance of Ely as well as the community's independence from external jurisdiction."[69] Judith, chaste and exceptional, also holds great potential as a model for monastic independence; in her singular militance, she is, as Ælfric implies, an even more adaptable figure for those resisting what Blanton calls "external jurisdiction."

Translating into Hagiographic Mode

In the previous chapter, I discussed the means by which Ælfric converts the purity of Jewish sexual law to the chastity of Christian life. His conversion of the Book of Judith to a Christian text operates through a similarly canny translation of purity, but in this case it is a translation of scrupulous Jewish observance, particularly *food* purity, into Christian sexual purity and thus of Biblical translation into the hagiography of a militant Old Testament saint. Where the *Judith*-poet ignores Jewish practice, Ælfric makes use of the Book of Judith's great concern with kosher law to create an Old Testament hagiography that explains chastity as the source of a sovereign exception.[70]

Like Ælfric's homiletic translations of Maccabees and Kings, the other Old Testament pieces in CCCC MS 303, *Judith* manifests the particular themes and much of the vocabulary that, as Godden and Brookes observe, generically mark Ælfric's hagiographies: for example, the wonder-working believer who, through God's power alone, triumphs against the *wælhreow* (bloodthirsty) invaders (as in lines 351 and 356).[71] The *Judith*-homily introduces Judith with the rich comment "Ða wæs on þære byrig, on þam ylcan timan, an ænlic wimman on wudewanhade Iudith gehaten, þæra heahfædera cynnes, swiðe gelefed mann on þone lyfigendan God, hlisfull on þeawum, rihtlice lybbende æfter Moyses æ, Manases laf" (lines 163–7; There was in the city at the same time a singular woman in widowhood called Judith, a descendant of the patriarchs, a person who believed strongly in the living God, famous for [her] virtues, living righteously according to the law of Moses, widow of Manasses). This passage situates her both narratively, in direct opposition to Nebuchadnezzar's/Holofernes's aggression (a pious *ænlic wimman* in this besieged city), and theologically/temporally (*rihtlice lybbende æfter Moyses æ*). Ælfric's biographical sketch abbreviates and shapes its Vulgate source to emphasize Judith's chastity and her regular life, and to flatten Jewish specificity. Noting that she is a wealthy landowner after her husband's death, the homily continues: "hi wunode on clænnysse æfter hire were on hyre upflore mid hire þinenum. Heo wæs swiðe wlitig, and wenlices hiwes, and heo fæste symle buton on freolsdagum, mid hæran gescryd to hire lice æfre, on Godes ege butan unhlisan" (lines 172–6; she lived in chastity after [the death of] her husband, with her maidservants on an upper floor. She was extremely beautiful, lovely in form, and she fasted constantly except on feast-days, her body always clad in a hair-shirt, in fear of God without ill-repute). This passage represents significant alteration to the Vulgate narrative, which also introduces its heroine as "Judith, vidua" (Judith, a widow; Judith 8:1) and gives her lineage,[72] the name of her late husband, and his manner of death. It then also describes her character and circumstances, as follows (in the Vulgate):

> Judith, [Manasseh's] relict, was a widow now three years and six months and she made herself a private chamber in the upper part of her house in which she abode shut up with her maids. And she wore

haircloth upon her loins and fasted all the days of her life except the sabbaths and new moons and the feasts of the house of Israel. And she was exceedingly beautiful, and her husband left her great riches and very many servants and large possessions of herds of oxen and flocks of sheep, and she was greatly renowned among all because she feared the Lord very much, neither was there any one that spoke an ill word of her. (Judith 8:4–8)[73]

In the Vulgate passage, the details of Judith's Jewish observance are crucial to a full account of her mode of life. Ælfric also aims for precision, but of a different kind. His homily retains Judith's location in her home and the presence of enslaved maidservants, but interpolates *clænnysse* (chastity), changing "she made herself a private chamber in the upper part of her house in which she abode shut up with her maids" to "hi wunode on clænnysse æfter hire were on hyre upflore mid hire þinenum." While the Biblical *Judith* communicates that Judith's steadfast observance of Jewish law includes chastity, the matter does not come up explicitly, as Clayton notes, until *after* Judith's feat.[74] Ælfric enhances the Vulgate language about Judith's beauty, adding to "swiðe wlitig," an invariable sign of chaste feminine virtue, the variation "wenlices hiwes." Ælfric also abbreviates "fasted all the days of her life except the sabbaths and new moons and the feasts of the house of Israel" to "heo fæste symle buton on freolsdagum." The Jewish specificities of fasting and feasting (that is, of the Jewish calendar of "sabbaths and new moons" and particular feasts) thus fall away, observances shared by medieval Christians (fasting in general and hair-shirts) remain, and sexual abstinence, a matter of perhaps more spiritual centrality to a medieval Christian than an antique Jewish audience, is foregrounded. As Ian Pringle observes, Ælfric sees Judith "as an example of monastic virtue."[75]

Ælfric's initial description of Judith conforms to a particular subgenre of hagiography: that of the sainted royal abbess. Although a number of such local cults were available (e.g., Sts. Hild, Mildthryth, and Sexburh), Ælfric wrote only one of these: the life of St. Æthelthryth, Abbess of Ely, in his collection *Lives of Saints*.[76] Ælfric marks St. Æthelthryth's distinguished lineage[77] and notes that she lives according to the strictest rule:

to anum mæle fæstende butan hit freols-dæg wære,
and heo syndrige gebedu swyðe lufode
and wyllen weorode and wolde seld-hwænne
hire lic baðian butan to heah-tidum
and ðonne heo wolde ærest ealle ða baðian

þe on ðam mynstre wæron and wolde him ðenian
mid hire þinenum and þonne hi sylfe baðian (lines 42–8)

restricting herself to one meal [daily] unless it was a feast-day, and she greatly loved solitary prayers and wore wool clothes and seldom bathed her body except on festival days, and then she would first bathe all of those who were in the monastery and would wait upon them with her servants and then bathe herself.[78]

All of the elements that appear here as markers of Æthelthryth's abbatical piety and sanctitude – lineage, solitude, sole authority over others in seclusion, fasting and prayer, and adhesion to the strictest form of regular life – also render Ælfric's Judith legible as a peerlessly pious woman in her own time. The similarities to Æthelthryth also highlight Judith's difference from the Christian saints (and therefore her theological utility as a pre-Christian). Gwen Griffiths describes Ælfric's Æthelthryth as a paradigmatic example of the "dependent and passive" character of women saints in Benedictine writing, reflective of a "fantasy of mute [sic] woman as the ideal."[79] As Griffiths observes, Ælfric's Æthelthryth speaks only to welcome the painful throat tumour that has replaced her prior love of rich necklaces.[80] We need not accept the idea that disability is akin to powerlessness, particularly within a hagiographic frame, to notice the stark contrast between Judith's and Æthelthryth's modes of sanctity in Ælfric's portrayals. If eager suffering, silence, and abjuration of secular glamour are Ælfric's requirements for sanctified Christian women, they do not seem to guide his depictions of Judith.[81] What are frequently described as Ælfric's attitudes to "women" are, in fact, attitudes to *Christian* women under a contemporary regime of sex and gender.[82] Similarly, the homily demonstrates a temporal difference in Ælfric's generally negative view of warcraft. Judith's acts of violence go far beyond what Ælfric finds generally acceptable for any Christian, finding their closest parallel in his work in the homily-translation of *Maccabees*.

Judith's hagiography is not, in orthodox terms, a *real* hagiography, because Judith is not a Christian saint. Yet as Ælfric notes, there is no prohibition on Old Testament saints:

Manega halgan wæron under Moyses æ,
ac we nabbað heora gemynd mid nanum mæsse-dæge,
butan þyssere gebroðra þe swa bealdlice ðrowodon (lines 203–5)

There were many saints under Moses's law, but we do not have any feast-days in their memories, except for these brothers who suffered so eagerly.[83]

114 Nothing Pure

What is remarkable is not *Judith*'s difference from conventional hagiographies, but how much it conforms to generic expectations. Even Judith's unconventional act of violence slots into a conventional hagiographic plot arc: at the gates of Bethulia, when she shows Holofernes's bloody head and announces her people's deliverance, she manifests a characteristic plot point in the life of a virgin saint:

> Undoð þas burhgatu! God sylf is mid us ... Heriað, ic bidde, mid blisse urne drihten, se þe ne forlæt on hine gelefende and þa þe hihtað on his micclum truwan, and on me gefylde his mildheortnesse þa þe he behet Israheles hirede; and he ofsloh nu to niht on minum handum his folces feond ... Godes engel soðlice me gescylde wið hine, þæt ic unwemme eft becom to eow; and God self ne geþafode þæt ic gescynd wurde, ac butan besmitennysse he asende me ongean, on his sige blissigende and on eowre alysednesse. (lines 262–77)

> Unlock the city gates! God Himself is with us ... Praise joyfully, I command, our Lord, who did not forsake His believers and those who trust in His great promises, and in me fulfilled his mercy, which He promised to the house of Israel. And tonight through my hands He killed the enemy of His people ... God's angel truly protected me against him, so that I have come back to you undefiled. And God Himself did not allow me to be shamed, but He sent me back without pollution, rejoicing in His victory and in your redemption.

Taking up the hagiographic mode, Ælfric's Judith emphasizes her role as God's instrument ("he ofsloh ... on minum handum") and her great acts as God's works ("on me gefylde"),[84] also central points in her Biblical speech.[85] Her role as God's agent appears to sweep Judith's execution of Holofernes into the category of divine acts, consistent with the statement that God has acted by her hand.[86] Judith also stresses that she has miraculously escaped sexual violence, a conventional feature of virgin saints' lives: God does not allow her to be "gescynd" or suffer "besmitennysse." On the contrary, in the homily it is Holofernes and his men who are "gescynd" by Judith's actions and Holofernes who "lið ... on bedde mid his blode besyled" (lines 307–9; lies ... in bed soiled with his blood).[87] As is usual in a saint's life, Judith's proofs of sanctity and of marvellous resistance to evil inspire a Gentile conversion, that of Achior.

Judith is doubly exceptional, both singular among women and temporally different from the other saints – that is, Jewish – and therefore has licence to behave outside of the bounds of Christian religious living. Within a rough hagiographic frame, Judith achieves spiritual glory for acts that would be unthinkable for Ælfric's Christian saints, including self-adornment and killing. Her style of speaking, too, lies outside the bounds of conventional hagiography. Judith's above-mentioned speech, condensed from a much longer Biblical conversation, is rich with the "utterances that command and advise" that Helen Damico identifies as characteristic of royal and divine speech in Old English literature.[88] These include imperatives such as *Undoð* and *Heriað*, corresponding to the Vulgate's "Aperite" (13:13) and "exaltate" (16:2), as well as a commanding rather than supplicatory *ic bidde*, which has no direct source in the Vulgate but appears to be Ælfric's original interpolation. This is precisely the sort of commanding tone that St. Birgitta of Sweden, theorist of the abbess's sovereign exception, will later use towards several popes, when she speaks in Christ's voice to order them to ratify her Rule, repent their corruptions, return the papacy to Rome, and so forth.[89] However, this form of speech is not characteristic of women saints in Old English prose hagiographies. (The anonymous life of bold St. Margaret constitutes one memorable exception.)[90]

In the Vulgate, the Israelites obey Judith's various commands at first slowly and then with increasing alacrity. Ælfric condenses the Biblical passage significantly, highlighting her direction of the action. In the homily, the people obey Judith quickly from the start: at her demand that they open the gates, "hi þa ardlice undydon þa gatu" (lines 264–5; then they immediately unlocked the gates). This is Ælfric's interpolation, creatively supplying action that is only implied in the Biblical account (unlocking the gates at Judith's command). After further speech, she issues a battle command:

> Asettað þis heafod on þam hehstan wealle, and gað eow gewæpnode, on Gode truwigende, nu on ærne mergen ut of þyssere byrig. Þonne beoð eowre fynd afyrhte for eow, þonne hi heafodleasne heora ealdorman findað, þonne mage ge gewyrcan eower word on heom. (lines 292–7)

> Set this head on the highest wall, and now go out armed from this city, trusting in God, in the early morning. Then your enemy will be afraid of you, when they discover their leader headless;[91] then you can fulfil your oath on them.

The people obey this military direction: "Hi dydon þa swa, sona on dægred, and gewæpnode ut ferdon mid folclicum truman, swiðe hlydende to þam ungeleaffullum" (lines 298–300; Then they did so, immediately at daybreak, and went out armed, with an army of the people, clamouring so loudly, to the unbelievers).

The explanation for Judith's empowerment, so to speak, as a subject, may be found in her temporal and ethnic difference from an Æthelthryth, which Ælfric evokes most explicitly in the final address on chastity: "ær Cristes acennednysse" (lines 366) Judith lives a form of regular and chaste life that authorizes autonomous spiritual action and direction over others. That is, "on ðæs godspelles timan" (line 367) and, more to the point, in the eleventh century, Judith's form of life and her authority translate into an abbatical form of power, anchored by chastity and command over self and others.[92] Judith is an early type of an abbess – or perhaps an abbot, since this text is apparently meant for a mixed audience who could interpret exempla across gender. And monastic audiences such as those Stephenson has posited for this homily could, no doubt, recognize an abbess when they saw one. The tenth and eleventh centuries were not the heyday of English women's monasteries: abbesses no longer ruled double houses of men and women as they had in the first centuries of English monastic life, and while many women may have lived under vows as *nunnan*, few lived in large or wealthy foundations. As Catherine Cubitt notes, the Benedictine Reform was in many ways demonstrably hostile to abbesses' political power and to the religious life of women.[93] Yet a broader European perspective indicates that sovereign abbesses were not an unknown relic of the distant past; on the Continent, their power was in some ways ascendant. For instance, at Gandersheim Abbey, home to Ælfric's near-contemporary Hrotsvit, the abbess achieved in 947, as Katharina M. Wilson notes, "the authority to have her own court of law, keep her own army, coin her own money, and hold a seat in the Imperial Diet."[94] If Old English authors of the tenth and eleventh centuries, particularly male monastic and ecclesiastical writers, are extraordinarily reluctant to portray such unvarnished power in the hands of Christian women, whether past or present, this reticence does not mean they could not vividly imagine or perhaps envy it. The exceptional Judith, made strange by her ancientness and by her Judaism, as well as by the acts of seduction and killing that would never be permitted to Christian women or to clerics, proves a distant enough figure to hold all the conceptual weight of a pure (in both senses), even saintly, self-sovereignty for monastic imitation.

This political thought-experiment in sacred clothing has several immediate applications. Ælfric asks his various readers to draw two more-or-less explicit morals from the homily: women under vows must see Judith as an example of chastity, and laymen must see her as an example of militance.[95] These messages, as Ian Pringle has demonstrated, do not contradict. In both cases, what is at issue is the alignment of self-rule with proper authority: religious women to chastity and their vows, warriors to discipline and the national defence. Each must throw off improper rule in the form of sin and invasion. Both messages must have seemed urgent during the Danish invasions, particularly, as Pringle observes, insofar as Ælfric and his contemporaries considered English sexual sin a factor in Danish victory.[96] As Rebecca Stephenson argues, however, Ælfric just as likely imagines a male monastic audience as the audiences he explicitly names.[97] The message to this audience is a conceptual extension of the first moral and accords with both: the condition of *ænlicnyss, that is, of personal and political independence, is Christian chastity. Sanctified authority, even or especially in a time of national crisis, is therefore properly monastic; it cannot truly rest in secular hands. This political message aligns with the tactful but persistent critique of secular kingship, and in particular its recurrent violent and power-hungry excesses, that Gabriella Corona and Rachel S. Anderson observe throughout Ælfric's work.[98] It is impossible to say whether Ælfric, who was probably not yet abbot at the time of *Judith*'s composition, envisioned this argument's full implications for monastic independence from secular (including episcopal) land grabs and governance.

It is often observed that the Book of Judith presents several problems to its medieval Christian translators and commentators: most intransigent among these are Jewish particularity, women's sexuality, and women's leadership.[99] This chapter has argued that (as with Job and Maccabees), Ælfric finds these features particularly exploitable in his creative translation: in *Judith*, "ær Cristes acennednysse" versus "on ðæs godspelles timan" sets up a space between Old Testament and contemporary times where Jewish observance can be translated into Christian chastity. Judith's complete alignment of her body, will, and speech with God's sovereignty is only possible under the signs of several forms of difference. Ælfric uses the figure of a sovereign Jewish woman to do what he will not when writing about Christian women: display the full force of God's power in the wonder-working hands of a sovereign holy woman. To do this, he converts Jewish purity to Christian chastity and female exceptionality to the sovereignty of chastity, a political form that promisingly opposes the headless figure of imperial and secular kingship.

5 Like Dogs and Wolves: Wulfstan as Biblical Translator

This chapter traces Wulfstan's canny redeployment of several modes and figures of translation, all of them centring on scenes of humiliation, conquest, and abasement. In his translation praxis, Wulfstan forges a passage of the Hebrew Bible, subverts the well-known translation trope of the captive woman until it is nearly unrecognizable, and uses dogs as figures of both supersession and of bad pastorship. What unifies these modes is an apparent multivocality straining towards univocality, where the voice of the people, the voice of the author, and the voice of God become indistinguishable. For the episcopal author, supersessionary translation serves and expresses a political theology in the sense Miguel Vatter uses the term, as "an answer to the question of who or what represents and bears the person of the state or of God."[1] In Wulfstan's hands, a Biblical figure of supersessionary sexual violence explains the necessity for episcopal rule.

Like Ælfric's *Judith*-homily, Wulfstan of York's much-revised political speech *Sermo Lupi ad Anglos* (Sermon of the Wolf to the English) elaborates a theory of English Christian sovereignty based, as Nicholas Howe demonstrated thirty years ago, on the skilled adaptation of Old Testament theo-politics.[2] Yet its most memorable passage, known to every scholar and nearly all students of Old English – has never, to my knowledge, been identified as an Old Testament translation:

> And scandlic is to specenne þæt geworden is to wide and egeslic is to witanne þæt oft doð to manege þe dreogað þa yrmþe, þæt sceotað togædere and ane cwenan gemænum ceape bicgað gemæne, and wið þa ane fylþe adreogað, an æfter anum and ælc æfter oðrum, hundum gelicost þe for fylþe ne scrifað, and syððan wið weorðe syllað of lande feondum to gewealde Godes gesceafte and his agenne ceap þe he deore gebohte.

And it is shameful to say what has too widely happened, and it is horrible to know what too many people have often done, who commit that crime, contribute together and buy a common woman as a common purchase, and commit filth against that one, one after another and each after the other, exactly like dogs who take no care for filth, and afterwards sell at a price out of the land, into the power of enemies, God's creation and His own purchase that He bought dearly.[3]

Wulfstan's capsule description of sexual crime – sexual assault and trafficking, in contemporary parlance – resonates by means of its temporal strategies: repetition that horrifies by transforming its object (a common woman as a common purchase; God's purchase, purchased by Englishmen and then by Danes), repetition that enacts the awful repetition it describes (one after another and each after the other), and the abbreviation of a constellation of Biblical references that give it a transhistorical scope. Within this passage are the Levitical litanies of sexual sins that can abrogate land title, causing one's enemies to inherit the land – one of Wulfstan's favourite themes; the Exodus 21 prohibition on reselling an enslaved woman, also creatively translated by King Alfred in his Prologue to the *Domboc*;[4] the sexual assault episode of Judges 19, the brutalization of a concubine as an index of national degradation.[5] Also encapsulated here are God's creation of human beings, Christ's redemption of humanity, and an array of Biblical dirty dogs, most conspicuously 2 Peter's parable (derived from Proverbs) of dogs returning to their vomit. Wulfstan may also be invoking, structurally, the prophetic texts, such as Ezekiel 16 and Ezekiel 23, in which God denounces ancient Israel in specifically sexual terms for its disobedience and promises heinous punishments of exile, famine, violence, humiliation, and slavery.[6] The scene also calls up any number of medieval analogues, including many very close to home. In the English woman trafficked and assaulted by dog-like English men, we see echoes of Jezebel, the Biblical queen humiliated and consumed, in Ælfric's words, "þurh fule hundas" (line 354; by filthy dogs).[7] This violence also previews the moment in 1036 when Ælfred *ætheling* and his followers lose life, freedom, and dignity to men the *Encomium Emmae Reginae* will call "worse than dogs" (*canibus deteriores*).[8] Wulfstan proposes, using the Biblical sources and invoking Gildas,[9] that the English in their sinfulness are akin to the Canaanites rightfully displaced by ancient Israel, to Israel justly punished with exile by God, and even to the superseded post-Incarnation Jews compared by their Christian successors to vomit-eating dogs. In Wulfstan's reading of the ongoing Danish conquest, the English, in their sin and greed, pass the land to the Danes as easily as they would sell on a woman who really belongs, like the land, to God and like the land is rightfully His to dispose of.

Wulfstan's legal and homiletic writings oppose both concubinage and sexual abuse, which were routine aspects of early English slavery, and the trafficking of Christians into non-Christian hands, since, as he notes in his 1018 legislation on this topic for Cnut, "beorge man georne þæt man þa sawla ne forfare þe Crist mid his agenum life gebohte" (we must take diligent care that we do not cause destruction of the souls that Christ paid for with his own life).[10] As *Sermo Lupi* indicates, a brisk international slave trade favoured women and children for both domestic and sexual labour. Indeed, Christopher Paolella finds nothing unusual in Wulfstan's story of the exploited woman sold on to new rapists; primary sources attest robustly to such practices, he observes, throughout early medieval European experiences of enslavement.[11]

Yet this is not mere reporting. Wulfstan's captive woman is a figure and object of supersessionary translation, who represents the question of God's sovereignty over land, law, and the bodies of human beings. Selectively and creatively translating the Old Testament, and identifying with ancient Israel, was not only a way that English Christians demonstrated spiritual supremacy over Jews and control over their legacy; it was also a key to English claims over Britain (a habit of mind inherited from the Britons they conquered, at least as represented by Gildas). Howe and others have catalogued an early medieval English identification with ancient Israel that proposes the fifth-century conquests as divinely underwritten and English Christians as national heirs to the covenant.[12] Wormald calls this the "Covenant thesis," and traces Wulfstan's elaborations of the thesis through his legislation and homilies to its "blunt logic" in the *Sermo Lupi*.[13] Here, Wulfstan draws self-consciously upon Gildas's description of a Britain conquered because it had "cast away fear of heaven and earth … to be ruled each man by his own contrivances and lusts" (abiecto caeli terraeque metu propriis adinventionibus aliquem et libidinibus regi).[14] As in Gildas and the Bible, the language of sexual depravity stands in not only for depravity as such but for a fundamental disturbance of the (gendered, sexualized) relations between people and God that are the foundation of legal sovereignty and land-right. In Biblical sexual economics, the people Israel's land-right, and the belonging of individuals to the people Israel, is particularly tied to the observation of certain laws; several passages in Leviticus warn specifically that the prostitution of Israelite women and the violation of other sexual taboos will sever these ties.[15] Wulfstan uses the Old Testament as a resource for stories of repeated sin and degradation as part of God's plan: as Joyce Lionarons notes, he "presents Old Testament history as a cycle of transgression and punishment that is inevitably followed by renewed transgression and further punishment."[16] This model would be crucial to state survival during the Danish conquest, since as Patrick Wormald indicates, it frames foreign conquests as divinely sanctioned, *temporary* punishments similar to those suffered by ancient Jews.[17] By this logic, there is no real contradiction in Wulfstan's horror at the Danish invasion and his subsequent participation in the Anglo-Danish administration, which has apparently been ordained to take possession of a sinful land through the well-known process of *translatio imperii*, with all of its supersessionary connotations.[18] The land and its people are God's to dispose of, and this property relation is an affirmation of the specialness of English Christians, of their intimacy with God.

The passage cited above appears only in the EI version of *Sermo Lupi*, the longest of three different versions all apparently written by Wulfstan within a short period. The EI *Sermo Lupi* (so called because it survives in the two manuscripts Wulfstan scholars call E and I)[19] is particulary notable, as Malcolm Godden notes, for two unique passages: the description of the enslaved *cwen[e]* and her dog-like rapists, and the citation of Gildas's Biblical view of history towards the end. Godden observes of the first addition: "The English are here seen to be appropriating the atrocities of the Vikings, abusing their own fellow-creatures; but their crime is far greater, since the woman whom they abuse is seen as the possession not just of a proud thegn but of God himself. It is, though, the Gildas passage which is important."[20] The contention of this chapter is not only that the abused human being at the centre of this text is key to reading Wulfstan's work, but also that these two issues – sovereignty over bodies, enslavement, and rape on the one hand, and translation, citation, and supersession on the other – are in fact inextricably linked.

Wulfstan as Forger and Translator

Wulfstan's significance as a translator begins, for this study, in the difficulty of defining his body of translation, which shades uneasily/fascinatingly into his career as lawmaker and, in Nicholas P. Schwartz's frank appellation, "forger" of historical laws. As Schwartz observes, Wulfstan created in the *Laws of Edward and Guthrum* "a fabricated source" that established "an 'historical' and authoritative code which he could mine for material to use in his later official lawcodes for both Æthelred and Cnut."[21] It is the boldest of Wulfstan's extant forgeries – in fact, Schwartz observes that it is "the only non-diplomatic textual forgery from the Anglo-Saxon period"[22] – but it is congruous with his general method of inventing imagined and erasing real sources. As Andrew Rabin notes, the ecclesiastical code scholars call *The Canons of Edgar* "may initially have been intended to be another of Wulfstan's 'forgeries.'"[23] Wulfstan was, in Rabin's terms, "a propagandist seeking historical precedent for current policy. And in the absence of such precedent, he appears to have felt little compunction about creating it. As a result, his tendency to manufacture documents (such as *The Laws of Edward and Guthrum*) or claim precedent where none may exist (as in *On the Ranks of People and Law* in *The Compilation on Status*) can blur the line between historical fact and fiction."[24] On the other hand, as Rabin notes, "unlike his contemporaries, [Wulfstan] only very rarely identifies his sources" – that is, his real sources.[25] Nor does his work present itself as interpretation, exegesis, or gloss on a Latin original. In one of his most extended acts of Biblical translation,[26] the homily *Be Godcundre Warnunge*, based on Leviticus 26, the archbishop provides a similar "fabricated source" by, as Jonathan Wilcox notes, presenting an improved Latin Biblical text that Wulfstan has in fact altered and epitomized freely.

The work the first compiler rubricates as *Be Godcundre Warnunge* (Bethurum 19/Napier 28) is apparently central to Wulfstan's political program and legacy, for it appears in four existing witnesses, including one of his own Commonplace Books (Cotton Nero A.i, fols 70–177) and continued to be read and copied into the late twelfth century, long after *Sermo Lupi* had lost its cachet.[27] *Be Godcundre Warnunge* appears to be a bilingual sermon, although it is a strange kind of sermon; Bethurum suggests that "[i]t was probably preached to the clergy as a model, for the first [Latin] part could hardly have meant anything to a popular audience."[28] It comprises three sections disguised as two: a Vulgate excerpt (Leviticus 26:3–12), followed by Wulfstan's own rendering of Leviticus 26:14–45, which Wilcox describes as a "paraphras[e] ... still in Latin but identifiably in his own words," followed by a creative English summary of the Levitical text that, as Bethurum observes, "adjusts the lesson to an English audience and substitutes English ideas of social relations for Hebrew, as in *heretoga, mundbora, þegnan*."[29] As Wilcox notes, "A work which looks at first glance like a straightforward translation of Leviticus XXVI with a brief homiletic conclusion is, in fact, a message carefully crafted by Wulfstan as a comment on his own days."[30] In the Commonplace Book, it precedes several law codes and sections of *The Institutes of Polity*, and is bound with a manuscript including Alfred's Mosaic Preface. The sermon reappears in combination with another Wulfstan piece (Bethurum 21/Napier 34), in Cambridge, Corpus Christi College MS 201, a manuscript that Mark Atherton calls "a mirror for a prince ... a coherent grand narrative of law-making and nation-building" that, Atherton suggests, generously incorporates Biblical material to assimilate Anglo-Danish rule into salvation history.[31] The manuscript context suggests that eleventh-century readers saw this homily as reuseable, relevant theo-political material within the rich English tradition of appropriating the Old Testament for secular rule.

Wulfstan's Latin edition of Leviticus 26:14–45, the portion Wilcox describes as a paraphrase, is instructive. In some ways, the structure (although not the details) of his alterations resembles those of the *Old English Heptateuch*'s Leviticus: Wulfstan abbreviates some verses to a single clause or two (e.g., 14 and 17), combines and consolidates others (e.g., 39–41), and omits the bulk (e.g., 34–8, predicting Israel's sustained rebellion through many initial rounds of punishment). What differentiates the passage is that this is not an interlingual but what we might call an intralingual translation; it is, as Wilcox observes, "identifiably" in Wulfstan's vocabulary and syntax rather than the Vulgate's.[32] For instance, he renders the Vulgate's "et corruetis coram hostibus vestris et subiciemini his qui oderunt vos; fugietis nemine persequente" (26:17; and you shall fall down before your enemies and shall be made subject to them that hate you; you shall flee when no man pursueth you)[33] as "et persequentur uos inimici uestri, et fugietis nullo persequente" (lines 28–9; and you will be pursued by your enemies, and you will flee pursued by no one),[34] a pithy formulation that shares with Wulfstan's late English style the characteristics of syntactic repetition, polysyndeton, and ironic reversal.[35] Wulfstan lavishly frames the adapted passage as an authentic excerpt from the Latin Bible: he introduces the Latin with the Old English comment: "God sylf gedihte swutele bysne and þus spæc on geardagum to Moyse þam heretogan" (lines 6–7; God himself plainly dictated [these] precepts and in antiquity spoke thus to Moses, the people's leader) and introduces the freely adapted portion (26:14–45) with the interpolation "dicit Dominus omnipotens. Et item Dominus dicit" (lines 24–5; says the almighty Lord. And the Lord also says), a piece of special pleading easily mistakable, on first reading or hearing, for *verbatim* Biblical language.[36] This is what Schwartz calls a "fabricated source": another of Wulfstan's minor forgeries, although easily detectable by a very learned contemporary.[37] The English translation, which Wulfstan introduces as an explanation of the Latin for the unlearned ("And se þe ne cunne þæt Leden understandan, hlyste nu on Englisc be suman dæle hwæt þæt Leden cwede," lines 42–4; And he who cannot understand the Latin, hear now in English something of what the Latin says) is not so much an explication but a concise, blistering prophecy in Wulfstan's fine rhetorical style, promising "gif ge þonne fram me hwyrfað eowre heortan and lara and laga mine forgymað oððe oferhogiað, þonne sceal eow sona weaxan to hearme wædl and wawa, sacu and wracu, here and hunger" (lines 59–62; And if you then turn your hearts away from me and neglect or scorn my teachings and my laws, then poverty and misery, instability and feuds, invasion and hunger must soon multiply as pain for you).[38] Wulfstan, here, reveals himself as a skilled translator of the Bible who is willing, as with his other sources, to forge originals and to rewrite passages in his own words without much of the humility topos we are used to from Ælfric. He does not announce what he is doing, yet he does not go to any trouble to hide it from learned contemporaries. He also demonstrates a knack for occupying multiple rhetorical positions within the same text, creating an authorial echo chamber where the voice of God and the voice of the humble translator converge.[39]

Wulfstan's Captive Woman: Translation and Humiliation

It is with an understanding of Wulfstan as skilful forger and politically engaged Biblical translator that I return to this famous scene of human degradation in *Sermo Lupi ad Anglos* to demonstrate the importance of humiliation, conquest, sexual violence, and human beastliness to Wulfstan's theories of translation. Wulfstan's passage translates and transmutes a particular Biblical passage that has become, since Origen, a common figure for translation – that of the captive woman. As I discuss in the introduction, Origen and Jerome identified translated texts with the war captive of Deuteronomy 21:10–13, a law describing how foreign women captured and enslaved in battle may be legally made into wives, and in the Christian West this glamourized image of wartime rape became a common figure for Christian translation of non-Christian sources. Wulfstan's *cwen[e]*, a stylized exemplar from a real class of contemporary enslaved people, is also a figure trafficked from the Hebrew Bible, not only multiply translated from her origins in Deuteronomy, but appearing in the *Sermo Lupi* as a figure of supersessionary translation and *translatio imperii*. Enslaved captives forced to move between cultures emerge at numerous other key sites in English vernacular literature: for example, Gregory's encounter with enslaved boys in the Old English translation of Bede and Ælfric's homily on St. Gregory,[40] and in *Beowulf* the funeral mourner who foretells "hyn[ð]o ond hæf(t)nyd" (line 3155a; abuse and captivity) for the Weder-Geats.[41] In general, the trafficked captive proves a figure not (or not only) for the translation of language but for the translation of power: the English conversion, the fall of the Geats. As such, they are not allegorical but metonymic figures, fictional and highly stylized condensations of the real experiences of captivity and misery that attend conquest.[42] In their metonymic relations to the Biblical-patristic captive woman trope, each of these captives also comments on the relationship of rhetoric and vernacularity to conquest and power – sometimes (as in *Beowulf* and the *Sermo Lupi*) a relationship of pure disenchantment.[43]

In the *Sermo Lupi*, *translatio imperii* manifests in the transfer of an abused woman without any of the mystifying glamour with which this trope appears in Origen, Jerome, and in many of their heirs. Wulfstan's woman undergoes no purification or adornment, nor is her sexual mistreatment glossed as marriage or reserved to one man or one people, nor does it represent military triumph; while the Biblical and patristic sources sacralize what is easily recognizable as, in M.I. Rey's terms, "genocidal rape,"[44] we are to understand that the captive of *Sermo Lupi* (like a Christian land overrun by non-Christians) is only profaned and debased, an object of pity; the act also degrades the bestial rapists, "hundum gelicost," who commit it.[45] While Ælfric makes little distinction between the theo-political concepts *anweald* and *geweald*, using both to refer to imperial and God-like power, *geweald* has, as discussed in chapter 4, a special connotation of grubby, illegitimate, abusive power: power only to hurt. Within *Sermo Lupi*, these canine abusers are joined by a slew of other English people debased by rape and human trafficking: noblewomen subjected to horrible sexual violence; children who fall into slavery as the result of poverty and crime; noblemen enslaved and murdered by those they have (legally) held in slavery; a group of captive Christians paraded publicly by Danish captors on their way out of the country. Wulfstan names the harms of these acts: mainly humiliation and loss of status to noblemen ("he on locað þe læt hine sylfne rancne and ricne and genoh godne ær þæt gewurde"; lines 115–17, he looks on, who before that had considered himself sufficiently valiant and powerful and worthy) and to Christian England as a whole ("us eallum to woroldscame"; line 122, [exposing] us all to humiliation before the world). Rape and enslavement, which Wulfstan describes in terms of harms to God and men (not women),[46] are the general condition of the people and land that do not pay God's dues, forget His laws, and thus fall into conquest. As Wulfstan, in the voice of Deuteronomy, prophesies in the English portion of *Be Godcundre Warnunge*, "ge beoð gesealde feondum to gewealde, þa eow geyrmað and swyþe geswencað" (lines 66–7; you will be given into the power [*gewealde*] of enemies, who will make you miserable and severely oppress you).[47] Wulfstan's "translation" of the captive woman, when read as a translation, does not participate in the traditional, triumphal identification of the writer with the captor-rapist or of the literary act with conquest. On the contrary, Wulfstan identifies both the captive woman and her bestial captors with the whole English people brought low by various acts of rape. He speaks for this collective in the first-person plural, both calling for and answering with the remedy that "us neod is" / "us þearf is" (lines 174, 186–7, 190; is necessary for us) in a univocal chorus that represents the whole sinful, humiliated English people and the solution to their plight.[48]

Wulfstan's own figurative identification with the captive extends further, for he is also enslaved – in a manner of speaking. His description of the woman as God's *agenne ceap* (and therefore legally ineligible for trafficking) evokes the widely used Old English epithet *godes þeowa[s]*, God's slaves, with which Wulfstan frequently describes clerics.[49] This term expresses, somewhat hyperbolically, both a real economic relation between the Church and its ministers, as Patricia M. Dutchak notes, and the specialness of the monastic and priestly class.[50] Wulfstan uses the term to assert the privileges and responsibilities of this class, most frequently admonishing them to chastity and obedience, as in Cnut's Oxford Legislation of 1018: "And ealle Godes þeowas we biddað and lærað, and huruþinga sacerdas, þæt hi Gode hiran and clænnesse lufian and beorgan him silfum wið Godes irre and wið ðone weallendan bryne, þe weallað on helle (And we command and direct all the slaves of God, and especially priests, that they obey God and love chastity and protect themselves against God's fury and against the blazing fire that rages in hell).[51] He uses the epithet with less frequency, but equal force, to admonish others for abusing them: "Godes þeowas syndan mæþe and munde gewelhwær bedælde ... þær cristene scoldan Godes lage healdan and Godes þeowas griðian" (*Sermo Lupi*, lines 33–7; God's slaves are everywhere deprived of status and protection ... where Christians must observe God's law and give sanctuary to God's slaves). Wulfstan not only authorizes himself to speak for this class, but counts himself as first among them, as when he legislates in Æthelred's name that "Godes þeowas – biscopas and abbudas, munecas and mynecena, preostas and nunnan – to rihte gebugan and regollice libban, and for eall Cristen folc þingian georne" (God's slaves, bishops and abbots, monks and nuns, priests and women under vows, submit to righteousness and live according to their rules and devotedly intercede for all Christian people).[52]

How can a bishop, a maker of laws in the king's name, also be enslaved? As Katherine Miller observes, "the association of 'real' slaves with the *servi Dei* does not seem to have perturbed Anglo-Saxon audiences, but was, indeed, critical to the understanding of the metaphor."[53]

In Ælfric's Passion of St. [Judas] Thomas, both Christ and the apostle assure the royal steward Abbanes that Thomas is "to soðan" (line 40; in truth) enslaved by Christ: "ic eom his þeowa and þa þing ne do / þe ic sylf geceose, ac þæt me sægð min hlaford" (lines 43–4; I am his slave and do not do the things that I myself choose, but what my Lord tells me).[54] Indeed, as a conservative and partially depoliticized interpretation of Paul's promulgation of "paradoxes of freedom in slavery and servitude in freedom," *servus Dei*, as Magennis notes, reinforces both the normalcy of slavery as an institution and the existing social hierarchy.[55] This hierarchy distinguishes between those who may become clerics or monastics, and thus be enjoined to chastity and certain rites of the body, and those who must be enslaved and thus unable to protect their bodies. Moreover, his previously discussed comments on priests' wives as "Nis ... ænig oðer þing" (nothing) but sexual temptations aligns him with the most draconian eleventh-century ecclesiastical attitudes towards these women, which would bolster priestly celibacy by reducing them to enslavement.[56] Since *servus Dei*, or *Godes þeow*, is both voluntary and ennobling, the role generally offers a fundamental contrast to mundane slavery; as Thomas later clarifies, "ic sylf-willes þrowige, for mines scippendes naman" (line 272; I suffer by my own will, for my Creator's name).[57] Indeed, to be enslaved to God is to be no earthly person's: it returns us to the political idea of self-sovereignty described in the previous chapter, of being bound to no earthly master except by one's own will or consent.

Wulfstan was not a person of little power, as enslaved people in England and its trading partners really were. In fact, his legal texts provide a record of extending episcopal sovereignty over free women and the truly enslaved, most notably through legislation nominally benefiting these groups. Corinne Saunders observes that while the ninth-century *Domboc*, the Laws of Alfred, records the crime of grabbing a nun, free woman, or lady "mid hæmeðþinge oððe on hire hrægl oððe on hire breost *butan hire leafe* gefo" (with sexual intentions by her garment or by her breast *without her permission*; emphasis mine), Wulfstan avoids the idea that sexual assault wrongs the victim herself by, among other things, violating her will.[58] Instead, as with the humiliated nobles in the *Sermo Lupi*, Wulfstan frames sexual assault only as harm against God, the state, and the affected free man – a free woman's husband or father, or the person who holds an unfree woman in bondage.[59] This is not to say that Alfred's policies are more anti-rape or proto-feminist than Wulfstan's, although both Saunders and Carole Hough see the *Domboc* in this light. The *Domboc* tacitly preserves enslavers' sexual prerogatives over enslaved women,[60] while, as Wyatt observes, Wulfstan treats the sexual exploitation of enslaved women with the same repugnance with which he views other forms of fornication, legislating somewhat narrowly against it in 2 Cnut II.[61] This legislation represents an extension of state and episcopal power over a form of sexual violence that, to this point, the law had barely named. It is beyond the capacity of any historian to judge whether Wulfstan foresaw successfully eliminating the sexual coercion of enslaved people while maintaining their enslavement, a task that the reader may consider both impossible and a moral contradiction. The attempt, at any rate, reveals the hope that unfree people might be able to maintain their chastity under greater Church supervision.[62]

Wulfstan's humane legislation and advocacy for what he calls *þrælriht*, the rights of the enslaved, affirm the status of enslaved people and their subjection, within this status, not only to their enslavers but also to the Church.[63] For instance, in 1009 Wulfstan calls a three-day national fast in response to Danish invasion, legislating in Æthelred's name, "Et sit omnis servus liber ab opere illis tribus diebus, quo melius ieiunare possit, et operetur sibimet quod vult" (And all slaves are to be freed from work on those three days so that they will be able to fast better and make what they wish for themselves). This apparently generous injunction harnesses the energies of enslaved Christians for (spiritual) national defence and subjects them to judicial punishment for failing to comply: "servus corio suo componat" (a slave is to be whipped), while free people must pay a fine.[64] In granting a certain form of mercy to enslaved people, the law also brings their bodies under the more direct control of the entwined church and state.[65]

Going to the Dogs

In calling the English rapists "hundum gelicost þe for fylþe ne scrifað," exactly like dogs who don't mind the filth they wallow in, Wulfstan is not only describing a generic descent from the bestial to the human. He also transmutes a well-known image from Proverbs and 2 Peter, that of the dogs who return to their vomit, which depends on a Hebrew Biblical understanding of dogs as unclean beasts.[66] Ælfric twice translates this idiom into Old English. In the homily on Ash Wednesday, Ælfric affirms, "se man þe æfter dædbote his manfullan dæda geedniwað, se gegremað God, and he bið þam hunde gelic, þe spiwð and eft ett þæt þæt he ær aspaw" (The one who after penitence returns to his sinful deeds enrages God, and he is like a dog who vomits and eats again what he vomited).[67] In his homily on the Fifth Sunday after Pentecost, Ælfric transitions from the gospel anecdote of Christ saving an adulterous woman (John 8) to the exemplum of the dirty dogs and pigs translated closely from 2 Peter 2:

> for ðan þe ælc man bið, þe geandet his synna,
> and þæt ylce eft deð his Drihtne on teonan,
> þam hunde gelic, þe geet his spiweðan,
> and ðam swine gelic, þe hit besylað eft æfter his þweale,
> and bið his ende wyrse þonne his angin wære (lines 230–4)

> because everyone who confesses his sins and does the same thing again to injure his Lord is like the dog who eats its vomit, and like the pig who fouls itself again after its bath, and his end will be worse than his beginning was.[68]

By linking an anecdote about sexual sin to the imagery of unclean dogs and pigs, Ælfric gestures towards the synecdochic relationship between species/alimentary uncleanness and unchastity seen elsewhere in his work and calls upon the frequent association between dogs' promiscuity in bodily matters and human sexual sinning.[69]

This sense of dogs as filthy and promiscuous eaters appears throughout Old English hagiography, where canine consumption of the human body is a recurrent index of ignominious violent death, a particularly disturbing variation on the food-of-worms imagery considered in chapter 2. In Ælfric's Passion of St. Vincent, Datianus unsuccessfully orders the desecration of the saint's corpse by dogs and other beasts:

> "Awyrpað nu his lic on anum wid-gillum felda,
> fugelum to æse and fulum hundum to mete,
> and þam wildeorum," and his wæl-hreowan þegnas swa dydon;
> sona geferedan þæt lic to þam feldan middan,
> and hit þar awurpon wild-deorum to mete (lines 234–8)

> "Now cast out his body onto a large field as carrion for birds and food for dirty dogs and for wild animals," and so his bloodthirsty followers did; they immediately carried that body to the middle of the field and threw it there as food for wild animals.[70]

This attempt and subsequent attempts at defilement fail because the body is too holy to be touched by beasts. In the Old English Martyrology entry on Milus and Senneus, Milus curses brothers who have persecuted him, "Tomorgen to þysse tyde yncer ægðer ofslyhð oðerne on þysse ylcan stowe, and hundas licciað eowre blod, and fugelas fretað incer flæsc, and yncer wif beoð on anum dæge wudewan (Tomorrow at this time, each of you two will kill the other in this same place, and dogs will lick your blood, and birds will eat your flesh, and your wives will be widows in the same day).[71] Similarly, in Ælfric's Ash Wednesday homily, a man who refuses to go to church for the special mass and intends to "his wifes brucan on þam unalyfedum timan" (enjoy his wife at that unlawful time) is consequently set upon by dogs (gestodon hine hundas hetelice swyðe; dogs very violently attacked him) and killed with his own spear. This last detail makes the moral as clear as possible – the man has killed and probably damned himself by following his own physical inclinations – but there is more to it. Here, untimeliness and impiety turn what would be lawful relations into unregulated sexual enjoyment (*brucan*), the realm of dogs and other beasts, so that the unshriven man's death by dogs allows him to properly die among them.[72] This is the same homily in which Ælfric translates the Proverbs version of the dogs returning to their vomit.

Bad Sovereignty: Abdication and Abjection

Ælfric's homiletic translation of the Old Testament Book of Kings, which forms part of the Lives of Saints collection in London, British Library, MS Cotton Julius E.vii, highlights the image of dogs eating tyrants and drinking their blood as punishment for sins against the land.[73] The punishment first appears in the Kings translation as threatened retribution for King Ahab and Queen Jezebel's unjust seizure (via corrupt judicial murder) of their neighbour Nabod's ancestral land. God threatens Ahab through the prophet Elijah:

> swa swa hundas lapodon Naboðes blod,
> swa hi sceolon lapian and liccian þin blod.
> Ic adilegie þinne hired and fordo þinne ofspring,
> forðan þe ðu me getyrgdest and min folc mistihtest,
> and Gezabel sceolon etan æl-grædige hundas   (lines 209–13)

> just as hounds licked up Nabod's blood, so too shall they lap up and lick your blood; I will destroy your household and kill your descendants, because you angered me and led my people astray, and ravenous dogs will devour Jezebel.[74]

This canine curse, which condenses a longer Biblical passage, is swiftly fulfilled when Ahab falls in battle, and as the army carries his body home, "his blod ða fleow binnon ðam cræte, / þæt liccodon hundas ða ða hi ham comon" (lines 225–6; his blood ran within the cart, so that dogs licked it when they came home). Ælfric selects these two details from a longer passage in 1 Kings 22, eliminating the two verses that separate flowing blood from hungry dogs and translating quite closely from the Latin (3 Kings 22:35–38; "fluebat autem sanguis plagae in sinum currus ... et linxerunt canes sanguinem eius"; and the blood ran out of the wound into the midst of the chariot ... and the dogs licked up his blood). As Ahab's sons succeed to his office, Jezebel does not repent but "manfullice leofode / on fulum forligere and on ælcere fracodnysse" (lines 270–1; lived wickedly in disgusting fornication and in every sin). Eventually God engineers a coup, "þæt ic beo gewrecen on þære awyrigendan Gezabel. / Heo bið hundum to mete, na bebyrged on eorðan" (lines 324–5; so that I may be revenged on that cursed Jezebel. She will be food for dogs, not buried in the ground).[75] As Stacy S. Klein notes of the prophecy, "In the Vulgate [4 Kings 9:7–10], Jezebel's death and subsequent consumption by dogs is simply one in a long list of retributive acts that God allots for the house of Ahab," but Ælfric eliminates most of this chilling passage in order to highlight the manner of Jezebel's impending death.[76]

Jezebel's queenly posture and adornment at her assassination mirror Judith's before she goes to Holofernes.[77] Jezebel, too, "stod uppon anre up-flora, ænlice geglencged, / and gehiwode hire eagan and hire neb mid rude" (lines 341–2; stood on an upper story, singularly adorned, and her eyes and her face made up with blush). While the Vulgate Jezebel "depinxit oculos suos stibio et ornavit caput suum et respexit per fenestram" (4 Kings 9:30; painted her face with stibic stone and adorned her head and looked out of a window), Ælfric adds *ænlice* and the (otherwise only implied) *up-flora* metonymic, in his work, of female sovereignty. While the upper floor of the Judith and Æthelthryth homilies is a cloistered place of regular life, piety, and self-mortification, Jezebel's is a window onto the world where she displays herself and views the realm she rules illegitimately. While Judith is chaste and "geglenged for nanre galnysse" (line 242; adorned for no lustful purpose), Jezebel uses both her power and her beauty to satisfy her adulterous desires. The punishment for abusing royal power is even more serious for Jezebel than for *Beowulf*'s Modthryth.[78] Although she sees Jehu coming, she is (like her son) killed from behind, thrown out the window by his goons, and then trampled by Jehu's horses. Eventually he orders her buried properly,

ac heo wæs eall freten,
butan þam handum anum and þam hæfde ufweardum,
and þam fotwylmum, þurh fule hunda   (lines 352–4)

but she was all eaten, except the hands alone and the upper part of her head and the soles of her feet, by filthy dogs.[79]

132   Nothing Pure

As the Biblical Jehu notes, this desecration of the body goes beyond what Jezebel deserves as a king's daughter. However, the association of dogs with sexual sin, rapacity, religious impurity, and the loss of power make this a fitting punishment for a bad sovereign who seized land improperly and wallowed, we are told, in sexual and theological adulteries.

The dogs who consume Jezebel and lick Ahab's blood dishonour the sovereign body by mutilating it and by making proper burial impossible. They destroy and erase traces of the body. They also associate misrule and sovereign deposition with dogs through a particularly humiliating gesture: the sovereign known for inappropriate appetites is now subject to canine rule and appetite. While sometimes they might feast together, dogs also eat cast-offs that are not even good enough for other wild animals, as we know from a line of Alfred's Prologue to the *Domboc* translated from Exodus: "Eal ðæt flæsc þæt wildeor læfen ne eten ge þæt, ac sellað hit hundum" (§39; All the meat that wild animals leave, do not eat it, but give it to dogs).[80] This is not simply an injunction against eating carrion; it is a principle of agricultural and species management. One allocates to domesticated or semi-wild dogs the trash of humans and wild predators.[81]

Dogs, Sheep Supersessionary Translation

The reason that dogs can symbolize abdicated sovereignty is that, within the theological sources of Old English prose, dogs are figures of supersession. The two familiar gospel sources for this association are the injunction in the Sermon on the Mount, rendered in the Vulgate as "Nolite dare sanctum canibus, neque mittatis margaritas vestras ante porcos, ne forte conculcent eas pedibus suis et conversi disrumpant vos" (Matthew 7:6; Give not that which is holy to dogs, neither cast ye your pearls before swine, lest they trample them under their feet, and turning upon you they tear you [italics removed]) and Christ's initial refusal to exorcise a demon from a Canaanite child: "Non sum missus nisi ad oves quae perierunt domus Israhel ... Non est bonum sumere panem filiorum et mittere canibus" (Matthew 15:24, 26; I was not sent but to the sheep that are lost of the house of Israel ... It is not good to take the bread of the children and to cast it to the dogs). As David M. Freidenreich observes, Christ has "no interest in ministering to Gentiles," but only to wayward Jewish "sheep"; the "bread" of his wisdom and miracles is for Jews ("the children") and not Gentiles ("dogs").[82] Christ relents when the girl's mother argues, "Etiam, Domine, nam et catelli edunt de micis quae cadunt de mensa dominorum suorum"

(Matthew 15:27; Yea, Lord, for the whelps also eat of the crumbs that fall from the table of their masters). Christ does not extend terms of equality to this Gentile woman,[83] but within the context of the "gustatory theology" discussed in greater detail in chapter 2, this episode has far-reaching implications for Gentile inclusion in the community of believers. The Judaean Jewish culture that produced Christ and the disciples discouraged commensality with non-Jews, and although Matthew does not include Jews and Gentiles at the same "table" here, the integration of these groups in table fellowship (as followers of Christ) and their corresponding separation from non-Christians will become, as Freidenreich notes, a central preoccupation of early Christianity.[84]

In the Gospel of Matthew, the "dogs" of the parable are Gentiles, and the children (and lost sheep who require pastorship) are Jews. By the late antique period, however, this image of Gentile debasement and Jewish belovedness had transmuted, thanks to St. John Chrysostom, into a powerful image of Christian supersession of Judaism. The association of dogs with Jews, which became a mainstay of anti-Jewish rhetoric by the twelfth century, dates to Chrysostom's bold fourth-century inversion of terms.[85] As Chrysostom explains: "Although those Jews had been called to the adoption of sons, they fell to kinship with dogs; we who were dogs received the strength ... to rise to the honor of sons ... Christ was speaking to the Canaanite woman when He called the Jews children and the Gentiles dogs. // But see how thereafter the order was changed about: they became dogs, and we became the children."[86] In Chrysostom's influential formulation, characteristic of an anti-Jewish project of extreme exegetical creativity,[87] the Jews have abdicated their position as God's children and "we" (Gentile Christians) have assumed it. These dogs now represent not only what is outside – Gentiles, in gospel terms – but what God has cast off, the rejection of His former beloved: Jews. Chrysostom's inversion became the standard, followed by writers including Bede and Aquinas.[88] As Irven M. Resnick notes, "Christian exegetes understood [these] important Gospel texts ... to be clear references to Jews."[89]

The gospel anecdote of the dogs and the children survives in three fairly similar Old English translations: in the Lindisfarne gospel glosses, in the Rushworth gospel glosses, and in Ælfric's homily on the Second Sunday in Lent. Ælfric closely follows Bede via Smaragdus, narrating the story of the Canaanite woman and explaining:

Þæt israhela folc wæs gyo geteald to godes bearnum, and hæðen folc geond ealle woruld to hundum, for heora fulum ðeawum; Nu is seo endebyrdnys þæra namena awend, mid ðam geleafan; Hi sind gehatene hundas, and we scep. Witodlice se witega cwæð be cristes ehterum, ðe hine acwealdon; Fela hundas me ymbe eodon; Se witega þurh godes gast het ða Iudeiscan cristes slagan hundas, þe hine mid facenfullum mode ymbe eodon; Eft crist sylf cwæð be us. Ic hæbbe oðre scep, þa ðe ne sind of ðyssere eowde, and ða ic sceal lædan, and hi gehyrað mine stemne.[90]

The people Israel were once considered to be God's children, and the pagan people throughout all the world as dogs because of their filthy practices. Now the order of these names is transformed by belief. They are called dogs, and we [are called] sheep. Indeed, the apostle said about Christ's persecutors, who killed him: Many dogs circled me. With God's spirit, the apostle called the Jewish killers of Christ dogs, who in deceitful spirit circled him. Again, Christ himself said about us, "I have other sheep, who are not of this flock, and I will lead them, and they will hear my voice."

Instead of simply reversing the terms dogs and children as Chrysostom does, Ælfric uses the gospel's third term, *scep*, to describe the Christian social body. In doing so, he follows Bede (via Smaragdus) in using not the reference to Jews as sheep in Matthew 15:24 ("I was not sent but to the sheep that are lost of the house of Israel") but rather a verse from John, which in context refers to Gentile believers: "Et alias oves habeo quae non sunt ex hoc ovili; et illas oportet me adducere, et vocem meam audient, et fiet unum ovile et unus pastor" (John 10:16; And other sheep I have that are not of this fold; them also I must bring, and they shall hear my voice, and there shall be one fold and one shepherd).[91] The interpolation of sheep is not only more inclusive of Gentiles than Matthew's usage; it also changes the meaning of *hundas*: where (Gentile) dogs were unclean and excluded in comparison to the Jewish children, here Jewish dogs are predatory in contrast, and in relation, to the lamb of God and to the faithful Christian flock. Ælfric also follows his proximate sources in combining the image of the dog from Matthew 15 with an unrelated canine image from Psalms ("quoniam circumdederunt me canes multi; concilium malignantium obsedit me"; for many dogs have encompassed me; the council of the malignant hath besieged me, Psalms 21:17). This subtle triangulation of Biblical canine and ovine imagery in Ælfric and his sources does not yet resemble the anti-Semitic dogpiles Resnick finds in twelfth-century controversial literature. Yet in Wulfstan we find the dogs of Exodus, Psalms, Kings, Proverbs/2 Peter, and Matthew in sophisticated collusion. It is from this constellation of metonymically related images – the dogs who return to their sin again and again, the dogs who eat what is abandoned, the supersessionary image of debased, hungry, filthy dogs who circle the helpless Christian in a pack – that the men who are "hundum gelicost" arise as an index of the people's corruption and susceptibility to conquest.

The Good Shepherd

Despite their different structures and audiences, Wulfstan's *Sermo Lupi* shares with his *Be Godcundre Warnunge* the skilled and highly selective translation of the Hebrew Bible in order to tie the Danish Conquest to England's sins against God. These homilies should also be seen as elaborating *theories* of supersessionary translation, as sophisticated as Ælfric's although less explicit. Wulfstan's framing performs, through translation and rhetoric about translation, a triple identification. The episcopal translator aligns himself with England as the humiliated (new) Israel, with the lupine pastor who guards the Christian flock against the rapacious dogs of sin and humiliation, and with the church that is both the bearer of salvation and the wounded object of the people's sin. In this final section, I turn to the question of the captive woman and to the flock as, in Wulfstan's words, God's *agenne ceap* (own purchase) to discuss the remedy at which Wulfstan's translations invariably arrive: the restoration of what is God's – that is, ecclesiastical sovereignty.

In the passage I have quoted above, the epithet "his agenne ceap þe he deore gebohte," indicates that these sex criminals wrong not primarily the woman but rather God, her robbed and defrauded purchaser. Wulfstan persistently elaborates a theory of God's human creation as property bought through Christ's sacrifice, and of the Church as keepers of that property, so much so that we understand his urgent injunction, in the *Sermo Lupi*, that Christians "Godes gerihta mid rihte gelæste" (line 27; should lawfully pay God's dues) and lament that "we forhealdað æghwær Godes gerihta ealles to gelome" (lines 29–30; we have everywhere, all too often, held back God's dues) as references to tithes, the withholding of which has exposed the nation to conquest.[92] In Wulfstan's judicial philosophy, protection of what we might call human rights relies on the principle that harm to Christians is harm to God and the Church; this explains, for instance, the inequality before the law of enslaved Christians and other enslaved people. The special purchase of clergy for God, discussed above, makes it equally logical to describe offences against monks, nuns, and priests as particular harms to God's rights.

Wulfstan elaborates this concept of God's property rights in Christians in part through – what else? – translation of the Old Testament, although it is far from a simple translation of the covenant between God and Israel into a New Covenant between Christ and the faithful. Nor is it, as Michael Treschow argues of Alfred's translation of an Exodus passage favouring enslaved Israelites into one favouring enslaved Christians, a kind of universalization of Jewish particularity.[93] On the contrary, it turns a characteristically frightening piece of prophetic exhortation into a theologically coherent rule about episcopal authority and the role of priests in eleventh-century England. In a recurrent passage adapted creatively from material in Ezekiel and Isaiah, Wulfstan describes bishops and priests as hired shepherds of God's sheep, charged with guarding the flock against the devil figured as a wolf or as a *werewulf* (man-wolf):

> Þonne motan þa hyrdas beon swiþe wacore and geornlice clypiende, þe wið þone þeodscaðan folce gescyldan sculan. Þæt syndon bisceopas and mæssepreostas þe godcunde heorde gewarian and bewerian sculon mid wislicre lare ... Ðeah ure heorda hwylc an sceap forgyme, we willað þæt he hit forgylde. And hwæt gefarað þonne æt Godes egeslican dome þa hyrdas, þe ne cunnon gehealdon þa godcundan heorde þe Crist mid his agenum life gebohte?

> Then those shepherds must be very vigilant and calling out adamantly, those who must guard people against the people's enemy. Those are the bishops and priests who must guard and defend the sacred herd with wise teaching ... Even if anyone neglects one sheep of our flock, we will [make] him pay compensation for it. And then at God's terrible judgment what will happen to the shepherds, who do not know how to protect the spiritual flock that Christ bought with his own life?[94]

Pastoral failures, according to this same passage, require an accounting. The ultimate source is Ezekiel 34:10: "Ecce: ego ipse super pastores; requiram gregem meum de manu eorum, et cessare eos faciam ut ultra non pascant gregem, nec pascant amplius pastores semet ipsos, et liberabo gregem meum de ore eorum, et non erit ultra eis in escam" (Behold: I myself come upon the shepherds; I will require my flock at their hand, and I will cause them to cease from feeding the flock any more, neither shall the shepherds feed themselves any more, and I will deliver my flock from their mouth, and it shall no more be meat for them). This piece of theological economics, translated from the Vulgate and adapted to describe English ecclesiastical rights and responsibilities, is so crucial to Wulfstan's sense of the Church's role in society that the passage appears four times in his work. It can be found twice in the *Institutes of Polity*, in Wulfstan's legislation for Cnut, and in a Latin-Old

English piece, similar in composition to *Be Godcundre Warnunge*, combining portions of Ezekiel and Isaiah.[95] Wulfstan uses the divine first-person plural (*"ure* heorda," *"we* willað"), implying that not only God but also the Church is also robbed and requires compensation from pastors for lost members of the flock.

The Church requires a financially and politically empowered episcopate, working in concert with secular leadership, to protect God's flock.[96] Indeed, as Jay Paul Gates notes, in Wulfstan's legal project bishops ideally have "responsibility for, and authority over, everyone," including secular lords and the king.[97] The pastoral imperative to speak and act comes directly from Isaiah, as Wulfstan notes, "Ealswa Issaias se witega hwilum be þam spræc: *Canes muti non ualentes latrare*. Ealswilce he cwæde þæt gemidlede hundas ne beorcað to nahte" (Just so the prophet Isaiah once said about this: *Silent dogs cannot bark*. Just so, he said that muzzled dogs do not bark at anything).[98] Here, Wulfstan follows Alcuin of York, King Alfred, and Ælfric in translating a passage from Isaiah to elide the failed human shepherd with a sheepdog who doesn't bark when the wolf comes near.[99] In the *Letter to Wulfsige*, Ælfric admonishes priests to remember, "*Canes muti non possunt latrare*; þa dumban hundas ne magon beorcan. We sceolon beorcan and bodigan þam læwedum, þe læs hy for larlyste losian sceoldan" (*Silent dogs cannot bark*; speechless dogs cannot bark. We must bark and preach to the unlearned, lest they be destroyed through ignorance).[100] In muzzling the dogs, Wulfstan departs from Alfred and Ælfric, both of whom describe the dogs as *dumb[an]*, a more literal translation of *muti* (silent or nonverbal).[101] As Lionarons observes, the image of the muzzle, of constraint, emphasizes the dogs' lack of self-control.[102] The dog is never a figure of successful protection – no pastor ever compares himself to a dog – but always of failure, impotence, and incapacity in the face of lupine success. It is, presumably, in opposition to these figures that Wulfstan nicknames himself *Lupus*. On its face a risky pun, this ironic nickname with which Wulfstan flamboyantly signs the *Sermo Lupi ad Anglos* indicates a pastor as powerful, and bold, as the ravening enemy: set a wolf to guard against one. The metaphor reaches back into the fantasy of wolf turned protector that Ælfric elaborates in the martyrdom of St. Edmund.[103] While Matthew E. Spears argues that early English thought makes wolves the particular sign of "tyrannical kings" and their cruelties,[104] the much-touted exemption of wolves from human affairs seems, in fact, to allow great moral flexibility. In particular, Wulfstan's nickname for himself, *Lupus*, which Keynes speculatively labels "a warning to [Wulfstan's] flock that he was out on the prowl," indicates that a pastor could proudly avow the ferocity and the sovereign associations of a wolf without being confused, in the people's minds, with the human wolves (and dogs) whom Wulfstan frequently names as threats to them.[105]

What makes the sex criminals in *Sermo Lupi* "hundum gelicost" is not only that they commit violence, or that they wallow in filth, but also that they steal (and abuse and sell) what is God's, just as wolves and dogs attack a flock and as the dogs of the parable eat the children's bread. Dogs have nothing that is properly theirs – everything they consume is stolen or cast off.[106] Violence and sexual impropriety – and their nexus at sexual violence and the trafficking of Christians – are property offences against God and therefore against ecclesiastical authority. Therefore, while one rhetorical effect of Wulfstan's mastery of Hebrew Biblical tropes of human bestiality, slavery, sexual violence, and property relations is to identify with the sinning and humiliated members of his congregation, another far more consequential effect is to identify the episcopal voice as a representative of the master whose flock is endangered both by ravening wild dogs and muzzled sheepdogs. That is, the bishop who calls out against sin is, by definition, the one authorized both to evaluate and collect God's debt. In the *Sermo Lupi*, where Wulfstan partially subverts the captive woman trope, he identifies himself with the humiliated body of the English people, presenting himself as another of God's enslaved, another of the English exposed to shame. Read in the context of his judicial philosophy, this identification goes even further: Wulfstan speaks for the church–state apparatus that represents – that is, the only institution authorized to represent and protect – powerless people who belong to God. This rhetorically dazzling reparative project, which finds juridical and authorial sovereignty in identifying with the enslaved and humiliated, becomes, in these terms, almost too familiar. Wulfstan's bold strategy of supersessionary translation differs from that of his contemporaries in that it minimizes difference, attempting fully to appropriate Jewish texts without a compensatory strategy of rejection or separation. For Wulfstan, author of Leviticus 26,[107] there is simply no need to distinguish between the fully appropriated and the superseded aspects of Jewish law, or for that matter between translation, exhortation, and legal code: there is no remnant of a prior text that survives and requires disposal.

Afterword: Cleansings

Can we now even speak of the formation of medieval English culture, or of the medieval English nation, without also discussing the Jews? Anti-Judaism has become undeniably central to the picture of medieval English national development and even of European colonialism, Islamophobia, and racism. Geraldine Heng's 2018 *The Invention of Race in the European Middle Ages*, for instance, demonstrates that English experiments in anti-Jewish racialization, discrimination, and ethnic cleansing in the twelfth and thirteenth centuries created some of the earliest models of European racism and race-based state terror.[1] *Nothing Pure* illuminates the paradoxical process by which the thirteenth-century dehumanization and othering of Jews was articulated well over a century earlier in the supersessionary translation of the Hebrew Bible, via the Septuagint and Vulgate, into Old English. In this conclusion, I wish to reflect on two images drawn from the Hebrew Bible, that of the captive woman and that of digestion and emesis, that have proven through-lines for this argument.

Nothing Pure

The book's title, *Nothing Pure*, is drawn from Origen's description of Jewish law as a woman captured in war and forced into concubinage, a metaphor that is itself drawn from a Deuteronomic law obsolete by Origen's time.[2] Origen's striking formulation of this image, which I have discussed at greater length in the introduction and chapter 5, transforms a Hebrew Biblical law into both a figure for and a model of the ethic of supersession translation. The Christian exegete must violently purify his captive, the Jewish text, because, as Origen observes in his seventh homily on Leviticus, "She has nothing in her head, nothing in her hands, lest she bring something unclean or dead either in her thoughts or in her deeds. For the women of our enemies have nothing pure because there is no wisdom among them with which something unclean was not mixed."[3] Since Jewish law and Jewish texts such as Leviticus contain "nothing pure" (*nihil ... mund[us]*) and are freighted with death and corruption, they must be hollowed out, evacuated of original content. Yet they are not wholly unclean either. Although they come from an enemy culture, they contain something of value. This particular Deuteronomic verse contains a streak of cruel xenophobic misogyny that Origen now deploys to redefine the Jews as alien foes.[4] This early Christian act of supersessionary translation, which has had an outsized influence on Western Christian theories of translation, sets up Jewish and Christian texts as the most intimate of enemies while foreshadowing the elements of appropriation, repudiation, and fantastic creativity that this book describes in the Old English supersessionary translations of the late tenth and early eleventh centuries. Indeed, although or perhaps because this law is archaic, and although the original passage does not itself refer to purity or cleansing, the captive figure metonymically contains the entire Hebrew Biblical theology of purity upon which Origen draws in order to label Jewish law "something unclean" (*immunditia aliqua*).

Although this is not a book about Origen, I wish as I close to draw further upon his provocative invocation of the woman/enemy/Jewish text in whom there is "nothing pure" – yet who is slated for purification and sacralized enjoyment. This supersessionary directive exemplifies what it urges. Here Origen appropriates from the Hebrew Bible, or Old Testament, what seems to be a directive about carnal purity in order to fully spiritualize it, to appropriate it into the house of the translator as fully Christian. Yet as I mention above, the Biblical law says nothing about purification; Origen is importing this concept so that he may translate and supersede it. Such sleights of hand are necessary to supersessionary translation, which must continually expose and misrepresent the original in order to convert it to a new meaning. In the relatively straightforward variety of supersessionary translation practised by the anonymous translators of the Old English Leviticus, form skilfully follows function; as in Steven F. Kruger's indelible image of the undead "Jewish body" reanimated by Christians for the purposes of banishment,[5] the prohibition against consuming blood surfaces only to vanish misleadingly within the superseded realm of animal sacrifice. Within this translation economy, the problem of accounting for a carnal remnant of Jewish practice becomes an opportunity to present parts of the Hebrew Bible as archaic and partial historical narrative, both Jewish textual corpse and Christian archive.

As a method, supersessionary translation is very well suited to the objectification, appropriation, and exoticization of an essentialized Jewish legalism. In reality, it is not unusual for a people to eat certain meats and not others, to segregate waste, to build elaborate houses of worship, and to prescribe sexual mores that suit their existing power structures. Medieval English Christians did all these things, and as I discuss in chapters 1 and 2, they relied heavily on Biblical laws for guidance. But this book has argued that purity structures are agile and productive, and that laws about food, sexuality, and the body translated from the Hebrew Bible or Septuagint, via the Vulgate, become something quite different in Old English. In Ælfric's translations, taxonomies of *kashrut* can be translated to consolidate the human as Christian. The Old English word *clæn*, which renders the Hebrew concept טָהוֹר (*tahor*) as it passes through Latin *mundus*, supports specifically monastic and ecclesiastical forms of celibacy.

Origen's fantasy of the captive woman's empty hands (*nihil in manibus*) strikingly contrasts with the image of the Biblical heroine Judith's hands, which hold a sword and, later, a vanquished foe's head. These hands appear in chapter 4 of this book as instruments of sacred political sovereignty that punish tyrannical rule: "he ofsloh nu to niht on minum handum his folces feond!" (lines 271–2; And tonight through my hands He killed the enemy of His people!) Her hands must be understood as the sacred instruments not only of execution but also of Holofernes's desecration and exposure. Judith's narrative appears here not as subversion or anti-type of the captive woman trope, for it too relies on the subjugation of women in wartime and the threat of rape.[6] Instead, this Jewish fiction becomes, in Old English via Latin translation, a piece of Benedictine political theology in which the tyrant's head, not the captive woman's, is filled with uncleanness, nothingness, and death. This chapter demonstrates that Ælfric's translation of Judith's Jewish observance into monastic and priestly chastity (and of her Biblical story into Old English hagiography) subvent his formulation of the *ænlic*, the multiply singular exception that can oppose *anweald*, unjust power. In linking supersessionary translation, the chaste body, and the sovereign exception, Ælfric experiments with the idea of abbatical sovereignty as divinely backed political force.

Finally, Origen's ascription of impure, valueless, deathly nullity to a nameless enemy woman (whom he names, however, as Jewish law) resonates with Wulfstan's generic description of a priest's wife as "Nis ... ænig oðer þing butan deofles grin" (nothing but a devil's snare),[7] as examined in chapter 3 of this book. As Susanna Drake notes, Origen's fantasy of reading/enslaving the captive woman is entwined with an argument for Christian celibacy; he locates carnality as both sexuality and literality in the "feminized, Jewish text" that must be purified by the chaste masculine Christian reader.[8] While Ælfric translates Jewish laws about marriage and circumcision as a temporally distant heterosexual ideal against which the decidedly non-heterosexual monastic family and the imposition of priestly celibacy appear as desirable supersessionary successors, Wulfstan's writing on the same topic locates sexual sin in impure vehicles faintly recognizable, in his description, as real women. Origen's apparently figurative endorsement of sexual violence and enslavement provides a glimpse of the material structures of violence that supported late antique and medieval societies, and evokes Wulfstan's identification with, and power over, the enslaved and abused in early eleventh-century England, which I have explored in chapter 5 as a key to his practice of supersessionary translation.

One can no more purify something through translation than through violence, since translation is by definition a complex relation with something external. In the case of supersessionary translation, it is a relation between the Jewish text and the Christian scholar who attempts to transmit, transform, and repudiate it. The title *Nothing Pure* is not a cry against religious structures such as kosher law or chastity, or against secular purity regimes such as food inspection, regular bathing, and separating one's recycling, nor against the material cleansings and separations required by any religious or secular form of life. When it comes to cultural purity, however, this book must return to the figure of the enslaved – who stands for but does not dissolve into the Christianized Jewish text – to insist on both the futility and the great cost of such cleansings.

Digestion and Emesis

It will not have escaped readers' notice that the matter of food is at the heart of supersessionary translation, and therefore is a thread that runs centrally through this book. So frequently a potent marker of Jewish–Christian–Muslim difference,[9] Scriptural food prohibitions emerge in the work of Ælfric as figures for Christian translation and as vehicles of Jewish dehumanization. However productive its metaphorical uses, food law also fails to shed its literal meanings, retaining value as a system of materially differentiating acceptable and unacceptable foodstuffs, as in the case of contaminated liquids. Religious segregation at table, a sometime Jewish practice taken up by early Christians, retains importance for Ælfric as a means of excluding heretics. Moreover, the observation of kosher law is a positive in the case of the Old Testament *halgan* (saints) Judith and Maccabees.

The supersessionary project of the translator is to find a way to spiritualize all these meanings, just as Christ's sacrifice and its repetition in the Eucharist spiritualizes the superseded Temple sacrifice – but that is no model, since the Eucharist, too, is bread and wine. Indeed, there is no real road map for this. Bede says that just as the cow regurgitates and rechews its cud, Caedmon turns Genesis into a sweet English-Christian Creation song, but he does not say that Caedmon turns cud into song.[10] Nor even does Origen, who redeems the at-first revolting (to him) Leviticus by claiming for it a deep spiritual meaning for Christians, turn away from the language of food; on the contrary, he says that while Jewish law might not be infant milk, it is digestible and tasty in its own way. As both John Penniman and Gillian Feeley-Harnik observe, theology *is* food, and vice versa.[11] But food is not only theology: food is life and what is beyond mere life. It counts out daily and seasonal time, it demarcates and holds the community, it makes and breaks the body. Digestion is, moreover, not only a figure for translation; it is, as J. Allan Mitchell observes, translation itself.[12] As scholars including Carolyn Walker Bynum, Geraldine Heng, and Karl Steel have observed, the sacred and profane implications of this gustatory translation animate medieval Christian thought.[13] Food matters. The solutions Ælfric and the anonymous translators find to the problems of Jewish food law therefore never actually do away with consumption, digestion, excretion, and commensality. On the contrary, for supersessionary translation, food is a site of compulsive appropriation and resignification between the Jewish and the Christian that can never be reduced to the false opposition of letter/flesh and spirit.

Let us return to Christian England's bad digestion. Heschel has asked how Christians can receive nourishment from Jewish law if, in supersessionary visions of Scriptural digestion, they are continually vomiting it. Bede would answer, no doubt, that there is a difference between the dogs that return to their filth and the kosher animals like cows and sheep that ruminate – that is, they regurgitate and then digest their food again, but do not expel it from their bodies first. In ambitiously linking the ecclesiastical history of the English to the history of creation, he likens Caedmon, whom Robert Stanton calls "the foundational English translator," to a beast chewing its cud. The tremendous political importance of the ruminant Caedmon, for Bede and for later English readers, is that his poem aligns the first act of English literature, which is also the first English translation of any part of the Old Testament from Latin, with the act of creation and the history of the English church with the history of the world.[14] Ælfric explains that when God instructs the Jews to eat those clean animals that chew their cud and to reject those, like pigs and dogs, that do not, this prefigures the eventual difference between Christians, who will become the holy ruminants, and Jews, who will become the unclean disbelievers. Wulfstan suggests that such abjections are mobile and transferable – they can travel from supersessionary translation to any object, including fellow English. In both authors, the imagery of digestion and emesis, and of clean and unclean beasts, transforms Hebrew Biblical metaphor into assertions of English Christian sovereignty. These images guide the cultural translation of Jewish texts into early English and eventually, I speculate, suggest a sovereign right to expel Jews not only from the Christian socius but also from the land.

The disgust and ambivalence with which anti-Jewish scholars medieval and modern have regarded Jewish traces in the English Christian past seem to draw authentically upon Hebrew Biblical idiom. I write here of the Biblical connection, which will become so salient in anti-Semitic metaphor, between gustatory disgust and the sovereign right of expulsion. As Brent Strawn observes, the Hebrew Bible understands nausea and vomiting as, primarily, a non-human (divine, terrestrial, and/or occasionally cetacean) judgment upon the human.[15] Vomiting is usually an expression of the land's rejection and disgust; it is also nearly always a forceful enactment of the separation between sacred and profane – or, speaking even more broadly, between what belongs and does not belong in a particular site or vessel – as in the case of Jonah, whom the whale rejects emetically more as an act of mercy than of disgust. This separation informs the Hebrew Bible, particularly the law codes. In the book of Leviticus, the legal narrative is punctuated with frequent discussions of what the land of Canaan will do, or what will happen to it, if the ancient Israelites do or don't follow the law. As Bible scholar Esias E. Meyer notes, Leviticus portrays the land as highly agential: "an actor with its own will," and a "subject of the kinds of verbs which do not always convey good news for the people living on it": becoming polluted, prostituting herself, resting, giving, taking pleasure, and most notably, vomiting.[16] In Leviticus, the people are repeatedly warned that lawlessness will result in the land expelling them, vomiting them out for making it unclean, messages that Wulfstan echoes and rewrites in his homilies. One Biblical warning is itself concerned with food. Following a list of sexual and other prohibitions, God warns:

> You shall faithfully observe all My laws and all My regulations, lest the land to which I bring you to settle in spew you out. You shall not follow the practices of the nation that I am driving out before you. For it is because they did all these things that I abhorred them and said to you: You shall possess their land, for I will give it to you to possess, a land flowing with milk and honey. I the LORD am your God who has set you apart from other peoples. So you shall set apart the clean beast from the unclean, the unclean bird from the clean. You shall not draw abomination upon yourselves through beast or bird or anything with which the ground is alive, which I have set apart for you to treat as unclean. You shall be holy to Me, for I the LORD am holy, and I have set you apart from other peoples to be Mine. (Leviticus 20:22–6)[17]

It is Jewish law itself – the sacrifices and food laws discussed in this very passage – that offends the supersessionary stomach, and yet English Christians themselves will, in many cases, digest and regurgitate Leviticus and reassert Christian authority over the Old Testament to structure their own laws, prohibitions, warnings, and exhortations. The book has located inflection points in Old English legal and religious writing for several political ideas that have been key to English national formation in the *longue durée*, suggesting that all of them are linked to Christian supersession of the Hebrew Bible and Old Testament. While I do not have the capacity to trace the full history of any of these concepts – histories that also stretch far outside of national boundaries – the book suggests a central role for supersessionary translation, and for appropriated and alienated versions of Jewish law, within the development of the English state. One such idea, elaborated in chapter 4, is political sovereignty rooted in chastity, a Christian idea translated from Jewish theology that forms the basis not only of abbatical claims to self-rule but also of the cults of virgin monarchs. Another, the subject of chapter 5, is the expansion of united church–state authority in the name of protecting the nation, identified rhetorically with its most vulnerable and exploited members, from sexual violence and humiliation. Finally, the subject of the entire book is the temporal non-belonging of those who follow superseded laws and the power of translation to establish sovereignty. *Nothing Pure* thus explains the temporal and racial logics that have allowed these same structures to be periodically re-activated. While this book is unable to reach into the post-Conquest period in order to trace the uptake, continuities, and discontinuities of these political concepts, in tracing the narrative strategies by which English culture imposed temporal distance on Jews, it provides a new literary-historical perspective on how the racialized supersession of Jews and other religious enemies became integral to a progressive national narrative.[18]

The idea that Jewish doctrine is bad food that ought to be thrown up, or (later) that Jews themselves nauseate the Christian social body, or that Jews themselves wallow in bodily waste, would become a medieval commonplace. The chronicler William of Hoveden, narrating London's 1189 anti-Jewish pogrom, calls upon the familiar Biblical image of a dog returning to its vomit to describe a lapsed Jewish convert to Christianity who had briefly survived the massacre.[19] Here, Judaism itself is the vomit, Jews the unclean dogs who consume it. Richard of Devizes uses a different emetic metaphor in his satirical discussion of the same massacre, noting that Winchester behaved with restraint towards its Jewish citizens: "It did not want to vomit forth the load on its stomach by which it was opposed, and took care of its bowels in the meantime, modestly concealing the trouble, till an opportune time when she might once and for ever evacuate the whole mass of disease."[20] Here Jews are bad, contaminated food that other neighbours cannot digest; they must be converted into vomit and feces for civic survival. Richard praises Winchester for not massacring its Jews as London, York, and other cities did in 1189–90 (a chaotic and immediate form of removal akin to vomit) but for digesting them properly and expelling them in an orderly and lawful way as if they were feces – not, perhaps, as well as a ruminant might digest, but properly enough. When Richard suggests that more violent civic bodies than Winchester vomited out their Jews, he uses a common Christian, anti-Jewish figure drawn from Leviticus as well as from other parts of the Hebrew Bible,[21] but he transfers the right to expel from the land itself to these bodies. As Heather Blurton has brilliantly demonstrated, these images must be read in concert with the *Cronicon*'s overall parodic engagement with digestive themes: Jews are not the only objects of England's (and its king's) improper eating and bad digestion.[22] Yet the idea of English Jews as indigestible and intolerable is no joke; it goes hand in hand, as Blurton and Anthony Bale demonstrate in their discussions of this flamboyant satire, with real pogroms and expulsions.

These alignments would pick up steam during the expulsion period of the thirteenth through fifteenth centuries, in which Christian monarchs and polities throughout the Christian West arrogated to themselves the powers held in Leviticus by God and the land: the power to expel. As Sara Ahmed explains of such doomed attempts to purify the social body, "Such an expulsion will never be over."[23] Such expulsion is marked by endless reassertions, both in texts and on people's bodies, of a separation that will never be accomplished – both because of the extensive reliance by Christianity on Judaism's theology and legal structures and because of the transitive power of hate, in which the same fears and hatreds, which do not go away with the first expulsion, must be renewed and, often, transferred to new internal enemies.

Notes

Introduction: A Brief History of Supersessionary Disgust

1 I use the term "Jewish law" here to encompass only those laws enumerated in the Hebrew Bible and discussed in the Septuagint, since the Talmud (late antique and medieval Jewish law, which considerably revised Biblical precepts) was more or less unknown to the writers I discuss in this book. I also, at times, use the term "Jewish" with a certain deliberate anachronism when referring to ancient Israelites real and imagined. I use "Jew" and "Jewish" in these ways not to essentialize Jewish law or to freeze it in time, nor to deny the changing concepts of peoplehood designated by the different terms, but rather to re-racinate, so to speak, what we alternatively call "Old Testament" and "Biblical" laws and to highlight their connections to living medieval and modern Judaisms.
2 Kruger, *The Spectral Jew*, esp. 11. Kruger draws the notion of spectrality from Derrida, *Specters of Marx*, esp. 1–60. See also Janet Thormann, for whom Kruger's concept of spectrality is crucial to understanding the role of Jews and Jewish textuality in Old English poetry and West Saxon politics. Thormann, "The Jewish Other," 1.
3 Biddick, *The Typological Imaginary*, 1–2, provides a helpful summary of supersessionary thinking.
4 Litvak, *The Un-Americans*, 70. Litvak refers to assimilated US Jews in the twentieth century.
5 All references to Ælfric's dates draw from Kleist, *The Chronology and Canon of Ælfric of Eynsham*. See also Clemoes, "The Chronology of Ælfric's Works."
6 See Pareles, "Giving Yiddish the Devil."
7 On anti-Semitism in Old English literature, see especially Scheil, *The Footsteps of Israel*; Lavezzo, *The Accommodated Jew*, 28–63; Zacher, "Jews and

Judaizing as Pathologies in the Anglo-Saxon Imagination"; Thormann; Younge, "The New Heathens"; Estes, "Reading Ælfric in the Twelfth Century."

8 This is a book about narrow, elite English Christian uses – in some readers' eyes, misuses – of Jewish texts, and not about Jewish traditions or texts in themselves. To essentialize Judaism as a single object or "faith" is to profoundly misunderstand the history of Judaisms; this is true as well for Christianities and Islams. See, *inter alia*, D. Boyarin, *Border Lines*; Hughes, *Shared Identities*; Becker and Reed, eds., *The Ways That Never Parted*. The reader will, I hope, pardon my use of "Jewish"/"Judaism" (and indeed "Christian"/"Christianity," although these terms are not exactly parallel). This is a form of shorthand that reflects the absence of real Jews and Judaisms, and to a certain degree of other Christianities, from the works I am discussing. Throughout the book, I refer to works in Jewish and religious studies that can be helpful to readers interested in the complexity of Judaism and other Abrahamic traditions.

9 K. Davis, "Boredom, Brevity and Last Things"; Stephenson, *The Politics of Language*, esp. 158–87; see also Stanton, *The Culture of Translation*, 145–56.

10 Anidjar, *Semites*, 5.

11 As Treharne and others demonstrate, the works I discuss in this study continued to be read, used, and copied into the twelfth century. See Treharne, "Making Their Presence Felt." On my use of "genocidal" to describe forced removal and mass killing, both judicial and extra-judicial, of Jews in thirteenth-century England, see Pareles, "Already/Never," 238n25. On Jewish racialization in twelfth- and thirteenth-century England in the context of the history of racism, see Heng, *The Invention of Race*, 27–31, 55–109; Heng, "England's Dead Boys." On medieval anti-Semitism in the history of racism, colonialism, and chattel slavery, see also J. Boyarin, *The Unconverted Self*, esp. 109–18; Wynter, "Unsettling," esp. 266; Gil Anidjar, *Blood*, 83–135; and M. Lindsey Kaplan, *Figuring Racism in Medieval Christianity*. On the centrality of Jews to medieval English identity formation and nation-building, see, *inter alia*, Barkey and Katznelson, "States, Regimes, and Decisions"; Lampert-Weissig, "The Transnational Wandering Jew"; A. Boyarin, *The Christian Jew and the Unmarked Jewess*; Lavezzo, *The Accommodated Jew*; Blurton, *Inventing William of Norwich*; Krummel, *Crafting Jewishness in Medieval England*; Strickland, "Edward I, Exodus, and England." On the relationship between racialization and colonialism in England prior to the Norman Conquest, see, *inter alia*, Lavezzo, *Angels on the Edge of the World*, 27–45, and Lumbley, "The 'Dark Welsh.'"

12 On temporal abjection in Expulsion-era anti-Jewish cultural work, see *inter alia*, Pareles, esp. 223–5.

13 J. Simpson, *Burning to Read*, esp. 2–9; Gow, "The Bible in Germanic," esp. 198–9; Gow, "The Contested History of a Book: The German Bible of the Later Middle Ages and Reformation in Legend, Ideology, and Scholarship"; Gow, "Challenging the Protestant Paradigm." See Daniell, *The Bible in English*, *passim*, 125, for an excellent example of the narrative equating vernacular Bible translation, the Protestant Reformation, and vigorous "intellectual freedom"; see Simpson, esp. 26–9, 117–18, 134–5, for a detailed refutation.
14 See Simpson, esp. 2–9, 26–8, 101–2.
15 In general, I use the term "Old Testament" rather than "Hebrew Bible" for the materials I discuss in this book. These are not synonyms but refer to corpora that differ in small, significant ways. The Book of Judith, a work I attend to in this study, is included in the Old Testament but not the Hebrew Bible (indeed, there is no reliably attested ancient Hebrew version at all). I also find it more appropriate to refer to the materials translated by Ælfric and his contemporaries as the Old Testament because they are drawn from the Vulgate and other Latin Christian versions of the Bible. For my purpose, "vernacular" translations are those that render Biblical materials into living languages. It is a historically relative term, encompassing the Vulgate at the time of its creation, but not in the tenth and eleventh centuries. As Frans van Liere, 184, points out, "The Latin Bible of the Middle Ages was, of course, itself a translation, intended to make the text of the Bible available for the average reader of the late Roman Empire." All Hebrew quotations and English translations from the Hebrew Bible are from *JPS*, unless otherwise marked. All Latin Vulgate Bible quotations and English translations thereof are from Edgar and Kinney, eds., *The Vulgate Bible: Douay-Rheims Translation*, unless otherwise marked. Septuagint sources can be found in the bibliography. All references to other Bibles are marked. All translations from Old and Middle English, unless otherwise cited, are my own. Translations from other languages, including my own translations, are attributed. I omit editorial marks when quoting modern editions of medieval texts and the Bible, and occasionally modify punctuation accordingly.
16 For a succinct discussion of the problem, see *inter alia*, Asad, *The Concept of Cultural Translation*.
17 Dube, "Consuming a Colonial Cultural Bomb," 41. Dube, 40–1 writes of her dismay and shame upon encountering the story of the demon(s) Legion, expelled by Christ in the gospels of Mark and Matthew, in Setswana: "There I found our sacred *Badimo* scared in front of another divine being: they trembled and begged Jesus to leave them alone ... My reading moment itself was a violent experience."
18 Meens, *Translating the Devil*, 56. See also Meyer, "Modernity and Enchantment," and Margaret Jolly's account of the strategy's limited

success. Jolly, "Devils, Holy Spirits, and the Swollen God." For an alternative view, see Solomon K. Avotri on a spiritually resonant translation of Mark 5:1–20 (311–25). Avotri, "The Vernacularization of Scripture and African Beliefs."

19 Niranjana, *Siting Translation*, 3. Said, *Orientalism*, esp. 1–48.
20 "When you take the field against your enemies, and the Lord your God delivers them into your power and you take them captive, and you see among the captives a beautiful woman and you desire her and would take her to wife, you shall bring her into to your house, and she shall trim her hair, pare her nails, and discard her captive's garb. She shall spend a month's time in your house lamenting her father and mother; after that you may come to her and possess her, and she shall be your wife. Then, should you no longer want her, you must release her outright. You must not sell her for money: since you had your will of her, you must not enslave her," Deut. 21:10–14 (JPS). However, Heszer observes, "It is clearly implied here that the woman remains a slave" in her captor's house and does not become a (free) wife. Hezser, *Jewish Slavery in Antiquity*, 193; here, Heszer provides an alternative translation of the Hebrew Biblical passage to clarify that sex, not marriage, is at issue.

By Origen's time, Jewish scholars were apparently troubled and embarrassed by the existence of this passage in the Torah, although some have rationalized it as intended to restrict, rather than encourage, wartime rape. See, *inter alia*, Diamond, "The Deuteronomic *Pretty Woman* Law." For a frank history of Jewish and Christian interpretations, see Wilke, who doubts that the law was ever in force and sees it as essentially allegorical. Wilke, "The Soul Is a Foreign Woman," esp. 130.

21 Origen, "Homily 7 [on Leviticus]" §6.7, 150.
22 Origen, "In Leviticum Homilia VII," §6. Although delivered in Greek, the Levitical homilies survive only in Rufinus's widely circulated Latin translation. That Bede had access to at least one of the *Homilies on Leviticus* suggests that early medieval English writers might have known the captive woman passage directly (see Lapidge, 221); several late eleventh-century insular witnesses also survive (see Gneuss and Lapidge nos. 239, 669, 745; pp. 191, 511, 536). The metaphor of the translated text as captive woman also circulated in Jerome's Letter 70 and Hrabanus Maurus's *De institutione clericorum*, both of which describe the text as Gentile rather than Jewish.
23 See, *inter alia*, Rey, "Reexamination of the Foreign Female Captive."
24 Dinshaw, *Chaucer's Sexual Poetics*, esp. 22–5; Lampert-Weissig, *Gender and Jewish Difference*, 41–2; Drake, *Origen's Veils*, esp. 832–3. On allegorical reading and the inseparability of racial and theological anti-Semitism, see Freinkel, "The Merchant of Venice."

25 See de Lubac, *Medieval Exegesis*, 211–24; Walton, "New Wine in Old Skins," 21. On the influence of patristic exegetical translation theories, see Copeland, *Rhetoric, Hermeneutics*, esp. 42–55.
26 This is not to say that English and Latin are not sometimes treated as "original" languages of divine inspiration, or that "original" is exactly equivalent to first; the Greek Septuagint is one example of a Bible text that is both translation and, from a certain perspective, original. See Seidman *Faithful Renderings*, 37–72, on early Jewish–Christian debates about the Septuagint.
27 See Seidman on Martin Luther's struggle to de-Judaize his famously accessible German-language Bible. Seidman, *Faithful Renderings*, 115–21, 129–33. See also the American Bible Society's W.A. Smalley on universalizing an "Old Testament rooted in the narrow self-view of a small ethnic group" and grappling with host-culture theology. Smalley, *Translation as Mission*, esp. 178.
28 Nida, *Toward a Science of Translating*, 167.
29 Jennings, *The Christian Imagination*, esp. 119–68. On the myth of Christianity's supersession of racial logic, see, *inter alia*, Buell, *Why This New Race*. See D. Boyarin on the reliance of Christian universalism upon "suppression of [Jewish] cultural difference." *A Radical Jew*, 26, 201–24.
30 Heschel, *The Aryan Jesus*, esp. 106–13; Gerdmar, "The National Socialist Bible." As Alon Confino notes, Nazis also physically destroyed Hebrew Scriptures in public spectacles. For a thoughtful discussion of the relationship of this destruction to the Holocaust's temporalities, see Confino, *A World without Jews*, esp. 115–41.
31 Derrida, "What Is a 'Relevant' Translation?"; Venuti, "Translating Derrida on Translation," 252. See, however, Chow, *Entanglements*, esp. 117. For an alternative reading, see Emmanuelle Ertel, "Derrida on Translation and his (Mis)reception in America."
32 See Drake, *Slandering the Jew*, 38–58, on Origen as an architect of supersession.
33 "In Numeros Homilia XXVII," §1.3.
34 "Homily 27," §1.3. This English translation is Scheck's in Origen, *Homilies on Numbers*, 168. One might translate "offenditur continuo animus, et quasi non suum refugit cibum" in any number of ways. I suggest "his spirit is immediately offended and he recoils as if it is not his proper food." Contemporary Protestant commentator Ephraim Radner translates this passage: "[P]rovide someone a reading from Leviticus, and at once the listener will gag and push it away as if it were some bizarre food. He came, after all, to learn how to honor God, to take in the teachings that concern justice and piety. But instead he is now hearing about the ritual of burnt sacrifices!" Radner is certainly stretching the point, but he accurately

154 Notes to pages 10–13

captures Origen's comparison of Leviticus to offensive food. Radner, *Leviticus*, 17.

35 See Daniell, *The Bible in English*, 5, for a contemporary account of "revulsion" provoked by "the details of [Israelite] tribal law." On Origen's theology of nourishment, see especially Penniman, *Raised on Christian Milk*, 109–37.

36 Penniman, esp. 5; Feeley-Harnik, *The Lord's Table*, esp. 107.

37 Heschel, "Theological Bulimia," 189. Heschel is drawing upon Kristeva; it is salutary to formulate the Christian–Jewish relation of translation as a mother–daughter relation rather than, as Jerome and Origen do, a relationship of rape.

38 Ahmed, *Strange Encounters*, 38–54; Ahmed, *The Cultural Politics of Emotion*, 82–100.

39 I generally avoid the use of "Anglo-Saxon" to describe early English people or Old English, and of "Anglo-Saxonist" to describe scholarship or scholars. I make exceptions in two cases: in quotations, which I leave unaltered, and when describing research that draws racialized connections between pre-Conquest English literature/history and modern English (or white settler) national character. Many scholars of Old English literature have been, in this sense, "Anglo-Saxonists." See Ellard, *Anglosaxon(ist) Pasts, Post Saxon Futures*, esp. 20–7. For an early critical use of "Anglo-Saxonism" to mean a theoretical orientation to the study of early English history and literature that promotes racism and imperialism, see Horsman, "Origins of Racial Anglo-Saxonism"; Horsman, *Race and Manifest Destiny*. See also, *inter alia*, Rambaran-Olm, "A Wrinkle in Medieval Time"; Rambaran-Olm and Wade, "The Many Myths of the Term 'Anglo-Saxon'"; Remein, "ISAS Should Probably Change Its Name"; Wilton, What Do We Mean by *Anglo-Saxon*?"

40 Soames, *The Anglo-Saxon Church*, 125.

41 Soames, 252–3.

42 See D. Boyarin, *The Jewish Gospels*, 102–28.

43 On long nineteenth-century medievalism, racism, and Anglo-American colonialism, see 201n45, above. See Fazioli, *The Mirror of the Medieval*, 71–92, on German imperialism and medieval studies before 1945. On "genteel" anti-Semitism as a key element of white Anglo-American respectability, see Julius, *Trials of the Diaspora*, esp. xxxix.

44 Fabian, *Time and the Other*, 31, emphasis removed.

45 See Krummel, *Medieval Postcolonial Jew*, esp. 1–28. As K. Davis notes, Bede institutes medieval Christian views of sacred time, "ground[ing] Christian political order by attaching it, by way of the *anno domini* and the biblical supersession of the New Testament over the Old Testament (which is also to say Christian history over Jewish history), to a division

in sacred time." He also shows that Christians must reify the movement of sacred time by participating in it – that is, observing the annual liturgy and the seasonal festivals that replay sacred history and in so doing hasten its longed-for resolution. K. Davis, *Periodization and Sovereignty*, 4. On secularized inheritance of supersessionary temporal modes, see especially Raz-Krakotzkin, "Secularism, the Christian Ambivalence Toward the Jews, and the Notion of Exile." See also, *inter alia*, Joshi, *White Christian Privilege*, 1; Gow and Valerio, "Editor's Note," ix. For more on Jewish timekeeping, including the salutary reminder that from a Jewish temporal perspective we do not inhabit a new millennium but the end of the monstrous fifty-ninth century, see Rosen, *The Holocaust's Jewish Calendars*, esp. 4. See Rubin, "Beyond Holocaust Time."

46 Nye, "Decolonizing the Study of Religion." As Anidjar remarks, "Orientalism operates ... as the epistemological foundation of, the very structuring principle (and power) behind, disciplinary and discursive divisions." Anidjar, "Secularism," 54. See also Anidjar, *Semites*, 39–63.

47 K. Davis, *Periodization and Sovereignty*, passim; Biddick, *The Typological Imaginary*, passim.

48 On the potentially grave implications of supersessionary thinking in early English studies, see esp. Rambaran-Olm, "A Wrinkle in Medieval Time," esp. 386–8; Hermann, *Allegories of War*, 101–18.

49 Raz-Krakotzkin, "Secularism, the Christian Ambivalence toward the Jews, and the Notion of Exile," esp. 293, argues persuasively that they cannot be.

50 Kamionkowski, *Leviticus*, xlvi. On the "guilty pleasures" of reading Leviticus ("full of lists, full of inexhaustible, demanding, meticulous details") as a child, see Akbari, "The Object of Devotion," 303–4.

51 Marsden, *The Text of the Old Testament*, 429.

52 For the many literary uses of repetition in the Hebrew Bible, including that of simple emphasis, see Walsh, *Style and Structure in Biblical Hebrew Narrative*, esp. 145–54. One common example of this device is the Hebrew מוֹת תָּמוּת (Genesis 20:7, *inter alia*), lit. "dying you shall die," but translated into English as "you shall die" (JPS) and "thou shalt surely die" (Douay-Rheims). See the *Interrogationes Sigewulfi* for an eschatological interpretation of this phrase, which the Latin Vulgate translates more literally as "morte morieris." MacLean, "Ælfric's Version of *Alcuini interrogationes*," 22–23.

53 Douglas, *Leviticus as Literature*, 18.

54 Douglas, 51. For another intricate theory of the literary unity of Leviticus, see Warning, *Literary Artistry in Leviticus*, esp. 178–80.

55 Withers, *The Illustrated Old English Hexateuch*, 54.

56 As Davis observes, "brevity" is an eschatological concept in Ælfric's work and is not reducible to mere consideration for his audience. K. Davis, "Boredom, Brevity, and Last Things," esp. 328.

57 K. Davis, 321.
58 Vatter, "The Political Theology of Carl Schmitt," 248.

1. Exsanguinating Leviticus: Supersessionary Translation in the *Old English Heptateuch*

1 For a history and rebuttal of the nearly axiomatic identification of literal translation with (Jewish) carnality, see Seidman, *Faithful Renderings*, 73–114.
2 Menzer, "The Preface as Admonition," esp. 23–4, 36–9. On Ælfric's anxiety, see especially Stanton, *The Culture of Translation*, 146, 156–66, 174–5. Stanton, 146, locates this anxiety not in Ælfric's psychology but in "tensions inherent in the very act of translation."
3 Stephenson, *The Politics of Language*, esp. 164–87.
4 Stanton, *The Culture of Translation*, 145, notes that Ælfric "consciously developed in an English context the idea of *sermo humilis*, or plain style, that was the goal of Latin religious writers from at least the time of Augustine." On simplicity in the Old English writing of the Benedictine Reform, see Stephenson, *The Politics of Language, passim*, esp. 28–30.
5 Stanton, *The Culture of Translation*, 137. The concept of "slavish literalism" draws from Origen's slur on the Christian and Jewish translator Aquila; for this remark in the context of Jewish–Christian translation controversies, see Seidman, *Faithful Renderings*, esp. 76–9.
6 Meeder, "The 'Liber ex lege Moysi,'" esp. 174.
7 See "Alfred's Prologue," in Jurasinski and Oliver, *The Laws of Alfred*, 220–73. Stanton, *The Culture of Translation*, 104, observes that this preface constitutes "[t]he first actual prose translation of any Latin scripture" into English. Bethurum includes *Be Godcundre Warnunge* (God's Threat to Sinning Israel, Bethurum 19) in Bethurum, *Homilies of Wulfstan*, 251–4. Rabin translates this homily in *Political Writings*, 173–6.
8 Clemoes, "Introduction," 48.
9 On the dating of MS Cotton Claudius B.iv, see Withers, "A Sense of Englishness," 340–7. The term "Heptateuch" is a play on "Pentateuch" and "Hexateuch" with no independent currency in Biblical studies.
10 Withers, *The Illustrated Old English Hexateuch*, 8, 298n21. See also Ker, *Catalogue of Manuscripts Containing Anglo-Saxon*, nos. 344, 142. Seven other partial witnesses exist, manuscripts and fragments that contain excerpts from and versions of primarily Genesis, Exodus, and the *Prefatio*; none of these contain Leviticus, Deuteronomy, or Joshua. See *OEH*, xxxiv–lxix, for details; see cxxxiii–cxxxv for Marsden's assertion about the grandparent text and a manuscript genealogical chart. On Genesis witnesses, see Richards, "Fragmentary Versions of Genesis in Old English Prose." In

addition, William L'Isle's seventeenth-century modern English translation of the Heptateuch survives as Oxford, Bodleian, MS. Laud Misc. 381.

11 These are the chapters that deal with, respectively, childbirth and circumcision; persons with skin diseases; the purification of lepers; genital discharge and menstruation; sin offerings; bans on illicit animal slaughter and blood consumption; prohibitions to maintain the purity of the priestly class, including a ban on priests with blemishes; appropriate offerings and consumers of the sacrifice; and vows and consecrations made by laypeople.

12 Modern chapter and verse divisions postdate the early Middle Ages, so references to them are for convenience. Likewise, the Latin text used by the Old English translators does not survive. Marsden has demonstrated that most of the text is based on a "good" Latin Vulgate or Vulgates linked strongly to the Theodulfian school of revisions, that a small part is based on a Vulgate linked to the separate Alcuinian tradition, and that Old Latin interpretive texts and liturgy (although not unreliable Old Latin Bibles) influenced some portions of the text (particularly Ælfric's interpolations). See Marsden, *The Text of the Old Testament*, 437–9, for a discussion of these sources. I use the contemporary Douay-Rheims edition of the Vulgate, which is close, but not identical, to the Latin original.

13 Marsden, *The Text of the Old Testament*, 429.

14 These exceptions are the Codex Amiatinus (Florence, Biblioteca Medicea Laurenziana, Amiatino I), a complete Bible copied and kept in Northumbria (at Wearmouth-Jarrow) until the early eighth century; a ninth-century complete Bible of which only New Testament fragments remain (as London, BL, Royal 1. E. VI + Canterbury, Cathedral Library, Add. 16 + Oxford, Bodleian Library, Lat. Bib. b. 2 (P)); and London, BL, Royal 1. E VII + VIII, the complete Bible Marsden calls "canine" in its size and weight. Another partial source, now in fragments, contains Numbers and Deuteronomy, and another fragment of Numbers exists in London, BL, Sloane 1086, no. 109. Marsden, 40–2.

15 In other words, this fragment has been separated apparently at random from its manuscript context and used more or less as wrapping paper. The two leaves consist respectively of Leviticus 14:46–15:16 (on the purity regulations surrounding leprosy and male emissions, ending just as the regulations about purification after copulation are beginning) and 26:5–28 (God's promises and curses dependent upon Israel's fidelity). See Marsden, 236–40 for further description of the manuscript context. Whether or not the apparently casual treatment of these pages is derogatory, their value is obviously not reducible to, and perhaps does not even depend upon, their content. The content does, however, indicate that whatever hesitation existed about sexual purity regulations in vernacular

158 Notes to pages 21–4

translation did not extend to the Latin context of the monastery. For another example of the somewhat mature themes that were apparently acceptable in Latin glosses, see the Canterbury Biblical commentaries, e.g., the speculation that Jacob grabbed and injured not the thigh of the angel he wrestled but actually his "uirilem," genitals (Bischoff and Lapidge, PentI.184, at 336; translation mine).

16 See Marsden, 394. On partial Bibles see also van Liere, *An Introduction to the Medieval Bible*, 20.
17 Marsden, 346.
18 A later hand adds this.
19 In Leviticus, Marsden, *The Text of the Old Testament*, 346, attributes some such omissions purely to homoeoteleuton (the longest, in 23:35–6, is eighteen words). Marsden, 349, notes (and I agree) that the two significant lacunae in Numbers "are not disruptive of sense." The later Old Testament books of this manuscript (including Kings, Job, and Proverbs) include many Latin interpolations; these seem not to be commentary, as in the case of the *Old English Heptateuch* translators' interpolations, but rather primarily Old Latin and Septuagint material. Marsden, 355–62.
20 *OEH*, 133.
21 Douglas, *Leviticus as Literature*, esp. 137–9.
22 See Pareles, "Giving Yiddish the Devil."
23 Mary Douglas's classic 1966 study *Purity and Danger* explains the Levitical separation of clean and unclean animals as abomination of category confusion, but her preface to the 2002 edition, xv–xvi retracts this patronizing framework, noting that the distinction is instead "part of an elaborate intellectual structure of rules that mirror God's covenant with his people" and "intricately model the body and the altar upon one another." Douglas develops this idea in a 2001 monograph, *Leviticus as Literature*, but the book is not as well-known and many scholars, even some Hebrew Biblical scholars, continue to cite and disseminate only her earlier conclusions.
24 Magennis, "No Sex Please," 8.
25 See Stephenson, *The Politics of Language*, 140–3, on the role of this passage in Ælfric's repudiation of clerical marriage.
26 Menzer, "The Preface as Admonition," 23–4, 37–8.
27 Barnhouse, "Shaping the Hexateuch Text," 95.
28 Rachel successfully hides her father's idols by sitting on them and, when he comes to search her tent, slyly apologizing, according to the Vulgate, "Let my lord not be angry that I cannot rise up before thee, because it has now happened to me according to the custom of women" (Gen. 31:35; Ne irascatur dominus meus quod coram te adsurgere nequeo, quia iuxta consuetudinem feminarum nunc accidit mihi). Compare Ælfric's

omission of the episode to the frank elaboration of the Canterbury Biblical commentaries, which gloss "Iuxta consuetudinem mulierum" (31:35) as ".i. menstrualem. Tunc/enim non est facilis cuilibet surgere uel ambulare; nec licet eam tangere alicui nisi ut cibum tantum quis ponat ante ipsam quae accipiat usque dum sanguis resistat" (PentI.181, at 334–5; that is, during menstruation. At that time, it is not easy for a woman to get up or to walk around; nor is it permissible for anyone to touch her, but that someone may place food – and nothing else – before her, which she may accept until the blood ceases). This comment is noteworthy not only because it apparently assumes a readership unfamiliar with menstruation but also because it seems to endorse Jewish laws on menstrual separation.

29 *OEH*, 44. See Barnhouse, "Shaping the Hexateuch Text," 96–7, 99. See Marsden, "Ælfric as Translator," for some other examples of Ælfric's alterations to Genesis.

30 Nor did the compilers of the Hexateuch shy away from visually portraying polygamy: Lamech's wives appear in an illumination to Genesis (9v) and, per Clemoes, "Introduction," 19, are also subtly indicated in a family tree; Abraham and Hagar are shown in bed together (27v); Esau is shown with two brides; and Jacob marries Rachel and Leah.

31 *OEH*, 42.

32 Lot's daughters' sexual sin, raping their father and conceiving children by him while he is asleep (possibly a kind of justice in the world of the text), is *not* omitted, as Marsden notes ("Ælfric as Translator," 341n68); moreover, the Hexateuch devotes three illustrations to it. The story was probably well known in pre-Conquest England; it is, for instance, the subject of Exeter Riddle 46. For a full discussion of Old English writing about Sodom, including a different interpretation of this passage, see Clark, *Between Medieval Men*, 85–129.

33 References to this poem are by line to Anlezark's edition of *Genesis* in *Old Testament Narratives*, 2–203. Likewise, compare to the late fourteenth-century *Middle English Metrical Paraphrase of the Old Testament*, which multiplies the crimes of Sodom and Gomorrah: "Thei drede not God in no degré, / bot lyfyd in lust and lecheré – / And that thei schewyd in syght to see – / and agaynst kynd most oncumly. / Foule is to declare / how ther werkyns was. / No syb ne spoussyd thai spare, / ne nowther lad ne las" (37.437–44, at 57; They did not fear God at all, but lived in lust and fornication, and they demonstrated that openly, and very immorally against nature. It is indecent to talk about what they did. They did not leave alone relatives or married people, boys or girls). Incest, adultery, and other taboo acts accompany the Sodomites' insatiable pansexual predations. In this version, Lot encourages the group to assault his daughters, but the speech is not reported directly: "Hys ennemys com on

ylka syd / and bad furth tho chylder two. / Hys doyghturs proferd he that tyd, / bot thei sayd nay, thei wold non of tho" (Gen. 50.591–4, at 62; His enemies came on each side and called forth those two lads. At that point, he offered his daughters, but they said no, they wanted none of them). The poem includes the sexual assault upon Lot by his daughters.

34 Magennis, "No Sex Please," 14.
35 In fact, apparent Old Latin influence in *Genesis A* demonstrates that its Biblical source was not, or at least not solely, a Vulgate. Marsden, *The Text of the Old Testament*, 443.
36 Douglas, *Leviticus as Literature*, 5.
37 In Carmichael's thesis, the laws are a direct response to the transgressions in these earlier stories, in circulation prior to the writing of Leviticus. Carmichael, *Illuminating Leviticus*, 9.
38 *OEH*, 133. Here I include Marsden's verse notations to demonstrate the exact number and length of verses included.
39 "Turpitudinem uxoris fratris tui non revelabis, quia turpitudo fratris tui est."
40 Translation is mine, with reference to Douay-Rheims.
41 Milgrom, *Leviticus 17–22*, 1515. See Milgrom, 1548–9, for a detailed discussion of this verse. See, however, Hezser, 193, who notes the legal ambiguity around marital language when it refers to unfree women.
42 See Unger, ed., *Stjórn*, 320, for the *Stjórn* text. For more on the *Stjórn*, including dating, see Kirby, *Bible Translation in Old Norse*, esp 51–73; Ernjaes, "The Bible in the Languages of Scandinavia," esp. 240–2, 249–50.
43 For these, see Jónsson, *Blóðskömm á Íslandi*, 10–11.
44 At the other extreme, the *Middle English Metrical Paraphrase of the Old Testament* goes so far as to omit Leviticus entirely and to reduce Deuteronomy to narrative passages. See Livingston, ed., *Middle English Metrical Paraphrase*, sections 219–23 at 118–19). Its version of the Noah story omits the reference to clean and unclean animals and the injunction not to eat with blood, section 29 at 55.
45 *OEH*, 134. This is precisely what Lot tries to do in the excised portion of Genesis 19; offering his daughters for the purpose of sexual assault would fall under the heading of prostituting them.
46 When young Abraham and Sarah travel to Egypt (as Abram and Sarai), they pose as brother and sister so that no one will kill Abram for Sarai. Pharoah takes Sarai into his harem of wives, but expels her when he is punished by God (Genesis 12:11–20). As Clemoes, "Introduction," 22, notes, the Old English emphasizes that Pharaoh pays Abram for her, and the Hexateuch depicts this.
47 Cham uncovers his father Noah's nakedness, leading to Noah's curse on his son Canaan (Genesis 9:21–7). Lot's daughters rape him and conceive Moab and Ammon (Genesis 19:31–8). In Genesis 20, Abraham performs

the same ruse, for the same reason, as in Egypt, and excuses it by saying that the brother–sister ruse was not completely a lie: Sarah is his half-sister by his father as well as his wife. This is apparently considered a weaker kinship relationship than sharing the same mother. It is unclear whether Abraham is telling the truth here, but the point is ambiguous enough that, as Carmichael notes, 20–2, the story seems to have inspired the Levitical prohibition on sex with paternal half-sisters. Father–daughter incest is not explicitly mentioned in Leviticus, but its prohibition is implied by Leviticus 6 (the blanket prohibition against sex with close relatives), 10 (the prohibition against sex with daughters' daughters on the grounds that they are closely related to daughters), and most of all 17 (the prohibition against sex with both a mother and her daughter). For a different perspective on the relationship of incest in Genesis to incest prohibitions in Leviticus, see Hepner, "Abraham's Incestuous Marriage with Sarah," 143–55.)

48 Carmichael, *Illuminating Leviticus*, 2. As Elizabeth Archibald observes, the early medieval Church was at this stage very sensitive, to a degree untenable in some localities, to incest with relatively distant relatives. Archibald, *Incest and the Medieval Imagination*, 34.

49 The Latin text of Gregory's letters is from *Gregorii I papae registrum epistolarum*, ed. Ewald and Hartmann; the translation is mine. I have also consulted Bede, *Ecclesiastical History of the English People*, ed. Sherley-Price.

50 Frantzen, *The Literature of Penance*, 117; Dinshaw, *Getting Medieval*, 9 refers to this as "dangerous knowledge"; see also Dinshaw, 212–13n22. The thirteenth-century *Ancrene Wisse* exemplifies this principle when urging anchorites to confess sexual sins committed alone or with other women. See *Ancrene Wisse*, ed. Hasenfratz, IV.343–5, 351–4:

> Ah sari mei ha beon the bute fere, other with, haveth swa i-fed cundel of hire galnesse – thet ich ne mei speoken of for scheome ne ne dear for drede, leste sum leorni mare uvel then ha con ant beo th'rof i-temptet … Ye, the of swucches nute nawt, ne thurve ye nawt wundrin ow, ne thenchen hwet ich meane, ah yeldeth graces Godd thet ye swuch uncleannesse nabbeth i-fondet, ant habbeth reowthe of ham the i swuch beoth i-fallen.

> But grieved may she be who without a companion, or with another, has thus nourished the pups of her lust – which I may not speak of for shame, nor dare to on account of fear, lest someone learn more evil than she had known and be tempted thereby … You, who know nothing of such things, you do not need to wonder or to think about what I mean, but give thanks to God that you have not tried such uncleanness, and have pity for those who have fallen into it.

162   Notes to pages 30–4

51 White was working under the contemporary assumption that Ælfric was the translator of the entire Old English Heptateuch.
52 White, *Ælfric*, 146.
53 Marsden, *The Text of the Old Testament*, 439.
54 Marsden, "Translation by Committee?," 53–63.
55 *OEH* Genesis 24:15–60 (L MS), at 50.
56 Withers, *The Illustrated Old English Hexateuch*, 170.
57 Roy Liuzza, ed., *The Old English Version of the Gospels*, 12–13. The subsequent Latin glossing of the Heptateuch is applied inconsistently throughout the book, so it is not necessarily consequential that the later hand does not apply any glossing to the story of Sodom or to Leviticus 18.
58 Barnhouse, "Shaping the Hexateuch Text," 92.
59 Barnhouse, 106.
60 Barnhouse, 108.
61 Milgrom, *Leviticus 1–16*, 2.
62 Marsden, *The Text of the Old Testament*, 405. See, however, Helen Gittos's warning against the assumption that Old English translations were meant for those with little Latin ability. Gittos, "The Audience for Old English Texts." Moreover, as Stephenson notes, even educated clerics used English, since "the inflated Latin style preferred by the [Benedictine] reformers … was very difficult to understand and, in some cases, required an English translation in order to make the text useful to its named audience of Benedictine monks." Stephenson, *The Politics of Language*, 14.
63 "Benedixitque Deus Noe et filiis eius. Et dixit ad eos, 'Crescite, et multiplicamini, et implete terram. Et terror vester ac tremor sit super cuncta animalia terrae et super omnes volucres caeli cum universis quae moventur in terra. Omnes pisces maris manui vestrae traditi sunt. Et omne quod movetur et vivit erit vobis in cibum. Quasi holera virentia tradidi vobis omnia, excepto quod carnem cum sanguine non comedetis, sanguinem enim animarum vestrarum requiram de manu cunctarum bestiarum, et de manu hominis, de manu viri et fratris eius requiram animam hominis. Quicumque effuderit humanum sanguinem, fundetur sanguis illius, ad imaginem quippe Dei factus est homo.'" Note that God makes this covenant not only with Noah and his descendants but also "with every living soul that is with you, as well in all birds as in cattle and beast of the earth that are come forth out of the ark, and in all the beasts of the earth" (ad omnem animam viventem quae est vobiscum, tam in volucribus quam in iumentis et pecudibus terrae cunctis quae egressa sunt de arca, et universis bestiis terrae; Gen. 9:10).
64 *OEH*, 23–4.
65 Some controversy follows the translation of Hebrew *nefesh* (נָפֶשׁ) as "life" rather than "soul" in God's dicta about blood in Genesis and Leviticus. Gil

Anidjar, noting that the Vulgate uses "anima" as opposed to "vita," argues that the shift to "life" originates in German Protestant Bible translations of the early modern period, and that the near-universal translation of this word as "life" in subsequent English translations, including those used by Jews and non-Protestant Christians, reflects a Lutheran theological interpretation that other traditions have unwittingly affirmed by carelessly adopting this mistranslation. The translation of "anima" as "lif" in this Old English passage, however, indicates that this purported mistranslation occurs in English prior to the Reformation. See Anidjar, "We Have Never Been Jewish," 56n72, on Luther's imposition of "Blut" to mean ancestry in his translation of Acts 17:26.

66 D. Biale, *Blood and Belief*, 10.
67 Milgrom, *Leviticus 17–22*, 1470.
68 Shannon, *The Accommodated Animal*, 60–1.
69 "Adolebitque ea sacerdos super altare in alimoniam ignis et suavissimi odoris. Omnis adeps Domini erit iure perpetuo in generationibus et cunctis habitaculis vestris; nec adipem omnino nec sanguinem omnino comedetis."
70 *OEH*, 131.
71 See Milgrom, *Leviticus 1–16*, 214–16.
72 "Homo quilibet de domo Israhel et de advenis qui peregrinantur inter eos si comederit sanguinem, obfirmabo faciem meam contra animam illius et disperdam eam de populo suo quia anima carnis in sanguine est et ego dedi illum vobis ut super altare in eo expietis pro animabus vestris et sanguis pro animae piaculo sit. Idcirco dixi filiis Israhel, 'Omnis anima ex vobis non comedet sanguinem nec ex advenis qui peregrinantur apud vos.'

"Homo quicumque de filiis Israhel et de advenis qui peregrinantur apud vos, si venatione atque aucupio ceperit feram vel avem quibus vesci licitum est, fundat sanguinem eius et operiat illum terra, anima enim omnis carnis in sanguine est. Unde dixi filiis Israhel, 'Sanguinem universae carnis non comedetis quia anima carnis in sanguine est, et quicumque comederit illum interibit.'"

73 See Milgrom, *Leviticus 17–22*, 1596–602, for classification.
74 "Non comedetis cum sanguine. Non augurabimini nec observabitis somnia. Neque in rotundum adtondebitis comam, nec radatis barbam. Et super mortuo non incidetis carnem vestram, neque figuras aliquas aut stigmata facietis vobis. Ego Dominus. Ne prostituas filiam tuam ne contaminetur terra et impleatur piaculo. Sabbata mea custodite, et sanctuarium meum metuite. Ego Dominus. Non declinetis ad magos, nec ab ariolis aliquid sciscitemini ut polluamini per eos. Ego Dominus, Deus vester. Coram cano capite consurge, et honora personam senis,

et time Dominum, Deum tuum. Ego sum Dominus." See, however, Carmichael's interpretation of 19:26 as a ban not on consuming blood itself but on conspiring at the dinner table to spill human blood. Carmichael, *Illuminating Leviticus*, 119–22.

75 *OEH*, 163. See the corresponding Vulgate passage: "What I command thee, that only do thou to the Lord. Neither add any thing nor diminish." (Quod praecipio tibi, hoc tantum facito Domino. Nec addas quidquam nec minuas; Deut. 12:32.)

76 "Si quis adipem qui offerri debet in incensum Domini comederit, peribit de populo suo. Sanguinem quoque omnis animalis non sumetis in cibo, tam de avibus quam de pecoribus. Omnis anima quae ederit sanguinem peribit de populis suis."

77 The entire Old English translation of chapter 7 is as follows: [7:17] "And gif þær hwæt to lafe bið ofer þa twegen dagas, forbærne hit man þæs þriddan dæges. [25] Gif hwa þæt smeru oððe þæt blod [ytt], þe bið Gode geoffrud, he sceal forwurðan. [31-2] Se swiðra boh and þa ribb sceal beon Aarones and his sunena of ðære offrunga þe man for gesibbsumnysse offrIað." *OEH*, 131. (And if anything is left as a remainder over two days, burn it on the third day. If anyone eats the fat or the blood that is offered to God, he shall perish. The right shoulder and the ribs shall be Aaron's and his descendants', for their peace offerings.)

78 In the homily on Job, Ælfric explains animal sacrifice as "gewunelic on ealdum dagum" (customary in the old days) but "nu unalyfedlic æfter cristes ðrowunge" (now unlawful after Christ's passion). "Dominica I in Mense Septembri Quando Legitur Job" (First Sunday in September: Job), *CHII* 260–7, at 265.

79 Anti-Semites later reconceived Jewish animal slaughter methods as both evidence and substance of bloodthirsty sacrifice; for a detailed discussion of this inversion, see D. Biale, *Blood and Belief*, esp. 126–31; John J. Hartman, "A Psychoanalytic View of Racial Myths in a Nazi Propaganda Film," 329–46. My thinking throughout this book has been profoundly influenced by European and North American campaigns against *halal* slaughter and *shechitah* (kosher slaughter) since 1933. See, *inter alia*, Klug, "Ritual Murmur"; Bergeaud-Blackler, "New Challenges for Islamic Ritual Slaughter," 965–80; Kushner, "Stunning Intolerance," 16–20. For an excellent summary of the current situation see Kanji, "Kosher and Halal Bans."

80 Spindler, ed., *Das altenglische Bussbuch*, 191–2.

81 Spindler, 192. I follow Frantzen in avoiding the designation "Penitential of Pseudo-Egbert." See Frantzen, *The Literature of Penance*, 133–4.

82 "An Edition of Ælfric's *Letter to Brother Edward*." 280. See also Clayton, "Letter to Brother Edward: A Student Edition," 31–46. Clayton argues

that a key concern of this letter is the maintenance of cultural boundaries between non-Christian invaders and English Christians.
83 Hagen, *Anglo-Saxon Food and Drink*, 186, 93, 194, 290–1.
84 "anima enim omnis carnis in sanguine est. Unde dixi filiis Israhel, 'Sanguinem universae carnis non comedetis quia anima carnis in sanguine est, et quicumque comederit illum interibit.'"

2. Men as Meat: Jewish Law and Orders of Being in Ælfric's Translations of Maccabees and Job

1 Clayton, *LS* 2:286.
2 Godden, "Biblical Literature," 216. See Ælfric, "*Prefatio* to Genesis," *OEH*, 3–7; Marsden, "Ælfric as Translator," 322; Wilcox, ed., *Ælfric's Prefaces*, 2–3.
3 As, for instance, in 1 Macc. 1:15, 1:51, 1:63, 1:64, 2:46, and 2 Macc. 6:10.
4 On Old Testament translations in this manuscript, see Brookes, "Life, but Not as We Know It." Substantial versions of the text appear in three additional collections dating from the eleventh and twelfth centuries: Cambridge, Corpus Christi College MS 198 and MS 303 (both complete witnesses), and Cambridge, University Library, MS Ii.1.33. For a convenient summary of the manuscript evidence, see Clayton, *LS* 2:388–9.
5 Jonathan A. Goldstein describes these books as "sharply different accounts" of the same historical period written by "bitter opponents." Goldstein, "Introduction," *II Maccabees*, 4. On Ælfric's skilful integration of the two books, see Zacher, "Anglo-Saxon Maccabees," 152–7.
6 In the context of the Danish threat, the homily's political implications probably do not need – for a contemporary audience – much explicit signposting. Zacher observes that he composed the text "when the Viking incursions had become intolerable and seemingly irreversible," 157. See also Godden, "Ælfric's Saints' Lives and the Problem of Miracles," esp. 302–5, and "Apocalypse and Invasion in Late Anglo-Saxon England."
7 Lee, "Ælfric's Treatment of Source Material," 170.
8 Eleazar's sympathetic executioners give him the option of simply *appearing* to eat pork, but he chooses death rather than allow a report that would weaken the resolve of younger people. Paul will later codify this principle: "Si enim propter cibum frater tuus contristatur, iam non secundum caritatem ambulas ... Bonum est non manducare carnem et non bibere vinum neque in quo frater tuus offenditur aut scandalizatur aut infirmatur" (Rom. 14:15, 21; But if because of thy meat thy brother be grieved, thou walkest not now according to charity ... It is good not to eat flesh and not to drink wine nor any thing whereby thy brother is offended or scandalized or made weak). On the Maccabees as Christian saints, see

Joslyn-Siemiatkoski, *Christian Memories of the Maccabean Martyrs, passim,* esp. 104–5, 143–55.
9 Ælfric, *Passio sanctorum Machabeorum* ("The Martyrdom of the Maccabees, Their Battles, and the Three Orders of Society"). Clayton, *LS* 2:282.
10 Lee, "Ælfric's Treatment of Source Material," 171–2.
11 Halbrooks, "Ælfric, the *Maccabees,* and the Problem of Christian Heroism," 269–70.
12 As Scheil notes, "þe Moyses forbead / Godes folce to þicgenne for þære gastlican gatacnunge" is Ælfric's original addition. Scheil, *The Footsteps of Israel,* 314n3.
13 "Maccabees." Clayton, *LS* 2: 282, 284.
14 Scheil, *Footsteps of Israel,* 317.
15 Scheil, 316. See Joslyn-Siemiatkoski, *Christian Memories of the Maccabean Martyrs, passim,* for exegetes prior to and after Ælfric who also, although in quite different ways, turn interpretation of the Maccabees to supersessionary and even openly anti-Semitic ends. Although Lee, "Ælfric's Treatment of Source Material," 168–70, does not find evidence of influence on this homily, Ælfric should be seen as contributing to the tradition.
16 Wilcox, "A Reluctant Translator in Late Anglo-Saxon England," esp. 6.
17 See Wynter, "No Humans Involved," 42–73; Wynter, "Unsettling the Coloniality of Being/Power/Truth/Freedom"; Agamben, *The Open,* 14–16. I use the term "manmade" deliberately, influenced by Sylvia Wynter's formulation of Man as the hegemonic modern subject who colonizes the category "humanity." On the emergence of the human as a racialized category, see, *inter alia,* Z.I. Jackson, *Becoming Human.*
18 Agamben argues that the late nineteenth-century discovery of the evolutionary division between apes and humans leads shortly to "the Jew, that is, the non-man produced within the man" (37). Wynter, on the other hand, calls the modern racialized conception of humanity a "reinvention" of the medieval category "Christian." Wynter, "Unsettling the Coloniality," 266. Agamben and Wynter refer to the postmedieval operations of scientific racism; for a comprehensive introduction to this massive and disturbing topic, see Saini, *Superior.* We can, however, trace the production of the human as Christian far earlier. On the medieval and early modern Christian identification of Jews with dogs and pigs, see especially Fabre-Vassas, *Singular Beast;* Stow, *Jewish Dogs;* Enders, "Homicidal Pigs"; Shachar, *The Judensau: A Medieval Anti-Jewish Motif and Its History;* Weidl, "Laughing at the Beast," 325–64; Resnick, "Good Dog/Bad Dog"; Pareles, "Already/Never".
19 Stow, *passim,* esp. 34–6.
20 Salisbury, *The Beast Within,* 60.

21 Halbrooks, "Ælfric, the *Maccabees*, and the Problem of Christian Heroism," 264.
22 Kruger, *The Spectral Jew*, 8.
23 The holiness code reveals that certain categories of persons (or persons with certain kinds of experiences) can also make food (and anything else they touch) unclean: menstruating women, lepers, men with nocturnal emissions, those who have handled the dead, and a number of others.
24 Douglas, *Leviticus as Literature*, 250. The holiness codes in Leviticus and Deuteronomy in fact betray divergent world views; in particular, the Levitical writers exclude but do not abhor or abominate impure objects. The differences are beyond the scope of this book; see Douglas, *Leviticus as Literature*, passim. It is worth noting that Douglas's conclusion that animals not suitable for consumption analogize peoples not chosen to the covenant replaces her earlier and much more widely known argument that unclean animals were improper to their classes ("matter out of place") and therefore abominable. Douglas, *Purity and Danger*, 67–71. Douglas in fact retracts this frequently cited argument about Levitical law, criticizing its circularity and its collapse of the concepts of abomination and exclusion. Douglas, in the 2002 preface to *Purity and Danger*, xii–xvi.
25 For more detail on Ælfric's Vulgate and Old Latin source material for this homily, see Lee, "Ælfric's Treatment of Source Material," 165–76. See also Marsden, *The Text of the Old Testament*, 398–401, on the Latin sources of Ælfric's Old Testament writings.
26 Filotas, *Pagan Survivals*, 108–10; Salisbury, *The Beast Within*, 55–6.
27 Spindler, *Das altenglische Bussbuch*, 192–3.
28 Steel, *How to Make a Human*, 68; see also Resnick, *Marks of Distinction*, 166–7; Feeley-Harnik, *The Lord's Table*, 19. On early Christianity as a form of Judaism, see *inter alia*, D. Boyarin.
29 Feeley-Harnik, 107, 167.
30 For pre-Rabbinic Hellenistic Jewish attitudes to food restrictions, including Alexandrian Jewish acceptance of commensality with non-Jews, see Freidenreich, *Foreigners and Their Food*, 31–46.
31 See especially Freidenreich, 87–8. Freidenreich notes that the movement for table-fellowship grew up after Christ's death; the Christ of the gospels is never shown eating with non-Jews, although he makes a point of eating with Jewish outcasts.
32 2 Macc. indicates that the pork was also "sacrificii carnibus" (2 Macc. 6.21; the flesh of the sacrifice), and Ælfric reveals an awareness of this twofold unlawfulness by translating the phrase as "offrung-spice" (93; sacrifice-bacon). "Maccabees." Clayton, *LS* 2:286. See Schwartz, *2 Maccabees*, 287–8. See Joslyn-Siemiatkoski, *Christian Memories of the Maccabean Martyrs*, 94, on Rupert of Deutz's treatment of this issue.

168   Notes to pages 49–50

33 *OEH*, 3–7.
34 Spindler, *Das altenglische Bussbuch*, 182.
35 Freidenreich, *Foreigners and Their Food*, 113–23, 191–6.
36 Freidenreich, 101–28.
37 Augustine, *Contra faustum*, 32.13. Augustine argues that the ban was a gesture of unity between the Jewish and gentile branches of the Church that symbolized the inclusion of all believers in Noah's covenant. In the absence of Jews, this ban is no longer in effect.
38 Freidenreich, *Foreigners and Their Food*, 113–23, 191–6; Stow, 3–22, 134–57.
39 Meens, "A Penitential Diet," 150.
40 "Si quis Christianus a perfidis Judaeis azima eorum accipit, vel alium quemlibet cybum, vel potum, et communicat impietatibus eorum … quia scriptum est: Omnia munda mundis, coinquinatis autem et infidelibus nihil est mundum, sed Omnia sunt communia." Wasserschleben, ed., *Die Bussordnungen der abendländischen Kirche*, 610–11. The English translation and Biblical citation are Freidenreich's, *Foreigners and Their Food*, 193–4. For an account of the widespread acceptance of taboos against consuming Jewish food in medieval western Christianity, see Freidenreich, 191–6. Stow, 6, writes that in the Middle Ages and by the Renaissance, "Exegetically, the Jew had become, and would continue to be seen as … the 'trampler' of the true Christian food."
41 Freidenreich, 194.
42 On the manuscripts and contexts, see van Rhijn and Saan, "Correcting Sinners, Correcting Texts."
43 Filotas, *Pagan Survivals*, 339.
44 Steel, *How to Make a Human*, 67–88. Steel cites as support the additional penitential preoccupation with (usually non-meat) food polluted by the scavengings, defecations, and other traces of animals. Such food is seen as unclean, but less so than carrion. Steel, 83–4, argues that "escalating levels of illicit animal agency correspond to escalating levels of pollution, and animals that killed and ate other animals exhibited the most agency … the chief concern is to preserve the difference between human and animal agency in the enormously important realm of violence against animals," that is, the creation and consumption of human food. Meens argues that the redeemability of many non-meat foods polluted by animals demonstrates the symbolic rather than hygienic importance of this category of food: that "one can purify food polluted by animals by sprinkling it with holy water and saying a prayer … shows that we are not dealing with matters of hygiene and health … but that the pollution was conceived first and foremost as a ritual feature needing a liturgical cure" (149).
45 Filotas, *Pagan Survivals*, 108–10; Salisbury, *The Beast Within*, 55–6. See especially the horse meat compromise in the *Kristni Saga* account of the

Icelandic conversion. Grønlie, *Íslendingabók*, 50. On the other hand, the Scriftboc seems at least equivocally to reject this taboo: "Nis horses flæsc forboden þeah ðe hi fela mægða þicgean nelle" (XXVII.34b; Horse flesh is not forbidden, although many groups will not eat it). Spindler, *Das altenglische Bussbuch*, 192.

46 "Maccabees," in Clayton, *LS* 2:284, 286.
47 "An Edition of Ælfric's *Letter*," 280. See also "Letter to Brother Edward: A Student Edition," where Clayton, ed., demonstrates the letter's preoccupation with maintaining cultural boundaries between non-Christian invaders and English Christians.
48 God does not give permission to eat flesh until the Noahic covenant: "And every thing that moveth and liveth shall be meat for you. Even as the green herbs have I delivered them all to you, saving that flesh with blood you shall not eat" (Gen. 9:3–4; Et omne quod movetur et vivit erit vobis in cibum. Quasi holera virentia tradidi vobis omnia, excepto quod carnem cum sanguine non comedetis).
49 Kruger, *The Spectral Jew*, 13.
50 "Dominica I in Quadragesima (The First Sunday in Lent)," *CHII* 61. As Godden notes, "Ælfric's point about sexual abstinence in Lent is not in the sources or analogues"; it is his own and he repeats it in two other homilies. Godden, *CH Introduction*, 93. Rather, it is a characteristic statement of the importance of chastity and in particular of Ælfric's tendency, discussed more fully in chapter 4, to make chastity the central message of food regulation.
51 Ælfric's *Item Alia* differentiating the three orders of society falls beyond the limits of this chapter; see Scheil, *Footsteps of Israel*, 324–30.
52 Bede, *The Old English Version of Bede's Ecclesiastical History*, 346. This closely translates Bede's Latin: "quasi mundum animal ruminando, in carmen dulcissimum conuertebat." Bede, *Ecclesiastical History* iv.24, at 418.
53 Scheil, *Footsteps of Israel*, 314–15n5.
54 "Quid si inmundi fuerint pisces?" / "Ego proiciam inmundos foras, et sumo mihi mundos in escam."
55 O'Neill, *First Fifty Psalms*, 116.
56 Grumett and Muers, *Theology on the Menu*, 83.
57 "In Ascensione Domini" (On the Lord's Ascension), *CHI* 349.
58 See Gregory, Homily 29. See also Ælfric's "Primus sermo de initio de creaturae" ([First] Sermon on the Origin of Creation): God "ne sealde nanum nytene ne nanum fisce nane sawle, ac heora blod is heora lif, and swa hraðe swa hi beoð deade, swa beoð hi mid ealle geendode" (*CHI* 182; gave no soul to any beast or fish, but their blood is their life and as soon as they are dead, so are they finished and all).
59 See also Augustine's dictum on the subordination of animals: "animalia inrationabilia recte dicimus in usus dari naturis excellentioribus"

170   Notes to pages 54–5

(Cunningham, trans., "A Treatise on the Origin of the Human Soul," 528; irrational animals are given by God to serve creatures possessing a higher nature). "Epistulum 166," 569.
60 Agamben, *The Open*, 14.
61 See Agamben, 14–16.
62 Magennis, *Anglo-Saxon Appetites*, 12.
63 *Ceorfan*, meaning "to carve" as well as "to cut," is often used for meat; *for-ceorfan*, "to carve off," is usually used in reference to body parts. For usage, see *DOE*, s.v. *for-ceorfan*.
64 "Maccabees," in Clayton, *LS* 2:288. These brothers are not unique among Ælfric's martyrs in facing cooking tortures, but they alone go mutely, like animals, to cooking deaths. Some Christian saints resist such tortures and choose more conventional forms of execution, e.g., St. George, who survives salting and boiling, and St. Dionysius, who survives a bed of coals, hungry beasts, and an oven ("Natale Sancti Georgii, Martyris" [Feast of Saint George the Martyr], Clayton, *LS* 2:52–65; "Passio Sancti Dionisii et Sociorum Eius" [The Passion of Saint Dionysius and His Companions], Clayton, *LS* 3:57–81). Others make a point of the Christian symbolism of cooking deaths: compare the Jewish brothers to the triumphant St. Laurence, for instance, who as a Christian saint turns his cooking death a lesson on appropriate and inappropriate sacrifices to God and on the separation of body and spirit, declaring, "Ic offrie me sylfne þam ælmihtigan gode on bræðe wynsumnysse, for þan ðe se gedrefeda gast is gode andfenge onsægednys" (I offer myself to the Almighty God in a fragrance of delight, because the troubled spirit is an acceptable sacrifice to God), and taunting the emperor: "efne ðu earming brædest ænne dæl mines lichaman, wend nu þone oþerne, and et" ("Passio Sancti Laurentii" [Passion of St. Laurence], *CHI* 425–6; Just as, you wretch, you have roasted one side of my body, now turn the other, and eat). On the salutary symbolism of St. Laurence's death, see, for example, Wogan-Browne and Burgess, "Introduction," in Wogan-Browne and Burgess, trans., *Virgin Lives and Holy Deaths*, xl–xliii; see also Wilcox, "Famous Last Words," 1–13. The martyred Jewish brothers of the Maccabees story undergo equally symbolic cooking deaths in their own context, but are denied St. Laurence's power of speech. Unlike Christian martyrs, they die silently and without choosing the time and manner of their death; they die like beasts rather than like saints. For more on the cooking tortures of male martyrs, see Mills, "Whatever you do is a delight to me!" and Mills, "Violence, Community and the Materialisation of Belief," 87–103, esp. 89–90.
65 As Nathan MacDonald demonstrates, the Hebrew Bible elsewhere portrays the elision of human and animal slaughter as a sign of the loss

of human community and order: in Judges, for instance, the application of sacrificial killing methods to humans represents a collapse of "the boundaries between animals and humans" that, hand in hand with the erasure of "boundaries between cultural domains affirmed elsewhere in the Old Testament," signals a state of extreme chaos in Israel. MacDonald, *Not Bread Alone*, 132. As Cary Wolfe observes, the species distinction that transforms animal butchery into what Derrida has labelled "a non-criminal putting to death" is in fact the necessary precondition for such murders. Derrida, "Eating Well" 112; Wolfe, *Animal Rites*, 6–7.

66 Deleuze, *Francis Bacon*, 20–1, emphasis in text. Agamben later appropriates this phrase as one definition of bare life, a condition of absolute vulnerability to violence. Agamben, *Homo Sacer*, 106. For an analysis of his adaptation of Deleuze's concept of the "zone of indiscernibility," see Gilson, "Zones of Indiscernibility."

67 Deleuze, 20–1.

68 As Derrida notes in a more optimistic vein, this zone of shared suffering and vulnerability can be conceptualized as a place of community and compassion for humans and animals. Derrida, *The Animal That Therefore I Am*, 28.

69 Tompkins, *Racial Indigestion*, 31.

70 "Maccabees," 2 :316.

71 "de corpore impii vermes scaturrirent, ac viventis in doloribus carnes eius effluerent, odore etiam illius et fetore exercitus gravaretur. Et qui paulo ante sidera esta contingere se arbitrabatur, eum nemo poterat propter intolerantiam fetoris portare" (2 Macc. 9:9–10; worms swarmed out of the body of this man, and whilst he lived in sorrow and pain, his flesh fell off, and the filthiness of his smell was noisome to the army. And the man that thought a little before he could reach to the stars of heaven, no man could endure to carry for the intolerable stench).

72 Antiochus dies of "tristitia" (sorrow, translation mine) in 1 Macc. 6:8; in 2 Macc. 9, he suffers both a fatal illness and a chariot accident. On Antiochus's death, see Africa, "Worms and the Death of Kings," esp. 7–9; D. R. Schwartz, "Why Did Antiochus Have to Fall (II Maccabees 9:7)?"

73 Schwartz, 264–5.

74 Hoek, "Violence and Ideological Inversion," 278. See Steel, *How Not to Make a Human*, 75–110, on worms and human death.

75 On the relationship of this manner of death to early medieval English capital punishment, see Marafioti, "Secular and Ecclesiastical Justice in Late Anglo-Saxon England," esp. 82, 117–18.

76 "Dominica I in Mense Septembri, Quando Legitur Job" (First Sunday in September: Job) *CHII* 265.

77 The *DOE* defines *forrotian* as "to rot away, decay" and gives both carnal (for instance, "of bodies/parts of bodies: to rot away, be corrupted," "of

wounds/sores: to fester, putrefy," "of water: to become stale or fetid,") and corresponding figurative ("of abstractions: to decay, decline, perish (over time)," and "of a name: to fall into contempt, become disgusting") uses. *DOE*, s.v. *forrotian*.

78 Aberth, *From the Brink of the Apocalypse*, 17–18.
79 Besserman, *The Legend of Job in the Middle Ages*, 39, 43, 65. See also Besserman, "A Note on the Source of Ælfric's Homily on the Book of Job," 248–52.
80 Tucker, "Rain on a Land Where No One Lives," 15.
81 Ælfric, *Libellus de veteri testamento et novo* (Treatise on the Old and New Testaments), *OEH*, 216. This work is also called the *Letter to Sigeweard*.
82 As Vicchio notes, in the Jewish tradition, this figure is "an angel in good standing in the heavenly court" whose special role is to argue with God – hence his title, which means "the accuser." He is not yet Satan in the Christian sense, the master of evil and chief demon. Vicchio, *Job in the Ancient World*, 74–5.
83 Vicchio, 5.
84 Vicchio, 34.
85 In light of Ælfric's obvious debt to Gregory and divergences from the *Moralia*, Besserman conjectures, "Having read and digested a large part (if not all) of Gregory's interpretation of the Book of Job, Ælfric incorporated in his own homily whatever its much abbreviated format and his limited pedagogical ends required." Besserman, "A Note on the Source of Ælfric's Homily," 251.
86 The Hebrew is מֵאֲנָה לִנְגּוֹעַ נַפְשִׁי הֵמָּה כִּדְוֵי לַחְמִי.
87 For some of the difficulties of interpretation and translation, see Alter, *The Wisdom Books*, 8.
88 The vibrant scholarly debate on Biblical Hebrew verb tense lies well outside the purview of this book, but see John Cook, "The Finite Verbal Forms in Biblical Hebrew Do Express Aspect."
89 Alter, *The Wisdom Books*, 31.
90 Alter, 31–32n7.
91 Kahn and Solomon, *Job's Illness*, 40.
92 Lee, "The Hungry Soul," 70–2.
93 Lee, 74–5.
94 "Numquid rugiet onager cum habuerit herbam? Aut mugiet bos cum ante praesepe plenum steterit? Aut poterit comedi insulsum quod non est sale conditum? Aut potest aliquis gustare quod gustatum adfert mortem?" Job 6:5–6.
95 "Dominica II in Adventum Domini" (Second Sunday in the Lord's Advent), *CHI* 525.

96 Filotas, 114.
97 Spindler, *Das altenglische Bussbuch*, 193.
98 Fulk and Jurasinski, eds., *The Old English Canons of Theodore*, A.38. See also Frantzen, *The Anglo-Saxon Penitentials*, for his online edition.
99 Fulk and Jurasinski, A.88.
100 Hagen, 442.
101 Ælfric, "Saint Basil," in Clayton, *LS* 1:90.
102 See, for instance, Aberth 7–42 for an account of this phenomenon.
103 Gregory, *Moralia in Job*, 7.11.
104 Kruger, *The Spectral Jew*, 4.
105 "Judaea quippe, vitam gentilium dedignata, eam dudum quasi tangere noluit, cujus societatem recipere sprevit; sed ad Redemptoris gratiam veniens, ab Israelitis infidelibus repulsa, dum per sanctos apostolos ad collectionem se gentium dilatat, quasi hoc in cibum esuriens accipit, quod indignum prius fastidiosa despexit ... prae angustia cibos quos dudum contempserat comedit, quae, repulsa Judaeorum duritia, gentiles suscipere populos quos despexerat concupiscit." Gregory, *Moralia in Job*, *PL* 75 773A; *Morals* 372.
106 Vicchio, *Job in the Medieval World*, 32. See Besserman, *Legend of Job*, esp. 52, 56.
107 Vicchio, 45.
108 Vicchio, 35.
109 Marsden, *The Text of the Old Testament*, 439.
110 *CHI* 266.
111 See Heb. 9.
112 *CHI* 267.
113 MacDonald, *Not Bread Alone*, 186.
114 See Agamben, *Homo Sacer*, esp. 15–29. Schmitt, *Political Theology*, esp. 36–7.
115 Tucker, "Rain on a Land Where No One Lives," 13.
116 See, for instance, the Old English *Physiologus*, which identifies the whale with the devil.
117 "An extrahere poteris Leviathan hamo, et fune ligabis linguam eius? Numquid pones circulum in naribus eius aut armilla perforabis maxillam eius? Numquid multiplicabit ad te preces aut loquetur tibi mollia? Numquid feriet tecum pactum, et accipies eum servum sempiternum? Numquid inludes ei quasi avi aut ligabis illum ancillis tuis? Concident eum amici? Divident illum negotiatores?"
118 For more on this elephantine insertion, see Thornbury, "Ælfric's Zoology," 150.

3. The Benedictine Invention of Heterosexuality: Jewish (Law's) Sexual Difference in Time

1 See Kruger, *The Spectral Jew*, esp. 88–9.
2 D. Boyarin, Itzkovitz, and Pellegrini, "Strange Bedfellows: An Introduction," 1–18, esp. 1–5. Matti Bunzl notes the "joint logic of social articulation" that produced (European) Jews as a racial category and gays as a sexual category in the same nineteenth-century moment. Bunzl, *Symptoms of Modernity*, 12. See also Bunzl, "Jews, Queers, and Other Symptoms," 321–41; Epstein, "Refrigerator Mothers and Sick Little Boys."
3 Seidman, "Fag-Hags and Bu-Jews," 263. Seidman, 255, 262, identifies a remarkably similar "coming-out scene" in Judith Butler's *Bodies That Matter*.
4 Sedgwick, *Epistemology of the Closet*, 83–90. As Sedgwick notes, neither of these models is inherently oriented towards queer liberation; for instance, while the universalizing position has empowered lesbian-feminists who see sexual liberation from men as a possibility for all women, Sedgwick notes that it is also a foundational assumption in the "gay panic defense," which excuses homophobic violence. Moreover, the idea of bisexual potentials does not necessarily create any recognition or even legibility for real bisexual and pansexual people.
5 D. Boyarin, "Othello's Penis," 254.
6 If this observation is noteworthy, it is only because, as Joseph Litvak notes, "the Americanization of the Jew has consisted precisely in *unlinking* Jews from women, homosexuals, and queers." Litvak, *The Un-Americans*, 52–3.
7 Fabre-Vassas, *The Singular Beast*, 8.
8 See, *inter alia*, D. Boyarin, *Unheroic Conduct*, esp. 1–13, 208–16; Drake, *Slandering the Jew*; DeVun, *The Shape of Sex*; Kruger, *Spectral Jew*, esp 19–109; Kruger, "Medieval Jewish/Christian Debate and the Question of Gender," 85–103.
9 On Jews as nonbinary, see DeVun, 70–98.
10 On this figure see, *inter alia*, Resnick, *Marks of Distinction*, esp. 203–5; D. Biale, *Blood and Belief*; 105; Kruger, *Spectral Jew*, 82–3.
11 See Zacher, "Jews and Judaizing as Pathologies in the Anglo-Saxon Imagination."
12 This medievally imagined Jewish heterosexual should not, of course, be confused with real medieval Jews; on the relationship between medieval European Jewish gender/sexual practices and Biblical interpretation, see Baumgarten, *Biblical Women and Jewish Daily Life in the Middle Ages*. On the contrary, the Jewish (Biblical) heterosexual is a rich resource for Church hegemony over sexuality and reproduction, which will include the eventual imposition of procreative heterosexuality and gender binaries over Christians and non-Christians alike.

13 Clark, *Between Medieval Men*, 22.
14 Riggs and Peel, *Critical Kinship Studies*, 54.
15 Ward, *Tragedy of Heterosexuality*, 3. It is not possible to adumbrate the very full feminist and queer literature on kinship here, but see n18.
16 Edelman, *No Future*, 2, 31; Long Chu, "Andrea Long Chu," interview by Blanchard.
17 Huber and Robertson, eds., *Hali Meithhad*, 27.2, 26.4.
18 On these issues see, among many other critiques, Roderick Ferguson, *Aberrations in Black*, and Leanne Betasamosake Simpson, *As We Have Always Done*, 84–118. It is worth noting that feminist, anti-racist, and anti-colonial critiques of heteropatriarchy (although not all critiques of heterosexuality!) assign significant value to the reproduction and care labour that every human relies upon but which is so frequently unpaid or underpaid, coerced, sentimentalized, denigrated, penalized, racialized, and gendered.
19 D. Boyarin, *A Radical Jew*, esp. 67–85, 196–200.
20 Drake, *Slandering the Jew*, 26.
21 Boyarin, *A Radical Jew*, 167.
22 Drake, *Slandering the Jew*, 11–13.
23 Pasternack, "The Sexual Practices of Virginity and Chastity in Aldhelm's De Virginitate," 94.
24 Weston, "Where Textual Bodies Meet," 231–46; Weston, "Reading the Textual Shadows of Anglo-Saxon Monastic Women's Friendships," esp. 68, 77. On the strong ties between monastic women and their secular families of origin, see J. Stevens, "Brothers and Sisters," esp. 7–16, 18–21.
25 Foucault, "Friendship as a Way of Life," 309.
26 Ælred of Rievaulx, *Spiritual Friendship*; Venarde, ed. and trans., *The Rule of Saint Benedict*, esp. §§2, 22, 69.
27 Foucault, "Friendship as a Way of Life," 309.
28 Symons, ed. and trans., *Regularis Concordia*, at 66, emphasis removed.
29 Moreover, monasteries depended on the work of artisans, servants, and enslaved people.
30 See also Jaeger, *Ennobling Love*, 31–32.
31 Saltzman, "Writing Friendship, Mourning the Friend in Late Anglo-Saxon Rules of Confraternity," 260, and see n26, above.
32 Karras, *Sexuality in Medieval Europe*, 38, 57–75.
33 Lochrie, *Heterosyncracies*, xiii. See also, *inter alia*, Tin, *The Invention of Heterosexual Culture*, esp. viii–xi.
34 Aldhelm, *Aldhelm: The Prose Works*, 62; "dulcia natorum pignora, nesciens coniugii illecebrosa consortia, fetosa quadam suauissimi suci concretione producit: ecclesia uero bis acuto testamentorum mucrone hominum uitaliter corda transuerberans hereditariam legitimae aeternitatis sobolem

casto uerbi fecundat semine." Aldhelm, *Aldhelmi Malmesbiriensis Prosa de Virginitate cum Glosa atque Anglosaxonica*, §V. On the influence of this text and, generally, of Aldhelm's writing upon the Benedictine writers, see, *inter alia*, Gretsch, *Intellectual Foundations*; Gwara, "Manuscripts of Aldhelm's 'Prosa de Virginitate'"; Stephenson, *The Politics of Language*.
35 Irigaray, *This Sex Which Is Not One*, 23–33.
36 Muñoz, *Cruising Utopia*.
37 Aldhelm, *The Prose Works*, 63; "flagrantis ambrosiae thimiama ac nardi spirantis olfactum uincat, uerum etiam ... uniuersam mundanae suauitatis dulcedinem opulentique luxus exquisita superet oblectamenta et haustum defruti despiciat" (Aldhelm, *Prosa*, §VI).
38 Aldhelm, 59–60; "adoptiuas regenerantis gratiae filias ex fecundo ecclesiasticae conceptionis utero spiritualis uerbi semine progenitas" (Aldhelm, *Prosa*, §II). In this analogy, the Word impregnates the fertile Church. See Lees and Overing, *Double Agents*, 111–24 for an extensive feminist reading of this passage.
39 Weston, "Queering Virginity," 22–4.
40 Kolve, "Ganymede/Son of Getron," 1056–9. Elliott takes a different view, contending that only clergy who "were widowers or had in some way assumed responsibility for any children they might have fathered" – that is, those who had already undergone heterosexual fatherhood – could experience parental feelings. Elliott, *Corrupter of Boys*, 232.
41 Clark, *Between Medieval Men*, 182.
42 See, *inter alia*, Kolve, "Ganymede/Son of Getron," 1041; Sauer, "Uncovering Difference," 135–6; Schroeder, "Queer Eye for the Ascetic Guy?" 333; Lochrie, *Heterosyncracies*, 26–70; Traub, *The Renaissance of Lesbianism in Early Modern England*, 62–5; Weston, "Virgin Desires," 98–100; Clark, 169, 203–6.
43 On the idea that any kind of sex between clergy or between a cleric and a parishioner is a form of spiritual abuse, as well as a contemporary (1048) assessment that such contacts were common and frequent, see Peter Damian's complaint, *The Book of Gomorrah*. Elliott has recently demonstrated the prevalence of sexual abuse within (male) medieval monasteries and throughout medieval clerical culture, in spite of regulations to the contrary, but has not found any similar evidence in female monasteries. Elliott, *passim* and 6, respectively. Regular life seems thus to have represented for some people (aristocratic girls and women) an escape from the ordinary sexual violence of (secular) patriarchal life, while exposing others (boys and young men) to greater violence.
44 Weston, "When Textual Bodies Meet," 233–5.
45 Betancourt, *Byzantine Intersectionality*, 89.
46 Betancourt, 120.

47 Like Betancourt, I "take [trans] existence for granted." Betancourt, 17. On the importance of doing so, see *inter alia*, Kim and Bychowski, "Visions of Medieval Trans Feminism."
48 See, *inter alia*, Betancourt, 125–9.
49 See Frantzen, *Before the Closet*, 81, on this chapel as a place of erotic temptation. For a chilling eroticization of non-consensual outing in a monastic environment, see Howie, *Claustrophilia*, 62–4.
50 There is a considerable body of scholarship interrogating whether these episodes are motivated by queer desire, and these works appear in the bibliography. A transgender studies perspective has simplified this question. On the dangerous (for trans people) myth of transmasculine irresistibility, see especially Adair and Aizura, "The Transgender Craze," esp. 47–51.
51 Clark, *Between Medieval Men*, 198, notes that it is unclear whether the brothers believe "that Smaragdus is a eunuch," which might (as Betancourt suggests) make him transfeminine in their eyes. As Clark observes, "the emphasis is on the fact that Smaragdus is *wlitig on ansyne*" (199), that is, beautiful. See, however, Lisa Weston's remark that Smaragdus's gender may be what the brothers find sexually compelling; Weston, "Saintly Lives," 401.
52 Clark, 199. See also Betancourt, *Byzantine Intersectionality*, 126. See, however, Elliott's discussion of Smaragdus in the context of a monastic culture that blames children and youth for attracting men's sexual attention. Elliott, *Corrupter of Boys*, 49–50.
53 "Saint Eugenia," Clayton, *LS* 1:44–73. In referring to Smaragdus and Eugenia, I use the naming and pronoun conventions established by Betancourt, who distinguishes between transmasculine figures, like Smaragdus, who choose to both live and die in their masculine identities and whose biographers affirm these identities with frequent use of masculine names and pronouns, and those, like Eugenia, whose masculine identities are more circumscribed and situational and who later live as women. For the former, I use he/him; for the latter, I use they/them. (I use he/him and she/her for apparently cisgender figures.) See Betancourt, 91. Betancourt uses feminine pronouns for Eugenia, but see Clark, 190, on Eugenia's gender markers in the Old English manuscripts.
54 The literature of romance will discover a similar preoccupation with transmasculinity in martial settings.
55 Jaeger, *Ennobling Love*, *passim*.
56 See also Jack Mallon's characterization of the monastic family as "an alternative to the heterosexual familial experience," a difference he locates in same-sex love. Mallon, "To Love and Be Loved," 94. See, however, Elliott, for the view that same-sex relations and sexual abuse

in the church became disordered substitutes for the heterosexual and biofamilial affections that clergy were prohibited. Elliott, *Corrupter of Boys*, esp. 231.
57 Cubitt, "Apocalyptic and Eschatological Thought in England," 5.
58 Unlike in modern Judaism, belonging in the ancient people Israel was patrilineal.
59 On the history of interpretation of the primordial blessing, see J. Cohen, *Be Fertile and Increase*. See Koltun-Fromm, *Hermeneutics of Holiness* on the interesting tradition of Moses's celibacy.
60 See J. Cohen, 232–4, 243–4.
61 J. Cohen, 251–9.
62 "The Chair of Saint Peter the Apostle," Clayton, *LS* 1:294.
63 See Cubitt, "Virginity and Misogyny," 4–5.
64 Cubitt, esp. 18.
65 See Lees and Overing, *Double Agents*, 127–32, for the thematic connections between *De virginitate* and the homilies of Ælfric.
66 *Die Hertenbriefe Ælfrics*, IV, §19.
67 Giorgio Agamben, *The Highest Poverty*, 110, emphasis removed.
68 "The Chair of Saint Peter," Clayton, *LS* 1:294. Neither Clayton nor Jayatilaka, "Lives 10 (Chair of St Peter)," gives a source for these lines but see Aldhelm, who allows that for "men of ancient times" (*ueteribus uiris*), "the licence of the ancient law benignly permitted nuptial bonds of marriage for the sake of a family of offspring and for propagating the progeny of descendants" (Aldhelm, *The Prose Works*, 78); "priscae legis licentia nuptiales thalamorum copulas pro nepotum prosapia et posterorum progenie propaganda clementer indulsit" (Aldhelm, *Prosa*, §XXII).
69 Stafford, "Queens, Nunneries, and Reforming Churchmen," 7–8.
70 Agamben, *The Time That Remains*, *passim*, esp. 53, 55, 68, 76. For an extended reading of Ælfric's eschatology with reference to both *The Chair of St. Peter* homily and Agamben's insights, see K. Davis, "Boredom and Brevity," 338–42.
71 K. Davis, 30–1.
72 Jost, ed., *Institutes of Polity*, §166. On the opprobrium suffered by priests' wives, see especially Elliott, *Corrupter of Boys*, 58–75.
73 *Hertenbriefe*; see Hill, "Authorial Adaptation."
74 See Trilling, "Sovereignty and Social Order," 58–9, on the usefulness of this rhetoric.
75 Lees, *Tradition and Belief*, 136. As Kathy Lavezzo and David Clark observe, Ælfric also studiously avoids references to same-gender sexuality except, as Clark notes, "in texts aimed at a uniquely clerical audience" (Lavezzo, "Gregory's Boys," 77–85; Clark, *Between Medieval Men*, 88).
76 *Hertenbriefe*, IV, §128–34.

77 "Primus Sermo de Initio Creaturae" ([First Homily] On the Origin of Creation), *CHI* 184.
78 Anlezark, "An Ideal Marriage," 195–6; Karkov, "Hagar and Ishmael," 208; *OEH*, Gen. 21:12. On the ambiguity of Hagar's legal status as wife, concubine, and enslaved woman, see, *inter alia*, Yoo, "Hagar the Egyptian," 215–35.
79 This is Paul's phrase, but in quoting it I do not mean to imply that Paul's own theology is reductively supersessionist. On the contrary, as Guido Baltes observes, "heart circumcision" as Paul uses it is a Hebrew Biblical concept that only connotes "negation of physical circumcision" beginning in the patristic era. Baltes, "Circumcision of the Heart," 98. On New Testament and patristic approaches to circumcision, see Jacobs, *Christ Circumcised*.
80 Zacher, "Circumscribing the Text," 82.
81 See J. Cohen, *Be Fertile and Increase*, esp. 96, 54. Indeed, as J. Cohen notes, 213, the Zohar will later use the term "covenant" as a "metonym[ic]" euphemism for men's sexuality or for the penis. Contemporary Jewish theologians resist the reduction of the covenant to heteropatriarchal reproductivity; for an overview of the issues, see S.D. Cohen, *Why Aren't Jewish Women Circumcised?* As Speiser notes, the Hebrew implies that Sarah separately receives the blessing of fertility and nationhood in Gen. 17:16. Speiser, trans., *Genesis*, 123, 125n16. However, this is not apparent in the Vulgate verse, which confers the blessing upon Isaac instead. On rabbinic law and gender, see, *inter alia*, D. Boyarin, *Carnal Israel*, and Strassfeld, *Trans Talmud*.
82 Just as in Latin and English, the same root word, בָּשָׂר (*basar*, flesh), links the Abrahamic covenant to the Noahic covenant in Gen. 9 (discussed at greater length in chapter 1), where it designates both the community of mortal (human and non-human) animals and meat permitted for consumption; σαρκὸς is a form of σάρξ, which the Septuagint often uses to translate בָּשָׂר. As Boyarin notes, σάρξ is the same word Paul uses in Rom. 9:3 to describe Jews as "τῶν συγγενῶν μου κατὰ σάρκα" (my kinsmen according to the flesh) and to transfer the covenant from Israel in the flesh (those who are "circumcised and genealogically Israelite") to Israel in the spirit (Jewish and non-Jewish Christ-followers). D. Boyarin, *Radical Jew*, 81; see also 65–85, esp. 77, and Drake, *Slandering the Jew*, 26.
83 D. Biale, "The God with Breasts," 252. Biale also calls attention to the connections between "El-Shaddai," God's appellation in this passage, and God's traditional feminine aspects. Glick, *Marked in Your Flesh*, 18.
84 "Dominica V in Quadragesima" (Fifth Sunday in Lent), *CHII* 133. On the relationship to Augustine and to Gen. 24:1–4, see *CHIntro*, 471.
85 *OEH*, 39–40.

86 See the corresponding Vulgate passage: "Hoc est pactum meum quod observabitis inter me et vos, et semen tuum post te : circumcidetur ex vobis omne masculinum: et circumcidetis carnem praeputii vestri, ut sit in signum foederis inter me et vos. Infans octo dierum circumcidetur in vobis, omne masculinum in generationibus vestris: tam vernaculus, quam emptitius circumcidetur, et quicumque non fuerit de stirpe vestra: eritque pactum meum in carne vestra in foedus aeternum. Masculus, cujus praeputii caro circumcisa non fuerit, delebitur anima illa de populo suo : quia pactum meum irritum fecit" (This is my covenant which you shall observe, between me and you, and thy seed after thee: all the male kind of you shall be circumcised. And you shall circumcise the flesh of your foreskin that it may be for a sign of the covenant between me and you. An infant of eight days old shall be circumcised among you, every man-child in your generations. He that is born in the house as well as the bought servant shall be circumcised and whosoever is not of your stock. And my covenant shall be in your flesh for a perpetual covenant. The male whose flesh of his foreskin shall not be circumcised, that soul shall be destroyed out of his people: because he hath broken my covenant; Gen. 17:10–14)

87 For a fuller discussion of Ælfric's treatment of circumcision passages in the *Old English Heptateuch*, see Zacher, "Circumscribing the Text," 97–9.

88 The note appears after Gen. 17:27, at *OEH*, 39.

89 For source analysis see Marsden, *CHIntro*, 45–53, and Godden, "Catholic Homilies 1.6."

90 This early homily (completed by 990; see Kleist, *Chronology*, 277) appears in the first series of *Catholic Homilies*. See Zacher's discussion, "Circumscribing the Text," 101–7.

91 "Octabas et Circumcisio Domini" (The Lord's Octave and Circumcision), *CHI* 225.

92 Zacher, "Circumscribing the Text," 96.

93 *CHIntro*, 48.

94 I am influenced in my translation of *holdne* as "generous" by Josephine Bloomfield. See Bloomfield, "Benevolent Authoritarianism in Klaeber's *Beowulf*," *passim*, esp. 148–50.

95 Zacher, "Circumscribing the Text," 111–12.

96 *CHI* 225.

97 These roles are, of course, hopelessly entangled, because Abraham is the patriarch of Hagar's line only through Sarah's domestic authority over Hagar's and (therefore) Ishmael's bodies.

98 Bede, "In Octava Nativitatis Domini," §1.2, lines 99–100. Translation is Martin and Hurst, *Homilies on the Gospels*, 107.

99 On the racial and national implications of circumcision's supersession by baptism, see Britton, *Becoming Christian*, 64–101. See also Biddick, *Typological Imaginary*, 91–104.
100 *CHI* 225–6. See Bede, lines 41–8. For the relationship to the source, see Marsden, *CHIntro*, 48–9; Godden, "Catholic Homilies 1.6".
101 As Baltes notes, 4–5, this interpretation has no basis in Jewish sources.
102 Translation Martin and Hurst, *Homilies on the Gospels*, 105. On this passage see Conor O'Brien, "Bede's Theology of Circumcision, Its Sources and Significance," esp. 595.
103 See Susanna Drake's discussion of "difference in times," 36.
104 See Freidenreich, *Foreigners and Their Food*, 87–100.
105 *OEH*, 21, 23; see Marsden, *The Text of the Old Testament*, 402–39 on the Latin sources of the *Old English Heptateuch*.
106 *OEH* Lev. 11.9–12, at 133.
107 See *Genesis A* in Anlezark, ed. and trans., *Old Testament Narratives*, line 1305.
108 See Momma, "Epanalepsis," 60.
109 *DOE*, s.v. *clænnes*.
110 Stafford, "Queens, Nunneries, and Reforming Churchmen," 7–8; Wright, "A New Latin Source for Two Old English Homilies," 252.
111 Ambrose, "The Theme of Lay *Clænnyss* in Ælfric's Letters," 8.
112 Ambrose, 6.
113 See Drake, *Slandering the Jew*, esp. 50–8, 78–98.
114 See Cubitt and Stafford for two classic assessments of Ælfric's relationship to Reform misogyny.

4. *Ænlic Wimman*: Judith and the Exception

1 All extracts from the *Judith*-homily are cited by line and refer to Lee's electronic edition. On the relationship between this interpolation and its apparent Latin source in MS. Boulogne-sur-Mer 63, see S. D. Lee, *Judith*, lines 2–21n and Raynes, "MS. Boulogne-sur-Mer 63 and Ælfric," 69–70. Gatch has edited the relevant texts in *Preaching and Theology in Anglo-Saxon England*," 134–46.
2 Gera, *Judith*, 38.
3 "Latin Preface," §2. Clayton, *LS* 1:4–5. This originally Alfredian rule about the expression of sovereignty in English must be properly understood as a *translation* principle, since it governs only what can be carried into the vernacular; see Stephenson, *The Politics of Language*, 29. As Davis notes, it is also a temporal principle; see K. Davis, "Boredom and Brevity," 327.
4 "Old English Preface," §4. Clayton, *LS* 1:10. As Catherine Cubitt notes, these lines implicitly liken the saints to Ælfric's patrons, who were "amongst the most senior of all the earthly king's thegns." Cubitt, "Ælfric's Lay Patrons," 165.

182 Notes to pages 94–7

5 Lee's source table accounts for lines translated directly from the Biblical source and lines interpolated by Ælfric. See Lee, "Source Tables," in *Ælfric's Homilies*. As we do not have the Vulgate manuscript Ælfric used, so any such accounting is subject to minor discrepancies. For the interpolations, it is possible that Ælfric used additional sources that are now lost. For more detail on Ælfric's Vulgate and Old Latin source material for this homily, see Lee, "Ælfric's Treatment of Source Material," 165–76. See also Marsden, *The Text of the Old Testament*, 398–401, on the Latin sources of Ælfric's Old Testament writings.
6 Like Peggy McCracken, I "use 'sovereignty' to insist on the coincidence of modern theoretical considerations ... and medieval literary texts." McCracken, *In the Skin of a Beast*, 7.
7 McCracken, *In the Skin of a Beast*, 97; Markell, *Bound by Recognition*, 12. Both Markell and McCracken are interested primarily in the *failure* of self-sovereignty as a fantasy.
8 *DOE* s.v. *anweald*.
9 Wright and Wright, *Old English Grammar*, 299, §568.
10 *DOE* s.v. *anweald*. See Momma, "Element by Element," 338. See also Bosworth-Toller, s.v. *an-wald*. For consistency with the style of this book rather than with the style of my references, I omit the macrons that indicate stress; these can be found in the dictionary entries but are not useful for distinguishing between the homonyms.
11 Momma, "Element by Element," esp. 338–41. Pauline Stafford attributes this meaning, "sole rule," to the Chronicle A entry on Æthelflæd's death. Stafford, *After Alfred*, 74.
12 Smith, *Land and Book*, 151.
13 *DOE,* s.v. *anweald*.
14 Godden, ed. and trans., *The Old English History of the World*, I.1–3, at 56, 58. See Kretzschmar, "Adaptation and *anweald*," for a perspective on the *anweald/rice* distinction in *Orosius* that differs from this chapter's line of argument.
15 *An Anglo-Saxon Dictionary Online*, ed. Bosworth and Toller, defines *geweald* as 1. "power, strength, might, efficacy, *potestas*"; 2. "power over any thing, empire, rule, dominion, mastery, sway, jurisdiction, government, protection, keeping, a bridle-bit" (s.v. *ge-weald*.) The *DOE* has not yet published an entry for this word.
16 *OEH*, 10.
17 Ælfric, *De Falsis Diis* (On the False Gods), in *Homilies of Ælfric*, ed. Pope, 2:678.
18 Ælfric, *Exameron Anglice*, 58.
19 *OEH*, 13.
20 Ælfric, "Praefatio" (Preface to the First Series) in *CHI* 176.

21 Ælfric, "Theodosius and Ambrose," in *Homilies of Ælfric,* ed. Pope, 2:762. Similarly, the prose Old English Martyrology refers to St. Clement's "helle geweald," authority over hell. *OEM,* 218.
22 Ælfric, "Inventio Sanctae Crucis" (Invention of the Holy Cross), in *CHII* 176.
23 "Natale Sanctorum Abdon et Sennes" (Saints Abdon and Sennes and the Letter of Christ to Abgar), Clayton, *LS* 2:264.
24 *DOE* s.v. *anweald.* For an overview of Wulfstan's idiosyncratic vocabulary in the context of standard Old English and the Benedictine Reform, see esp. Dance, "Sound, Fury, and Signifiers."
25 Wulfstan, *Be Godcundre Warnunge* (Bethurum 19), in Bethurum, *Homilies of Wulfstan,* 253.
26 "Genesis," in Anzelark, ed., *Old Testament Narratives,* 170. See chapters 5 and 3, respectively.
27 *OEM,* 148.
28 Ælfric has adapted this dialogue into his own idiom from the Vulgate, where Nebuchadnezzar announces that "cogitationem suam in eo esse ut omnem terram suo subiugaret imperio" (his thoughts were to bring all the earth under his empire [italics removed]) and "Quod dictum ... placuisset omnibus" (this saying pleased them all), Judith 2:3–4.
29 Paul Szarmach suggests that the speech is "singular in its moral stupidity." Szarmach, "Ælfric's *Judith,*" 84. The laudatory phrase appears once elsewhere in Ælfric's work, in a context that underlines the irony of its appearance in *Judith*: "Þa cwæð eall þæt folc þæt he ænlice spræce" (line 111; Then that people all said that he spoke peerlessly). "Kings," Clayton, *LS* 2:146). Here, the people of Israel are praising the prophet Elijah for publicly denouncing their tyrannical rulers' flirtation with polytheism.
30 See Lee, notes to *Judith* lines 43–9, lines 49–54, on Ælfric's approach to the source; see also Judith 2:12–17.
31 "Yehudit" in its Septuagint Greek context is the feminine form of "Jew." See, *inter alia,* Gera, *Judith,* 11 and 255.
32 Gera points out that "[w]hile Holophernes may see Nebuchadnezzar as the only real god, the author makes certain that the readers of [the Book of] Judith will not share this view at any point in the story," 7. The same can be said of the readers of the *Judith*-homily.
33 For the relationship between the interpolation and Achior's speech, see Cooper, "Judith in Late Anglo-Saxon England," 173–4.
34 Stephenson, "Judith as Spiritual Warrior," 85.
35 Szarmach calls it a "motif word." Szarmach, "Ælfric's *Judith,*" 83.
36 "St. Thomas," Clayton, *LS* 3:270.
37 "De Septem Dormientibus" "The Seven Sleepers," in Skeat *LS* 2 489–541, at 538; *DOE* s.v. *ænlic.* According to the *Dictionary, ænlic* here glosses Latin *unigenite.*

38 "Symbolum apostolorum," in Sisam, ed., *The Salisbury Psalter*, 304–5.
39 Three non-Ælfrician texts (Alfred's Old English translations of Boethius and of Augustine's *Soliloquies*; Vercelli Homily VII) use versions of the term "ænlic wif" to mean something like "excellent wife" or "beautiful woman" without the same connotations of singularity. In all of these cases, the context is marriage or male desire and in only one case (that of Eurydice in the *Boethius*) does the phrase refer to a specific woman. Irvine and Godden, ed., *The Old English Boethius*, 270.
40 Fulk, Bjork, and Niles, eds., *Klaeber's* Beowulf, 66.
41 See Bloomfield, "Diminished by Kindness," 183–203.
42 *DOE* s.v. *ænlic*. Erin Sebo and Cassandra Schilling, however, observe that "it makes more sense to understand 'ænlic' as referring to Modthryth's excellence, rather than her beauty." Sebo and Schilling, "Modthryth and the Problem of Peace-Weavers," 644.
43 Judith, who keeps several people enslaved, evades this charge by the standards of her texts. For more on slavery in Judith, see Glancy, "The Mistress-Slave Dialectic," esp. 82–6; Hezser, *Jewish Slavery in Antiquity*, *passim*. See also McCracken on the feminine "fantasy that self-sovereignty also promises sovereignty over others" in medieval romance. McCracken, *In the Skin of a Beast*, 125; see 97–125. Wyatt conjectures that in early medieval England, both powerful women and monastic institutions gained status, just as powerful men long had, through the acquisition of women and girls (*Slaves and Warriors*, 190, 281).
44 When St. Lucy sees St. Agatha in a dream-vision, Agatha calls out to her from "betwux engla werodum, ænlice gefretewode" (line 260; among bands of angels, singularly adorned). "Saint Agatha and Saint Lucy," Clayton, *LS* 1:268.
45 Cubitt, "Virginity and Misogyny," 6.
46 "Saint Agnes and Saints Constantia and Gallicanus," Clayton, *LS* 1:222. On this passage in context, see, *inter alia*, Gulley, *The Displacement of the Body*, 37–49; McDaniel, "Agnes among the Anglo-Saxons." See also Clayton's comparison of Ælfric's *Judith* to his passion of St. Agatha. Clayton, "Ælfric's *Judith*," 223.
47 Clayton, 223.
48 See Clayton, 223.
49 Zacher, *Rewriting the Old Testament*, 138.
50 Tal Ilan compellingly argues for the Book of Judith, as well as the Book of Esther and the story of Susanna, as "propaganda" for Shelamzion's reign. Ilan, *Integrating Women into Second Temple History*, esp. 127–33, at 150–1. Gera, who dates the Book to the period between 161 BCE and 63 BCE, suggests instead that "the fictional Judith and the historical Shelamzion ... share a common influence" in Queens Cleopatra II and

Cleopatra III of Egypt. Gera, *Judith*, 42, 38–9. As Gera observes, Judith is also a recognizable "composite" or double of more than a dozen Biblical figures, most obviously her near predecessor Judah Maccabee, another allegorical figure of militant Jewish righteousness. Gera 39–40, 41, 51–2, *passim*. Figures from ancient Greek writing, including Hera, Helen of Troy, Tomyris, and Artemisia, also contribute to the composite. Gera 57, 65–72.
51 Gera, esp. 9–10.
52 Gera, 10.
53 See Klein, "Ælfric's Sources and His Gendered Audiences," 133–4. As Brookes notes, Ælfric's epithets for Jezebel align her with the persecuting tyrants of his hagiographies. "Life, but Not as We Know It," 148.
54 Gera, *Judith*, 99.
55 Salmesvuori, *Power and Sainthood*, 162.
56 Birgitta, *The Revelations of St. Birgitta of Sweden*, IV. 136.
57 As a political philosophy articulated by powerful women such as Birgitta and by their many male supporters (including, possibly, the supporters of Shelamzion of Judaea, if they composed or used the Biblical book), the concept of feminine sovereign exceptionality does not aim to advance gender equality. On the contrary, the potency of ancient Jewish and premodern Christian women who need not submit to men is predicated on the unfreedom and supposed defencelessness of women in general, and indeed on the production of *woman* itself as a normative category of sexual and reproductive property. Moreover, as Dube observes regarding Rahab and Judith, it is compatible with the particular subjugation of colonized and racialized women. Dube, "Rahab Says Hello to Judith," 156. These are features rather than bugs of these premodern discourses of feminine sovereignty, which did not and could not adhere to the modern feminist-humanist assumption, trenchantly critiqued by Saba Mahmood, that every ambitious woman advances or even seeks the liberation of all women. Mahmood, *Politics of Piety*, esp. 1–17.
58 Schmitt, *Political Theology*, esp. 36–7. For recent Jewish critiques of Schmittian political theology, with particular attention to its reliance on Jewish abjection and disappearance, see, *inter alia*, Gross, *Carl Schmitt and the Jews*; Nirenberg, *Aesthetic Theology and Its Enemies*.
59 Heschel, "The Slippery Yet Tenacious Nature of Racism," 13.
60 Schmitt, *Political Theology*, 5.
61 Zacher, *Rewriting the Old Testament*, esp. 17–24. Erin Forbes observes that the poem's Judith herself "in certain ways fulfills Schmitt's definition of the sovereign"; specifically, she is the one who takes the exceptional decision to assassinate Holofernes. Forbes, "Sovereign Poetics," 17. The part of the story depicting the decision is in fact missing from the poem, but in the Biblical account Judith both decides and acts with the consent

of the elders, a collaborative process that the homily emphasizes. Seeking counsel is not the behaviour of a Schmittian sovereign, a dictator who unilaterally usurps the power of an absent God, but as Rachel S. Anderson notes, it is essential kingly behaviour in Ælfric's world. See Anderson, "Ælfric's Kings," esp. 23.

62 Vatter, "The Political Theology of Carl Schmitt," 248.
63 On the "crisis" context of Judith's actions, see Ilan, *Integrating Women into Second Temple History*, 150–1.
64 This point is even more explicit in the Septuagint; the Vulgate differs from that text in several important ways. For a thorough discussion of Judith's "hand" as a theopolitical instrument, see Wills, *Judith*, 289–91; Gera, *Judith*, 318.
65 Gera, 458.
66 Stafford, "The Portrayal of Royal Women," 146–7.
67 See Erin V. Casey-Williams on the "politicized manifestation of chastity – an insistence on the impenetrability and non-subordination of the sovereign body natural, as well as body politic" in early modern literature about queenship (Casey-Williams, "The Queen's Three Bodies," 43–4).
68 Dube, "Rahab Says Hello to Judith," 156.
69 Blanton, *Signs of Devotion*, 139, 153; see also Blanton, "*Tota integra, tota incorrupta*," 233, 245; Stafford, "The Portrayal of Royal Women," 146–7.
70 As Momma notes, "Elements of Judaism that are missing from the extant poem include dietary laws, priesthood, the temple, and (most importantly of all) circumcision, which the poet has managed to leave unmentioned by omitting the character of Achior." Momma, "Epanalepsis," 60.
71 See Brookes, "Life, but Not as We Know It," esp. 147–9; Godden, "Experiments in Genre," 279–80; see Corona, "Ælfric's Schemes and Tropes," esp. 302–8, on Ælfric's florid descriptions of tyrants.
72 As Gera notes, this "elaborate genealogy" marks Judith to early readers as a fictional "character." Gera, *Judith*, 28; and see esp. 26–38, 171–3, 176–7, on the obvious fictionality of the geography and historical setting.
73 "erat ... Iudith, relicta eius, vidua iam annis tribus et mensibus sex et in superioribus domus suae fecit sibi secretum cubiculum in quo cum puellis suis clausa morabatur.

Et habens super lumbos suos cilicium ieiunabat omnibus diebus vitae suae praeter sabbata et neomenias et festa domus Israhel. Erat autem eleganti aspectu nimis, cui vir suus reliquerat divitias multas et familiam copiosam ac possessiones armentis boum et gregibus ovium plenas, et erat haec in omnibus famosissima quoniam timebat Dominum valde, nec erat qui loqueretur de illa verbum malum."
74 Clayton, "Ælfric's *Judith*," 223.

75 Pringle, "Judith," 95.
76 *The Life of St. Æthelthryth* survives in the eleventh-century *LS* collection London, British Library, MS Cotton Julius E.vii; in Cambridge, University Library, MS Ii.1.33; and in a partial witness. See Clayton, *LS* 2:343–5, 379.
77 Anna hatte hyre fæder, East Engla cynincg, / swyðe Cristen man, swa swa he cydde mid weorcum, / and eall his team wearð gewurðod þurh God" (lines 5–7; Her father was called Anna, king of the East Anglians, a very Christian person just as he demonstrated with his deeds, and his entire family attained honour through God).
78 "Saint Æthelthryth," in Clayton, *LS* 2:194, 196.
79 Griffiths, "Reading Ælfric's Saint Æthelthryth as a Woman," 35, 45. Critical disability studies scholars have challenged the conventional equation between voice and agency. See, for instance, Troeung, *Refugee Lifeworlds* and Smilges, *Queer Silence*.
80 Griffiths, 46–7; "Saint Æthelthryth," lines 52–61, in Clayton, *LS* 2:198.
81 Some non-Ælfrician Old English hagiography depicts women and gender non-conforming saints in violent *spiritual* battle. Most notable among these are St. Margaret, who brutally beats and tortures a racialized devil, and St. Perpetua, who in the *OEM* "mætte þa heo wæs on mædenhade þæt heo wære on wæres hiwe, ond ðæt heo hæfde sweord on handa, ond ðæt heo stranglice fuhte mid þy. Þæt wæs eall eft on hire martyrdome gefylled, ða heo mid werlice geðohte deofol oferswiðde ond þa hæþnan ehteras" (dreamed when she was a girl that she had a masculine appearance and that she had a sword in her hands, and that she fought powerfully with it. That was all fulfilled later in her martyrdom, when with a masculine mind she overcame the devil and the heathen persecutors). Clayton and Magennis, ed. and trans., *The Old English Lives of St. Margaret*, 124. *OEM*, 62.
82 It is not within the scope of this book to critique the historical categories "woman" and "man," as others have so elegantly done, but I will note that it would not be correct to multiply our errors and imagine that Ælfric saw non-Christian women as a meaningful category or extended his admiring attitude towards Judith to her medieval Jewish descendants.
83 *Maccabees*, Clayton, *LS* 2.294. On the Maccabees as Christian saints, see Joslyn-Siemiatkoski, *Christian Memories of the Maccabean Martyrs, passim*, esp. 104–5, 143–55.
84 See Brookes, "Life, but Not as We Know It," 149.
85 In contrast, the *Judith*-poem entirely omits the theme of Judith's hands.
86 Far from diminishing her individual significance, Judith's role as God's agent licenses her to carry out His will according to her decision; see Forbes, "Sovereign Poetics," 25–7. See Lees and Overing, 251, who theorize a holy woman's agency in extreme religious action as "her own interpretation of the demands of heroic obedience to the will of God."

87 For more on this passage, see Klein, "Ælfric's Gendered Audiences," 115–16. As Klein notes, Ælfric's interpolated language about shame posits Holofernes's unchastity as the wellspring of his loss of command and his army's humiliation.
88 Damico, *Beowulf and the Grendel-kin*, 207; see Damico, 204–84, esp. 257–64.
89 See, for instance, "On Eleven Misdeeds of Pope Gregory XI," in which Birgitta intervenes in the Great Schism in tones of prophetic command: "Come, then, and do not delay! Come not with your customary pride and worldly pomp, but with all humility and ardent love! As soon as you have thus come, uproot, pluck out and destroy all the vices of your court! Separate yourself from the counsel of carnal-minded and worldly friends and follow humbly the spiritual counsel of my friends. Approach, then, and be not afraid. Get up like a man and clothe yourself confidently in strength! Start to reform the church that I purchased with my own blood in order that it may be reformed and led back spiritually to its pristine state of holiness, for nowadays more veneration is shown to a brothel than to my Holy Church" (lines 13–15, *The Revelations of St. Birgitta of Sweden*, II. 255). Although Birgitta's own Rule demands her obedience to popes, the authority she allocates to herself in the name of Christ also, apparently, means that in real terms she chooses the ecclesiastical authorities she will obey. (These revelations do not exhaust Birgitta's extensive political writings, which also address kings, archbishops, and other authorities.)
90 In the Cotton Tiberius A.iii version of her life, St. Margaret physically and verbally assaults a devil, telling him "Gewit fram minum magþhad!" (Get away from my virginity!) and commands an unwilling executioner to carry out her beheading, on pain of damnation. Clayton and Magennis, ed., *The Old English Lives*, 124, 134.
91 See Gera, *Judith*, 396–7 on the relationship of this beheading to its cultural context and intertexts. One valence is political: "with Holophernes's death the vast Assyrian army loses its head, their commander"; Gera, 396.
92 On the temporality of these terms in the homily, see Hostetler, "Nimað eow bysne be þyssere Iudith," 160.
93 Cubitt, "Virginity and Misogyny," *passim*. On this complicated issue, see also, *inter alia*, Stafford, "Queens, Nunneries, and Reforming Churchmen"; Scheck, *Reform and Resistance*; Bugyis, *The Care of Nuns*. On Ælfric's attitudes, see especially Cubitt.
94 Wilson, *Hrotsvit of Gandersheim*, 6. Women in this era also occasionally held independent secular power, as Æthelflæd and, briefly, Ælfwynn did in Mercia in the early tenth century.
95 See Clayton, "Ælfric's *Judith*," for a sceptical reading of the moral on chastity. For identification of these women as vowesses rather than cloistered (monastic) nuns, see further Foot, *Veiled Women*, 109. On the

possibility that the *swustor* (line 372; sister) to whom Ælfric addresses this discussion of unchaste vowesses is herself a monastic woman, see Stephenson, "Judith as Spiritual Warrior," 82–3.
96 Pringle, "Judith," esp. 91, 97.
97 Stephenson, "Judith as Spiritual Warrior," 82–5. On Ælfric's usual presumption of a masculine audience, see Cubitt, "Virginity and Misogyny," esp. 17; Treharne, "The Invisible Woman," 191–208. See also Lees and Overing, *Double Agents*, 169, on "identification across as well as within the sexes" in Ælfric's hagiographies. As Robert Stanton notes of the bilingual prefaces, Ælfric's work often assumes multiple audiences. Stanton, *The Culture of Translation*, 170-1.
98 Corona, "Ælfric's Schemes and Tropes," esp. 316–19; Anderson, "Ælfric's Kings," *passim*.
99 See, *inter alia*, Clayton, "Ælfric's *Judith*," 220–5.

5. Like Dogs and Wolves: Wulfstan as Biblical Translator

1 Vatter, "The Political Theology of Carl Schmitt," 248.
2 Howe, *Migration and Mythmaking in Anglo-Saxon England*, 8–32.
3 Wulfstan, *Sermo Lupi ad Anglos*, in Bethurum, *Homilies of Wulfstan*, lines 85–91.
4 See Jurasinski, "Slavery, Learning and the Law of Marriage in Alfred's Mosaic Prologue," 45–64. On this law in its Biblical context, see Hezser, *Jewish Slavery in Antiquity*, 92–3.
5 See MacDonald, *Not Bread Alone*, 130–2. Ælfric does not translate this episode, which resembles the events that Wulfstan narrates but culminates in the sacrifice and mutilation of the concubine; Nicholas Ansell opines that among Biblical texts it "is matched in horror only by the crucifixion" (Ansell, "This Is Her Body," 114).
6 See Drake, *Slandering the Jew*, 15. If the parallel is intentional, then Wulfstan has noticeably altered the terms: where God calls Israel His foster daughter and wife, a sexual possession who has voluntarily become promiscuous and who therefore deserves a humiliating fate (see esp. Ezek. 16), Wulfstan locates sin and punishment in the men who sexually exploit a woman who belongs to God.
7 "Kings," Clayton, *LS* 2:162.
8 A. Campbell and Keynes, eds., *Encomium Emmae Reginae*, 44–5. Translation is Alistair Campbell's.
9 *Sermo Lupi*, lines 176–9.
10 Cnut's Oxford Legislation of 1018 (Cnut 1018), §6, in Rabin, *Old English Legal Writings*, 212.
11 Paolella, *Human Trafficking in Medieval Europe*, 143–68, esp. 164. On patterns of enslavement in early medieval England and its neighbours, see also

190 Notes to pages 120–1

Wyatt, "Reading between the Lines" and Wyatt, *Slaves and Warriors in Medieval Britain and Ireland*.

12 Howe, *Migration and Mythmaking in Anglo-Saxon England*, passim. See also, *inter alia*, Wormald, *The Making of English Law*, 462–3; Wormald, "*Engla Lond*: The Making of an Allegiance," esp. 14–15; Scheil, *The Footsteps of Israel*, 19, 101–91; Zacher, *Rewriting the Old Testament in Anglo-Saxon Verse*, passim, esp. 14–18; Harris, *Race and Ethnicity*, esp. 108.

13 Wormald, *The Making of English Law*, 465.

14 Gildas, *The Ruin of Britain*, 17 and 90. On the Gildas passage in context, see Rabin, "Wolf's Testimony," 406–8.

15 The relevant commandments in the Vulgate include: "Ne prostituas filiam tuam ne contaminetur terra et impleatur piaculo … Ego Dominus" (Lev. 19:29–30; Make not thy daughter a common strumpet lest the land be defiled and filled with wickedness … I am the Lord), and after an enumeration of interconnected sexual sins in Lev. 20: "Custodite leges meas atque iudicia, et facite ea ne et vos evomat terra quam intraturi estis et habitaturi. Nolite ambulare in legitimis nationum quas ego expulsurus sum ante vos omnia enim haec fecerunt et abominatus sum eos. Vobis autem loquor, 'Possidete terram eorum, quam dabo vobis in hereditatem, terram fluentem lacte et melle.' Ego Dominus, Deus vester, qui separavi vos a ceteris populis" (Lev. 20:22–4; Keep my laws and my judgments, and do them lest the land into which you are to enter to dwell therein vomit you also out. Walk not after the laws of the nations which I will cast out before you, for they have done all these things, and therefore I abhorred them. But to you I say, "Possess their land which I will give you for an inheritance, a land flowing with milk and honey." I am the Lord your God, who have separated you from other people). See also Lev. 18:24–30.

16 Lionarons, *The Homiletic Writings of Archbishop Wulfstan*, 85; see also 157.

17 Wormald, "Archbishop Wulfstan," 23; see also Atherton, "Cambridge, Corpus Christi College 201," 469. On the relationship between this theory of historically fulfilled (cyclical) divine justice and Wulfstan's well-known apocalypticism see, *inter alia*, Godden, "Apocalypse and Invasion," 153–6; Roach, "Apocalypse and Atonement," esp. 746–51.

18 On the relevance of *translatio imperii* to pre-Conquest political formulations, see Leneghan, "*Translatio imperii*," 656–705.

19 These are Oxford, Bodleian Library, Hatton 113 (E) and London, British Library, Cotton Nero A.i (I). EI is not necessarily the last version; for a thorough summary of the debate see Lionarons, *The Homiletic Writings of Archbishop Wulfstan*, 149–63. Cotton Nero A.i., discussed further below, is a reference collection compiled at Worcester or York for Wulfstan's use and which continued to accrete material, is one of Wulfstan's own Commonplace Books. The manuscript and a full list of contents can be

viewed at the British Library's Digital Manuscripts collection online. On Cotton Nero A.i and the development of Wulfstan's legal thinking, see Wormald, *The Making of English Law*, 198–203. For some intriguing thoughts on its composition and use, see Wilcox, "The Wolf at Work," 146–7.
20 Godden, "Apocalypse and Invasion," 150.
21 Schwartz, "Wulfstan the Forger," *passim*, 223. See Whitelock, "Laws of Edward and Guthrum."
22 Schwartz, 222n20.
23 Rabin, "Introduction," *Old English Legal Writings*, xxiv. Rabin observes, however, that while *The Laws of Edward and Guthrum* "is manifestly a forgery, Wulfstan almost certainly did not intend this – or any of his other 'forgeries' … to be taken at face value" (Rabin, xiv).
24 Rabin, xiv.
25 Rabin, xxi.
26 An even longer bilingual document translating selections from Isaiah and Jeremiah into rhythmical prose survives in several manuscripts; Dorothy Bethurum edits this as *Incipit de Visione Isaie Prophete quam Vidit Super Iudam et Hierusalem* (Bethurum 11); Bethurum, *Homilies of Wulfstan*, 211–20, and see 331–3. See Lionarons, *The Homiletic Writings of Archbishop Wulfstan*, 147–8, on this text. For more of Wulfstan's Biblical translation, see also Bethurum 16a and especially 16b, described in more detail below.
27 The other three manuscripts are CCCC 201, Oxford, Bodleian Library; MS Junius 121 (eleventh century); London, Lambeth Palace, MS 487 (late twelfth century).
28 Bethurum, *Homilies of Wulfstan*, 355.
29 Wilcox, "Wulfstan and the Twelfth Century," 88; Bethurum, 354.
30 Wilcox, 88. See also Lionarons, *The Homiletic Writings of Archbishop Wulfstan*, 148–9.
31 Atherton, "Cambridge, Corpus Christi College 201," esp. 451, 469. See Wormald, *The Making of English Law*, 204–10.
32 As Bethurum suggests, Wulfstan may also be borrowing from Deut. 28. Bethurum, *Homilies of Wulfstan*, 355n26–31.
33 As elsewhere, the Vulgate Latin and English translation are Douay-Rheims (Dumbarton Oaks edition).
34 Wulfstan, *Be Godcundre Warnunge* (Bethurum 19) in Bethurum, *Homilies of Wulfstan*, 252. Translation is mine.
35 On Wulfstan's singular style see, *inter alia*, Lionarons, *The Homiletic Writings of Archbishop Wulfstan*, esp. 9–11; Bethurum, 87–98; Whitelock, "Laws of Edward and Guthrum," 6–11; Dance, "Sound, Fury, and Signifiers," 54–61; Ogawa, "Syntactical Revision in Wulfstan's Rewritings of Ælfric."

36 *Be Godcundre Warnunge*, in Bethurum, 251–2. Translation is mine.
37 On the availability of Leviticus in eleventh-century England, see chapter 1.
38 Bethurum, *Homilies of Wulfstan*, 253. Ælfric, too, has translated a portion of this passage of Leviticus into alliterative prose, not as part of the Heptateuch project but in the *Lives of Saints* piece *De Oratione Moysi*; the style is also literary but could never be mistaken for Wulfstan's. See "On the Prayer of Moses for Mid-Lent Sunday," lines 156–75, in *LS*, 2:36–8. See Godden, "Apocalypse and Invasion," 134–5, on this passage in its context.
39 On ventriloquism of God's voice as a source of Wulfstan's authority, see Lionarons, *The Homiletic Writings of Archbishop Wulfstan*, 94. See Wilcox, "Wolf at Work," 142–3, for a fascinating example of Wulfstan's meticulous selection of personal pronouns.
40 Bede, *The Old English Version of Bede's Ecclesiastical History*, 96, lines 6–33; "Sancti Gregori Pape" (St. Gregory the Great) in *CH2*, 72–80. On this episode see especially Lavezzo, "Gregory's Boys"; Lees, "In Ælfric's Words"; Chazelle, "The Power of Oratory," 39–46.
41 Fulk, Bjork, and Niles, *Klaeber's Beowulf*, 107. Interpolations are the editors'. For these and other examples of women trafficked in war in Old English writing, see Saunders, "Women and Warfare," esp. 193–6; see also Saunders, *Rape and Ravishment*, esp. 38.
42 On metonymy in Old English, see Overing, *Language, Sign, and Gender in Beowulf*, esp. 33–67.
43 On the fate of Beowulf's people and the limits of human language, see Pareles, "What the Raven Told the Eagle," 174–7.
44 See, *inter alia*, Rey, "Reexamination of the Foreign Female Captive." On slavery and concubinage in the Hebrew Bible and in ancient Judaism, see Hezser, *Jewish Slavery in Antiquity*, *passim*, esp. 191–201.
45 *Sermo Lupi*, lines 88–90.
46 Saunders, *Rape and Ravishment*, 44–45.
47 *Be Godcundre Warnunge*, in Bethurum, 253.
48 As Lionarons notes, Wulfstan expertly toggles in his homilies between the rhetorical voices of external "authority figure fit to instruct his congregation," which may include the "borrow[ed]" voice of God, and "humble fellow Christian who must also follow the instructions he gives" (Lionarons, *The Homiletic Writings of Archbishop Wulfstan*, 94; see also 116).
49 *Godes þeow* expresses the Biblical and Latin Christian concept *servus Dei* (forms of which, as Hugh Magennis notes, maintain currency in early medieval Anglo-Latin). Magennis, "*Godes Þeow* and Related Expressions," 146–7. *Þeow* can be translated as "servant," but is, in Katherine Miller's terms, "the unmarked, conventional term for a chattel slave" in West Saxon texts such as the West Saxon gospels. Miller, "The Semantic Field of Slavery," 63.

50 Dutchak suggests that for Wulfstan the servitude or even slavery of priests to God is no metaphor. Dutchak, "The Church and Slavery," 36–7.
51 Cnut's Oxford Legislation of 1018 (Cnut 1018), §11.1, in *Old English Legal Writings*, 214. In the same volume, see also I Cnut, §6.1, 232–52, at 240.
52 5 Æthelred, §4.1, 148.
53 Miller, "The Semantic Field of Slavery," 69.
54 "St. Thomas," Clayton, *LS* 3:268.
55 Magennis, 142n7, 144–45. See Wyatt, *Slaves and Warriors in Medieval Britain and Ireland*, 254–8; Glancy, *Slavery in Early Christianity*, 96–9, for the St. Thomas episode in context.
56 See esp. F. Griffiths, "Wives, Concubines, or Slaves."
57 Clayton, *LS* 3:282. Katherine O'Brien O'Keeffe's extended discussion of monastic obedience as a "product of choice" highlights the difference between the voluntary submission of elite Christians to their respective rules and the situation of enslaved people. O'Keeffe, *Stealing Obedience*, 7.
58 Saunders, *Rape and Ravishment*, esp. 41, 43–5. "The Laws of Alfred" §20, in Jurasinski and Oliver, eds., *The Laws of Alfred*. See also §13, 307, and 307n62. See Hough, "Alfred's *Domboc* and the Language of Rape."
59 Saunders observes that, particularly in its discussion of how assaults on noblewomen affect noblemen, "The *Sermo Lupi* demonstrates how completely a recognition of the political impact of rape may be detached from any evident concern over the rights of women per se," 43–4. Nevertheless, the reminder in *Sermo Lupi* that an assault survivor is precious to God is about as close as Wulfstan ever comes to, in Wyatt's terms, acknowledging laywomen's "humanity" (Wyatt, *Slaves and Warriors in Medieval Britain and Ireland*, 286).
60 The *Domboc*'s penalty for unwanted sexual touch applies only to nuns and sexually continent free women, according to their rank. By specifying only that an enslaved man or third party may not rape an enslaved woman (§29, at 320), and that the penalty for doing so is to be paid to the enslaver, the *Domboc* makes clear that there is no crime for a free man in sex, whether consensual or non-consensual, with a woman he enslaves. Indeed, Wyatt proposes that at the time of Alfred "no legal conception existed" for this crime (Wyatt, 155).
61 "Gif wiffæst wer hine forlicge be his agenre wylne, þolige þære and bete for hine sylfne wið God and wið men" (2 Cnut §54, at 282; If a married man has illicit sex with his own female slave, let him be deprived of her and make amends for himself to God and society); see Wyatt 286, 286n190.
62 My brief consideration of the relationship between state authority and sexual violence benefits from the influence of abolitionist and anti-colonial feminisms. While I cannot do justice to this topic here, Jaleel, *The Work of Rape*, 174–86, provides an excellent summary of the key issues. See also,

inter alia, Deer, *The Beginning and End of Rape*; A. Davis, *Abolition. Feminism. Now.*; L. B. Simpson, "Not Murdered, Not Missing"; A. Smith, *Conquest*; A. O. Harris, "Heteropatriarchy Kills."
63 On the definition of *þrælriht* see esp. Miller, "The Semantic Field of Slavery," 245–7. Wulfstan uses this term only in the *Sermo Lupi*, to describe one of the forms of order that has been violated.
64 7 Æthelred §2.3, 2.4, in *Old English Legal Writings*, 182–3. Translation is Rabin's. See also, *inter alia*, the penalties in 2 Cnut §45.1–3 for working, or forcing an enslaved person to work, on a holy day, 278. See further Kirkland, "Coercion on Holy Days in the Middle Ages," esp. 235–7.
65 The scale of enslavement in the eleventh-century English Church can be judged by Wyatt's observation that Wulfstan of York's nephew Bishop Wulfstan II of Worcester, an outspoken opponent of the slave trade, "continued to maintain around 472 slaves on his monastic demesne in the West Midlands" (Wyatt, *Slaves and Warriors in Medieval Britain and Ireland*, 30).
66 In the Vulgate, "Sicut canis qui revertitur ad vomitum suum, sic inprudens qui iterat stultitiam suam" (Prov. 26:11; As a dog that returneth to his vomit, so is the fool that repeateth his folly); "Contigit enim eis illud veri proverbii: 'Canis reversus ad suum vomitum,' et 'Sus lota in volutabro luti'" (2 Pet. 2:22; For that of the true proverb hath happened to them: "The dog is returned to his own vomit," and "The sow that was washed to her wallowing in the mire"). On the uncleanness of dogs in the Hebrew Bible, see *inter alia*, Stone, *Reading the Hebrew Bible with Animal Studies*, 54–8.
67 "Shrove Sunday," Clayton, *LS* 2:6. This homily appears in Skeat as "In Caput Ieiunii" (Ash Wednesday).
68 "Dominica V Post Pentecosten" (Fifth Sunday after Pentecost), in Pope, ed., *Homilies of Ælfric*, 2:507. See Pope, 2:496, 2:507n230–4. See Alfred, who writes in his translation of Gregory's *Cura Pastoralis*: "Be ðæm is awriten ðæt se hund wille etan ðæt he ær aspaw, & sio sugu hi wille sylian on hire sole æfterðæmðe hio aðwægen bið. Hwæt, se hund wile aspiwan ðone mete ðe hine hefegað on his breostum, & ðæt ilce ðæt he for hefignesse aspaw, ðonne he hit eft frit." (About that it is written that the dog will eat what he vomited before, and the sow will soil her mire after she gets cleaned. So the dog will vomit the food that sits heavy in his chest, and then he will eat it again, that same thing that he vomited because of its heaviness.) *King Alfred's West Saxon Version*, 491.
69 See Resnick, "Good Dog/Bad Dog," esp. 77–8; Sophia Menache notes the "peculiar association" of dogs and sex workers in the Bible and Talmud. Menache, "Dogs," 23, 29, 30, 32.
70 "Saint Vincent," Clayton, *LS* 3:312.
71 *OEM*, 214.
72 "Shrove Sunday," Clayton, *LS* 2:12.

Notes to pages 130–4   195

73 The text appears in one additional witness: Oxford, Bodleian Library, MS Hatton 115.
74 "Kings," Clayton, *LS* 2:154.
75 "Kings," Clayton, *LS* 2:154, 158, 160.
76 Klein, *Ruling Women*, 140.
77 See chapter 4.
78 See chapter 4.
79 "Kings," Clayton, *LS* 2:162. On the connotations of *fretan*, see Magennis, *Anglo-Saxon Appetites*, 74–8.
80 "Alfred's Prologue," in Jurasinski and Oliver, *The Laws of Alfred*, 256. In the Vulgate, this is "Carnem quae a bestiis fuerit praegustata, non comedetis, sed proicietis canibus" (Ex. 22:31; The flesh that beasts have tasted of before, you shall not eat, but shall cast it to the dogs). For Alfred's Latin Biblical source(s), see Marsden, *Text of the Old Testament*, 402.
81 On the role of this prescription in Christian–Jewish dispute, see Resnick, *Marks of Distinction*, 150; Stow, *Jewish Dogs*, 17, 155–56. On street dogs and their eating habits in colonial and anti-colonial thinking, see Boisseron, *Afro-Dog*, 81–119.
82 Freidenreich, *Foreigners and Their Food*, 88.
83 See Coogan, Brettler, Newsom, and Perkins, ed., *The New Oxford Annotated Bible*, NT31, n15.21–28.
84 Although the importance of this issue in the New Testament has perpetuated the belief that all ancient Jews observed segregation from Gentiles at meals, Freidenreich, *Foreigners and Their Food*, 31–46, observes that in fact these restrictions were, at the time, likely particular to Hellenistic Jews in Judaea.
85 See Drake, *Slandering the Jew*, 83–4; Stow, *Jewish Dogs*, 4.
86 Chrysostom, *Homilies against Judaizing Christians*. I.II.1–2, at 5–6. On the career of this identification, see Stow, esp. 3–36; Stow, "The Bread, the Children and the Dogs"; Resnick, "Good Dog/Bad Dog."
87 See Drake, *Slandering the Jew*, 78–98. Drake, 94, notes that Chrysostom also productively revisits canine identification in an exhortation to chase Jews as hounds might. See Chrysostom, *Homilies Against Judaizing Christians* II.I.4, at 36. For an argument against reading Chrysostom as anti-Jewish, see Harkins's introduction to Chrystosom, xxvi–l.
88 On Bede's anti-Semitic interpretation of this verse, see Scheil, *The Footsteps of Israel*, 89–90.
89 Resnick, "Good Dog/Bad Dog," 70.
90 "Dominica Secunda in Quadragesima" (The Second Sunday in Lent), *CHII* 70.
91 The ninth-century Abbot Smaragdus of St. Mihiel included excerpts from Bede in his *Collectiones in Epistola et Evangelia*. See Smaragdus *PL* 102, 131C. On the relationship to the sources, see Marsden, *CHIntro* 399–403, esp. 399, 402; see also Godden, "Catholic Homilies 2.8."

92 *Sermo Lupi*, 268.
93 Treschow, "The Prologue to Alfred's Law Code," 95.
94 *Institutes of Polity* 2 §16, in *Old English Legal Writings*, 76.
95 See *Institutes of Polity* 1 §6, *Institutes of Polity* 2 §10, and I Cnut §26.3, in *Old English Legal Writings*, at 44–6, 68–70, and 252, respectively; and *Verba Ezechielis Prophete de Pastoribus non Recte Agentibus* and *Verba Ezechiel Prophete de Pigris aut Timidis vel Neglegentibus Pastoribus*, Bethurum 16a/16b (also known as Napier 41), *Homilies of Wulfstan*, 239 and 240–1. See also Lionarons, *The Homiletic Writings of Archbishop Wulfstan*, 111–13, and Wilcox, "The Wolf on Shepherds," 399–400, 402–3, on Bethurum 16b. On Wulfstan's repeated use of this passage, see Bethurum, 348–9. On the pastoral metaphor in Wulfstan's Commonplace Books, see Elliott, "Wulfstan's Commonplace Book Revised," *passim*. See O'Camb, "Isidorean Wolf Lore," for an intriguing reading of this passage in the context of Old English lupine imagery and rights of sanctuary, esp. 693–4.
96 See Lionarons, 98–100, for a concise summary of the specific threats to ecclesiastical finances and authority to which Wulfstan is responding, including taxes, raiding, and royal seizure.
97 Gates, "Preaching, Politics and Episcopal Reform," 94.
98 *Verba Ezechielis*, 240.
99 The Vulgate passage is "Omnes bestiae agri, venite ad devorandum, universae bestiae saltus. Speculatores eius caeci omnes; nescierunt universi, canes muti non valentes latrare, videntes vana, dormientes et amantes somnia (All ye beasts of the field, come to devour, all ye beasts of the forest. His watchmen are all blind; they are all ignorant, dumb dogs not able to bark, seeing vain things, sleeping and loving dreams, Isaiah 56: 9–10).
100 Brief I, §62–3 (*Letter to Wulsige*), in *Hertenbriefe*, 15. Ælfric also cites this figure in the letter's preface at *Hertenbriefe*, 1; and in *Sermo de Die Judicii* 2:597–8, lines 173–4.
101 See *King Alfred's West-Saxon Version of Gregory's Pastoral Care*: "Dumbe hundas ne magon beorcan," lines 17, 89. Similarly, the Old English Rule of Chrodegang translates the Latin as "Dum[b]e hundas ne magon beorcan." Napier, §77.3, at 84. See s.v. *mutus*, in Latham, Howlett, and Ashdowne, *Dictionary of Medieval Latin from British Sources*.
102 Lionarons, *The Homiletic Writings of Archbishop Wulfstan*, 113; Gates, "Preaching, Politics and Episcopal Reform," 98, suggests an identification or parallel between the muzzled dog and the *werewulf*.
103 "Saint Edmund," in Clayton, *LS* 3:188. See also McCracken, *In the Skin of a Beast*, 48.
104 Spears, *Identifying with the Beast*, 161; see also Steel, *How Not to Make a Human*, 56–8.

105 Keynes, "A Note on Anglo-Saxon Personal Names," 22. Spears notes the deliberate irony of the nickname and attributes Wulfstan's licence to his sense of temporality: "In this time of peril, in a world rapidly approaching collapse, a wolf who would normally threaten to devour a sinful people was now attempting to protect them," 7. See Spears 6–7 and 7n22 for more on the canine and lupine in Wulfstan; Rabin, "Wolf's Testimony," 404–6, for more on *Lupus*.
106 See Dayan, *The Law Is a White Dog*, 209–52, on the status of dogs in Anglo-American law.
107 I use "author" here in the sense of Jorge Luis Borges's well-known short story "Pierre Menard," where it designates the creator of a brilliant work of plagiarism.

Afterword: Cleansings

1 Heng, *The Invention of Race*, 27–31, 55–109. See Introduction, n11. On the English "nation," see especially Krummel, 14–15; K. Davis, "National Writing in the Ninth Century."
2 "When you take the field against your enemies, and the Lord your God delivers them into your power and you take them captive, and you see among the captives a beautiful woman and you desire her and would take her to wife, you shall bring her into to your house, and she shall trim her hair, pare her nails, and discard her captive's garb. She shall spend a month's time in your house lamenting her father and mother; after that you may come to her and possess her, and she shall be your wife. Then, should you no longer want her, you must release her outright. You must not sell her for money: since you had your will of her, you must not enslave her," Deut. 21:10–14 (JPS). See Introduction, n19.
3 "In Leviticum Homilia VII," §6.7; Origen, "Homily 7 [on Leviticus]" §6.7, in *Homilies on Leviticus, 1–16*, 150. See Introduction, 6–8.
4 As Denise K. Buell observes, Origen's "universalizing argument relies on rather than opposes ethnic reasoning," 82.
5 Kruger, *The Spectral Jew*, 13.
6 See *inter alia*, Dube, "Rahab Says Hello to Judith," esp. 149–50; Saunders, *Rape and Ravishment*, 138–39.
7 Jost, ed., *Institutes of Polity*, §166.
8 Drake, "Origen's Veil," 833–4, at 833.
9 See Freidenreich, *Foreigners and Their Food*, passim.
10 Bede iv.24, 418.
11 Penniman, *Raised on Christian Milk*, esp. 5; Feeley-Harnik, *The Lord's Table*, esp. 107.

12 Mitchell, *Becoming Human*, 145, 160–1. Mitchell draws upon Cochran, "Object-Oriented Cookery," 313.
13 See especially Bynum, *Resurrection of the Body*; Heng, *Empire of Magic*, 25–61; Steel, *How to Make a Human*, 108–18. See also Ælfric's emphatic citation of what seems to be Leviticus 7:14 in the *Letter to Brother Edward*: "Ælc ðæra manna ðe blod ytt sceal losian of his folce, beo he inlenda, beo he ælðeodig, forþan ðe on þam blode is þæs nytenes lif." (Any man who eats blood shall be lost from his people, whether he be native or foreign, because a beast's life is in the blood.) "An Edition of Ælfric's *Letter to Brother Edward*," 280.
14 Stanton, *The Culture of Translation*, 174; Lees and Overing, *Double Agents*, 22.
15 Strawn, "On Vomiting," esp. 447–9.
16 Meyer, "People and Land in the Holiness Code," 448.
17 It is essential to remember that, according to Hebrew Biblical law, while *failing* to separate what is holy/chosen/sacred from what is profane/freed/mundane constitutes serious wrongdoing and is abhorrent to God, these profane things (such as bodily emissions and contact with the dead, which pollute the sanctuary; work, which may not be done on the Sabbath; unclean animals that people may not eat) are not *themselves* sinful, wrong, or abhorrent.

The other crucial passage on vomit follows the list of sexual prohibitions: "Do not defile yourselves in any of those ways, for it is by such that the nations that I am casting out before you defiled themselves. Thus the land became defiled; and I called it to account for its iniquity, and the land spewed out its inhabitants. But you must keep My laws and My rules, and you must not do any of those abhorrent things, neither the citizen nor the stranger who resides among you; for all those abhorrent things were done by the people who were in the land before you, and the land became defiled. So let not the land spew you out for defiling it, as it spewed out the nation that came before you" (Lev. 18:24–8). See Strawn 447–52 on these two passages and their relationship to the Hebrew Bible's ecological themes.
18 On the inheritance of Christian supersession by post-Christian secular states, see especially Asad, *Secular Translations*, 13–54.
19 de Hoveden, *Chronica magistri Rogeri de Houedene*, 13.
20 Translated by Mundill, *The King's Jews*, 76. "Noluit indigeriem qua premebatur imparata periculo sui per partes uiolenter euomere, cauitque uisceribus, dissimulans interim modeste (uel phisice) molestiam, donec oportuno medendi tempore totam liceat sibi morbi materiam simul et semel egerere" Richard of Devizes, *Cronicon Ricardi*, 3.
21 See Zacher's similar comment on Vercelli VII in "Jews and Judaizing as Pathologies in the Anglo-Saxon Imagination," 274.

22 Blurton, "Richard of Devizes's *Cronicon*," esp. 275–9. See also Bale, "Richard of Devizes and Fictions of Judaism," esp. 58–60. As Bale notes, "the *Cronicon*'s version of these images suggests that Judaism is 'inside' Christianity ... If the Winchester Christians are disgusted at the matter within, Richard suggests that they should literally be disgusted with themselves" (60).
23 Ahmed, *Cultural Politics of Emotion*, 98.

Bibliography

Primary Texts

Ælfric. *Ælfric's Catholic Homilies: The First Series Text*. Edited by Peter Clemoes. EETS s.s. 17. Oxford: Oxford University Press, 1997.
– *Ælfric's Catholic Homilies: The Second Series Text*. Edited by Malcolm Godden. EETS s.s. 5. Oxford: Oxford University Press, 1979.
– *Ælfric's Colloquy*. Edited by G.N. Garmonsway. Revised ed. Exeter: University of Exeter Press, 1991.
– *Ælfric's Homilies on Judith, Esther, and the Maccabees*. Edited by Stuart D. Lee, 1999. https://users.ox.ac.uk/~stuart/kings/main.htm.
– *Ælfric's Lives of Saints*. 2 vols. Edited by W. W. Skeat and translated by Gunning Wilkinson, and Skeat. EETS o.s. 94 and 114. London: Oxford University Press, 1966.
– *Ælfric's Prefaces*. Edited by Jonathan Wilcox. Durham Medieval Texts 9. Durham, NJ: University of Durham Department of English, 1994.
– *Die Hirtenbriefe Ælfrics in altenglischer und lateinischer Fassung*. Edited by Bernhard Fehr. Darmstadt, Germany: Wissenschaftliche Buchgesellschaft, 1966.
– "An Edition of Ælfric's *Letter to Brother Edward*." Edited by Mary Clayton. In *Early Medieval English Texts and Interpretations: Studies Presented to Donald G. Scragg*, edited by Elaine Treharne and Susan Rosser, 263–83. Tempe, AZ: ACMRS Press, 2002.
– *Exameron Anglice, or The Old English Hexameron*. Edited by Samuel J. Crawford. Darmstadt: Wissenschaftliche Buchgesellschaft, 1968.
– *Homilies of Ælfric: A Supplementary Collection*. 2 vols. Edited by John C. Pope. EETS o.s. 259 and 260. London: Oxford University Press, 1967 and 1968.
– "Letter to Brother Edward: A Student Edition." Edited by Mary Clayton. *Old English Newsletter* 40 (2007): 31–46.

Bibliography

- *Old English Lives of Saints*. Edited and translated by Mary Clayton and Juliet Mullins. 3 vols. Dumbarton Oaks Medieval Library 59. Cambridge, MA: Harvard University Press, 2019.

Ælfric Bata. *Anglo-Saxon Conversations: The Colloquies of Ælfric Bata*. Edited by Scott Gwara and David Porter. Woodbridge, UK: Boydell & Brewer, 1997.

Ælred of Rievaulx. "De Spiritali Amicitia." Edited by A. Hoste. In *Aelredi Rievallensis Opera Omnia I: Opera Ascetica*, edited by Hoste and C.H. Talbot, 279–350. Corpus Christianorum Continuatio Medievalis 1. Turnhout, Belgium: Brepols, 1971.

- *Spiritual Friendship*. Edited by Marsha L. Dutton and translated by Lawrence C. Braceland. Cistercian Fathers Series 5. Collegeville, MN: Liturgical Press, 2010.

Aldhelm of Malmesbury. *Aldhelm: The Prose Works*. Translated by Michael Lapidge and Michael Herren. Cambridge, UK: D.S. Brewer, 1979.

- *Aldhelmi Malmesbiriensis Prosa de Virginitate cum Glosa atque Anglosaxonica*. Edited by Scott Gwara. Corpus Christianorum Series Latina 124A. Turnhout, Belgium: Brepols, 2001.

Alfred of Wessex. *King Alfred's West Saxon Version of Gregory's Pastoral Care*. Edited and translated by Henry Sweet. EETS o.s. 45 and 50. London: N. Trubner and Co., 1871–72.

Alter, Robert, trans. *The Wisdom Books: Job, Proverbs, and Ecclesiastes: A Translation with Commentary*. New York: W.W. Norton, 2010.

Anlezark, Daniel, ed. and trans. *Old Testament Narratives*. Dumbarton Oaks Medieval Library 7. Cambridge, MA: Harvard University Press, 2011.

Augustine. *Answer to Faustus, a Manichean*. Edited by Boniface Ramsey and translated by Roland J. Teske. Hyde Park, NY: New City Press, 2007.

- *Contra faustum manichaeum*. Edited by Joseph Zycha, 251–797. Corpus Scriptorum Ecclesiasticorum Latinorum 25/1. Vienna: F. Tempsky, 1891.

- *Epistulum 166: De originae animae hominis*. Edited by Alois Goldbacher, 545–85. Corpus Scriptorum Ecclesiasticorum 44. Vienna: F. Tempsky, 1904.

- "A Treatise on the Origin of the Human Soul, Addressed to Jerome." In *Nicene and Post-Nicene Fathers of the Christian Church*, edited by Philip Schaff and translated by J.G. Cunningham, vol. 1, 523–32. Grand Rapids: Eerdmans, 1983.

Bede. *Bede's Ecclesiastical History of the English People*. Edited by Bertram Colgrave and R.A.B. Mynors. Oxford: Clarendon Press, 1969.

- *De temporum ratione*. Edited by Christopher Jones. Corpus Christianorum Series Latina 123B. Turnhout, Belgium: Brepols, 1997.

- *Ecclesiastical History of the English People: With Bede's Letter to Egbert and Cuthbert's Letter on the Death of Bede*. Translated by Leo Sherley-Price. London: Penguin, 2003.

- *Homilies on the Gospels, Book One: Advent to Lent*. Translated by Lawrence T. Martin and David Hurst. Kalamazoo, MI: Cistercian Publications, 1991.
- "In Octava Nativitatis Domini." In *Bedae Venerabilis Opera*, edited by David Hurst, vol. 3, 73–9. CCSL 122. Turnhout, Belgium: Brepols, 1955.
- *The Old English Version of Bede's Ecclesiastical History of the English People*. Edited by Thomas Miller. Vol. 2. EETS o.s. 96. London: N. Trubner, 1892.
- *The Reckoning of Time*. Translated by Faith Wallis. 2nd revised ed. Liverpool: Liverpool University Press, 2004.

Bethurum, Dorothy, ed. *The Homilies of Wulfstan*. Oxford: Clarendon Press, 1957.

Birgitta of Sweden. *The Revelations of St. Birgitta of Sweden. Vol. 2, Liber Caelestis, Books IV–V*. Edited by Bridget Morris and translated by Denis Searby. Oxford: Oxford University Press, 2008.
- Vol. 4, *The Heavenly Emperor's Book to Kings, the Rule, and Minor Works*. Edited by Bridget Morris and translated by Denis Searby. Oxford: Oxford University Press, 2015.

Bischoff, Bernhard, and Michael Lapidge. *Biblical Commentaries from the Canterbury School of Theodore and Hadrian*. Cambridge: Cambridge University Press, 1994.

Blake, E. O., ed. *Liber Eliensis*. Camden Third Series 92. London: Royal Historical Society, 1962.

Cameron, Angus, Ashley Crandell Amos, and Antoinette DiPaolo Healey, eds. *Dictionary of Old English: A to I Online*. Toronto: Dictionary of Old English Project, 2018.

Campbell, Alistair, and Simon Keynes, eds. *Encomium Emmae Reginae*. Cambridge: Cambridge University Press, 1998.

Chrysostom, John. *Homilies against Judaizing Christians*. Translated by Paul W. Harkins. Washington, DC: Catholic University Press, 2010.

Clayton, Mary, and Hugh Magennis, eds. and trans. *The Old English Lives of St. Margaret*. Cambridge: Cambridge University Press, 1994.

Coogan, Michael D., Marc Z. Brettler, Carol Newsom, and Pheme Perkins, eds. *The New Oxford Annotated Bible with the Apocrypha*. 4th ed. New York: Oxford University Press, 2010.

Damian, Peter. *The Book of Gomorrah*. Translated by Pierre J. Payer. Waterloo, ON: Wilfred Laurier University Press.

de Hoveden, Roger. *Chronica magistri Rogeri de Houedene*. Edited by William Stubbs. Vol. 3. Camrbidge: Cambridge University Press, 2012.

Dodwell, C.R., and Peter Clemoes, eds. *The Old English Illustrated Hexateuch: British Museum Cotton Claudius B. IV*. Early English Manuscripts in Facsimile 18. Copenhagen: Rosenkilde and Bagger, 1974.

Fairweather, Janet, trans. *Liber Eliensis: A History of the Isle of Ely from the Seventh Century to the Twelfth*. Woodbridge, UK: Boydell, 2005.

Frantzen, Allen J. *The Anglo-Saxon Penitentials: A Cultural Database*. Published 2007. Accessed 2014. http://www.anglo-saxon.net/penance/.

Fulk, R.D., Robert E. Bjork, and John D. Niles, eds. *Klaeber's Beowulf and the Fight at Finnsburg*. 4th ed. Toronto: University of Toronto Press, 2008 [1950].

Fulk, R. D., and Stefan Jurasinski, eds. *The Old English Canons of Theodore*. EETS s.s. 25. Oxford: Oxford University Press, 2012.

Gildas. *Gildas: The Ruin of Britain and Other Works*. Edited and translated by Michael Winterbottom. Chichester: Phillimore and Co. Ltd., 1978.

Godden, Malcolm, ed. and trans. *The Old English History of the World: An Anglo-Saxon Rewriting of Orosius*. Dumbarton Oaks Medieval Library 44. Cambridge, MA: Harvard University Press, 2016.

Goldstein, Jonathan A., ed. and trans. *II Maccabees: A New Translation with Introduction and Commentary*. The Anchor Yale Bible Series, vol. 41A. New York: Doubleday, 1983.

Gregory. *Gregorii I Papae Registrum Epistolarum*. Edited by Paulus Ewald and Ludovicus M. Hartmann. Vol. 2. München: Monumenta Germaniae Historica, 1899.

– Homily 29. *PL* 76. Edited by J.P. Migne, cols 1213–19. Patrologiae Cursus Completus. Series Latina 76. Paris, 1857.

– *Moralia in Job*. Edited and translated by Charles Marriott. Vol. 1. Oxford: John Henry Parker and London: J.G.F. and J. Rivington, 1844.

Grønlie, Siân, ed. and trans. *Íslendingabók, Kristni Saga: The Book of the Icelanders, the Story of the Conversion*. London: Viking Society for Northern Research, 2006.

Hasenfratz, Robert, ed. *Ancrene Wisse*. Kalamazoo, MI: Medieval Institute Publications, 2000.

Healey, Antonette DiPaolo, ed. *Dictionary of Old English Web Corpus*. Toronto: Dictionary of Old English Project, 2009.

Huber, Emily Rebekah, and Elizabeth Robertson, eds. "Hali Meithhad." In *The Katherine Group MS Bodley 34*, edited by Huber and Robertson. Kalamazoo, MI: Medieval Institute Publications, 2016.

Irvine, Susan, and Malcolm R. Godden, eds. *The Old English Boethius: With Verse Prologues and Epilogues Associated with King Alfred*. Dumbarton Oaks Medieval Library 19. Cambridge, MA: Harvard University Press, 2012.

JPS Hebrew-English Tanakh: The Traditional Hebrew Text and the New JPS Translation. 2nd ed. Philadelphia, Jerusalem: The Jewish Publication Society, 1999 [1985].

Jurasinski, Stefan, and Lisi Oliver, eds. and trans. *The Laws of Alfred: The Domboc and the Making of Anglo-Saxon Law*. Cambridge: Cambridge University Press, 2021.

Klinck, Anne L., ed. *Old English Elegies*. Montreal and Kingston: McGill-Queen's University Press, 1992.

Kramer, Johanna, Hugh Magennis, and Robin Norris, eds. and trans. *Anonymous Old English Lives of Saints*. Cambridge, MA: Harvard University Press, 2020.

Liuzza, Roy, ed and trans. *Beowulf: Facing Page Translation*. 2nd ed. Peterborough, ON: Broadview Press, 2012.

– ed. *The Old English Version of the Gospels*. Vol. 1. EETS o.s. 304. Oxford: Oxford University Press, 1994.

Livingston, Michael, ed. *The Middle English Metrical Paraphrase of the Old Testament*. Kalamazoo, MI: Medieval Institute Publications, 2011.

MacLean, George E., ed. "Ælfric's Version of *Alcuini interrogationes Sigeuulfi in Genesin*." *Anglia* 7 (1884): 1–59.

Marsden, Richard, ed. *The Old English Heptateuch and Ælfric's Libellus de Veteri Testamento et Novo*. EETS o.s. 330. Oxford: Early English Text Society, 2008.

Napier, Arthur, ed. *The Old English Version of the Enlarged Rule of Chrodegang Together with the Latin Original*. EETS o.s. 150. London: Keegan Paul, 1916.

Neusner, Jacob, ed. and trans. *Esther Rabbah I: An Analytical Translation*. Atlanta: Scholars Press, 1989.

O'Neill, Patrick, ed. *King Alfred's Old English Prose Translation of the First Fifty Psalms*. Cambridge, MA: Medieval Academy of America, 2001.

Origen. "Homily 7." In *Homilies on Leviticus, 1–16*, edited and translated by Gary Wayne Barkley, 129–52. Washington, DC: Catholic University of America Press, 1990.

– "Homily 27." In *Homilies on Numbers*, translated by Thomas P. Scheck and edited by Christopher A. Hall, 168–83. Downers Grove, IL: IVP Academic, 2009.

– "In Leviticum Homilia VII." In *Origenis Opera Omnia*, edited by J.P. Migne, vol. 12 of *Patrologiæ Cursus Completus: Patrologiæ Græcæ*, Imprimerie Catholique, 1862. Cols. 475–92.

– "In Numeros Homilia XXVII." In *Origenis Opera Omnia* edited by J.P. Migne, vol. 12 of *Patrologiæ Cursus Completus: Patrologiæ Græcæ*, Imprimerie Catholique, 1862. Cols. 780–801.

Rauer, Christine, ed. *The Old English Martyrology: Edition, Translation and Commentary*. Cambridge, UK: Boydell & Brewer, 2013.

Richard of Devizes. *Cronicon Ricardi Divisensis de Tempore Regis Richardi Primi*. Edited and translated by John T. Appleby. London: Thomas Nelson, 1963.

Sisam, Celia, and Kenneth Sesam, eds. *The Salisbury Psalter: Edited from Salisbury Cathedral MS. 150*. EETS o.s. 242. London: Oxford University Press, 1959.

Smaragdus of St. Mihiel. "Evangelium Matthaei, Cap. XV." In *Collectiones in Epistolas et Evangelia*, edited by J. P. Migne. Corpus Corporum, 1851.

Speiser, E. A., trans. *Genesis: A New Translation with Introduction and Commentary*. The Anchor Yale Bible Series, vol. 1. New Haven: Yale University Press, 1964.

Spindler, Robert, ed. *Das Altenglische Bussbuch (sog. Confessionale Pseudo-Egberti)*. Leipzig: Bernhard Tauchnitz, 1934.

Swain, Larry J., ed. and trans. "Ælfric of Eynsham's Letter to Sigeweard: An Edition, Translation and Commentary." PhD diss., University of Illinois, 2009. ProQuest (3364640).

Symons, Dom Thomas, ed. and trans. *Regularis Concordia Anglicae Nationis Monachorum Sanctimonialiumque: The Monastic Agreement of the Monks and Nuns of the English Nation.* London: Thomas Nelson, 1953.

Treharne, Elaine M., ed. *The Old English Life of St. Nicholas with the Old English Life of St. Gile*s. Leeds: Leeds Studies in English, 1997.

Unger, Carl Rikard, ed. *Stjórn: Gammelnorsk Bibelhistorie fra Verdens Skabelse til det babyloniske.* Christiania: Feilberg & Landmark, 1862.

Venarde, B.L., ed. and trans. *The Rule of Saint Benedict.* Cambridge, MA: Harvard University Press, 2011.

The Vulgate Bible: Douay-Rheims Translation. Edited by Swift Edgar and Angela M. Kinney, 6 vols. Cambridge, MA: Harvard University Press, 2010–13.

Warner, Rubie D.-N. *Early English Homilies from the Twelfth-Century MS. Vesp. D. XIV.* EETS o.s. 152. Oxford: Oxford University Press, 1917.

Wasserschleben, F.W.H., ed. *Die Bussordnungen der abendländischen Kirche.* Halle, Germany: Graeger, 1851.

Westcott, Brooke Foss, and Fenton John Anthony Hart, eds. *The New Testament in the Original Greek.* Vol. 1. Cambridge: Cambridge University Press, 2010 [1881].

Wevers, John William, ed. *Genesis* (Septuaginta: Vetus Testamentum Graecum 1). Göttingen: Vandenhoeck & Ruprecht, 1974.

William of Malmesbury. *Saints' Lives: Lives of SS. Wulfstan, Dunstan, Patrick, Benignus and Indract.* Edited by M. Winterbottom and R.M. Thomson. Oxford: Oxford Medieval Texts, 2002.

Wogan-Browne, Jocelyn, and Glyn S. Burgess, trans. *Virgin Lives and Holy Deaths: Two Exemplary Biographies for Anglo-Norman Women: The Life of St. Catherine; The Life of St. Lawrence.* London: Everyman, 1996.

Wulfstan. *Die "Institutes of Polity, Civil and Ecclesiastical": Ein Werk Erzbischof Wulfstans von York.* Edited by Karl Jost. Bern: Francke, 1959.

– *Old English Legal Writings.* Edited and translated by Andrew Rabin. Cambridge, MA: Harvard University Press, 2020.

– *The Political Writings of Archbishop Wulfstan of York.* Edited and translated by Andrew Rabin. Manchester: Manchester University Press, 2015.

Secondary Texts

Aberth, John. *From the Brink of the Apocalypse: Confronting Famine, War, Plague and Death in the Later Middle Ages.* New York: Routledge, 2013.

Abulafia, Anna Sapir. *Christians and Jews in the Twelfth-Century Renaissance.* Abington: Routledge, 1995.

Adair, Cassius, and Aren Aizura. "'The Transgender Craze Seducing Our [Sons]'; or, All the Trans Guys Are Just Dating Each Other." *TSQ* 9 (2022): 44–64.
Adams, Jonathan, and Cordelia Heß. *Antisemitism in the North: History and State of Research*. Berlin: De Gruyter, 2020.
Africa, Thomas. "Worms and the Death of Kings: A Cautionary Note on Disease and History." *Classical Antiquity* 1 (1982): 1–17.
Agamben, Giorgio. *The Highest Poverty: Monastic Rules and Form-of-Life*. Translated by Adam Kotsko. Redwood City, CA: Stanford University Press, 2004.
– *Homo Sacer: Sovereign Power and Bare Life*. Translated by D. Heller-Roazen. Redwood City, CA: Stanford University Press, 1998.
– *The Open: Man and Animal*. Translated by Kevin Attell. Redwood City, CA: Stanford University Press, 2004.
– *The Time That Remains: A Commentary on the Letter to the Romans*. Translated by Patricia Dailey. Redwood City, CA: Stanford University Press, 2005.
Ahmed, Sara. *Cultural Politics of Emotion*. Edinburgh: Edinburgh University Press, 2014.
– *Strange Encounters: Embodied Others in Post-Coloniality*. London: Routledge, 2013.
Akbari, Suzanne Conklin. *Idols in the East: European Representations of Islam and the Orient: 1100–1450*. Ithaca, NY: Cornell University Press, 2009.
– "The Object of Devotion: Fundamentalist Perspectives on the Medieval Past." *Religion and Literature* 42 (2010): 299–315.
Ambrose, Shannon O. "Addressing Jewish Alterity in the Literature of Anglo-Saxon England." In *Jews in Medieval England: Teaching Representations of the Other*, edited by Miriamne Ara Krummel and Tison Pugh. 23–36. Cham, Switzerland: Palgrave Macmillan, 2017.
– "The Theme of Lay *Clænnyss* in Ælfric's Letters to Sigeweard, Sigefyrð and Brother Edward." *Mediaevalia* 35 (2014): 5–21.
Anderson, Rachel S. "Ælfric's Kings: Political Hagiography in Anglo-Saxon England." PhD diss., Indiana University, 2004.
– "The Old Testament Homily: Ælfric as Biblical Translator." In *The Old English Homily: Precedent, Practice, and Appropriation*, edited by Aaron J. Kleist, 121–42. Turnhout: Brepols, 2007.
Anidjar, Gil. *Blood: A Critique of Christianity*. New York: Columbia University Press, 2014.
– "Secularism." *Critical Inquiry* 33 (2006): 52–77.
– *Semites: Race, Religion, Literature*. Redwood City, CA: Stanford University Press, 2008.
– "We Have Never Been Jewish: An Essay in Asymmetric Hematology." In *Jewish Blood: Reality and Metaphor in History, Religion, and Culture*, edited by Mitchell Hart, 31–56. London: Routledge, 2009.
Anlezark, Daniel. "An Ideal Marriage: Abraham and Sarah in Old English Literature." *Medium Aevum* 69 (2000): 187–210.

- "Of Boys and Men: Anglo-Saxon Literary Adaptations of the Book of Daniel." In *Childhood and Adolescence in Anglo-Saxon Literary Culture*, edited by Susan Irvine and Winfried Rudolf, 244–69. Toronto: University of Toronto Press, 2018.
Ansell, Nicholas. "This Is Her Body … Judges 19 as Call to Discernment." In *Tamar's Tears: Evangelical Engagements with Feminist Old Testament Hermeneutics*, edited by Andrew Sloane, 112–70. Eugene, OR: Pickwick Publications, 2012.
Archibald, Elizabeth. *Incest and the Medieval Imagination*. Oxford: Oxford University Press, 2001.
Arthur, Ciaran. "Postural Representations of Holofernes in the Old English Judith: The Lord Who Was Laid Low." *English Studies* 94 (2013): 872–82.
Asad, Talal. "The Concept of Cultural Translation in British Social Anthropology." In Writing Culture: The Poetics and Politics of Ethnography, edited by James Clifford and George E. Marcus, 141-64. Berkeley: University of California Press, 1986.
- *Secular Translations: Nation-State, Modern Self, and Calculative Reason*. New York: Columbia University Press, 2018.
Ashton-Cross, D.I.C. "Liability for Animals in Roman Law." *The Cambridge Law Journal* 17 (1959): 189–92.
- "Liability in Roman Law for Damage Caused by Animals." *Cambridge Law Journal* 11 (1953): 395–403.
Astell, A. W. "Holofernes's Head: *tacen* and Teaching in the Old English *Judith*." *Anglo-Saxon England* 18 (1989): 117–34.
Atherton, Mark. "Cambridge, Corpus Christi College 201 as a Mirror for a Prince: *Apollonius of Tyre*, Archbishop Wulfstan and King Cnut." *English Studies* 97, no. 5 (2016): 451–72.
Avotri, Solomon K. "The Vernacularization of Scripture and African Beliefs: The Story of the Gerasene Demoniac among the Ewe of West Africa." In *The Bible in Africa: Transactions, Trajectories, and Trends*, edited by Gerald O. West and Musa W. Dube, 311–25. Leiden: Brill, 2000.
Bach, Alice. *Women, Seduction, and Betrayal in Biblical Narrative*. Cambridge: Cambridge University Press, 1997.
Bahar, Shirly. "Coming Out as Queen: Jewish Identity, Queer Theory, and the *Book of Esther*." *Studies in Gender and Sexuality* 13 (2012): 167–78.
Bale, Anthony P. "Richard of Devizes and Fictions of Judaism." *Jewish Culture and History* 3 (2001): 55–72.
Baltes, Guido. "'Circumcision of the Heart' in Paul: From a Metaphor of Torah Obedience to a Metaphor of Torah Polemics?" In *The Challenge of the Mosaic Torah in Judaism, Christianity, and Islam*, edited by Antti Laato, 88–112. Leiden: Brill, 2020.

Barkey, Karen, and Ira Katznelson. "States, Regimes, and Decisions: Why Jews Were Expelled from Medieval England and France." *Theory and Society* 40 (2011): 475–503.

Barnhouse, Rebecca. "Shaping the Hexateuch Text for an Anglo-Saxon Audience." In *The Old English Hexateuch*, edited by Rebecca Barnhouse and Benjamin C. Withers, 91–108. Kalamazoo, MI: Medieval Institute Publications, 2000.

Barnhouse, Rebecca, and Benjamin C. Withers, eds. *The Old English Hexateuch: Aspects and Approaches*. Kalamazoo, MI: Medieval Institute Publications, 2000.

Baumgarten, Elisheva. *Biblical Women and Jewish Daily Life in the Middle Ages*. Philadelphia: University of Pennsylvania Press, 2022.

Bautch, Richard J. "Reading Judith, Tobit and Second Maccabees as Responses to Hegemony." In *Intertextual Explorations in Deuterocanonical and Cognate Literature*, edited by Jeremy Corley and Geoffrey David Miller. 157–74. Berlin: De Gruyter, 2019.

Baxter, Stephen. "Archbishop Wulfstan and the Administration of God's Property." In *Wulfstan, Archbishop of York: The Proceedings of the Second Alcuin Conference*, edited by Matthew Townend, 161–205. Turnhout, Belgium: Brepols, 2004.

Becker, Adam H., and Annette Yoshiko Reed, eds. *The Ways That Never Parted: Jews and Christians in Late Antiquity and the Early Middle Ages*. Minneapolis: Fortress Press, 2003.

Beem, Charles. *The Lioness Roared: The Problems of Female Rule in English History*. New York: Palgrave Macmillan, 2006.

Bernau, Anke. "The Translation of Purity in the Old English Lives of St Eugenia and St Euphrosyne." *Bulletin of the John Rylands Library* 86 (2004): 11–37.

Bernstein, Melissa Joy. "Concealment and Revelation: Fatherhood in the Literature of Anglo-Saxon England." PhD diss., University of Rochester, 2004.

Besserman, Lawrence L. *The Legend of Job in the Middle Ages*. Cambridge, MA: Harvard University Press, 1979.

— "A Note on the Source of Ælfric's Homily on the Book of Job." *English Language Notes* 10 (1973): 248–52.

Betancourt, Roland. *Byzantine Intersectionality: Sexuality, Gender and Race in the Middle Ages*. Princeton: Princeton University Press, 2020.

Biale, David. *Blood and Belief: The Circulation of a Symbol between Jews and Christians*. Berkeley: University of California Press, 2007.

— "The God with Breasts: El Shaddai in the Bible." *History of Religions* 21 (1982): 240–56.

Biale, Rachel. *Women and Jewish Law: The Essential Texts, Their History, and Their Relevance for Today*. New York: Schocken, 1995.

Biddick, Kathleen. *Make and Let Die: Untimely Sovereignties*. Goleta, CA: punctum books, 2016.

- "Paper Jews: Inscription/Ethnicity/Ethnography." *Art Bulletin* 78 (1996): 594–9.
- *The Typological Imaginary: Circumcision, Technology, and History*. Philadelphia: University of Pennsylvania Press, 2003.

Biggs, Frederick M. "'Righteous People According to the Old Law': Ælfric on Anne and Joachim." *Apocrypha* 17 (2006): 151–77.

Binyam, Yonatan. "Anti-Judaism Versus Anti-Semitism: The Racialization of Jews in Late Antiquity." *Literature Compass* 20 (2023): e12698.

Blair, John. *The Church in Anglo-Saxon Society*. Oxford: Oxford University Press, 2005.

Blanton, Virginia. *Signs of Devotion: The Cult of St. Æthelthryth in Medieval England, 695–1615*. University Park, PA: Penn State University Press, 2007.

- "*Tota integra, tota incorrupta*: The Shrine of St. Æthelthryth as Symbol of Monastic Autonomy." *Journal of Medieval and Early Modern Studies* 32 (2002): 227–67.

Bloomfield, Josephine. "Benevolent Authoritarianism in Klaber's *Beowulf*: An Editorial Translation of Kingship." *MLQ* 60 (1999): 129–59.

- "The Bourgeois Family in *Beowulf*: Frederick Klaeber and Sentimental Kinship." *Nineteenth Century Contexts* 17 (1993): 34–52.
- "Diminished by Kindness: Frederick Klaeber's Rewriting of Wealhtheow." *Journal of English and Germanic Philology* 93 (1994): 183–20.

Blud, Victoria. *The Unspeakable, Gender and Sexuality in Medieval Literature, 1000–1400*. Cambridge, UK: D.S. Brewer, 2017.

Blurton, Heather. *Inventing William of Norwich: Thomas of Monmouth, Antisemitism, and Literary Culture, 1150–1200*. Philadelphia: University of Pennsylvania, 2022.

- "Richard of Devizes's *Cronicon*, Menippean Satire, and the Jews of Winchester." *Exemplaria* 22 (2010): 265–84.

Bogaert, Anthony F. *Understanding Asexuality*. Lanham, MD: Rowman & Littlefield, 2012.

Boisseron, Bénédicte. *Afro-Dog: Blackness and the Animal Question*. New York: Columbia University Press, 2018.

Borges, Jorge Luis. "Pierre Menard, Author of the *Quixote*." In *Collected Fictions: Jorge Luis Borges*, translated by Andrew Hurley, 88–95. New York: Penguin Putnam, 1998.

Borrell, Agustí. "Abraham and His Offspring in the Pauline Writings." *History and Identity* 2 (2006): 359–68.

Bosworth, Joseph, Thomas Northcote Toller, Christ Sean, and Ondrej Tichy, eds. *An Anglo-Saxon Dictionary Online*. Prague: Faculty of Arts, Charles University, 2019. https://bosworthtoller.com.

Boyarin, Adrienne Williams. *The Christian Jew and the Unmarked Jewess: The Polemics of Sameness in Medieval English Anti-Judaism*. Philadelphia: University of Pennsylvania Press, 2021.

Boyarin, Daniel. *Border Lines: The Partition of Judaeo-Christianity*. Philadelphia: University of Pennsylvania Press, 2004.
– *Carnal Israel: Reading Sex in Talmudic Culture*. Berkeley: University of California Press, 1995.
– *The Jewish Gospels: The Story of the Jewish Christ*. New York: New Press, 2012.
– "Othello's Penis: or, Islam in the Closet." In *Shakesqueer: A Queer Companion to the Complete Works of Shakespeare*, edited by Madhavi Menon, 254–62. New York: Duke University Press, 2011.
– *A Radical Jew: Paul and the Politics of Identity*. Berkeley: University of California Press, 1997 [1994].
– *Unheroic Conduct: The Rise of Heterosexuality and the Invention of the Jewish Man*. Berkeley: University of California Press, 1997.
Boyarin, Daniel, Daniel Itzkovitz, and Ann Pellegrini, eds. *Queer Theory and the Jewish Question*. New York: Columbia University Press, 2003.
– "Strange Bedfellows: An Introduction." In *Queer Theory and the Jewish Question*, edited by Daniel Boyarin, Daniel Itzkovitz, and Ann Pellegrini, 1–18. New York: Columbia University Press, 2003.
Boyarin, Jonathan. "Reading Exodus into History." *New Literary History* 23 (1992): 523–54.
– *The Unconverted Self: Jews, Indians, and the Identity of Christian Europe*. Chicago: University of Chicago Press, 2009.
Boynton, Susan, and Diane J. Reilly, ed. *The Practice of the Bible in the Middle Ages: Production, Reception, and Performance in Western Christianity*. New York: Columbia University Press, 2011.
Bretzke, James T. *Consecrated Phrases: A Latin Theological Dictionary*. Collegeville, MN: Liturgical Press, 2013.
Britton, Dennis Austin. *Becoming Christian: Race, Reformation, and Early Modern English Romance*. New York: Fordham University Press, 2014.
Brookes, Stewart. "Ælfric's Adaptation of the Book of Esther: A Source of Some Confusion." In *Essays on Anglo-Saxon and Related Themes in Memory of Lynne Grundy*, edited by Jane Roberts and Janet Nelson, 37–63. Exeter: Kings College London Centre for Late Antique and Medieval Studies, 2000.
– "Life, but Not as We Know It: Ælfric's Adaptation of the Book of Kings as Saint's Life." *Academia.edu*. Accessed January 31, 2022. https://www.academia.edu/14985046/Life_but_Not_as_We_Know_It_%C3%86lfric_s_Adaptation_of_the_Book_of_Kings_as_Saint_s_Life.
– "Reading Between the Lines: The Liturgy and Ælfric's *Lives of Saints* and Homilies." *Leeds Studies in English* (2011): 17–28.
Buell, Denise Kimber. *Why This New Race: Ethnic Reasoning in Early Christianity*. New York: Columbia University Press, 2005.

Bugyis, Katie Ann-Marie. *The Care of Nuns: The Ministries of Benedictine Women in England during the Central Middle Ages*. Oxford: Oxford University Press, 2019.

Bullough, Vern L. "The Sin against Nature and Homosexuality." In Bullough and Brundage, *Sexual Practices*, 55–71. Buffalo: Prometheus, 1982.

– "Transvestivism in the Middle Ages." In Bullough and Brundage, *Sexual Practices*, 43–54.

Bullough, Vern L., and James Brundage, ed. *Sexual Practices and the Medieval Church*. Amherst: Prometheus, 1982.

Bunzl, Matti. "Jews, Queers, and Other Symptoms: Recent Work in Jewish Cultural Studies." Review Essay. *GLQ* 6 (2000): 321–41.

– *Symptoms of Modernity: Jews and Queers in Late-Twentieth-Century Vienna*. Berkeley: University of California Press, 2004.

Burgeau-Blackler, Florence. "New Challenges for Islamic Ritual Slaughter: A European Perspective." *Journal of Ethnic and Migration Studies* 33 (2007): 965–80.

Burgwinkle, William E. *Sodomy, Masculinity and Law in Medieval Literature: France and England, 1050–1230*. Cambridge: Cambridge University Press, 2004.

Burke, Kevin J., and Avner Segall. *Christian Privilege in U.S. Education: Legacies and Current Issues*. New York: Routledge, 2017.

Bynum, Caroline Walker. *The Resurrection of the Body in Western Christianity, 200–1336*. New York: Columbia University Press, 1995.

Cain, Christopher M. "'þæt is on englisc': Performing Multilingualism in Anglo-Saxon England." In *Imagining Medieval English: Language Structures and Theories, 500–1500*, edited by Tim William Machan, 81–99. Cambridge: Cambridge University Press, 2016.

Campbell, Emma. *Medieval Saints' Lives: The Gift, Kinship, and Community in Old French Hagiography*. Cambridge, UK: D.S. Brewer, 2008.

– "Political Animals: Human/Animal Life in *Bisclavret* and *Yonec*." *Exemplaria* 25 (2013): 95–109.

– "Translating Gender in Thirteenth-Century French Cross-Dressing Narratives: *La Vie de Sainte Euphrosine* and *Le Roman de Silence*." *Journal of Medieval and Early Modern Studies* 49 (2019): 233–64.

Canton, William. *A History of the British and Foreign Bible Society*. Vol. 1. London: John Murray, 1904.

Carmichael, Calum M. *Illuminating Leviticus: A Study of Its Laws and Institutions in the Light of Biblical Narratives*. Baltimore: Johns Hopkins University Press, 2006.

Casey-Williams, Erin V. "The Queen's Three Bodies: Representations of Female Sovereignty in Early Modern Women's Writing, 1588–1688." PhD diss., State University of New York Albany, 2015.

Caviness, Margaret H. "Of Arms and the Woman in Medieval Europe: Fact. Fiction. Fantasy." *FKW // Zeischrift für Geschlechterforschung und Visuelle Kultur* 54 (2013): 54–75.

Cerling, Rebecca King. "Learning to Talk: Colloquies and the Formation of Childhood Monastic Identity in Late Anglo-Saxon England." In *Literary Cultures and Medieval and Early Modern Childhoods*, edited by Naomi J. Miller and Diane Purkiss, 21–35. Cham, Switzerland: Palgrave Macmillan, 2019.

Chakrabarty, Dipesh. *Provincializing Europe: Postcolonial Thought and Historical Difference*. Princeton: Princeton University Press, 2008.

Chamberlain, David. "*Judith*: A Fragmentary and Political Poem." In *Anglo-Saxon Poetry: Essays in Appreciation for John C. McGalliard*, edited by Lewis E. Nicholson and Delores Warwick Frese, 135–59. Notre Dame: University of Notre Dame Press, 1975.

Chandler, Nahum Dimitri. *X – The Problem of the Negro as a Problem for Thought*. New York: Fordham University Press, 2014.

Chazelle, Celia. "The Power of Oratory: Rereading the Whitby *Liber Beati Gregorii*." *Traditio* 76 (2021): 29–77.

Chen, Mel Y. *Animacies: Biopolitics, Racial Mattering, and Queer Affect*. Durham, NC: Duke University Press, 2012.

Chow, Rey. *Entanglements, or Transmedial Thinking about Capture*. Durham, NC: Duke University Press, 2012.

Clark, David. *Between Medieval Men: Male Friendship and Desire in Early Medieval English Literature*. Oxford: Oxford University Press, 2009.

Clark, Stephanie. *Compelling God: Theories of Prayer in Anglo-Saxon England*. Toronto: University of Toronto Press, 2018.

Clayton, Mary. "Ælfric's *De Virginitate*." *Notes and Queries* 32 (1985): 8–10.

– "Ælfric's *Esther*: A *Speculum Reginæ*?" In *Text and Gloss: Studies in Insular Learning and Literature Presented to Joseph Donovan Pheifer*, edited by Helen Conrad O'Brian, Anne Marie D'Arcy, and John Scattergood, 89–101. Dublin: Four Courts Press, 1999.

– "Ælfric's *Judith*: Manipulative or Manipulated?" *Anglo-Saxon England* 23 (1994): 215–27.

– "Blood and the Soul in Ælfric." *Notes and Queries* 54 (2007): 1–3.

Clemoes, Peter. "The Chronology of Ælfric's Works." In *The Anglo-Saxons: Studies in Some Aspects of Their History and Culture Presented to Bruce Dickins*, edited by Clemoes, 212–47. London: Bowes and Bowes, 1959. Reprinted as "The Chronology of Ælfric's Works." *Old English Newsletter Subsidia* 5 (1980): 2–37.

– "Introduction." In *The Old English Illustrated Hexateuch: British Museum Cotton Claudius B. IV*, edited by C.R. Dodwell and Peter Clemoes, 13–73. Copenhagen: Rosenkilde and Bagger, 1974.

Clover, Carol. "Regardless of Sex: Men, Women, and Power in Early Northern Europe." *Representations* 44 (1993): 1–28.

Cochran, John. "Object Oriented Cookery." *Collapse* 7 (2011): 299–329.

Cohen, Jeffrey J. "The Flow of Blood in Medieval Norwich." *Speculum* 79 (2004): 26–65.

Cohen, Jeremy. *"Be Fertile and Increase, Fill the Earth and Master It": The Ancient and Medieval Career of a Biblical Text*. Ithaca, NY: Cornell University Press, 1989.
– *Living Letters of the Law: Ideas of the Jew in Medieval Christianity*. Berkeley: University of California Press, 1999.
– *The Rule of Peshat: Jewish Constructions of the Plain Sense of Scripture and Their Christian and Muslim Contexts*, 900–1270. Philadelphia: University of Pennsylvania Press, 2020.
Cohen, Shaye J.D. *Why Aren't Jewish Women Circumcised? Gender and Covenant in Judaism*. Berkeley: University of California Press, 2005.
Coleman, Julie. "Lexicology and Medieval Prostitution." In *Lexis and Texts in Early English: Studies Presented to Jane Roberts*, edited by Christian J. Kay and Louise M. Sylvester, 69–87. Amsterdam: Rodopi, 2001.
– "Sexual Euphemism in Old English." *Neuphilologische Mitteilungen* 93 (1992): 93–98.
Collins, John J. *The Invention of Judaism: Torah and Jewish Identity from Deuteronomy to Paul*. Oakland: University of California Press, 2017.
Confino, Alon. *A World without Jews: The Nazi Imagination from Persecution to Genocide*. New Haven, CT: Yale University Press, 2014.
Cook, John. "The Finite Verbal Forms in Biblical Hebrew Do Express Aspect." *Journal of the Ancient Near Eastern Society* 30 (2006): 21–35.
Cooper, Tracey-Anne. "Judith in Late Anglo-Saxon England." In *The Sword of Judith: Judith Studies across the Disciplines*, edited by Kevin Brine and Henrike Lachnemann, 169–96. Cambridge, UK: Open Book Publishers, 2010.
Copeland, Rita. *Rhetoric, Hermeneutics, and Translation in the Middle Ages: Academic Traditions and Vernacular Texts*. Cambridge: Cambridge University Press, 1995 [1991].
Corona, Gabriella. "Ælfric's Schemes and Tropes: *Amplificatio* and the Portrayal of Persecutors." In *A Companion to Ælfric*, edited by Hugh Magennis and Mary Swan, 297–320. Leiden and Boston: Brill, 2009.
– "Ælfric's (Un)Changing Style: Continuity of Patterns from the Catholic Homilies to the *Lives of Saints*." *Journal of English and Germanic Studies* 107 (2008): 169–89.
Corradini, Erika. "The Composite Nature of Eleventh-Century Homiliaries: Cambridge, Corpus Christi College, 421." In *Textual Cultures: Cultural Texts*, edited by Orietta Da Rold and Elaine Treharne, 5–19. Woodbridge, UK: Boydell and Brewer, 2010.
Crabtree, Pam J. "A Note on the Role of Dogs in Anglo-Saxon Society: Evidence from East Anglia." *International Journal of Osteoarchaeology* 25 (2015): 976–80.
Crane, Susan. *Animal Encounters: Contacts and Concepts in Medieval Britain*. Philadelphia: University of Pennsylvania Press, 2013.

Cross, James E. "The Elephant to Alfred, Ælfric, Aldhelm, and Others." *Studia Neophilologica* 37 (1965): 367–73.
Cross, James E., and Alan Brown. "Literary Impetus for Wulfstan's *Sermo Lupi*." *Leeds Studies in English* 20 (1989): 271–91.
Cubitt, Catherine. "Ælfric's Lay Patrons." In *A Companion to Ælfric*, edited by Hugh Magennis and Mary Swan, 165–92. Leiden and Boston: Brill, 2009.
– "Apocalyptic and Eschatological Thought in England around the Year 1000." *Transactions of the Royal Historical Society* 25 (2015): 27–52.
– "On Living in the Time of Tribulation: Archbishop Wulfstan's *Sermo Lupi ad Anglos* and Its Eschatological Context." In *Writing, Kingship, and Power in Anglo-Saxon England*, edited by Rory Naismith and David A. Woodman, 202–33. Cambridge: Cambridge University Press, 2017.
– "Virginity and Misogyny in Tenth- and Eleventh-Century England." *Gender and History* 12 (2000): 1–32.
Damico, Helen. *Beowulf and the Grendel-kin: Politics and Poetry in Eleventh-Century England*. Morgantown: West Virginia University Press, 2014.
Dance, Richard. "Sound, Fury and Signifiers; or Wulfstan's Language." In *Wulfstan, Archbishop of York: The Proceedings of the Second Alcuin Conference*, edited by Matthew Townend, 29–61. Turnhout, Belgium: Brepols, 2004.
Daniell, David. *The Bible in English: Its History and Influence*. New Haven, CT: Yale University Press, 2003.
Davis, Angela, et al. *Abolition. Feminism. Now.* Chicago: Haymarket Books, 2022.
Davis, Bruce James. "The Art of Translation in the Age of Æthelwold: A Legacy of King Alfred." PhD diss., Arizona State University, 2002.
Davis, Kathleen. "Boredom, Brevity and Last Things: Ælfric's Style and the Politics of Time." In *A Companion to Ælfric*, edited by Hugh Magennis and Mary Swan, 321–44. Leiden and Boston: Brill, 2009.
– *Deconstruction and Translation*. Vol. 8. London: Routledge, 2001.
– "Intralingual Translation and the Making of a Language." In *A Companion to Translation Studies*, edited by Sandra Bermann and Catherine Porter, 586–98. Chichester, UK: John Wiley & Sons, 2014.
– "National Writing in the Ninth Century: A Reminder for Postcolonial Thinking about the Nation." *Journal of Medieval and Early Modern Studies* 28 (1998): 611–37.
– *Periodization and Sovereignty: How Ideas of Feudalism and Secularization Govern the Politics of Time*. Philadelphia: University of Pennsylvania Press, 2008.
Dayan, Colin. *The Law Is a White Dog: How Legal Rituals Make and Unmake Persons*. Princeton: Princeton University Press, 2013.
De Jong, Mayke. *In Samuel's Image: Child Oblation in the Early Medieval West*. Leiden: Brill, 1996.

De Lubac, Henri. *Medieval Exegesis, Vol. 1: The Four Senses of Scripture*. Grand Rapids: Eerdmans, 1998.

Deer, Sarah. *The Beginning and End of Rape: Confronting Sexual Violence in Native America*. Minneapolis: University of Minnesota Press, 2015.

DeGregorio, Scott. "*Interpretatio Monastica*: Biblical Commentary and the Forging of Monastic Identity in the Early Middle Ages." In *Latinity and Identity in Anglo-Saxon Literature*, edited by Rebecca Stephenson and Emily V. Thornbury, 38–53. Toronto: University of Toronto Press, 2016.

Dekker, Kees. "Pentecost and Linguistic Self-Consciousness in Anglo-Saxon England: Bede and Ælfric." *The Journal of English and Germanic Philology* 104 (2005): 345–72.

Deleuze, Gilles. *Francis Bacon: The Logic of Sensation*. Translated by Daniel W. Smith. Minneapolis: University of Minnesota Press, 2003.

Deleuze, Gilles, and Félix Guattari. *A Thousand Plateaus: Capitalism and Schizophrenia*. Translated by Brian Massumi. Minneapolis: University of Minnesota Press, 1987.

Deloria, Philip J. *Playing Indian*. New Haven, CT: Yale University Press, 1998.

Derrida, Jacques. *The Animal That Therefore I Am*. Translated by David Wills. New York: Fordham University Press, 2008.

– *The Beast and the Sovereign*. Translated by Geoffrey Bennington. 2 Vols. Chicago: University of Chicago Press, 2009–2011.

– "'Eating Well,' or the Calculation of the Subject: An Interview with Jacques Derrida." In *Who Comes after the Subject?* edited by Eduardo Cadava, Peter Connor, and Jean-Luc Nancy, 96–119. New York: Routledge, 1991.

– *Specters of Marx: The State of the Debt, the Work of Mourning and the New International*. Translated by Peggy Kamuf. New York and London: Routledge, 2006.

– "What Is a 'Relevant' Translation?" Translated by Lawrence Venuti. *Critical Inquiry* 27 (2001): 174–200.

DeVun, Leah. "Animal Appetites." *GLQ: A Journal of Lesbian and Gay Studies* 20 (2014): 461–90.

– *The Shape of Sex: Nonbinary Gender from Genesis to the Renaissance*. New York: Columbia University Press, 2021.

Diamond, James A. "The Deuteronomic 'Pretty Woman' Law: Prefiguring Feminism and Freud in Nahmanides." *Jewish Social Studies* 14, no. 2 (2008): 61–85.

DiNapoli, Robert. *An Index of Theme and Image to the Homilies of the Anglo-Saxon Church: Comprising the Homilies of Ælfric, Wulfstan, and the Blickling and Vercelli Codices*. Hockwold cum Wilton, Norfolk: Anglo-Saxon Books, 1995.

Dinshaw, Carolyn. *Chaucer's Sexual Poetics*. Madison: University of Wisconsin Press, 1989.

– *Getting Medieval: Sexualities and Communities, Pre-and Postmodern*. Durham, NC: Duke University Press, 1999.

- *How Soon Is Now? Medieval Texts, Amateur Readers, and the Queerness of Time.* Durham, NC: Duke University Press, 2012.
- "Pale Faces: Race, Religion, and Affect in Chaucer's Texts and Their Readers." *Studies in the Age of Chaucer* 23 (2001): 19–41.

Discenza, Nicole Guenther. *The King's English: Strategies of Translation in the Old English Boethius.* New York: State University of New York Press, 2005.

Doane, A. N., and William P. Stoneman. *Purloined Letters: The Twelfth Century Reception of the Anglo-Saxon Illustrated Hexateuch (British Library, Cotton Claudius B. iv).* Tempe: Arizona Centre for Medieval and Renaissance Studies, 2011.

Dockray-Miller, Mary. "Female Community in the Old English *Judith.*" *Studia Neophilologica* 70 (1998): 165–72.

Douglas, Mary. *In the Wilderness: The Doctrine of Defilement in the Book of Numbers.* Sheffield, UK: JSOT Press, 1993.
- *Leviticus as Literature.* Oxford: Oxford University Press, 1999.
- *Purity and Danger: An Analysis of Concept of Pollution and Taboo.* London: Routledge Classics, 2002.

Drake, Susanna. "Origen's Veils: The *Askēsis* of Interpretation." *Church History* 83 (2014): 815–42.
- *Slandering the Jew: Sexuality and Difference in Early Christian Texts.* Philadelphia: University of Pennsylvania Press, 2013.

Dube, Musa W. "Consuming a Colonial Cultural Bomb: Translating *Badimo* into 'Demons' in the Setswana Bible (Matthew 8.28–34; 15.22; 10.8)." *Journal for the Study of the New Testament* 73 (1999): 33–58.
- "Rahab Says Hello to Judith: A Decolonizing Feminist Reading." In *The Postcolonial Biblical Reader*, edited by R. S. Sugirtharajah, 142–58. Malden, MA: Blackwell, 2006.

Dumitrescu, Irina. *The Experience of Education in Anglo-Saxon Literature.* Cambridge: Cambridge University Press, 2018.

Dutchak, Pat. "The Church and Slavery in Anglo-Saxon England." *Past Imperfect* 9 (2001–2003): 25–42.

Edelman, Lee. *No Future: Queer Theory and the Death Drive.* Durham, NC: Duke University Press, 2004.

Edwards, Jennifer C. *Superior Women: Medieval Female Authority in Poitiers' Abbey of Sainte-Croix.* Oxford: Oxford University Press, 2019.

Ellard, Donna Beth. *Anglosaxon(ist) Pasts, Post Saxon Futures.* Goleta, CA: Punctum Books, 2019.

Elliott, Dylan. *The Corrupter of Boys: Sodomy, Scandal, and the Medieval Clergy.* Philadelphia: University of Pennsylvania Press, 2020.

Elliott, Michael D. "Wulfstan's Commonplace Book Revised: The Structure and Development of 'Block 7,' on Pastoral Privilege and Responsibility." *The Journal of Medieval Latin* 22 (2012): 1–48.

Enders, Jody. "Homicidal Pigs and the Antisemitic Imagination." *Exemplaria* 14 (2002): 201–38.

Ernjaes, Bodil. "The Bible in the Languages of Scandinavia." In *The New Cambridge History of the Bible: From 600 to 1450*, edited by Richard Marsden and E. Ann Matter, 239–59. Cambridge: Cambridge University Press, 2012.

Ertel, Emmanuelle. "Derrida on Translation and His (Mis)Reception in America." *Revue Trahir* 2 (2011): 1–18.

Esler, Philip. "Ludic History in the Book of Judith: The Reinvention of Israelite Identity?" *Biblical Interpretation* 10 (2002): 107–43.

Estes, Heide. "Abraham and the Northmen in *Genesis A*: Alfredian Translations and Ninth-Century Politics." *Medievalia et Humanistica* 33 (2007): 1–13.

– "Feasting with Holofernes: Digesting Judith in Anglo-Saxon England." *Exemplaria* 15 (2003): 325–50.

– "Lives in Translation: Jews in the Anglo-Saxon Literary Imagination." PhD diss., New York University, 1998.

– "Reading Ælfric in the Twelfth Century: Anti-Judaic Doctrine Becomes Anti-Judaic Rhetoric." In *Imagining the Jew in Anglo-Saxon Literature and Culture*, edited by Samantha Zacher, 265–79. Toronto: University of Toronto Press, 2016.

Fabian, Johannes. *Time and the Other: How Anthropology Makes Its Object*. New York: Columbia University Press, 2002 [1983].

Fabre-Vassas, Claudine. *The Singular Beast: Jews, Christians, and the Pig*. Translated by Carol Volk. New York: Columbia University Press, 1997.

Falkeid, Unn. "The Political Discourse of Birgitta of Sweden." In *A Companion to Birgitta of Sweden and Her Legacy in the Later Middle Ages*, edited by Maria H. Oen, 80–102. Leiden: Brill, 2019.

Fay, Jacqueline (Stodnick). "Bodies of Land: The Place of Gender in the *Old English Martyrology*." In *Writing Women Saints in Anglo-Saxon England*, edited by Paul E. Szarmach, 30–52. Toronto: University of Toronto Press, 2013.

Fazioli, K. Patrick. *The Mirror of the Medieval: An Anthropology of the Western Historical Imagination*. New York and Oxford: Berghahn Books, 2017.

Feeley-Harnik, Gillian. *The Lord's Table: The Meaning of Food in Early Judaism and Christianity*. Washington, DC: Smithsonian Institution Scholarly Press, 1994 [1981].

Fellows, Mary Louise. "Aethelgifu's Will as Hagiography." In *Writing Women Saints in Anglo-Saxon England*, edited by Paul E. Szarmach, 82–102. Toronto: University of Toronto Press, 2013.

Fenn, Eric. "The Bible and the Missionary." In *The Cambridge History of the Bible: The West from the Reformation to the Present Day*, edited by S.L. Greenslade, vol. 3, 383–407. Cambridge: Cambridge University Press, 1963.

Filotas, Bernadette. *Pagan Survivals, Superstitions and Popular Cultures in Early Medieval Pastoral Literature*. Toronto: Pontifical Institute of Mediaeval Studies, 2005.

Finkelstein, Ari. *The Specter of the Jews: Emperor Julian and the Rhetoric of Ethnicity in Syrian Antioch*. Oakland: University of California Press, 2018.

Fleming, Damian. "Hebrew Words and English Identity in Educational Texts of Ælfric and Byrhtferth." In *Latinity and Identity in Anglo-Saxon Literature*, edited by Rebecca Stephenson and Emily Thornbury, 138–57. Toronto: University of Toronto Press, 2016.

Flight, Tim. "Aristocratic Deer Hunting in Late Anglo-Saxon England: A Reconsideration, Based upon the *Vita S. Dvnstani*." *Anglo-Saxon England* 47 (2017): 311–31.

Fonrobert, Charlotte Elisheva. *Menstrual Purity: Rabbinic and Christian Reconstructions of Biblical Gender*. Redwood City, CA: Stanford University Press, 2000.

Foot, Sarah. *Veiled Women, Vol. 1, the Disappearance of Nuns from Anglo-Saxon England*. London: Routledge, 2000.

Forbes, Erin. "Sovereign Poetics: From Exception to Apocrypha." *Expositions* 9, no. 2 (2015): 16–34.

Forbes, Helen Foxhall. "Affective Piety and the Practice of Penance in Late-Eleventh-Century Worcester: The Address to the Penitent in Oxford, Bodleian Library, Junius 121." *Anglo-Saxon England* 44 (2015): 309–45.

Foucault, Michel. "Friendship as a Way of Life." In *Foucault Live (Interviews 1966–84)*, edited by Sylvère Lotringer, 203–10. New York: Semiotext(e), 1989.

Fox, Michael. "Ælfric's *Interrogationes Sigewulfi*." In *Old English Literature*, edited by Michael Fox and Manish Sharma, 25–63. Toronto: University of Toronto Press, 2012.

Fox, Michael, and Manish Sharma, eds. *Old English Literature and the Old Testament*. Toronto: University of Toronto Press, 2012.

Frantzen, Allen J. *Before the Closet: Same-Sex Love from Beowulf to Angels in America*. Chicago: University of Chicago Press, 1998.

– *Desire for Origins: New Language, Old English, and Teaching the Tradition*. New Brunswick, NJ: Rutgers University Press, 1990.

– *The Literature of Penance in Anglo-Saxon England*. New Brunswick, NJ: Rutgers University Press, 1983.

Freccero, Carla. "Carnivorous Virility; or, Becoming-Dog." *Social Text* 29 (2011): 177–95.

– "A Race of Wolves." *Yale French Studies* 127 (2015): 110–23.

Freidenreich, David M. *Foreigners and Their Food: Constructing Otherness in Jewish, Christian, and Islamic Law*. Berkeley: University of California Press, 2011.

Freinkel, Lisa. "The Merchant of Venice: Modern Anti-Semitism and the Veil of Allegory." In *Shakespeare and Modernity: Early Modern to Millennium*, edited by Hugh Grady, 122–41. London: Routledge, 2000.

Gaca, Kathy L. *The Making of Fornication: Eros, Ethics, and Political Reform in Greek Philosophy and Early Christianity*. Berkeley: University of California Press, 2003.

Ganim, John M. *Medievalism and Orientalism: Three Essays on Literature, Architecture, and Cultural Identity*. New York: Palgrave Macmillan, 2005.
Gatch, Milton McG. "MS Boulogne-Sur-Mer 63 and Ælfric's First Series of Catholic Homilies." *JEGP* 65 (1966): 482–90.
– *Preaching and Theology in Anglo-Saxon England: Ælfric and Wulfstan*. Toronto: University of Toronto Press, 1977.
Gates, Jay Paul. "Preaching, Politics and Episcopal Reform in Wulfstan's Early Writings." *Early Medieval Europe* 23 (2015): 93–116.
Gaunt, Simon. "Straight Minds / 'Queer' Wishes in Old French Hagiography: *La Vie de Sainte Euphrosine*." *GLQ* 1 (1995): 439–57.
Geller, Jay. *Bestiarium Judaicum: Unnatural Histories of the Jews*. New York: Fordham University Press, 2017.
Gera, Deborah Levine. *Judith*. Berlin: De Gruyter, 2013.
Gerdmar, Anders. "The National Socialist Bible: 'Die Botschaft Gottes': Theological Legitimation of Antisemitism." In *Confronting Antisemitism from the Perspectives of Christianity, Islam, and Judaism*, edited by Armin Lange, Kerstin Mayerhofer, Dina Porat, and Lawrence H. Schiffman, 155–83. Berlin and Boston: De Gruyter, 2020.
Gerrard, Daniel M.G. *The Church at War: The Military Activities of Bishops, Abbots and Other Clergy in England, c. 900–1200*. London: Routledge, 2016.
Gesenius, William, and Francis Brown. *A Hebrew and English Lexicon of the Old Testament*. Oxford: Clarendon, 1952.
Gilson, Erinn Cunniff. "Zones of Indiscernibility: The Life of a Concept from Deleuze to Agamben." *Philosophy Today* 51 (2007): 98–106.
Gittos, Helen. "The Audience for Old English Texts: Ælfric, Rhetoric and 'the Edification of the Simple.'" *Anglo-Saxon England* 43 (2014): 231–66.
Glancy, Jennifer A. "The Mistress-Slave Dialectic: Paradoxes of Slavery in Three LXX Narratives." *Journal for the Study of the Old Testament* 21 (1996): 71–87.
– *Slavery in Early Christianity*. Oxford: Oxford University Press, 2002.
Glick, Leonard B. *Marked in Your Flesh: Circumcision from Ancient Judea to Modern America*. Oxford: Oxford University Press, 2005.
Gneuss, Helmut. *Ælfric of Eynsham: His Life, Times, and Writings*. Translated by Michael Lapidge. Kalamazoo, MI: Medieval Institute Publications, 2009.
Gneuss, Helmut, and Michael Lapidge. *Anglo-Saxon Manuscripts: A Bibliographical Handlist of Manuscripts and Manuscript Fragments Written or Owned in England up to 1100*. Toronto: University of Toronto Press, 2014.
Godden, Malcolm R. "Ælfric and Anglo-Saxon Kingship." *The English Historical Review* 102 (1987): 911–15.
– ed. *Ælfric's Catholic Homilies: Introduction, Commentary and Glossary*. EETS s.s. 18. Oxford: Oxford University Press, 2000.
– "Ælfric's Changing Vocabulary." *English Studies* 61 (1980): 206–23.

- "Ælfric's Saints' Lives and the Problem of Miracles." In *Old English Prose: Basic Readings*, edited by Paul E. Szarmach, 287–309. New York: Garland, 2000.
- "Apocalypse and Invasion in Late Anglo-Saxon England." In *From Anglo-Saxon to Early Middle English: Studies Presented to E.G. Stanley*, edited by Godden, Douglas Gray, and Terry Hoad, 130–62. Oxford: Clarendon, 1994.
- "Biblical Literature: The Old Testament." In *The Cambridge Companion to Old English Literature*, 2nd ed., edited by Malcolm Godden and Michael Lapidge, 214–33. Cambridge: Cambridge University Press, 2013.
- "Catholic Homilies 1.6 (C.B.1.1.7)." *Fontes Anglo-Saxonici: World Wide Web Register*, 1997. https://arts.st-andrews.ac.uk/fontes/.
- "Catholic Homilies 2.8 (C.B.1.2.9)." *Fontes Anglo-Saxonici: World Wide Web Register*, 1997. https://arts.st-andrews.ac.uk/fontes/.
- "Experiments in Genre." In *Holy Men and Holy Women: Old English Prose Saints' Lives and Their Contexts*, edited by Paul E. Szarmach, 261–88. Albany, NY: State University of New York Press, 1996.

Gooch, Peter D. *Dangerous Food: I Corinthians 8–10 in Its Context*. Waterloo, ON: Wilfrid Laurier University Press, 1993.

Gossett, Che. "Blackness, Animality, and the Unsovereign." In *Walls Turned Sideways: Artists Confront the Justice System*, edited by Risa Puleo, 56–63. Houston: Contemporary Arts Museum Houston; Miami: [NAME] Publications, 2018.

Gow, Andrew Colin. "The Bible in Germanic." In *The New Cambridge History of the Bible: From 600 to 1450*, edited by Richard Marsden and E. Ann Matter, 198–216. Cambridge: Cambridge University Press, 2012.
- "Challenging the Protestant Paradigm: Bible Reading in Lay and Urban Contexts of the Later Middle Ages." In *Scripture and Pluralism: Reading the Bible in the Religiously Plural Worlds of the Middle Ages and Renaissance*, edited by Thomas J. Heffernan and Thomas E. Burman, 161–91. Leiden: Brill, 2005.
- "The Contested History of a Book: The German Bible of the Later Middle Ages and Reformation in Legend, Ideology, and Scholarship." *The Journal of Hebrew Scriptures* 9 (2009): 1–37.

Gow, Andrew, and Nakita Valerio. "Editor's Note. In Critiquing Secularism." Edited by Andrew Gow and Nakita Valerio. Special Issue, *Past Imperfect* 21 (2019): i–xii.

Gretsch, Mechthild. *Ælfric and the Cult of the Saints in Late Anglo-Saxon England*. Cambridge: Cambridge University Press, 2006.
- "Ælfric, Language and Winchester." In *A Companion to Ælfric*, edited by Hugh Magennis and Mary Swan, 109–37. Leiden and Boston: Brill, 2009.
- *The Intellectual Foundations of the Benedictine Reform*. Cambridge: Cambridge University Press, 1999.
- "Winchester Vocabulary and Standard Old English: The Vernacular in Late Anglo-Saxon England." *Bulletin of the John Rylands University Library of Manchester* 83 (2001): 41–87.

Griffith, Mark. "Bigamy and the Bible in Ælfric's *Preface to Genesis*." *Notes and Queries* 64 (2017): 370–5.

Griffiths, Fiona. *Nuns' Priests' Tales: Men and Salvation in Medieval Women's Monastic Life*. Philadelphia: University of Pennsylvania Press, 2018.

– "Wives, Concubines, or Slaves? Peter Damian and Clerics' Women." *EME* 30 (2022): 266–90.

Griffiths, Gwen. "Reading Ælfric's Saint Æthelthryth as a Woman." *Parergon* 10 (1992): 35–49.

Gross, Raphael. *Carl Schmitt and the Jews: The "Jewish Question," the Holocaust, and German Legal Theory*. Translated by Joel Golb. Madison: University of Wisconsin Press, 2007.

Gruber, Ruth Ellen. *Virtually Jewish: Reinventing Jewish Culture in Europe*. Berkeley: University of California Press, 2002.

Grumett, David, and Rachel Muers. *Theology on the Menu: Asceticism, Meat and Christian Diet*. London: Routledge, 2010.

Gulley, Alison. *The Displacement of the Body in Ælfric's Virgin Martyr Lives*. Farnham, UK: Ashgate, 2014.

Gustafson, Timothy Alan. "Ælfric Reads Esther: The Cultural Limits of Translation." PhD diss., University of Iowa, 1995.

Gwara, Scott. "Manuscripts of Aldhelm's 'Prosa de Virginitate' and the Rise of Hermeneutic Literacy in Tenth-Century England." *Studi Medievali* 35 (1994): 101–59.

Haber, Tom Burns. "Canine Terms Applied to Human Beings and Human Events: Part II." *American Speech* 40 (1965): 243–71.

Hagen, Ann. *Anglo-Saxon Food and Drink: Production, Processing, Distribution, and Consumption*. Hockwold cum Wilton, Norfolk: Anglo-Saxon Books, 2006.

Halbrooks, John. "Ælfric, the Maccabees, and the Problem of Christian Heroism." *Studies in Philology* 106 (2009): 263–84.

Hall, Thomas N. "Ælfric As Pedagogue." In *A Companion to Ælfric*, edited by Hugh Magennis and Mary Swan, 193–216. Leiden and Boston: Brill, 2009.

– "Preaching at Winchester in the Early Twelfth Century." *The Journal of English and Germanic Philology* 104 (2005): 189–218.

Harris, Angela O. "Heteropatriarchy Kills: Challenging Gender Violence in a Prison Nation." *Washington University Journal of Law and Policy* 37 (2011): 13–65.

Harris, Stephen. *Race and Ethnicity in Anglo-Saxon Literature*. New York: Routledge, 2003.

Hartman, John J. "A Psychoanalytic View of Racial Myths in a Nazi Propaganda Film: *Der Ewige Jude* (The Eternal Jew)." *Journal of Applied Psychoanalytic Studies* 2 (2000): 329–46.

Hartman, Megan E. "A Drawn-Out Beheading: Style, Theme, and Hypermetricity in the Old English Judith." *The Journal of English and Germanic Philology* 110 (2011): 421–40.

Hastings, Adrian. "Special Peoples." *Nations and Nationalism* 5 (1999): 381–96.
Hawk, Brandon W. "Ælfric's Genesis and Bede's *Commentarius in Genesim.*" *Medium Aevum* 85 (2016): 208–16.
– "Biblical Apocrypha as Medieval World Literature." *The Medieval Globe* 6 (2020): 49–83.
– "Isidorian Influences in Ælfric's Preface to Genesis." *English Studies* 95 (2014): 357–66.
– *Preaching Apocrypha in Anglo-Saxon England*. Toronto: University of Toronto Press, 2018.
Hayes, Christine Elizabeth. *Gentile Impurities and Jewish Identities: Intermarriage and Conversion from the Bible to the Talmud*. Oxford: Oxford University Press, 2002.
Hazony, Yoram. *The Dawn: Political Teachings of the Book of Esther*. Jerusalem: Shalem Press, 1995.
Henderson, George. "The Joshua Cycle in BM Cotton MS. Claudius B. IV." *Journal of the British Archaeological Association* 31 (1968): 38–59.
Heng, Geraldine. *Empire of Magic: Medieval Romance and the Politics of Cultural Fantasy*. New York: Columbia University Press, 2003.
– "England's Dead Boys: Telling Tales of Christian-Jewish Relations before and after the First European Explusion of the Jews." *MLN* 127 (2012): S54–58.
– *The Invention of Race in the European Middle Ages*. Cambridge: Cambridge University Press, 2018.
Hepner, Gershon. "Abraham's Incestuous Marriage with Sarah a Violation of the Holiness Code." *Vetus Testamentum* 53 (2003): 143–55.
Heschel, Susannah. *The Aryan Jesus: Christian Theologians and the Bible in Nazi Germany*. Princeton: Princeton University Press, 2008.
– "The Slippery yet Tenacious Nature of Racism: New Developments in Critical Race Theory and Their Implications for the Study of Religion and Ethics." *Journal of the Society of Christian Ethics* 35 (2015): 3–27.
– "Theological Bulimia: Christianity and Its Dejudaization." In *After the Passion Is Gone: American Religious Consequences*, edited by J. Shawn Landres and Michael Berenbaum, 177–92. Walnut Creek, CA: AltaMira, 2004.
Heydeman, Gerda. "The People of God and the Law: Biblical Models in Carolingian Legislation." *Speculum* 95 (2020): 89–131.
Hezser, Catherine. *Jewish Slavery in Antiquity*. Oxford: Oxford University Press, 2005.
Hill, Joyce. "Ælfric: His Life and Works." In *A Companion to Ælfric*, edited by Hugh Magennis and Mary Swan, 35–65. Leiden and Boston: Brill, 2009.
– "Ælfric's Manuscript of Paul the Deacon's Homiliary: A Provisional Analysis." In *The Old English Homily: Precedent, Practice, and Appropriation*, edited by Aaron J. Kleist, 67–96. Turnhout, BE: Brepols, 2007.

- "Archbishop Wulfstan: Reformer?" In *Wulfstan, Archbishop of York: The Proceedings of the Second Alcuin Conference*, edited by Matthew Townend, 309–24. Turnhout, BE: Brepols, 2004.
- "Authorial Adaptation: Ælfric, Wulfstan, and the Pastoral Letters." In *Text and Language in Medieval English Prose: A Festschrift for Tadao Kubouchi*, edited by Akio Oizumi, Jacek Fisiak, and John Scahill, 63–75. Frankfurt, DE: Peter Lang, 2005.
- "The Dissemination of Ælfric's *Lives of Saints*: A Preliminary Survey." In *Holy Men and Holy Women: Old English Prose Saints' Lives and Their Contexts*, edited by Paul E. Szarmach, 235–59. Albany: State University of New York Press, 1996.
- "Translating the Tradition: Manuscripts, Models and Methodologies in the Composition of Ælfric's Catholic Homilies." *Bulletin of the John Rylands Library* 79 (1997): 43–66.
- "Two Anglo-Saxon Bishops at Work: Wulfstan, Leofric and Cambridge, Corpus Christi College MS 190." In *Patterns of Episcopal Power: Bishops in Tenth and Eleventh Century Western Europe*, edited by Ludger Körntgen and Dominik Waßenhoven, 145–61. Berlin: De Gruyter, 2011.
- "Two Micro-Texts in Ælfric's *Catholic Homilies*: A Puzzle Revisited." *Anglo-Saxon Micro-Texts*, edited by Ursula Lenker and Lucia Kornexl, 131–41. Berlin: De Gruyter, 2019.

Hobson, Jacob. "Exegetical Theory and Textual Communities in Late Anglo-Saxon England." PhD diss., University of California, Berkeley, 2017.

Hoek, Michelle. "Violence and Ideological Inversion in the Old English Soul's Address to the Body." *Exemplaria* 10 (1998): 271–85.

Horowitz, Elliott. "Circumcised Dogs from Matthew to Marlowe." *Prooftexts: A Journal of Jewish Literary History* 27 (2007): 531–45.

Horsman, Reginald. "Origins of Racial Anglo-Saxonism in Great Britain before 1850." *Journal of the History of Ideas* 37 (1976): 387–410.

- *Race and Manifest Destiny: The Origins of American Racial Anglo-Saxonism*. Cambridge, MA: Harvard University Press, 1981.

Hostetler, Margaret. "'Nimað eow bysne be þyssere Iudith': Deictic Shifting and Didactic Christian Discourse in Ælfric's Judith." *Studia Neophilologica* 76 (2004): 152–64.

Hough, Carole. "Alfred's *Domboc* and the Language of Rape: A Reconsideration of Alfred Ch. 11." *Medium Ævum* 66 (1997): 1–27.

Howe, Nicholas. *Migration and Mythmaking in Anglo-Saxon England*. Notre Dame: University of Notre Dame Press, 2001 [New Haven, CT: Yale University Press, 1989].

Howie, Cary. *Claustrophilia: The Erotics of Enclosure in Medieval Literature*. New York: Palgrave Macmillan, 2007.

Hsy, Jonathan. *Trading Tongues: Merchants, Multilingualism, and Medieval Literature*. Columbus: Ohio State University Press, 2013.

Hughes, Aaron W. *The Invention of Jewish Identity: Bible, Philosophy, and the Art of Translation*. Bloomington: Indiana University Press, 2011.

– *Shared Identities: Medieval and Modern Imaginings of Judeo-Islam*. New York: Oxford University Press, 2017.

Ilan, Tal. *Integrating Women into Second Temple History*. Tübingen, DE: Mohr Siebeck, 1999.

Irigaray, Luce. *This Sex Which Is Not One*. Translated by Catherine Porter. Ithaca, NY: Cornell University Press, 1985.

Irvine, Susan E. *Uncertain Beginnings: The Prefatory Tradition in Old English*. Cambridge, UK: Department of Anglo-Saxon, Norse and Celtic, University of Cambridge, 2017.

Israel, Hephzibah. "Translating the Sacred: Colonial Constructions and Postcolonial Perspectives." In *A Companion to Translation Studies*, edited by Sandra Bermann and Catherine Porter, 557–69. Chichester, UK: John Wiley & Sons, 2014.

Jackson, Peter. "Ælfric and the Purpose of Christian Marriage: A Reconsideration of the Life of Æthelthryth, Lines 120–30." *Anglo-Saxon England* 29 (2000): 235–60.

Jackson, Zakiyyah Iman. *Becoming Human: Matter and Meaning in an Antiblack World*. New York: New York University Press, 2020.

Jacobs, Andrew. *Christ Circumcised: A Study in Early Christian History and Difference*. Philadelphia: University of Pennsylvania Press, 2012.

Jaeger, Stephen C. *Ennobling Love: In Search of a Lost Sensibility*. Philadelphia: University of Pennsylvania Press, 1999.

Jaleel, Rana. *The Work of Rape*. Durham, NC: Duke University Press, 2021.

Jayatilaka, Rohini. "Lives 10 (Chair of St Peter) (C.B.1.3.11)." *Fontes Anglo-Saxonici: World Wide Web Register*, 1997. https://arts.st-andrews.ac.uk/fontes/.

Jennings, Willie James. *The Christian Imagination: Theology and the Origins of Race*. New Haven, CT: Yale University Press, 2010.

Jolly, Katherine L. *Popular Religion in Late Saxon England: Elf Charms in Context*. Chapel Hill: University of North Carolina Press, 1996.

Jolly, Margaret. "Devils, Holy Spirits, and the Swollen God: Translation, Conversation and Colonial Power in the Marist Mission, Vanuatu, 1887–1934." In *Conversion to Modernities: The Globalization of Christianity*, edited by Peter van der Veer, 231–62. New York: Routledge, 1995.

Jones, Christopher A. "Ælfric and the Limits of 'Benedictine Reform.'" In *A Companion to Ælfric*, edited by Hugh Magennis and Mary Swan, 67–108. Leiden and Boston: Brill, 2009.

- "Monastic Identity and Sodomitic Danger in the *Occupatio* by Odo of Cluny." *Speculum* 82 (2007): 1–53.
- "Wulfstan's Liturgical Interests." In *Wulfstan, Archbishop of York: The Proceedings of the Second Alcuin Conference*, edited by Matthew Townend, 325–52. Turnhout, BE: Brepols, 2004.

Jónsson, Már. "Blóðskömm á Íslandi 1270–1870." PhD diss., University of Iceland, 1993.
- "Defining Incest by the Word of God: Northern Europe 1520–1740." *History of European Ideas* 18 (1994): 853–67.
- "Incest and the Word of God: Early Sixteenth Century Protestant Disputes." *Archiv für Reformationsgeschichte* 85 (1994): 96–118.

Joshi, Khyati Y. *White Christian Privilege: The Illusion of Religious Equality in America*. New York: New York University Press, 2021.

Joslyn-Siemiatkoski, Daniel. *Christian Memories of the Maccabean Martyrs*. New York: Palgrave Macmillan, 2009.

Julius, Anthony. *Trials of the Diaspora: A History of Anti-Semitism in England*. Oxford: Oxford University Press, 2010.

Jurasinski, Stefan. "Noxal Surrender, the *Deodand*, and the Laws of King Alfred." *Studies in Philology* 111 (2014): 195–224.
- *The Old English Penitentials and Anglo-Saxon Law*. Cambridge: Cambridge University Press, 2015.
- "The Old English Penitentials and the Law of Slavery." In *English Law before Magna Carta: Felix Liebermann and Die Gesetze der Angelsachen*, edited by Stefan Jurasinki, Lisi Oliver, and Andrew Rabin, 97–118. Leiden: Brill, 2010.
- "Slavery, Learning and the Law of Marriage in Alfred's Mosaic Prologue." *Secular Learning in Anglo-Saxon England*, edited by László Sándor Chardonnens and Bryan Carella, 45–64. Leiden: Brill, 2012.

Kahn, Jack H., and Hester Solomon. *Job's Illness: Loss, Grief, and Integration: A Psychological Interpretation*. Oxford: Pergamon Press, 1975.

Kamionkowski, S. Tamar. *Leviticus*. Edited by Lauress Wilkins Lawrence. Wisdom commentary. Vol. 3. Collegeville, MN: Liturgical Press, 2018.

Kanji, Azeezah. "Kosher and Halal Bans: Fur-Washing Factory Farming's Brutality." *Al Jazeerah, Opinion*, November 3, 2021. https://www.aljazeera.com/opinions/2021/11/3/kosher-and-halal-bans-fur-washing-factory-farmings-brutality.

Kantorowicz, Ernst H. *The King's Two Bodies: A Study in Mediaeval Political Theology*. Princeton: Princeton University Press, 1957.

Kao, Wan-Chuan. "Identitarian Politics, Precarious Sovereignty." In *Race, Revulsion, and Revolution*, edited by M. Rambaran-Olm, M.B. Leake, and Micah Goodrich. Special issue, *Postmedieval* 11 (2020): 371–83.

Kaplan, Gregory. "Power and Israel in Martin Buber's Critique of Carl Schmitt's Political Theology." In *Judaism, Liberalism, and Political Theology*, edited by Randi Rashkover and Martin Kavka, 155–77. Bloomington: Indiana University Press, 2013.

Kaplan, M. Lindsay. *Figuring Racism in Medieval Christianity*. New York: Oxford University Press, 2019.

Karkov, Catherine E. "The Body of St Æthelthryth: Desire, Conversion and Reform in Anglo-Saxon England." In *The Cross Goes North: Processes of Conversion in Northern Europe, AD 300–1300*, edited by Martin Carver, 397–411. Woodbridge, UK: Boydell Press, 2005.

– "Hagar and Ishmael: The Uncanny and the Exile." In *Imagining the Jew in Anglo-Saxon Literature and Culture*, edited by Samantha Zacher, 197–218. Toronto: University of Toronto Press, 2016.

– "The Mother's Tongue and the Father's Prose." *Parallax* 18 (2012): 27–37.

– *The Ruler Portraits of Anglo-Saxon England*. Woodbridge, UK: Boydell Press, 2004.

Karras, Ruth Mazo. *Sexuality in Medieval Europe: Doing unto Others*. New York: Routledge, 2005, 2017.

Kelber, Werner H. "Roman Imperialism and Early Christian Scribality." In *The Postcolonial Biblical Reader*, edited by R.S. Sugirtharajah, 96–111. Malden, MA: Blackwell, 2006.

Ker, N.R. *Catalogue of Manuscripts Containing Anglo-Saxon*. Oxford: Clarendon Press, 1957.

Keynes, Simon. "An Abbot, an Archbishop, and the Viking Raids of 1006–7 and 1009–12." *Anglo-Saxon England* 36 (2007): 151–220.

– "A Note on Anglo-Saxon Personal Names." In *St. Wulfsige and Sherborne: Essays to Celebrate the Millenium of the Benedictine Abbey, 998–1998*, edited by Katherine Barker, 20–3. Oxford: Oxbow Books, 2005.

Kim, Dorothy. "The Historiographies of Premodern Critical Race Studies and Jewish Studies." *The Cambridge Journal of Postcolonial Literary Inquiry* 9 (2022): 139–48.

– "Reframing Race and Jewish/Christian Relations in the Middle Ages." *Transversal* 13 (2015): 52–64.

Kim, Dorothy, and M.W. Bychowski. "Visions of Medieval Trans Feminism: An Introduction." *Medieval Feminist Forum* 55 (2019): 6–41.

Kim, Susan. "Bloody Signs: Circumcision and Pregnancy in the Old English *Judith*." *Exemplaria* 11 (1999): 285–307.

Kirby, Ian J. *Bible Translation in Old Norse*. Geneva, CH: Libraire Droz, 1986.

Kirkland, J. S. "Coercion on Holy Days in the Middle Ages." *Journal of Law and Religion* 36 (2021): 230–54.

Klein, Stacy S. "Ælfric's Sources and His Gendered Audiences." *Essays in Medieval Studies* 13 (1996): 111–19.

– "Beauty and the Banquet: Queenship and Social Reform in Ælfric's *Esther*." *The Journal of English and Germanic Philology* 103 (2004): 77–105.

- "Introduction: Feminism and Early English Studies Now." In *New Readings on Women and Early Medieval English Literature and Culture*, edited by Helene Scheck and Christine E. Kozikowski, 1–20. Leeds: Arc Humanities Press, 2019.
- *Ruling Women: Queenship and Gender in Anglo-Saxon Literature*. Notre Dame: University of Notre Dame, 2006.

Kleist, Aaron J., ed. "Assembling Ælfric: Reconstructing the Rationale Behind Eleventh and Twelfth-Century Compilations." In *A Companion to Ælfric*, edited by Hugh Magennis and Mary Swan, 369–98. Leiden and Boston: Brill, 2009.
- *The Chronology and Canon of Ælfric of Eynsham*. Woodbridge, UK: Boydell & Brewer, 2019.
- "A Fourth Ælfrician Commonplace Book? Vestiges in Cambridge, Corpus Christi College 190." *Journal of English and Germanic Philology* 118 (2019): 31–72.
- *The Old English Homily: Precedent, Practice, and Appropriation*. Turnhout, BE: Brepols, 2007.

Kleist, Aaron J., and Robert Upchurch, eds. *Ælfrician Homilies and Varia*. 2 Vols. Cambridge, UK: D.S. Brewer, 2022.

Klug, Brian. "Ritual Murmur: The Undercurrent of Protest against Religious Slaughter of Animals in Britain in the 1980s." *Patterns of Prejudice* 23 (1989): 16–28.

Koltun-Fromm, Naomi. *Hermeneutics of Holiness: Ancient Jewish and Christian Notions of Sexuality and Religious Community*. Oxford: Oxford University Press, 2010.

Kolve, V. A. "Ganymede/Son of Getron: Medieval Monasticism and the Drama of Same-Sex Desire." *Speculum* 73 (1998): 1014–67.

Konshuh, Courtnay. "*Anraed* in Their *Unraed*: The Æthelredian Annals (983–1016) and Their Presentation of King and Advisors." *English Studies* 97 (2016): 140–62.

Kosmin, Paul J. *Time and Its Adversaries in the Seleucid Empire*. Cambridge, MA: Harvard University Press, 2018.

Kretzschmar, William A. "Adaptation and *Anweald* in the Old English Orosius." *Anglo-Saxon England* 16 (1987): 127–45.

Kritsch, Kevin R. "Fragments and Reflexes of Kingship Theory in Ælfric's Comments on Royal Authority." In *Ræd Revisited*, edited by Kristen Carella and László Sándor Chardonnens. Special issue, *English Studies* 97 (2016): 163–85.

Kruger, Steven F. "Becoming Christian, Becoming Male?" In *Becoming Male in the Middle Ages*, edited by Jeffrey J. Cohen and Bonnie Wheeler, 21–41. New York: Routledge, 2015.
- "Conversion and Medieval Sexual, Religious, and Racial Categories." In *Constructing Medieval Sexuality*, edited by Karma Lochrie, James Schultz,

and Peggy McCracken, 158–79. Minneapolis: University of Minnesota Press, 1997.
- "Convert Orthodoxies: The Case of Guillaume de Bourges." In *Jewish/Christian/Queer: Crossroads and Identities*, edited by Frederick S. Roden, 47–66. London: Routledge, 2009.
- "Medieval Christian (Dis)identifications: Muslims and Jews in Guibert of Nogent." *New Literary History* 28 (1997): 185–203.
- "Medieval Jewish/Christian Debate and the Question of Gender: Gilbert Crispin's *Disputatio Iudei et Christiani*." In *Intersections of Gender, Religion and Ethnicity in the Middle Ages*, edited by Cordelia Beattie and Kirsten A. Fenton, 85–103. London: Palgrave Macmillan, 2011.
- "Racial/Religious and Sexual Queerness in the Middle Ages." *Medieval Feminist Forum* 16 (1993): 32–6.
- *The Spectral Jew: Conversion and Embodiment in Medieval Europe*. Minneapolis: University of Minnesota Press, 2006.

Krummel, Miriamne Ara. *Crafting Jewishness in Medieval England: Legally Absent, Virtually Present*. New York: Palgrave Macmillan, 2011.

Kushner, Tony. "Stunning Intolerance: A Century of Opposition to Religious Slaughter." *Jewish Quarterly* 36 (1989): 16–20.

Lachs, Samuel Tobias. *A Rabbinic Commentary on the New Testament: The Gospels of Matthew, Mark, and Luke*. Hoboken, NJ: KTAV Publishing House, 1987.

Lampert[-Weissig], Lisa. *Gender and Jewish Difference from Paul to Shakespeare*. Philadelphia: University of Pennsylvania Press, 2004.
- "The Transnational Wandering Jew and the Medieval English Nation." *Literature Compass* 13/12 (2016): 771–83.

Langeslag, P. S. "Reverse-Engineering the Old English Book of Judges." *Neophilologus* 100 (2016): 303–14.

Lapidge, Michael. *The Anglo-Saxon Library*. Oxford: Oxford University Press, 2006.

Larsen, David. Introduction to *Names of the Lion*, by Al-Ḥusayn ibn Aḥmad Ibn Khālawayh, vii–xxv. Translated by Larsen. Seattle: Wave Books, 2017.

Latham, R.E., David R. Howlett, and Richard K. Ashdowne. *The Dictionary of Medieval Latin from British Sources*. In *Logeion*. Updated March 2017. https://logeion.uchicago.edu/mutus.

Lavelle, Ryan. "*Ine* 70.1 and Royal Provision in Anglo-Saxon Wessex." In *Kingship, Legislation and Power in Anglo-Saxon England*, edited by G. Owen-Crocker and B.W. Schneider, 259–73. Woodbridge, UK: Boydell, 2013.

Lavezzo, Kathy. *The Accommodated Jew: English Antisemitism from Bede to Milton*. Ithaca and London: Cornell University Press, 2016.
- *Angels on the Edge of the World: Geography, Literature, and English Community, 1000–1534*. Ithaca and London: Cornell University Press, 2006.
- "Gregory's Boys: Ælfric and the Homoerotic Production of English Whiteness." *Old English Newsletter* 29 (1996).

Lee, Heidi Oberholtzer. "'The Hungry Soul': Sacramental Appetite and the Transformation of Taste in Early American Travel Writing." *Early American Studies* 3 (2005): 65–93.

Lee, Stuart. "Ælfric's Treatment of Source Material in His Homily on the Books of the Maccabees." *Bulletin of the John Rylands University Library of Manchester* 77 (1995): 165–76.

Lees, Clare A. "In Ælfric's Words: Conversion, Vigilance, and the Nation in Ælfric's *Life of Gregory the Great*." In *A Companion to Ælfric*, edited by Hugh Magennis and Mary Swan, 271–96. Leiden and Boston: Brill, 2009.

– *Tradition and Belief: Religious Writing in Late Anglo-Saxon England*. Minneapolis: University of Minnesota Press, 1999.

Lees, Clare A., and Gillian R. Overing. *Double Agents: Women and Clerical Culture in Anglo-Saxon England*. Philadelphia: University of Pennsylvania Press, 2001.

LeGoff, Jacques. *The Medieval Imagination*. Chicago: University of Chicago Press, 1988.

Lehtipuu, Outi. "'Receive the Widow Judith, Example of Chastity': The Figure of Judith as a Model Christian in Patristic Interpretations." In *Biblical Women in Patristic Reception*, edited by Agnethe Siquans, 186–219. Göttingen, DE: Vandenhoeck & Ruprecht, 2017.

Lemke, Andreas. "Fear-Mongering, Political Shrewdness or Setting the Stage for a 'Holy Society'? Wulfstan's *Sermo Lupi ad Anglos*." *English Studies* 95 (2014): 758–76.

Leneghan, Francis. "*Translatio imperii*: The Old English *Orosius* and the Rise of Wessex." *Anglia* 133 (2015): 656–705.

Lert, Erika Nagy. "Fault in the Law: The Influence of the Penitentials on the Anglo-Saxon Legal System." *The Catholic Lawyer* 31 (1987): 264–76.

Lionarons, Joyce Tally. *The Homiletic Writings of Archbishop Wulfstan*. Woodbridge, UK: Boydell & Brewer, 2010.

Litvak, Joseph. *The Un-Americans: Jews, the Blacklist, and Stoolpigeon Culture*. Durham, NC: Duke University Press, 2009.

Liuzza, Roy M. "Who Read the Gospels in Old English?" In *Words and Works: Studies in Medieval English Language and Literature in Honour of Fred C. Robinson*, edited by Peter S. Baker and Nicholas Howe, 3–24. Toronto: University of Toronto Press, 1998.

Lochrie, Karma. *Heterosyncrasies: Female Sexuality When Normal Wasn't*. Minneapolis: University of Minnesota Press, 2005.

Long, Lynne. *Translating the Bible: From the 7th to the 17th Century*. Farnham, UK: Ashgate, 2002.

Long Chu, Andrea. "Andrea Long Chu Is the Cult Writer Changing Gender Theory." Interview by Sessi Kuwabara Blanchard. *Vice*, November 9, 2018. https://www.vice.com/en/article/ev74m7/andrea-long-chu-interview-avital-ronell-gender.

Lumbley, Coral. "The 'Dark Welsh': Color, Race, and Alterity in the Matter of Medieval Wales." *Literature Compass* 16 (2019): e12538.
– "Imperatrix, Domina, Rex: Conceptualizing the Female King in Twelfth-Century England." *Medieval Feminist Forum* 55 (2019): 64–99.
MacDonald, Nathan. *Not Bread Alone: The Uses of Food in the Old Testament*. Oxford: Oxford University Press, 2008.
Magennis, Hugh. *Anglo-Saxon Appetites: Food and Drink and Their Consumption in Old English and Related Literature*. Dublin: Four Courts Press, 1999.
– "Contrasting Narrative Emphases in the Old English Poem Judith and Ælfric's Paraphrase of the Book of Judith." *Neuphilologische Mitteilungen* 96 (1995): 61–6.
– "Gender and Heroism in the Old English Judith." In *Writing Gender and Genre in Medieval Literature: Approaches to Old and Middle English Texts*, edited by Elaine Treharne, 5–18. Cambridge, UK: D.S. Brewer, 2002.
– "*Godes þeow* and Related Expressions in Old English: Contexts and Uses of a Traditional Literary Figure." *Anglia-Zeitschrift für englische Philologie* 116 (1998): 139–70.
– "'Listen Now All and Understand': Adaptation of Hagiographical Material for Vernacular Audiences in the Old English Lives of St. Margaret." *Speculum* 71 (1996): 27–42.
– "'No Sex Please, We're Anglo-Saxons'? Attitudes to Sexuality in Old English Prose and Poetry." *Leeds Studies in English* 26 (1995): 1–27.
– "Warrior Saints, Warfare, and the Hagiography of Ælfric of Eynsham." *Traditio* 56 (2001): 27–51.
Magennis, Hugh, and Mary Swan, eds. *A Companion to Ælfric*. Leiden and Boston: Brill, 2009.
Mahmood, Saba. *Politics of Piety: The Islamic Revival and the Feminist Subject*. Princeton: Princeton University Press, 2005.
– *Religious Difference in a Secular Age: A Minority Report*. Princeton: Princeton University Press, 2016.
Maitland, Sarah. *What Is Cultural Translation?* London: Bloomsbury, 2017.
Major, Tristan. "Ælfric, Boulogne-Sur-Mer 63, and the Institutio Canonicorum Aquisgranensis." *Notes and Queries* 67 (2020): 172–4.
– *Undoing Babel: The Tower of Babel in Anglo-Saxon Literature*. Toronto: University of Toronto Press, 2018.
Mallon, Jack. "'To Love and Be Loved:' The Medieval Monastic Community as Family, 400–1300." MA thesis, University of Guelph, 2015.
Marafioti, Nicole. "Secular and Ecclesiastical Justice in Late Anglo-Saxon England." *Speculum* 94 (2019): 774–805.
Markell, Patchen. *Bound by Recognition*. Princeton: Princeton University Press, 2009.

Markus, Robert A. *Christianity and the Secular*. Notre Dame: University of Notre Dame Press, 2006.
Marsden, Richard. "Ælfric as Translator: The Old English Prose *Genesis*." *Anglia* 109 (1991): 319–58.
– "'Ask What I Am Called': The Anglo-Saxons and Their Bibles." In *The Bible as Book: The Manuscript Tradition*, edited by John L. Sharpe III and Kimberly Van Kampen, 145–76. London and New Castle: Oak Knoll Press, 1998.
– "Latin in the Ascendant: The Interlinear Gloss of Oxford, Bodleian Library, Laud. Misc. 509." In *Latin Learning and English Lore: Studies in Anglo-Saxon Literature for Michael Lapidge*, edited by Katherine O'Brien O'Keeffe and Andy Orchard, vol. 2, 132–52. Toronto: University of Toronto Press, 2005.
– *The Text of the Old Testament in Anglo-Saxon England*. Cambridge: Cambridge University Press, 1995.
– "Translation by Committee? The 'Anonymous' Text of the Old English Hexateuch." In *The Old English Hexateuch: Aspects and Approaches*, edited by Rebecca Barnhouse and Benjamin C. Withers, 41–89. Kalamazoo, MI: Medieval Institute Publications, 2000.
Marsden, Richard, and E. Ann Matter, eds. *The New Cambridge History of the Bible: From 600 to 1450*. Cambridge: Cambridge University Press, 2012.
McCracken, Peggy. *In the Skin of a Beast: Sovereignty and Animality in Medieval France*. Chicago: University of Chicago Press, 2017.
– "Translation and Animals in the *Lais* of Marie de France." *Australian Journal of French Studies* 46 (2009): 238–49.
McDaniel, Rhonda L. "Agnes among the Anglo-Saxons: Patristic Influences in Anglo-Latin and Anglo-Saxon Versions of the Passi of St. Agnes, Virgin and Martyr." In *Writing Women Saints in Anglo-Saxon England*, edited by Paul E. Szarmach, 217–48. Toronto: University of Toronto Press, 2013.
– *The Third Gender and Ælfric's* Lives of Saints. Kalamazoo, MI: Medieval Institute Publications, 2018.
Medovoi, Leerom, and Elizabeth Bentley, eds. *Religion, Secularism, and Political Belonging*. Durham, NC: Duke University Press, 2021.
Meeder, Sven. "The *Liber ex lege Moysi*: Notes and Text." *The Journal of Medieval Latin* 19 (2009): 173–218.
Meens, Rob. *Penance in Medieval Europe, 600–1200*. Cambridge: Cambridge University Press, 2014.
– "A Penitential Diet." In *Medieval Christianity in Practice*, edited by Miri Rubin, 144–50. Princeton: Princeton University Press, 2009.
– "Pollution in the Early Middle Ages: The Case of the Food Regulations in Penitentials." *Early Medieval Europe* 4 (1995): 3–19.
Menache, Sophia. "Dogs: God's Worst Enemies?" *Society and Animals* 5 (1997): 23–44.

Menzer, Melinda. "The Preface as Admonition: Ælfric's Preface to Genesis." In *The Old English Hexateuch: Aspects and Approaches*, edited by Rebecca Barnhouse and Benjamin C. Withers, 15–39. Kalamazoo, MI: Medieval Institute Publications, 2000.

Meyer, Birgit. "Modernity and Enchantment: The Image of the Devil in Popular African Christianity." In *Conversion to Modernities: The Globalization of Christianity*, edited by Peter van der Veer, 199–230. New York: Routledge, 1995.

– *Translating the Devil: Religion and Modernity among the Ewe in Ghana*. Edinburgh: Edinburgh University Press, 1999.

Meyer, Esias E. "People and Land in the Holiness Code: Who Is YHWH's Favorite?" *Old Testament Essays* 28 (2015): 433–50.

Milgrom, Jacob. *Leviticus 1–16: A New Translation with Introduction and Commentary*. Anchor Bible. Vol. 3. New Haven, CT: Yale University Press, 2001.

– *Leviticus 17–22: A New Translation with Introduction and Commentary*. Vol. 3a. New Haven, CT: Yale University Press, 2000.

– *Leviticus 23–27: A New Translation with Introduction and Commentary*. New Haven, CT: Yale University Press, 2001.

Mills, Robert. "Gender, Sodomy, Friendship, and the Medieval Anchorhold." *Journal of Medieval Religious Cultures* 36 (2010): 1–27.

– "Violence, Community and the Materialisation of Belief." In *A Companion to Middle English Hagiography: Texts and Contexts*, edited by Sarah Salih, 87–103. Cambridge, UK: D.S. Brewer, 2006.

– "Visibly Trans? Picturing Saint Eugenia in Medieval Art." *Transgender Studies Quarterly* 5 (2018): 540–64.

– "'Whatever You Do Is a Delight to Me!': Masculinity, Masochism and Queer Play in Representations of Male Martyrdom." *Exemplaria* 13 (2001): 1–37.

Miller, Katherine Leah. "The Semantic Field of Slavery in Old English: *Wealh, Esne, Þræl.*" PhD diss., University of Leeds, 2014.

Miller, William Ian. *The Anatomy of Disgust*. Cambridge, MA: Harvard University Press, 1998.

Minkoff, Harvey. "Some Stylistic Consequences of Ælfric's Theory of Translation." *Studies in Philology* 73 (1976): 29–41.

Mitchell, J. Allan. *Becoming Human: The Matter of the Medieval Child*. Minneapolis: University of Minnesota Press, 2014.

Miyashiro, Adam. "'Our Deeper Past': Race, Settler Colonialism, and Medieval Heritage Politics." *Literature Compass* 16 (2019): e12550.

Momma, Haruko. "Darkness Edible: Soul, Body, and Worms in Early Medieval English Devotional Literature." In *Darkness, Depression, and Descent in Anglo-Saxon England*, edited by Ruth Wehlau, 237–54. Kalamazoo, MI: Medieval Institute Publications, 2019.

– "'Element by Element': Glosses, Loan Translations, and Lexical Enrichment in Old English." In *Litterarum Dulces Fructus: Studies in Early Medieval Latin Culture in Honour of Michael W. Herren for His 80th Birthday*, edited by Scott G. Bruce, 323–45. Turnhout, BE: Brepols, 2021.
– "Epanalepsis: A Retelling of the Judith Story in the Anglo-Saxon Poetic Language." *Studies in the Literary Imagination* 36 (2003): 59–73.
– *From Philology to English Studies: Language and Culture in the Nineteenth Century*. Cambridge: Cambridge University Press, 2012.
– "Rhythm and Alliteration: Styles of Ælfric's Prose Up to the *Lives of Saints*." In *Anglo-Saxon Styles*, edited by Catherine E. Karkov and George Hardin Brown, 253–69. Albany: State University of New York Press, 2003.
Moore, Stephen D. "Retching on Rome: Vomitous Loathing and Visceral Disgust in Affect Theory and the Apocalypse of John." *Biblical Interpretation* 22 (2014): 503–28.
Morrison, Susan S. *The Literature of Waste: Material Ecopoetics and Ethical Matter*. New York: Palgrave Macmillan, 2015.
Morton, Nicholas. "The Defence of the Holy Land and the Memory of the Maccabees." *Journal of Medieval History* 36 (2010): 275–93.
Mullally, Erin. "The Cross-Gendered Gift: Weaponry in the Old English Judith." *Exemplaria* 17 (2005): 255–84.
Mundill, Robin R. *The King's Jews: Money, Massacre and Exodus in Medieval England*. London: Bloomsbury, 2010.
Muñoz, José Esteban. *Cruising Utopia: The Then and There of Queer Futurity*. New York: New York University Press, 2009.
Mustafa, Nawal, and Matthea Westerduin. "Exploring New Vocabularies in Conversations about Religion, Race, Politics, and Justice." In *Transforming Bodies and Religions: Powers and Agencies in Europe*, edited by Mariecke van den Berg, Lieke L. Schrijvers, Jelle O. Wiering, and Anne-Marie Korte, 135–54. London: Routledge, 2020.
Newman, Barbara. *From Virile Woman to WomanChrist: Studies in Medieval Religion and Literature*. Philadelphia: University of Pennsylvania Press, 1995.
– *Medieval Crossover: Reading the Secular against the Sacred*. Notre Dame: University of Notre Dame Press, 2013.
Ng, Su Fang. "Hobbes and the Bestial Body of Sovereignty." In *Feminist Interpretations of Thomas Hobbes*, edited by Nancy J. Hirschmann and Joanne H. Wright, 83–101. University Park, PA: Penn State University Press, 2021.
Nichols, Ann Eljenholm. "*Awendan*: A Note on Ælfric's Vocabulary." *The Journal of English and Germanic Philology* 63 (1964): 7–13.
Nida, Eugene A. *Toward a Science of Translating: With Special Reference to Principles and Procedures Involved in Bible Translating*. Leiden: Brill, 1964.

Nielsen, Kirsten. "Construction of Meaningful Contexts on War, Lions, Dogs, Birds and a Vineyard." *Scandinavian Journal of the Old Testament* 21 (2007): 218–27.
Nijhuis, Letty Jantje. "'Deor and nytenu mid us': Animals in the Works of Ælfric." PhD diss., University College Cork, 2008.
Niles, John D. *The Idea of Anglo-Saxon England 1066–1901: Remembering, Forgetting, Deciphering, and Renewing the Past*. Chichester, UK: John Wiley & Sons, 2015.
Niranjana, Tejaswini. *Siting Translation: History, Post-Structuralism, and the Colonial Context*. Berkeley: University of California Press, 1992.
Nirenberg, David. *Aesthetic Theology and Its Enemies: Judaism in Christian Painting, Poetry, and Politics*. Lebanon, NH: Brandeis University Press, 2015.
– "'Judaism' as Political Concept: toward a Critique of Political Theology.'" *Representations* 128 (Fall 2014): 1–29.
Norris, Robin, ed. *Anonymous Interpolations in Ælfric's Lives of Saints*. Kalamazoo, MI: Medieval Institute Publications, 2011.
Norris, Robin. "Genre Trouble: Reading the Old English *Vita* of Saint Euphrosyne." In *Writing Women Saints in Anglo-Saxon England*, edited by Paul E. Szarmach, 121–39. Toronto: University of Toronto Press, 2013.
Norris, Robin J., Renée R. Trilling, and Rebecca Stephenson. Introduction to "A Feminist Renaissance in Early Medieval English Studies." *English Studies* 101 (2020): 1–5.
Nye, Malory. "Decolonizing the Study of Religion." *Open Library of Humanities* 5 (2019): 43.
O'Brien, Conor. "Bede's Theology of Circumcision, Its Sources and Significance." *The Journal of Theological Studies* 67 (2016): 594–613.
O'Camb, Brian. "Isidorean Wolf Lore and the *felaf* æcne deor of Maxims I.C: Some Rhetorical and Legal Contexts for Recognising Another Old English Wulf in Sheep's Clothing." *English Studies* 97 (2016): 687–708.
O'Donnell, Thomas. "The Old English *Durham*, the *Historia de sancto Cuthberto*, and the Unreformed in Late Anglo-Saxon Literature." *Journal of English and Germanic Philology* 113 (2014): 131–55.
O'Keeffe, Katherine O'Brien. *Stealing Obedience: Narratives of Agency and Identity in Later Anglo-Saxon England*. Toronto: University of Toronto Press, 2012.
– "Three English Writers on Genesis: Some Observations on Ælfric's Theological Legacy." *Ball State University Forum* 19 (1978): 69–78.
Ogawa, Hiroshi. "Syntactical Revision in Wulfstan's Rewritings of Ælfric." In *English Historical Linguistics and Philology in Japan*, edited by Jacek Fisiak and Akio Oizumi, 215–28. Berlin and New York: De Gruyter Mouton, 1998.
Oliver, Lisi. *The Beginnings of English Law*. Toronto: University of Toronto Press, 2002.

Olsen, Alexandra Hennessey. "Inversion and Political Purpose in the Old English *Judith*." *English Studies* 63 (1982): 289–93.

Olsen, Glenn W. *Of Sodomites, Effeminates, Hermaphrodites, and Androgynes: Sodomy in the Age of Peter Damian*. Toronto: Pontifical Institute of Mediaeval Studies, 2011.

Orchard, Andy. "Crying Wolf: Oral Style and the *Sermones Lupi*." *Anglo-Saxon England* 21 (1992): 239–64.

– *Pride and Prodigies: Studies in the Monsters of the Beowulf-Manuscript*. Toronto: University of Toronto Press, 2003.

Otzen, Benedikt. *Tobit and Judith*. London: Sheffield Academic Press, 2002.

Overing, Gillian R. *Language, Sign, and Gender in Beowulf*. Carbondale and Edwardsville, IL: Southern Illinois University Press, 1990.

Paolella, Christopher. *Human Trafficking in Medieval Europe*. Amsterdam: Amsterdam University Press, 2020.

Pareles, Mo. "Already/Never: Jewish-Porcine Conversion in the Middle English Children of the Oven Miracle." *Philological Quarterly* 98 (2019): 221–42.

– "Giving Yiddish the Devil: How Missionary Translation Reckons with Demons in the Yiddish New Testament." *Literature and Theology* 26 (2012): 144–59.

– "Jewish Heterosexuality, Queer Celibacy? Ælfric Translates the Old Testament Priesthood." *Postmedieval* 8 (2017): 292–306.

– "Men as Meat: Exploiting Jewish Law in Ælfric's Translation of Maccabees." *Exemplaria* 27 (2015): 187–204.

– "What the Raven Told the Eagle: Animal Language and the Return of Loss in *Beowulf*." In *Dating Beowulf: Studies in Intimacy*, edited by Daniel C. Remein and Erica Weaver, 164–86. Manchester: Manchester University Press, 2020.

Pasternack, Carol Braun. "The Sexual Practices of Virginity and Chastity in Aldhelm's *De Virginitate*." In *Sex and Sexuality in Anglo-Saxon England: Essays in Memory of Daniel Gillmore Calder*, edited by Daniel Gillmore Calder, Carol Pasternack, and Lisa M. C. Weston, 93–120. Tempe: Arizona Center for Medieval and Renaissance Studies, 2004.

Pelteret, David A. E. *Slavery in Early Mediaeval England from the Reign of Alfred until the Twelfth Century*. Woodbridge, UK: Boydell Press, 1995.

Penniman, John David. *Raised on Christian Milk: Food and the Formation of the Soul in Early Christianity*. New Haven, CT: Yale University Press, 2017.

Pluskowski, Alexander. *Wolves and the Wilderness in the Middle Ages*. Woodbridge, UK: The Boydell Press, 2006.

Pons-Sanz, Sara M. "The Etymology of the Word-Field of Old English *hōre* and the Lexico-Cultural Climate of Eleventh-Century England." *Nottingham Medieval Studies* 55 (2011): 23–48.

– "A Reconsideration of Wulfstan's Use of Norse-Derived Terms: The Case of Þræl." *English Studies* 88 (2007): 1–21.

Poole, Kristopher. "Gone to the Dogs? Negotiating the Human-Animal Boundary in Anglo-Saxon England." In *Archaeologies of Rules and Regulation: Between Text and Practice*, edited by Barbara Hausmair, Ben Jervis, Ruth Nugent, and Eleanor Williams, 238–53. New York: Berghahn Books, 2018.

Pringle, Ian. "Judith: The Homily and the Poem." *Traditio* 31 (1975): 83–97.

Pulsiano, Phillip, and Elaine M. Treharne. *A Companion to Anglo-Saxon Literature*. Oxford: Blackwell, 2001.

Rabin, Andrew. "Evidence for Wulfstan's Authorship of the Old English *Að*." *Neuphilologische Mitteilungen* 111(2010): 43–52.

– "Female Advocacy and Royal Protection in Tenth Century England." *Speculum* 84 (2009): 261–88.

– "Holy Bodies, Legal Matters: Reaction and Reform in Ælfric's *Eugenia* and the Ely Privilege." *Studies in Philology* 110, no. 2 (2013): 220–65.

– "The Reception of Kentish Law in the Eleventh Century: Archbishop Wulfstan as Legal Historian." In *Languages of the Law in Early Medieval England: Essays in Memory of Lisi Oliver*, edited by Stefan Jurasinski and Andrew Rabin, 225–39. Louvain, BE: Peeters, 2019.

– "The Wolf's Testimony to the English: Law and the Witness in the *Sermo Lupi ad Anglos*." *JEGP* 105 (2006): 388–414.

– "Wulfstan at London: Episcopal Politics in the Reign of Æthelred." *English Studies* 97 (2016): 186–206.

Radner, Ephraim. *Leviticus*. Grand Rapids, MI: Brazos Press, 2008.

Rajak, Tessa. *Translation and Survival: The Greek Bible of the Ancient Jewish Diaspora*. Oxford: Oxford University Press, 2009.

Rajendran, Shyama. "Undoing 'the Vernacular': Dismantling Structures of Raciolinguistic Supremacy." *Literature Compass* 16 (2019): e12544.

Rambaran-Olm, Mary. "A Wrinkle in Medieval Time: Ironing Out Issues Regarding Race, Temporality, and the Early English." *New Literary History* 52 (2021): 385–406.

Rambaran-Olm, Mary, and Erik Wade. "The Many Myths of the Term 'Anglo-Saxon.'" *Smithsonian Magazine*, July 2021.

Rasmussen, Ann Marie. "Babies and Books: The Holy Kinship as a Way of Thinking about Women's Power in Late Medieval Northern Europe." In *Founding Feminisms in Medieval Studies: Essays in Honor of E. Jane Burns*, edited by Laine E. Doggett and Daniel E. O'Sullivan, 205–18. Cambridge, UK: D.S. Brewer, 2016.

Raynes, Enid. "MS. Boulogne-sur-Mer 63 and Ælfric." *Medium Ævum* 26 (1957): 65–73.

Raz-Krakotzkin, Amnon. "Secularism, the Christian Ambivalence toward the Jews, and the Notion of Exile." In *Secularism in Question: Jews and Judaism in Modern Times*, edited by Ethan B. Katz and Ari Joskowicz, 276–98. Philadelphia: University of Pennsylvania Press, 2015.

Regan, Catharine A. "Retrieving the Typological Dimension in Ælfric's Easter Homily." In *Typology and English Medieval Literature*, edited by Hugh T. Keenan, 289–305. New York: AMS Press, 1992.

Reinhard, Ben. "Wulfstan and the Reordered Polity of Cotton Nero A.i." In *Law | Book | Culture in the Middle Ages*, edited by Thom Gobbitt, 51–70. Leiden: Brill, 2021.

Remein, Daniel C. "Auden, Translation, Betrayal: Radical Poetics and Translation from Old English." *Literature Compass* 8 (2011): 811–29.

– "ISAS Should Probably Change Its Name." Paper delivered at the 52nd International Congress on Medieval Studies, Kalamazoo, MI, May 2017.

Resnick, Irven M. "Good Dog/Bad Dog: Dogs in Medieval Religious Polemics." *Enarratio* 18 (2013): 70–97.

– *Marks of Distinction: Christian Perceptions of Jews in the High Middle Ages*. Washington, DC: Catholic University of America Press, 2012.

Rey, M.I. "Reexamination of the Foreign Female Captive: Deuteronomy 21:10–14 as a Case of Genocidal Rape." *Journal of Feminist Studies in Religion* 32 (2016): 37–53.

Richards, Mary P. "Fragmentary Versions of Genesis in Old English Prose: Context and Function." In *The Old English Hexateuch: Aspects and Approaches*, edited by Rebecca Barnhouse and Benjamin C. Withers, 145–63. Kalamazoo, MI: Medieval Institute Publications, 2000.

Richards, Thomas. *The Imperial Archive: Knowledge and the Fantasy of Empire*. London: Verso, 1993.

Ridyard, Susan. *The Royal Saints of Anglo-Saxon England: A Study of West Saxon and East Anglian Cults*. Cambridge: Cambridge University Press, 1988.

Riggs, Damien W., and Elizabeth Peel. *Critical Kinship Studies: An Introduction to the Field*. London: Palgrave Macmillan, 2016.

Roach, Catherine M. *Happily Ever After: The Romance Story in Popular Culture*. Bloomington: Indiana University Press, 2016.

Roach, Levi. "Apocalypse and Atonement in the Politics of Æthelredian England." *English Studies* 95 (2014): 733–57.

Rogers, Will. "Dismembering Gender and Age: Replication, Rebirth, and Remembering in *The Phoenix*." In *Reconsidering Gender, Time and Memory in Medieval Culture*, edited by Elizabeth Cox, Liz Herbert McAvoy, and Roberta Magnani, 163–78. Cambridge, UK: D.S. Brewer, 2015.

Rosaldo, Renato. *Culture and Truth: The Remaking of Social Analysis*. Boston: Beacon Press, 1989.

Rosen, Alan. *The Holocaust's Jewish Calendars: Keeping Time Sacred, Making Time Holy*. Bloomington: Indiana University Press, 2019.

Rossello, Diego. "Hobbes and the Wolf-Man: Melancholy and Animality in Modern Sovereignty." *New Literary History* 43 (2012): 255–79.

Rubin, Eli. "Beyond Holocaust Time." Review of *The Holocaust's Jewish Calendars*, by Alan Rosen. *The Lehrhaus*, August 8, 2019. https://thelehrhaus.com/culture/beyond-holocaust-time/.
Said, Edward. *Orientalism*. New York: Vintage, 1994.
Saini, Angela. *Superior: The Return of Race Science*. Boston: Beacon Press, 2019.
Salisbury, Joyce E. *The Beast within: Animals in the Middle Ages*. New York: Routledge, Chapman and Hall, 1994.
Salmesvuori, Päivi. *Power and Sainthood: The Case of Birgitta of Sweden*. New York: Palgrave Macmillan, 2014.
Saltzman, Benjamin A. *Bonds of Secrecy: Law, Spirituality, and the Literature of Concealment in Early Medieval England*. Philadelphia: University of Pennsylvania Press, 2019.
– "Writing Friendship, Mourning the Friend in Late Anglo-Saxon Rules of Confraternity." *Journal of Medieval and Early Modern Studies* 41 (2011): 258–63.
Sanders, E.P. *Paul, the Law, and the Jewish People*. Minneapolis: Fortress, 1983.
Sauer, Michelle M. "Queer Time and Lesbian Temporality in Medieval Women's Encounters with the Side Wound." In *Medieval Futurity: Essays for the Future of a Queer Medieval Studies*, edited by Will Rogers and Christopher Michael Roman, 199–219. Berlin: De Gruyter, 2020.
– "Uncovering Difference: Encoded Homoerotic Anxiety within the Christian Eremitic Tradition in Medieval England." *Journal of the History of Sexuality* 19 (2010): 133–52.
Saunders, Corinne J. *Rape and Ravishment in the Literature of Medieval England*. Cambridge, UK: D.S. Brewer, 2001.
– "Women and Warfare in Medieval English Writing." In *Writing War: Medieval Literary Responses to Warfare*, edited by Saunders, Francoise Le Saux, and Neil Thomas, 187–212. Woodbridge, UK: Boydell and Brewer, 2004.
Scheck, Helene. *Reform and Resistance: Formations of Female Subjectivity in Early Medieval Ecclesiastical Culture*. Albany: State University of New York Press, 2008.
Scheil, Andrew P. *The Footsteps of Israel: Understanding Jews in Anglo-Saxon England*. Ann Arbor: University of Michigan Press, 2004.
– "Somatic Ambiguity and Masculine Desire in the Old English *Life of Euphrosyne*." *Exemplaria* 11 (1999): 345–61.
– "Transition and Renewal: Jews and the Church Year in Anglo-Saxon England." In *Imagining the Jew in Anglo-Saxon Literature and Culture*, edited by Samantha Zacher, 108–27. Toronto: University of Toronto Press, 2016.
Schmitt, Carl. *Political Theology: Four Chapters on the Concept of Sovereignty*. Translated by George Schwab. Chicago: University of Chicago Press, 2005.
Schroeder, Caroline T. "Queer Eye for the Ascetic Guy? Homoeroticism, Children, and the Making of Monks." *Late Antique Egypt. Journal of the American Academy of Religion* 77 (2009): 333–47.

Schultz, James A. "Heterosexuality as a Threat to Medieval Studies." *Journal of the History of Sexuality* 15 (2006): 14–29.

Schwartz, Daniel R. "Why Did Antiochus Have to Fall (II Maccabees 9:7)?" In *Heavenly Tablets: Interpretation, Identity, and Tradition in Ancient Judaism*, edited by Lynn LiDonnici and Andrea Lieber, 257–65. Leiden: Brill, 2007.

Schwartz, Nicholas P. "Rulers and the Wolf: Archbishop Wulfstan, Anglo-Saxon Kings, and the Problems of His Present." PhD diss., University of New Mexico, 2015.

– "Wulfstan the Forger: The 'Laws of Edward and Guthrum.'" *Anglo-Saxon England* 47 (2018): 219–46.

Scott, Penelope. "Symbolic Illness and the Construction of Virginities in Ælfric's *Lives of Saints*." *English Studies* 100 (2019): 959–79.

Sebo, Erin, and Cassandra Schilling. "Modthryth and the Problem of Peace-Weavers: Women and Political Power in Early Medieval England." *English Studies* 102 (2021): 637–50.

Sedgwick, Eve Kosofsky. *Epistemology of the Closet*. Berkeley: University of California Press, 1990.

– *Touching Feeling*. Durham, NC: Duke University Press, 2003.

Seidman, Naomi. "Fag-Hags and Bu-Jews: Toward a (Jewish) Politics of Vicarious Identity." In *Insider/Outsider: American Jews and Multiculturalism*, edited by David Biale, Michael Galchinsky, and Susannah Heschel, 254–67. Berkeley: University of California Press, 1998.

– *Faithful Renderings: Jewish-Christian Difference and the Politics of Translation*. Chicago: University of Chicago Press, 2006.

Shachar, Isaiah. *The Judensau: A Medieval Anti-Jewish Motif and Its History*. London: Warburg Institute, 1974.

Shannon, Laurie. *The Accommodated Animal: Cosmopolity in Shakespearean Locales*. Chicago: University of Chicago Press, 2013.

Shepard, Dorothy M. *Introducing the Lambeth Bible: A Study of Texts and Imagery*. Turnhout, BE: Brepols, 2007.

Shyovitz, David I. *A Remembrance of His Wonders: Nature and the Supernatural in Medieval Ashkenaz*. Philadelphia: University of Pennsylvania Press, 2017.

Simpson, James. *Burning to Read: English Fundamentalism and Its Reformation Opponents*. Cambridge, MA: Harvard University Press, 2007.

Simpson, Leanne Betasamosake. *As We Have Always Done: Indigenous Freedom through Radical Resistance*. Minneapolis: University of Minnesota Press, 2021.

Smalley, William A. *Translation as Mission: Bible Translation in the Modern Missionary Movement*. Macon, GA: Mercer University Press, 1991.

Smilges, J. Logan. *Queer Silence: On Disability and Rhetorical Absence*. Minneapolis: University of Minnesota Press, 2022.

Smith, Andrea. *Conquest: Sexual Violence and American Indian Genocide*. Durham, NC: Duke University Press, 2015.

Smith, Linda Tuhiwai. *Decolonizing Methodologies: Research and Indigenous Peoples*. London: Zed Books, 1999.

Smith, Scott Thompson. *Land and Book: Literature and Land Tenure in Anglo-Saxon England*. Toronto: University of Toronto Press, 2012.

Smoot, William Tanner. "Sacred Memory and Monastic Friendship in Eadmer of Canterbury's *Vita S. Oswaldi*." *Revue bénédictine* 130 (2020): 354–88.

Sneddon, Clive R. "The Bible in French." In *The New Cambridge History of the Bible: From 600 to 1450*, edited by Richard Marsden and E. Ann Matter, 251–67. Cambridge: Cambridge University Press, 2012.

Soames, Henry. *The Anglo-Saxon Church: Its History, Revenues and General Character*. London: John W. Parker, 1844.

Sobecki, Sebastian. "Muddy Waters: *Unclæne* Fish in Ælfric's Colloquy." *Neuphilologische Mitteilungen: Bulletin de la Société Néophilologique/Bulletin of the Modern Language Society* 107 (2006): 285–9.

Spears, Matthew E. "Identifying with the Beast: Animality, Subjectivity, and Society in Anglo-Saxon England." PhD diss., Cornell University, 2017.

Stafford, Pauline. *After Alfred: Anglo-Saxon Chronicles and Chorniclers, 900–1150*. Oxford: Oxford University Press, 2020.

– "The Portrayal of Royal Women in England, Mid-Tenth to Mid-Twelfth Centuries." In *Medieval Queenship*, edited by John Carmi Parsons, 143–67. New York: Palgrave Macmillan, 1998.

– "Queens, Nunneries, and Reforming Churchmen: Gender, Religious Status, and Reform in Tenth- and Eleventh-Century England." *Past and Present* 163 (1999): 3–35.

Stahuljak, Zrinka. *Bloodless Genealogies of the French Middle Ages: Translatio, Kingship, and Metaphor*. Gainesville: University Press of Florida, 2005.

Stanley, E.G. "Ælfric on the Canonicity of the Book of Judith: '*hit stent on leden þus on ðære bibliothecan*.'" *Notes and Queries* 32 (1985): 439.

Stanton, Robert. *The Culture of Translation in Anglo-Saxon England*. Cambridge, UK: D.S. Brewer, 2002.

Steel, Karl. *How Not to Make a Human: Pets, Feral Children, Worms, Sky Burial, Oysters*. Minneapolis: University of Minnesota Press, 2019.

– *How to Make a Human: Animals and Violence in the Middle Ages*. Columbus: Ohio State University Press, 2011.

Steinweis, Alan E. *Studying the Jew: Scholarly Antisemitism in Nazi Germany*. Cambridge, MA: Harvard University Press, 2006.

Stephenson, Rebecca. "Assuming Virginity: Tradition and the Naked Narrative in Ælfric's Homily on the Assumption of the Virgin." In *Writing Women Saints in Anglo-Saxon England*, edited by Paul E. Szarmach, 103–20. Toronto: University of Toronto Press, 2013.

– "Judith as Spiritual Warrior: Female Models of Monastic Masculinity in Ælfric's *Judith* and Byrhtferth's *Enchiridion*." *English Studies* 101 (2020): 79–95.
– *The Politics of Language: Byrhtferth, Ælfric, and the Multilingual Identity of the Benedictine Reform*. Toronto: University of Toronto Press, 2015.
Stevens, Jane. "Brothers and Sisters: Women and Monastic Life in Eighth-Century England and Frankia." *Dutch Review of Church History* 82 (2002): 1–34.
Stevens, Paul. "'Leviticus Thinking' and the Rhetoric of Early Modern Colonialism." *Criticism* (1993): 441–61.
Stone, Ken. *Reading the Hebrew Bible with Animal Studies*. Redwood City, CA: Stanford University Press, 2017.
Stow, Kenneth R. *Jewish Dogs: An Image and Its Interpreters*. Redwood City, CA: Stanford University Press, 2006.
Strawn, Brent A. "On Vomiting: Leviticus, Jonah, Ea(a)rth." *The Catholic Biblical Quarterly* 74 (2012): 445–64.
Strassfeld, Max K. *Trans Talmud: Androgynes and Eunuchs in Rabbinic Literature*. Berkeley: University of California Press, 2022.
Strickland, Debra Higgs. "Edward I, Exodus, and England on the Hereford World Map." *Speculum* 93 (2018): 420–69.
Swain, Larry J. "Ælfric of Eynsham's Letter to Sigeweard: An Edition, Translation and Commentary." PhD diss., University of Illinois at Chicago, 2009.
Swan, Mary. "Constructing Preacher and Audience in Old English Homilies." In *Constructing the Medieval Sermon*, edited by Roger Andersson, 177–88. Turnhout, BE: Brepols, 2007.
– "Identity and Ideology in Ælfric's Prefaces." In *A Companion to Ælfric*, edited by Hugh Magennis and Mary Swan, 247–69. Leiden and Boston: Brill, 2009.
– "Mobile Libraries: Old English Manuscript Production in Worcester and the West Midlands, 1090–1215." In *Essays in Manuscript Geography: Vernacular Manuscripts of the English West Midlands from the Conquest to the Sixteenth Century*, edited by Wendy Scase, 29–42. Turnhout, BE: Brepols, 2007.
– "Preaching Past the Conquest: Lambeth Palace 487 and Cotton Vespasian A. XXII." In *The Old English Homily: Precedent, Practice, and Appropriation*, edited by Aaron J. Kleist, 403–23. Turnhout, BE: Brepols, 2007.
Swan, Mary, and Elaine M. Treharne, eds. *Rewriting Old English in the Twelfth Century*. Cambridge: Cambridge University Press, 2000.
Szarmach, Paul E. "Ælfric's *Judith*." In *Old English Literature and the Old Testament*, edited by Michael Fox and Manish Sharma, 64–88. Toronto: University of Toronto Press, 2012.
– "Ælfric's Women Saints: Eugenia." In *New Readings on Women in Old English Literature*, edited by Helen Damico and Alexandra Hennessey Olsen, 146–57. Bloomington: Indiana University Press, 1990.

Thomson, Stephen. "Whatever: Giorgio Agamben's Gender Trouble." *Textual Practice* 35 (2021): 787–807.
Thormann, Janet. "The Jewish Other in Old English Narrative Poetry." *Partial Answers: Journal of Literature and the History of Ideas* 2 (2004): 1–19.
Thornbury, Emily. "Ælfric's Zoology." *Neophilologus* 92 (2008): 141–53.
Thundy, Zacharaias P. "*Afrisc Meowle* and the Old English *Exodus*." *Neophilologus* 64 (1980): 297–306.
Timofeeva, Olga. "Translating the Texts Where *et verborum ordo mysterium est*: Late Old English Idiom vs. *ablativus absolutus*." *The Journal of Medieval Latin* 18 (2008): 217–29.
Tin, Louis-Georges. *The Invention of Heterosexual Culture*. Translated by Michaël Roy. Cambridge, MA: MIT Press, 2012.
Tinti, Francesca. "Benedictine Reform and Pastoral Care in Late Anglo-Saxon England." *Early Medieval Europe* 23 (2015): 229–51.
– *Sustaining Belief: The Church of Worcester from c. 870 to c. 1100*. Farnham, UK: Ashgate, 2010.
Tomasch, Sylvia. "Postcolonial Chaucer and the Virtual Jew." In *The Postcolonial Middle Ages*, edited by Jeffrey Jerome Cohen, 243–60. New York: St. Martin's Press, 2000.
Tompkins, Kyla Wazana. *Racial Indigestion: Eating Bodies in the 19th Century*. New York: New York University Press, 2012.
Townend, Matthew, ed. *Wulfstan, Archbishop of York: The Proceedings of the Second Alcuin Conference*. Turnhout, BE: Brepols, 2004.
Traub, Valerie. *The Renaissance of Lesbianism in Early Modern England*. Cambridge: Cambridge University Press, 2002.
Treharne, Elaine M. "The Bishop's Book: Leofric's Homiliary and Eleventh-Century Exeter." In *Early Medieval Studies in Memory of Patrick Wormald*, edited by Stephen Baxter, Catherine Karkov, Janet L. Nelson, and David Pelteret, 521–37. London: Routledge, 2016.
– "The Canonization of Ælfric." In *English Now: Selected Papers from the 20th IAUPE Conference in Lund*, edited by Marianne Thormählen, 1–13. Lund, SE: Lund University, 2007.
– "The Invisible Woman: Ælfric and His Subject Female." *Leeds Studies in English* 37 (2006): 191–208.
– *Living through Conquest: The Politics of Early English, 1020–1220*. Oxford: Oxford University Press, 2012.
– "Making Their Presence Felt: Readers of Ælfric, c. 1050–1350." In *A Companion to Ælfric*, edited by Hugh Magennis and Mary Swan, 399–422. Leiden and Boston: Brill, 2009.
Treschow, Michael. "The Prologue to Alfred's Law Code: Instruction in the Spirit of Mercy." *Florilegium* 13 (1994): 79–110.

Trilling, Renée R. *The Aesthetics of Nostalgia: Historical Representation in Old English Verse*. Toronto: University of Toronto Press, 2009.

– "Sovereignty and Social Order: Archbishop Wulfstan and the Institutes of Polity." In *The Bishop Reformed: Studies of Episcopal Power and Culture in the Central Middle Ages*, edited by John S. Ott and Anna Trumbore Jones, 74–101. Farnham, UK: Ashgate, 2007.

Troeung, Y-Dang. *Refugee Lifeworlds: The Afterlife of the Cold War in Cambodia*. Philadelphia: Temple University Press, 2022.

Tucker, Gene M. "Rain on a Land Where No One Lives: The Hebrew Bible on the Environment." *Journal of Biblical Literature* 116 (1997): 3–17.

Upchurch, Robert K. "A Big Dog Barks: Ælfric of Eynsham's Indictment of the English Pastorate and *Witan*." *Speculum* 85 (2010): 505–33.

– "For Pastoral Care and Political Gain: Ælfric of Eynsham's Preaching on Marital Celibacy." *Traditio* 59 (2004): 39–78.

van Liere, Frans. *An Introduction to the Medieval Bible*. Cambridge: Cambridge University Press, 2014.

van Rhijn, Carine, and Marjolijn Saan. "Correcting Sinners, Correcting Texts: A Context for the *Paenitentiale pseudo-Theodori*." *Early Medieval Europe* 14 (2006): 23–40.

Vanderputten, Steven. *Dark Age Nunneries: The Ambiguous Identity of Female Monasticism, 800–1050*. Ithaca, NY: Cornell University Press, 2018.

Vatter, Miguel. *Living Law: Jewish Political Theology from Hermann Cohen to Hannah Arendt*. Oxford: Oxford University Press, 2021.

– "The Political Theology of Carl Schmitt." In *The Oxford Handbook of Carl Schmitt*, edited by Jens Meierhenrich and Oliver Simons, 245–68. New York: Oxford University Press, 2016.

Venuti, Lawrence. "Translating Derrida on Translation: Relevance and Disciplinary Resistance." *The Yale Journal of Criticism* 16 (2003): 237–62.

– *The Translator's Invisibility: A History of Translation*. Abington, UK: Routledge, 2018.

Vernon, Matthew X. *The Black Middle Ages: Race and the Construction of the Middle Ages*. Cham, CH: Palgrave Macmillan, 2018.

Vicchio, Stephen J. *Job in the Ancient World. Vol. 1, Images of the Biblical Job: A History*. Eugene, OR: Wipf & Stock, 2006.

– *Job in the Medieval World. Vol. 2, Images of the Biblical Job: A History*. Eugene, OR: Wipf & Stock, 2006.

Viswanathan, Gauri. *Masks of Conquest: Literature Study and British Rule in India*. New York: Columbia University Press, 1989.

Walker, Jonathan. "The Transtextuality of Transvestite Sainthood: Or, How to Make the Gendered Form Fit the Generic Function." *Exemplaria* 15 (2003): 73–110.

Walsh, Jerome T. *Style and Structure in Biblical Hebrew Narrative*. Collegeville, MN: The Liturgical Press, 2001.

Walton, Audrey Rochelle. "*Gehyre se ðe Wille*: The Old English 'Exodus' and the Reader as Exegete." *English Studies* 94 (2013): 1–10.
– "New Wine in Old Skins: Vernacular Typology in Medieval English Literature, 590–1390." PhD diss., Columbia University, 2015.
Ward, Jane. *The Tragedy of Heterosexuality*. New York: New York University Press, 2020.
Warning, Wilfried. *Literary Artistry in Leviticus*. Leiden: Brill, 1999.
Waterhouse, Ruth. "Affective Language, Especially Alliterating Qualifiers, in Ælfric's Life of St. Alban." *Anglo-Saxon England* 7 (1978): 131–48.
Watt, Diane. "A Fragmentary Archive: Migratory Feelings in Early Anglo-Saxon Women's Letters." *Journal of Homosexuality* 64 (2017): 415–29.
Weaver, Erica. "Hybrid Forms: Translating Boethius in Anglo-Saxon England." *Anglo-Saxon England* 45 (2016): 213–38.
Weidl, Birgit. "Laughing at the Beast: The *Judensau*: Anti-Jewish Propaganda and Humor from the Middle Ages to the Early Modern Period." In *Laughter in the Middle Ages and Early Modern Times: Epistemology of a Fundamental Human Behavior*, edited by Albrecht Classen, 325–64. Berlin and New York: Walter de Gruyter, 2010.
Weiler, Björn. "Clerical *admonitio*, Letters of Advice to Kings and Episcopal Self-Fashioning, c. 1000–c. 1200." *History* 102 (2017): 557–75.
Weston, Lisa M.C. "Queering Virginity." *Medieval Feminist Forum* 36 (2003): 22–4.
– "Reading the Textual Shadows of Anglo-Saxon Monastic Women's Friendships." *Magistra* 14 (2008): 68–78.
– "The Saintly Female Body and the Landscape of Foundation in Anglo-Saxon Barking." *Medieval Feminist Forum* 43 (2007): 12–25.
– "Virgin Desires: Reading a Homoerotics of Female Monastic Community." In *The Lesbian Premodern*, edited by Noreen Giffney, Michelle M. Sauer, and Diane Watt, 93–104. New York: Palgrave Macmillan, 2011.
– "Where Textual Bodies Meet: Anglo-Saxon Women's Epistolary Friendships." In *Fundamentals of Medieval and Early Modern Culture: Friendship in the Middle Ages and Early Modern Age: Explorations of a Fundamental Ethical Discourse*, edited by Albrecht Classen and Marilyn Sandidge, 231–46. Berlin: De Gruyter, 2011.
Whitaker, Cord J. *Black Metaphors: How Modern Racism Emerged from Medieval Race-Thinking*. Philadelphia: University of Pennsylvania Press, 2019.
– "Race-ing the Dragon: The Middle Ages, Race and Trippin' into the Future." *Postmedieval* 6 (2015): 3–11.
White, Caroline Louisa. *Ælfric: A New Study of His Life and Writings*. Boston: Lamson, Wolffe, and Co, 1898.
Whitelock, Dorothy. "Two Notes on Ælfric and Wulfstan." *The Modern Language Review* 38 (1943): 122–26.

- "Wulfstan and the Laws of Cnut." *The English Historical Review* 63 (1948): 433–52.
- "Wulfstan and the So-Called Laws of Edward and Guthrum." *The English Historical Review* 56 (1941): 1–21.
- "Wulfstan's Authorship of Cnut's Laws." *The English Historical Review* 70 (1955): 72–85.

Wilcox, Jonathan. "Famous Last Words: Ælfric's Saints Facing Death." *Essays in Medieval Studies* 10 (1994): 1–13.
- "Old English Translation." In *Translation – Theory and Practice: A Historical Reader*, edited by Daniel Weissbort and Astradur Eysteinsson, 34–46. Oxford: Oxford University Press, 2006.
- "A Reluctant Translator in Late Anglo-Saxon England: Ælfric and Maccabees." *Proceedings of the Medieval Association of the Midwest* 2 (1994): 1–18.
- "The Wolf at Work: Uncovering Wulfstan's Compositional Method." In *Manuscripts in the Anglo-Saxon Kingdoms: Cultures and Connections*, edited by Claire Breay, Joanna Story, and Eleanor Jackson, 141–53. Dublin: Four Courts, 2021.
- "The Wolf on Shepherds: Wulfstan, Bishops, and the Context of the *Sermo Lupi ad Anglos*." In *Old English Prose: Basic Readings*, edited by Paul E. Szarmach, 395–418. New York: Garland, 2000.
- "Wulfstan and the Twelfth Century." In *Rewriting Old English in the Twelfth Century*, edited by Mary Swan and Elaine M. Treharne, 83–97. Cambridge: Cambridge University Press, 2000. Reprinted in *Classical and Medieval Literature Criticism* 59 (2003): 342–9.
- "Wulfstan's *Sermo Lupi ad Anglos* as Political Performance: 16 February 1014 and Beyond." In *Wulfstan, Archbishop of York: The Proceedings of the Second Alcuin Conference*, edited by Matthew Townend, 375–96. Turnhout, Belgium: Brepols, 2004.

Wilke, Carsten L. "הנשמה היא 'אישה זרה' שונות ואלגוריה פסיכולוגית מן הזוהר ועד החסידות / The Soul Is a Foreign Woman: Otherness and Psychological Allegory from the '*Zohar*' to Hasidism." *Iggud: Selected Essays in Jewish Studies* (2005): 129–39. http://www.jstor.org/stable/23531304.

Wills, Lawrence M. *Judith*. Minneapolis: Fortress Press, 2019.

Wilson, Katharina. *Hrotsvit of Gandersheim: A Florilegium of Her Works*. Cambridge, UK: D.S. Brewer, 1998.

Wilton, David. "What Do We Mean by Anglo-Saxon? Pre-Conquest to the Present." *JEGP* 119 (2020): 425–56.

Withers, Benjamin C. *The Illustrated Old English Hexateuch, Cotton Claudius B.iv: The Frontier of Seeing and Reading in Anglo-Saxon England*. Toronto: University of Toronto Press, 2007.
- "A 'Secret and Feverish Genesis': The Prefaces of the Old English Hexateuch." *The Art Bulletin* 81 (1999): 53–71.

- "A Sense of Englishness: Claudius B.iv, Colonialism, and the History of Anglo-Saxon Art in the Mid-Twentieth Century." In *The Old English Hexateuch: Aspects and Approaches*, edited by Rebecca Barnhouse and Benjamin C. Withers, 317–50. Kalamazoo, MI: Medieval Institute Publications, 2000.
- "Unfulfilled Promise: The Rubrics of the Old English Prose Genesis." *Anglo-Saxon England* 28 (1999): 111–39.

Wolfe, Cary. *Animal Rites: American Culture, the Discourse of Species, and Posthumanist Theory*. Chicago: University of Chicago Press, 2003.

Wormald, Patrick. "Archbishop Wulfstan: Eleventh-Century State-Builder." In *Wulfstan, Archbishop of York: The Proceedings of the Second Alcuin Conference*, edited by Matthew Townend, 9–27. Turnhout, Belgium: Brepols, 2004.
- "*Engla Lond*: The Making of an Allegiance." *Journal of Historical Sociology* 7 (1994): 1–24.
- *The Making of English Law: King Alfred to the Twelfth Century*. Malden, MA: Blackwell, 1999.

Wright, Charles D. "*Genesis A* ad litteram." In *Old English Literature and the Old Testament*, edited by Michael Fox and Manish Sharma, 121–71. Toronto: University of Toronto Press, 2012.
- "A New Latin Source for Two Old English Homilies (Fadda I and Blickling I): Pseudo-Augustine, Sermo App. 125 and the Ideology of Chastity in the Anglo-Saxon Benedictine Reform." In *Source of Wisdom: Studies in Old English and Early Medieval Latin in Honour of Thomas D. Hill*, edited by Charles D. Wright, Thomas N. Hall, and Frederick M. Biggs, 239–65. Toronto: University of Toronto Press, 2007.

Wright, Joseph, and Elizabeth Mary Wright. *Old English Grammar*. 2nd ed. Oxford: Horace Hart, 1914.

Wyatt, David. "Reading between the Lines: Tracking Slaves and Slavery in the Early Middle Ages." In *Viking-Age Trade: Silver, Slaves and Gotland*, edited by Jacek Gruszczyński, Marek Jankowiak, and Jonathan Shepard, 17–39. London: Routledge, 2020.
- *Slaves and Warriors in Medieval Britain and Ireland, 800–1200*. Leiden: Brill, 2009.

Wynter, Sylvia. "No Humans Involved: An Open Letter to My Colleagues." *Forum N.H.I.: Knowledge for the 21st Century* 1 (1994): 46–73.
- "Unsettling the Coloniality of Being/Power/Truth/Freedom: Towards the Human, after Man, Its Overrepresentation – an Argument." *CR: The New Centennial Review* 3 (2003): 257–337.

Yamamoto, Dorothy. *The Boundaries of the Human in Medieval English Literature*. Oxford: Oxford University Press, 2000.

Yeager, Stephen M. *From Lawmen to Plowmen: Anglo-Saxon Legal Tradition and the School of Langland*. Toronto: University of Toronto Press, 2014.

Yoo, Philip. "Hagar the Egyptian: Wife, Handmaid, and Concubine." *Catholic Biblical Quarterly* 78 (2016): 215–35.
Yoon, Hyaesin. "Disappearing Bitches: Canine Affect and Postcolonial Bioethics." *Configurations* 24 (2016): 351–74.
Younge, George. "Monks, Money, and the End of Old English." *New Medieval Literatures* 16 (2016): 39–82.
– "The New Heathens: Anti-Jewish Hostility in Early English Literature." *Essays and Studies* 68 (2015): 124–47.
Zacher, Samantha. "Anglo-Saxon Maccabees: Political Theology in Ælfric's *Lives of Saints*." In *Old English Lexicology and Lexicography: Essays in Honor of Antonette diPaolo Healey*, edited by Maren Clegg Hyer, Haruko Momma, and Samantha Zacher, 143–58. Rochester, NY: Boydell & Brewer, 2020.
– "Circumscribing the Text: Views on Circumcision in Old English Literature." In *Old English Literature and the Old Testament*, edited by Michael Fox and Manish Sharma, 89–118. Toronto: University of Toronto Press, 2012.
– ed. *Imagining the Jew in Anglo-Saxon Literature and Culture*. Toronto: University of Toronto Press, 2016.
– "Jews and Judaizing as Pathologies in the Anglo-Saxon Imagination: Toward a Theory of Early Somatic Anti-Judaism." In *The Anonymous Old English Homily: Sources, Composition, and Variation*, edited by Winfried Rudolf and Susan Irvine, 257–86. Leiden: Brill, 2020.
– *Rewriting the Old Testament in Anglo-Saxon Verse: Becoming the Chosen People*. London: Bloomsbury, 2013.
– "Sir Gowther's Canine Penance: Forms of Animal Asceticism from Cynic Philosophy to Medieval Romance." *The Chaucer Review* 52 (2017): 426–55.
– "The Source of Vercelli VII: An Address to Women." In *New Readings in the Vercelli Book*, edited by Zacher and Andy Orchard, 98–149. Toronto: University of Toronto Press, 2009.

Index

adultery, 27, 28, 159n33; clerical marriage as, 81

Ælfric of Eynsham, 4, 16–18, 142–3, 144, 187n82, 189n97; and anxiety, 19, 156n2; and chastity/celibacy, 66, 77–83, 91–2, 107, 108–10, 128–9, 130, 141, 169n50, 178n75, 188n87; and hagiography, 43–4, 104–6, 112–15, 170n64; as *OEH* translator, 19, 20, 22–6, 28, 32–3, 34–6, 85, 90–1, 96, 162n51; and sovereignty, 93–4, 95, 96–7, 101–6, 107, 115–17, 141, 185–6n61, 188n87; and style, 19, 56, 85, 97, 115, 124, 155n56, 156n4, 185n53, 192n38; as translator (excluding *OEH*), 19, 42–3, 46–7, 64–5, 85–90, 93–5, 109–17, 128–9, 133–5, 141, 142, 166n15, 172n85, 182n5, 183n29, 192n38. *See also* Ælfrician texts; Bible references; Genesis; *Old English Heptateuch*

Ælfrician texts: *Catholic Homilies*: Preface to the First Series, 97; Sermon on the Origin of Creation, 169n58; Lord's Octave and Circumcision, 83–4, 85–90; St. Laurence, Second Sunday in the Lord's Advent, 59–60; On the Lord's Ascension, 53–4; First Sunday in Lent, 52, 169n50; Second Sunday in Lent, 133–4; Fifth Sunday in Lent 84–5, 179n84; Invention of the Holy Cross, 97; First Sunday in September: Job, 56–8, 63–4, 65, 164n78, 172n85; *Colloquy*, 52, 169n54; *Esther*, 42–3; *First Old English Letter to Wulfstan*, 79, 81–3; *Hexameron* 96; *Letter to Brother Edward*, 39–40, 51–2, 164–5n82, 169n47, 198n13; *Letter to Wulfsige*, 137; *Judith*-homily, 17–18, 90, 93–5, 98–106, 108–17, 183nn28–29, 183n32, 185–6n61, 186n72; *Lives of Saints*: Latin Preface, 93; Old English Preface, 94, 181n4; *LS* 2 (Eugenia), 74–6, 177n53; *LS* 3 (Basil), 60–1; *LS* 7 (Agnes), 104–5, 184n46; *LS* 8 (Agatha and Lucy), 184n44, 184n46; *LS* 9 (Chair of St. Peter), 78, 80–1, 178n68, 178n70; *LS* 11 (Shrove Sunday/Ash Wednesday), 128, 130; *LS* 12 (*Oratio Moysi*, Prayer of Moses), 192n38; *LS* 13 (George), 170n64; *LS* 17 (Kings), 111, 130–2, 183n29, 185n53; *LS* 20 (Æthelthryth),

Ælfrician texts (*continued*)
112–3, 187n76, 187n77; *LS* 22 (Abdon and Sennes), 97; *LS* 23 (Maccabees), 17, 42–7, 51–3, 54–6, 61, 62–3, 64–5, 111, 113, 143, 165n4–6, 166n13, 166n15, 167n32, 170n64; *LS* 27 (Dionysius), 170n64; *LS* 29 (Edmund), 137; *LS* 32 (Thomas), 103, 127; *LS* 33 (Vincent), 129; Seven Sleepers, 103; *OEH* (see *Old English Heptateuch*); supplementary homilies (ed. Pope): Pope 13 (*Fifth Sunday after Pentecost*), 128–9; Pope 21 (*De Falsis Diis*), 96; Pope 26 (Theodosius and Ambrose), 97

Ælred of Rielvaux, 71

ænlicnyss, 17–18, 98–9, 101–6, 183n29, 183n37

Æthelthryth, St.: and *Liber Eliensis*, 110. See also Ælfrician texts, *Lives of Saints, LS* 20 (Æthelthryth)

Agamben, Giorgio, 54, 63, 80, 81, 166n18, 171n66

Ahmed, Sara, 11, 147

Aldhelm, 72–3, 175–6n34, 176nn37–8, 178n68

Alfred, *Prologue to the Domboc*, 20, 119, 132; *Domboc*, 127, 193n60

animals (non-human): dogs, 46, 118–20, 128–35, 137–8, 143–4, 194n66, 194n69, 195n80, 196n99; elephant, 64–5; fish, 22, 33, 34, 35, 77–8, 91, 96, 169n58; and human dominion, 53–7, 62–5, 96, 130–2, 137–8; pigs, 42, 129, 132, 166n18; and racialization/anti-Semitism, 46, 132–5, 146, 166n18; sheep, 112, 132–5, 136; whales, 64, 65, 144, 173n116; wolves, 136, 137–8, 197n104; worms, 55–7, 171n71

anweald/geweald, 17, 95–101, 104, 125, 141, 182n15, 183n21, 184n39, 184n42, 184n44

Apostolic Decree, 47–8, 49–50, 52

Augustine, 8, 50, 78, 84, 168n37, 169n59, 179n84, 184n39

"bearing fruit for death," 69–70. *See also* temporalities, heterosexual/reproductive

Bede, 52, 86, 87–9, 124, 133–4, 143–4, 152n22, 154n45, 169n52, 195n91

Benedictine Reform, 4, 5; 17ish, 70–1; 77ish, 110; and anti-feminism, 116; and style, 5, 91, 156n4, 162n62. *See also Benedictine Rule; Regularis Concordia*

Benedictine Rule, 71

Beowulf, 98, 104, 124–5

Bible: individual books (as entries). *See* Bible references; manuscripts

Bible references: Genesis 1:28 (primordial blessing), 54, 65, 77–8, 96; 3:16, 96; 7:2, 91; 8:20, 91; 9:1–17 (Noahic covenant), 33, 34–5, 51, 162n63, 162–3n65, 169n48, 179n82; 9:21–7, 160n47; 12:11–20, 160n46; 16:3, 18; 17:1–23 (circumcision), 84–86, 179n81, 180n86; 19:5, 24; 19:8, 24, 89, 160n45; 19:31–8, 160–1n47; 20:7, 155n52; 20:13–4, 24, 160–1n40; 24:15–60; 31:35, 158–9n28; Exodus 7:18, 57; 7:21, 57; 12:2–11, 31, 62; 21:7–13, 119; 22:31, 132, 195n80; Leviticus 3:16–17, 35, 36, 163n69; 7:17–32, 38–9, 162–3n65, 198n13, 164nn76–7; 10:10, 32; 11:9–12, 22, 91; 14:46–15:16, 157–8n15; 17:10–16, 35, 36–7, 40, 163n2, 165n84; 18:6–30, 27, 29, 160n39, 198n17; 19:2–3, 21; 19:26–32, 28, 35, 37, 40, 163–4n74,

190n15; 20:10, 27; 20:22–6, 145, 190n15; 23:35–6, 158n19; 26:3–45, 122–4, 157–8n15; Deuteronomy 12:23, 35, 38; 12:32, 35, 37–8, 164n75; 21:10–14 (captive woman), 7, 28, 124, 152n20, 197n2; Judges 19:29, 119, 170–1n65; 1 Kings 22, 130–1; 3 Kings 22:35–38; 131; 4 Kings 9:7–10, 131; 9:30, 131; Isaiah 56:10: 9–10, 137, 196n99; Ezekiel 16, 119; 23, 119; 34:10, 136; Psalms 16:14, 52–3; 21:17, 134; Proverbs 26:11, 194n66; 27:7, 59, 119; Job 6:5–6, 59, 172n94; 6:7, 58–9, 61; 40:20–5, 64, 176n117; Judith 2:18–3:15, 99; 8:1, 111; 8:4–8, 111–2, 186n73; 8:9–10, 101; 9:9–27, 100, 107; 13:13–9, 108, 115; 13:22–3, 108; 15:10–11, 108–9; 16:2, 115; 16:7, 108; 16:16, 108; 1 Macc. 6:8, 171n72; 2 Macc. 6.21; 2 Macc. 9:7–10, 171nn71–2; Matthew 5:8, 90; 7:6, 132; 12:43, 90; 15:24–7, 132–4; Luke 11:24, 90, 14:11, 109; John 8, 129; 10:16, 134; Acts 15:29 (Apostolic Decree), 48; 17:26, 162–3n65; Romans 2:29, 83; 9:3, 179n82; 14:14, 47–8; 14:15/21, 165–6n8; Tit 1:15, 50, 51; 2 Peter 2:22: 119, 129, 194n66
Birgitta of Sweden, 107, 115, 188n89
blood, 26, 57, 105, 114, 130–1, 158–9n28, 162–3n65, 169n58, 188n89; prohibition on consuming, 11–12, 17, 33–41, 47, 48, 51–2, 157n11, 163–4n74, 164n77, 169n48, 198n13
Butler, Judith, 174n3

captive woman trope, 7–8, 18, 124–6, 138, 139–42, 152n22
chastity/celibacy, 91, 126–8, 129, 142, 169n50; and heterosexuality, 68–70;

and monasticism, 5, 17, 66, 72–3, 112, 116–17, 141; and saints' lives, 104–5, 114, 188n90; and sovereignty, 17, 94, 107–11, 116–17, 145, 188n87; and supersession, 68, 72, 77–83, 90, 94
Christ, 48, 57, 70, 78, 88–9, 103, 104–5, 120, 127, 132–4, 135–6, 151n17, 167n31, 188n89
Chrysostom, John, 67, 92, 133, 195n87
circumcision, 26, 28, 43, 72, 83–90, 179n79, 179n81, 179n82, 180n86, 181n99, 186n70
clænnys, 91–2, 108–12, 110–11, 139–41, 142
clergy, 126, 135; abbesses/abbots/abbacy, 70, 75–6, 88, 94–5, 106–7, 110, 112–13, 115, 116, 126, 145; bishops and episcopal office, 18, 76, 80, 117, 126–8, 135–8, 194n65; Christian priests and pastorship, 23, 33, 79–81, 126–7, 136, 137, 189n95, 193n50; and clerical marriage/priests' wives, 79–83, 91–2, 127; monasticism/monks 17, 32–3, 68–80, 184n43; nuns, 70, 73, 74, 126, 127, 175n24, 188–99n95, 193n60; priests in Hebrew Bible, 24, 28, 31, 32–3, 35, 36, 72, 79–81, 82–3, 84, 91–2, 136, 137, 157n11, 186n70; as *servus dei*, 126–7, 192n49; vowesses and women religious, 76, 109–10, 116–17, 126, 188–99n95
cultural translation, 4–5, 5–10, 19, 44–7, 93

Danes and Danish invasion, 42, 47, 117, 118–23, 125–6, 128, 164–5n82, 165n6
dehumanization. *See* animals, and human dominion; animals, and racialization/anti-Semitism

252   Index

demons/devils/Satan: Biblical, 56, 58, 90, 132, 151n17, 172n82; in hagiography, 187n81, 188n90; and harrowing of hell, 89; and mistranslation, 6–7, 151n17; in *Old English Physiologus*, 173n116; in Wulfstan, 81, 97, 136

Deuteronomy: and curses/warnings, 125–6; in Heptateuch mss, 156n10, 157n14; and holiness/purity regulations, 37–8, 45, 47, 167n24; translation into Middle English, 160n44; translation into Old English, 37–8, 45, 91, 124–5, 125–6. *See also* Bible references; captive woman trope

Douglas, Mary, 15, 22, 26, 47, 158n23, 167n24

Encomium Emma Reginae, 119
expulsions: of demons, 151n17; of feces, 143–4, 146; in Hebrew Bible, 144–5, 198n17; Jewish (European), 5, 146–7. *See also* vomit

faithful translation, 16, 19
fatherhood, 68, 73; abbatical/monastic/priestly, 71, 73, 76; and Abraham, 83–90, 180n97; and (hetero)patriarchy, 73, 84, 127; secular (medieval), 40, 73, 76, 176n40

feminisms: abolitionist/decolonial, 193–4n63; and female sovereignty, 185n57; lesbian-, 174n4; and reproductive labour, 175n18

food and eating: Christian regulations, 11–12, 47–51, 52, 60, 63, 168–9n45; commensality, 49, 133, 142–3; famine and starvation, 17, 52–3, 57, 59–61, 62, 123–4; fasting, 52, 111–13, 128; and feasting, 63, 111–13, 167n31; food metaphors, 10–11, 40–1, 48, 58–9, 72–3, 142–6; food refusal, 44, 55, 58–9, 60–1; gustatory conversion, 59, 61; *halal* (Muslim food regulations), 164n79; humans as food, 55–7, 65, 129–32; *kashrut* (Jewish food regulations), 17, 42–3, 44–5, 46–7, 52–3, 56, 63, 91, 141, 142, 143; *shechitah* (kosher slaughter), 38, 55, 164n79

Foucault, Michel, 70–1

Genesis: Cædmon's hymn, 143; Creation, 77–8, 96, 143; in Heptateuch mss, 20, 156–7n10; in Hexateuch illustrations, 159n30; and sexual transgressions, 22–6, 160nn45–6, 160–1n47; translation, 31, 34–6, 40, 83, 84–8, 91, 96–7, 162–3n35. *See also* Ælfric, as *OEH* translator; Bible references; circumcision; incest; Luther, Martin; Noahic covenant; polygyny; sacrifice; Sodom and Gomorrah; individual characters (as entries)

Genesis A (poem), 25–6, 68, 86–7, 91, 97, 98, 159n33, 160n35

Gregory I (Pope): *Cura Pastoralis*, 194n68, 196n101; and enslaved boys, 124; *Homily 29*, 53–4; letters, 29; *Moralia in Job*, 57, 58, 59, 61–2, 172n85, 173n105

Hagar, 83, 88, 159n30, 179n78, 180n97
heterosexuality, 66–72, 73–4, 174n12, 175n18, 177–8n56; as curse, 68; and Hebrew Bible, 17, 77–8, 172, 179n81; proper to Biblical Jews, 79–90, 92, 142
Holocaust, 9, 153n30, 154–5n45

imperialism, 6–7, 8, 74–5; and *Judith*-homily, 93–4, 95–101, 117, 183n28; and *Maccabees*, 42, 43; and medieval studies, 154n39, 154n43; in Old English *Orosius*, 95–6. *See also anweald/geweald*; sovereignty
incest, 23, 24, 26–9, 69, 80–1, 159n32, 159–60n33, 160n39, 160–1nn45–8
Isaac (Biblical), 31, 84, 179n81
Ishmael (Biblical), 85, 180n97
Islam, 48, 83, 142, 150n8; and Islamophobia, 49, 79, 139, 146

Jacob (Biblical): and the angel, 157–8n15; and marriage, 23, 159n30
Jerome, 8, 77, 78, 124, 152n22
Jezebel, 106, 119, 130–2, 185n53. *See also* Ælfrician texts, *Lives of Saints*; Ælfrician texts, *LS* 17 (Kings); Kings (Biblical book)
Job (Biblical book), 57, 58–9, 61–2, 63–4; medieval reception, 57–8, 64, 172n85
Judith (Biblical book), 5, 106, 107–8, 141, 184–5n50; medieval reception, 106–7, 110, 185n57. *See also* Ælfrician texts, *Judith*-homily
Judith (poem), 94, 187n85

Kings (Biblical book), 106, 130–2, 158n19. *See also* Ælfrician texts, *Lives of Saints*; Ælfrician texts, *LS* 17 (Kings); Bible references; Jezebel
kinship, 68, 69–70, 71, 73–4. *See also* fatherhood; heterosexuality; motherhood; queer reproduction

Leviticus, 147; in Anglo-Latin Bibles and fragments, 21, 157n14, 157–8n15, 158n19; and curses/warnings, 144–5, 157–8n15, 164n77, 190n15; in Heptateuch mss, 156n10, 162n57; and (non-sexual) holiness/purity laws, 21, 144–5, 157–8n15, 167n24; and literary qualities, 15–16, 155n50, 158n23, 167n24; and Luther, 162–3n65; as metonymic of Jewish law, 10–11, 140; and Middle English, 160n44; as problem text, 10–11, 14–15, 140, 143, 153–4n34; and sexual transgressions, 21, 26–9, 119, 120, 144–5, 160n37, 160–1n47, 198n17; translation into Old English, 15–17, 20, 21, 26–8, 29–3, 86, 91, 122–4, 140, 164n77, 190n15, 192n38. *See also* Bible references; expulsions; incest; manuscripts, Durham Cathedral Library, C. IV. 7; Wulfstan, *Be Godcundre Warnunge*
Liber ex lege Moysi, 20
literalism, 19–20, 45, 142, 156n5
Luther, Martin, 6, 162–3n65

Maccabees (Biblical books), 43–4, 56, 165n5, 165–6n8, 171n72; medieval reception, 44, 16566n8. *See also* Bible references; Ælfrician texts, *Lives of Saints*; Ælfrician texts, *LS* 23 (Maccabees)
manuscripts: BL MS Cotton Nero A.i, 122, 190–1n19; BL MS Cotton Tiberius A.iii, 188n90; BL MS Royal 1. E. VII + VIII (Northumbrian Royal Bible), 21, 157–8n15; Bodleian, MS Hatton 115, 195n73; Bodleian, MS Junius 121, 191n27; Bodleian, MS Laud Misc. 381 (L'Isle), 156–7n10; Bodleian, MS Misc

254 Index

manuscripts (*continued*)
509 (Old English Heptateuch), 16, 20–1, 31; Cambridge: Corpus Christi College (CCC), MS 190, 50; CCC MS 198, 165n4; CCC MS 201, 122–3, 191n27; CCC MS 303, 165n4; Durham Cathedral Library, MS C.IV 7, 21, 157–8n15; Florence Medicea Laurenziana Library, Codex Amiatinus, 157n14; glossing, 162n57; illustrations, 159n30, 159n32, 160n46; Lambeth Palace, MS 487, 191n27; London: British Library, MS Cotton Claudius B.iv (Illustrated Hexateuch), 20–1, 31; Oxford: Bodleian, MS Hatton 113, 190–1n19; University Library, MS Ii.1.33, 165n4, 187n76
Masoretic (Hebrew) text, 15, 57, 58–9, 78, 84, 141, 151n15, 155n52, 162–3n65, 172n86, 179n82
menstruation, 24, 28, 157n11, 158–9n28, 167n23; and Jewish men, 67
Middle English Metrical Paraphrase of the Old Testament, 159n33, 160n44
motherhood, 69, 70, 160–1n47; abbatical/monastic, 70, 73–4, 88, 90; and Eve, 96; as relationship of Judaism to Christianity, 11, 154n37; and Sarah, 87–8, 89–90

Nazism, 9, 153n30, 164n79
Nida, Eugene, 8, 9
Noahic covenant, 33–6, 51–2, 169n48, 179n82
numbers: in Anglo-Latin Bibles, 157n14, 158n19; in *OEH* mss, 20–1; in Old English translation, 22, 91

Old English Heptateuch, 4, 9–92, 15–16, 16–17, 19–41, 62, 85; *Libellus de Veteri Testamento et Novo* (*Letter to Sigeweard*), 20, 57, 172n81; *Preface to Genesis*, 20, 22–4, 28, 49; style, 5, 16–17, 19–20. *See also* Ælfric, as *OEH* translator; Bible references; individual books (as entries); manuscripts
Old English Life of St. Smaragdus (Euphrosyne), 74–6, 177nn51–3
Old English Lives of St. Margaret, 115, 187n81, 188n90
Old English Martyrology: Abdon and Sennes, 98; Clement, 183n21; Milus and Senneus, 129–30; Perpetua, 187n81; and trans/gender-fluid saints, 74–5, 187n81
Origen, 7–8, 10, 124, 139–42, 143, 153n32, 153–4n34, 156n5, 197n4

Penitentials, 11–12, 17, 48, 50, 60, 168n44; Canons of Theodore, 48, 60; Old English Penitential, 39; pseudo-Theodore, 50, 168n40; Scriftboc, 39, 48, 49, 60, 168–9n45; and sexuality, 29, 49
polygyny, 22–4, 27, 77, 83, 159n30, 160n46

queerness, 17, 68–77, 174n4, 174n6
queer reproduction, 68–70, 72–4
queer theory, 66–8, 70–1, 72, 73, 175n18

Rachel (Biblical), 24, 158–9n28, 159n30
racism: and anti-racism, 175n18; and anti-Semitism, 5, 9–14, 46, 139, 146, 150n11, 153n29, 154n79, 166n18, 174n2; and colonialism/imperialism, 9–14, 150n11, 155n46, 166n17, 185n57; and medieval studies, 12, 154n39

Rebecca (Biblical), 31
Regularis Concordia, 71
Richard of Devizes, 146, 198n20, 199n22

sacrifice: and Eucharist, 62–3, 80–1, 135, 143; in Hebrew Bible/Old Testament, 10, 15, 16, 30–1, 32, 36–8, 43, 47, 58, 80–1, 83, 84, 145, 153–4n34, 157n11, 164n78, 170–1n65; and martyrdom, 170n64; polytheistic, 48, 49–50, 55, 167n32; in translation, 10, 15, 17, 30–1, 36, 38, 62–4, 140, 167n32
Sarah (Biblical): as matriarch, 87–8, 89–90, 179n81, 180n97; and sexuality, 24, 28, 160n46, 160–1n47
secularism, 13–14, 66, 154–5n45, 198n18
Sedgwick, Eve, 67, 174n4
Septuagint, 149n1, 151n15, 153n26, 158n19, 179n82; and Job, 57; and Judith, 90, 94, 107, 183n31, 186n64
sexual abuse/violence, 97–8; and abolitionist/decolonial feminisms, 193–4n62; Biblical, 7–8, 24–6, 119, 124–5, 139–42, 152n20, 160–1n47; and English law, 127–8, 193nn60–1; and enslavement, trafficking, 120, 124–5, 127–8, 193nn60–1; in Judith, 148; in religious/monastic life, 74, 177–8n56; in secular life, 69; in *Sermo Lupi*, 98, 118–21, 124–6, 138, 142, 145, 193n59. *See also anweald/geweald*; captive woman trope; slavery/enslavement; incest
slavery/enslavement, 142; of Christians, 135–6; early medieval, 127–8, 179n29, 193nn60–1, 194nn63–4; in Hebrew Bible/Old Testament, 7, 28, 112, 119, 152n20, 184n43, 189n11; in *Sermo Lupi*, 119–21, 124–6, 135, 138, 194n63; and *servus dei*, 126–7, 192n49, 193n50, 193n57. *See also* captive woman trope
Sodom and Gomorrah, 24–6, 89, 98, 159–60n33, 162n57
sovereignty, 17–18, 93–102, 103–4, 116–17, 141, 145, 182n6; and abbatical/ecclesiastical office, 88, 89–90, 106–7, 115–17, 127–8, 135–8; and Abrahamic covenant, 87–90; and chastity, 108–10, 186n67; divine, 63–4, 93–4, 97, 101–2, 107–10, 117, 120–1; and exception, 63–4, 103–4, 106–10, 185–6n61; feminine, 106–8, 131, 185n57; forfeited/abdicated, 131–2; and human dominion, 65; imperial, 93, 94, 95–100, 101–2; and right to expel, 144, 147
Stjórn, 27

Talmud, 149n1, 194n69
temporalities: apocalyptic, 59–60; crisis, 16, 106, 117, 197n105; gay/queer 70, 73; heterosexual/reproductive, 69, 83; incarnational, 81, 89–90, 110, 154–5n45; Jewish, 154–5n45; and literary style, 5, 16, 119, 181n3, 197n105; messianic, 81; monastic, 70–1; "Old Testament," 120–1; ritual, 130, 143, 154–5n45, 158–9n28
temporal othering/difference, 4, 5, 6, 12–14, 23–4, 77, 79–81, 83, 85, 89–90, 110, 145–6, 154–5n45; and Judith's singularity, 113, 114, 116, 117
tôrôt, 32

translatio imperii, 121, 124–5
transmasculine saints (Eugenia, Smaragdus [Euphrosyne]), 74–7, 177nn50–3

vernacularity, 5, 32–3, 124–5, 151n15
vomit, 119, 128–30, 143–6, 190n15, 194n66, 198n17

Wulfstan, 4; *Be Godcundre Warnunge*, 20, 97–8, 122–4, 125, 135, 156n7; and composition, 121, 190–1n19; and forgery, 121–4, 138, 191n23; *Institutes of Polity*, 122, 136; legislation, 120, 121–2, 126–8, 136, 193n61; and misogyny, 81–2, 141–2, 193n59; *Sermo Lupi*, 18, 98, 118–21, 124–8, 135–8, 189n6, 193n59, 194n63; and style, 118–19, 123–4, 183n24, 191n35, 192n39, 192n48; and theo-politics, 18, 118–21, 127–8, 135–8; and translation, 5–6, 20, 118, 122–4, 124–6, 135–7, 138, 191n26, 196n95; *Verba Ezechielis* (Bethurum 16a/b), 136–7
Wynter, Sylvia, 46, 166n17

Milton Keynes UK
Ingram Content Group UK Ltd.
UKHW011020230224
438306UK00046B/102/J